THE CAMBRIDGE COMPANION TO NINETEENTH-CENTURY AMERICAN POETRY

This *Companion* is the first critical collection devoted solely to American poetry of the nineteenth century. It covers a wide variety of authors, many of whom are currently being rediscovered. A number of anthologies in the recent past have been devoted to the verse of groups such as Native Americans, African-Americans, and women. This volume offers essays covering these groups as well as more familiar figures such as Dickinson, Whitman, Longfellow, and Melville. The contents are divided between broad topics of concern, such as the poetry of the Civil War or the development of the "Poetess" role and articles featuring specific authors such as Edgar Allan Poe or Sarah Piatt. In the past two decades a growing body of scholarship has been engaged in reconceptualizing and reevaluating this largely neglected area of study in US literary history. This *Companion* reflects and advances this spirit of revisionism.

KERRY LARSON is Professor of English at the University of Michigan. He is the author of *Whitman's Drama of Consensus* (1988) and *Imagining Equality in Nineteenth-Century American Literature* (2008) as well as numerous articles.

A complete list of books in the series is at the end of this book

D0862896

THE CAMBRIDGE
COMPANION TO
NINETEENTH-
CENTURY AMERICAN
POETRY

EDITED BY
KERRY LARSON

CAMBRIDGE
UNIVERSITY PRESS

CAMBRIDGE UNIVERSITY PRESS
Cambridge, New York, Melbourne, Madrid, Cape Town,
Singapore, São Paulo, Delhi, Tokyo, Mexico City

Cambridge University Press
The Edinburgh Building, Cambridge CB2 8RU, UK

Published in the United States of America by Cambridge University Press, New York

www.cambridge.org
Information on this title: www.cambridge.org/9780521145800

First published 2011

Printed in the United Kingdom at the University Press, Cambridge

A catalogue record for this publication is available from the British Library

ISBN 978-0-521-76369-1 Hardback
ISBN 978-0-521-14580-0 Paperback

CONTENTS

CONTRIBUTORS

STEPHEN BURT is an associate professor at Harvard University. He has published *Randall Jarrell and His Age* (2002), *The Forms of Youth: Twentieth-Century Poetry and Adolescence* (2007), and *Close Calls with Nonsense: Reading New Poetry* (2009). The author of three books of poetry, he is also the editor of *Randall Jarrell on W. H. Auden* (2005) and the co-editor of *The Art of the Sonnet* (2010).

MAX CAVITCH is an associate professor at the University of Pennsylvania. He is the author of *American Elegy: The Poetry of Mourning from the Puritans to Whitman* (2007) as well as recent and forthcoming essays on Emma Lazarus, Stephen Crane, Emily Dickinson, Anne Gilchrist, Walt Whitman, the theory of poetic genres, and the nineteenth-century globalization of meters.

STEPHEN CUSHMAN is Robert C. Taylor Professor of English at the University of Virginia. In addition to publishing four books of poetry, he is the author of *William Carlos Williams and the Meanings of Measure* (1985), *Fictions of Form in American Poetry* (1993), and *Bloody Promenade: Reflections on a Civil War Battle* (1999). He is General Editor of the *Princeton Encyclopedia of Poetry and Poetics*, 4th edition.

VIRGINIA JACKSON is UC Endowed Chair of Rhetoric and Communication at UC Irvine. She has written *Dickinson's Misery: A Theory of Lyric Reading* (2005) and has another book forthcoming entitled *Before Modernism: Nineteenth-Century American Poetry in Public*. The author of several articles on nineteenth-century poetry, she has also co-edited, with Yopie Prins, *Lyric Theory Reader* (forthcoming).

JOHN D. KERKERING teaches at Loyola University, Chicago. A contributor to the *Cambridge History of Literary Criticism* (vol. VI, forthcoming) as well as to the forthcoming *Cambridge History of American Poetry*, he is the author of *The Poetics of National and Racial Identity in Nineteenth-Century American Literature* (2003).

MARY LOUISE KETE is an associate professor of English at the University of Vermont and the author of *Sentimental Collaborations: Mourning and Middle-Class*

Identity in Nineteenth-Century America (2000). Her current work-in-progress is *Slavish Ekphrasis: Representation, Slavery and the Liberal Self.*

CRISTANNE MILLER is Edward H. Butler Professor of English at the State University of New York, Buffalo. She is the author of *Emily Dickinson: A Poet's Grammar* (1987), *Marianne Moore: Questions of Authority* (1995), and *Cultures of Modernism: Marianne Moore, Mina Loy, Else Lasker-Schuler. Gender and Literary Community in New York and Berlin* (2005). Her edited volumes include *Feminist Measures: Soundings in Poetry and Theory* (1994), *The Emily Dickinson Handbook* (1998), and *Words for the Hour: A New Anthology of American Civil War Poetry* (2005).

ROBERT DALE PARKER is James M. Benson Professor of English at the University of Illinois, Champaign-Urbana. He is the author of *Faulkner and the Novelistic Imagination* (1985), *The Unbeliever: The Poetry of Elizabeth Bishop* (1988), *"Absalom, Absalom": The Questioning of Fictions* (1991), *The Invention of Native American Literature* (2003), and *How To Interpret Literature* (2008). He is also the editor of *The Sound the Stars Make Rushing Through the Sky: The Writings of Jane Johnston Schoolcraft* (2007) and *Changing Is Not Vanishing: A Collection of American Indian Poetry to 1930* (2011).

DONALD PEASE is the Ted and Helen Geisel Third Century Professor in the Humanities at Dartmouth College, New Hampshire. He is the author of *Visionary Compacts: American Renaissance Writings in Cultural Context* (1987) and *Theodor SEUSS Geisel (Lives and Legends)* (2010). The co-editor of *American Renaissance Reconsidered* (1985) and *The Cultures of US Imperialism* (1993), he is the editor of several other volumes and has published over seventy articles on American and British literature.

ELIZABETH RENKER is a professor of English at the Ohio State University. She is the author of *Strike Through the Mask: Herman Melville and the Scene of Writing* (1996) and *The Origin of American Literature Studies: An Institutional History* (2007). Her current project reexamines the literary history of American verse from 1870 to 1910.

ELIZA RICHARDS is an associate professor of English at the University of North Carolina, Chapel Hill. The author of *Gender and the Poetics of Reception in Poe's Circle* (2004), she is currently working on the book-length project *Correspondent Lines: Poetry and Journalism in the US Civil War.* Her edition of a collection of essays, *Dickinson in Context*, is also forthcoming.

JESS ROBERTS is an associate professor of English at Albion College. She is the co-editor, with William Spengemann, of *Nineteenth-Century American Poetry* (1996) and has published articles on Civil War print culture, nineteenth-century antholo-gies of infant elegies, and the erotics of incest.

IVY G. WILSON is an associate professor of English at Northwestern University, where he teaches the literatures of the black diaspora and US literary studies with an emphasis on African-American culture. He is the author of *Specters of Democracy: Blackness and the Aesthetics of Nationalism* (2011) and has edited a selection of the poetry of Albery Allson Whitman (2009) and co-edited that of James Monroe Whitfield (2011).

CHRONOLOGY

1805   Lewis and Clark expedition reaches the Pacific coast

1807   The Boston Athenaeum (eventually encompassing a library, museum, and laboratory) founded

        Joel Barlow, *The Columbiad*

1808   USA and Britain officially ban the international slave trade, but internal trade continues

1809   Philip Freneau, *Poems Written and Published During the American Revolutionary War*

1810   Census: 7,240,000

1812   War of 1812 (1812–1815)

        American Antiquarian Society founded in Worcester, Massachusetts

1813   Washington Allston, *The Sylphs of the Seasons*

1814   British burn the White House; Britain and USA sign peace treaty

        Francis Scott Key, "The Star-Spangled Banner"

1815   *The North American Review* begins publication

        Philip Freneau, *A Collection of Poems on American Affairs*

        Lydia Huntley (later Sigourney), *Moral Pieces in Prose and Verse*

1816   First Seminole War (1816–1818) between federal troops and Native Americans assisted by runaway slaves

1817   William Cullen Bryant, "Thanatopsis"

1818   William Cullen Bryant, "To a Waterfowl"

        John Neal, *Battle of Niagara*

        Samuel Woodworth, "The Bucket"

1819   Spain cedes Florida to USA

        First steam ship, the *Savannah*, crosses the Atlantic from Georgia to Liverpool

        Richard Henry Wilde, "The Lament of the Captive"

1820   Missouri Compromise makes Missouri a slave state and legalizes slavery in all territories south of the 36°30' Parallel

        Census: 9,634,000

        Maria Gowen Brooks, *Judith, Esther, and Other Poems*

1821   First public high school opens in Boston

        The Saturday Evening Post begins weekly publication in Philadelphia

        Richard Henry Dana, "The Dying Raven"

1822   American colony of Liberia established in Africa

        Henry Rowe Schoolcraft appointed government agent for Indian affairs in the Great Lakes region

        The anthology *Specimens of the American Poets* published in London

        William Cullen Bryant, *Poems*

        Philip Freneau, "On the Civilization of the Western Aboriginal Country"

        Lydia Huntley Sigourney, *Traits of the Aborigines*

1823   Monroe Doctrine rebuffs European interference and expansion of colonies

The New-York Mirror and Ladies' Literary Gazette (1823–1857) founded

1824   *The United States Literary Gazette* (1824–1826) founded

1825   Erie Canal opens passage from Great Lakes to Atlantic Ocean

Thomas Cole moves to New York City, establishes reputation as landscape painter

Henry Wadsworth Longfellow and Nathaniel Hawthorne graduate from Bowdoin College

The first American "gift book" anthology, *The Atlantic Souvenir* (1825–1831), appears in time for the holiday season

1826   Nashoba, colony for free African Americans, established on the outskirts of Memphis, Tennessee

Henry Rowe Schoolcraft and Jane Johnston Schoolcraft create and circulate the manuscript journal *The Literary Voyager* (1826–1827)

The Casket (renamed *Graham's Magazine* in 1841) begins publication

George Moses Horton, *The Hope of Liberty*

1827   Cherokee Nation establishes its constitution (1827–1828) and founds newspaper, *The Cherokee Phoenix*

First publication of *The Talisman*, an annual gift book

Edgar Allan Poe, *Tamerlane and Other Poems*

Nathaniel Parker Willis, *Sketches*

1828   Andrew Jackson elected president

"Jim Crow" minstrel character introduced in Louisville, Kentucky

1829   Edgar Allan Poe, *Al Aaraaf, Tamerlane, and Other Poems*

1830   Indian Removal Act passed

Census: 12,866,000

Sarah Josepha Hale, "Mary Had a Little Lamb"

1831   Nat Turner leads slave rebellion in Virginia

Abolitionist journal *The Liberator* founded by William Lloyd Garrison

1832   Andrew Jackson reelected president

Fanny Kemble tours America with her father's theatrical company

William Ticknor and John Allen found publishing house Allen and Ticknor in Boston

1833   The British Emancipation Act abolishes slavery in Britain's colonies

The Knickerbocker (1833–1865) begins publication in New York

Maria Gowen Brooks, *Zophiel, or the Bride of Seven*

1834   *The Ladies' Companion* (1834–1844) begins publication in New York

Lydia Huntley Sigourney, *Poems*

1835   Second Seminole War (1835–1842)

Grimké sisters lecture against slavery

Edgar Allan Poe takes position as editor of the *Southern Literary Messenger* (1834–1864), a post he holds until 1837

Alexis de Tocqueville, *Democracy in America*

1836   Thomas Cole completes series of paintings, *The Course of Empire*

Bronson Alcott, *Conversations with Children on the Gospels* (first volume)

Ralph Waldo Emerson, *Nature*

Oliver Wendell Holmes, *Poems*

1837   Financial depression brings widespread bank and business closures

The Gentleman's Magazine, later *Burton's Gentleman's Magazine* (1837–1840), founded in Philadelphia

United States Magazine and Democratic Review (1837–1849) founded in New York.

1838   "Trail of Tears" forces the Cherokee west to present-day Oklahoma

Underground Railroad formally organized

Ralph Waldo Emerson delivers Divinity School Address at Harvard

Henry Wadsworth Longfellow, "A Psalm of Life"

1839   Slave revolt on the Spanish ship the *Amistad*, off the eastern seaboard

Louis Daguerre develops early form of photography in France

Margaret Fuller initiates her "Conversations," seminars for Boston women

The Liberty Bell (1839–1857), a semi-annual gift book, begins publication

Henry Wadsworth Longfellow, *Voices of the Night*

Jones Very, *Essays and Poems*

1840   Census: 17,000,000

The Dial is published in its first incarnation (1840–1844)

William Cullen Bryant (editor), *Selections from the American Poets*

1841   Cooperative community Brook Farm established near West Roxbury, Massachusetts

New York Tribune founded

Edgar Allan Poe edits *Graham's Magazine*

Ralph Waldo Emerson, *Essays: First Series*

Lydia Huntley Sigourney, *Pocahontas and Other Poems*

1842   Rufus Griswold (editor), *The Poets and Poetry of America*

Henry Wadsworth Longfellow, *Ballads and Other Poems; Poems on Slavery*

1843   Bronson Alcott establishes short-lived utopian community at Fruitlands, in Massachusetts

William Ellery Channing, *Poems*

1844   Samuel Morse invents telegraph

Joseph Smith, founder of Mormon Church, is killed in Illinois

Margaret Fuller becomes book reviewer for the *New-York Tribune*

Christopher Pearse Cranch, *Poems*

Ralph Waldo Emerson, *Essays: Second Series* (including "The Poet")

Fanny Kemble, *Poems*

1845   Annexation of Texas

Journalist John O'Sullivan coins the phrase "Manifest Destiny"

The New York Times established
Stephen Foster, "Old Folks at Home" (song)
Herman Melville, *Moby Dick*

1852   Franklin Pierce elected president
Charles Baudelaire publishes first of his critical studies of Poe
The Memoirs of Margaret Fuller (including poems)
Alice Cary, *Lyra and Other Poems*

1853   New York and Chicago linked by railroad
Putnam's Monthly Magazine (1853–1857) begins publication
Stephen Foster, "My Old Kentucky Home" (song)
J. M. Whitfield, *America and Other Poems*
Sarah Helen Whitman, *Hours of Life and Other Poems*

1854   Kansas–Nebraska Act repeals Missouri Compromise
Republican Party founded, bringing together anti-slavery parties
James T. Fields enters full partnership with William Ticknor under the
     imprint Ticknor & Fields
Henry David Thoreau, *Walden*
Frances Ellen Watkins Harper, *Poems on Miscellaneous Subjects*

1855   Henry Wadsworth Longfellow, *Song of Hiawatha*
Maria White Lowell, *Poems*
Walt Whitman, *Leaves of Grass*

1856   Walt Whitman, *Leaves of Grass* (2nd edition)

1857   Supreme Court's Dred Scott ruling denies citizenship to African
     Americans
Atlantic Monthly (1857–)
Harper's Weekly (1857–1916)

1858   Abraham Lincoln delivers "A House Divided" speech
Oliver Wendell Holmes, *The Autocrat of the Breakfast Table*
Henry Wadsworth Longfellow, *The Courtship of Miles Standish*

1859   John Brown's raid on Harpers Ferry and subsequent execution

1860   Abraham Lincoln elected president
Census: 31,443,000
South Carolina secedes from Union
Pony Express runs from Missouri to California
William Dean Howells and John James Piatt, *Poems of Two Friends*
Thomas Buchanan Read, *Complete Poetical Works*
Edmund Clarence Stedman, *Poems Lyrical and Idyllic*
John Greenleaf Whittier, *Home Ballads*
Walt Whitman, *Leaves of Grass* (3rd edition)

1861   American Civil War (1861–1865)
First printed version of "John Brown's Body"
Ada Isaacs Mencken first performs title role in *Mazeppa*, in Albany,
     New York

1862   Lincoln issues Emancipation Proclamation

Emily Dickinson writes over 360 poems, 4 of which she encloses in a
    letter to Thomas Wentworth Higginson

Emerson delivers address at Henry David Thoreau's funeral

Julia Ward Howe, "The Battle Hymn of the Republic"

1863   Lincoln delivers "Gettysburg Address"

1865   Lincoln assassinated

    13th Amendment abolishes slavery

    Walt Whitman, *Drum Taps*; *Sequel to Drum Taps*

1866   Herman Melville, *Battle-Pieces and Aspects of the War*

    John Greenleaf Whittier, *Snow-Bound: A Winter Idyl*

1867   Reconstruction Acts grant African-American males right to vote

    First important collection of spirituals, *Slave Songs of the United States*,
    is published

    Ralph Waldo Emerson, *May-Day and Other Pieces*

    Emma Lazarus, *Poems and Translations*

    Henry Wadsworth Longfellow (translator), *The Divine Tragedy*

    James Russell Lowell, *The Biglow Papers (Second Series)*

1868   Congress approves 8-hour workday for federal employees

1869   First transcontinental railroad is completed

    Frances Ellen Watkins Harper, *Moses: A Story of the Nile*

1870   Census: 38,553,000

    Scribner's Monthly founded

    Helen Hunt Jackson, *Verses by H.H.*

1872   Frances Ellen Watkin Harper, *Sketches of Southern Life*

    Celia Thaxter, *Poems*

1873   Comstock Act defines contraceptive information as "obscene"

    William Dean Howells, *Poems*

1874   Ralph Waldo Emerson (editor), *Parnassus*

    Sarah Morgan Piatt, *A Voyage to the Fortunate Isles*

    G. D. Pike, *The Jubilee Singers of Fisk University*

1876   Ralph Waldo Emerson, *Selected Poems*

    Henry Wadsworth Longfellow (editor), *Poems of Places* (31 volumes,
    1876–1879

    Herman Melville, *Clarel: A Poem and Pilgrimage in the Holy Land*

    Walt Whitman, *Leaves of Grass* (Centennial Edition)

1877   Sidney Lanier, *Poems*

    Edmund Clarence Stedman, *Hawthorne and Other Poems*

    Constance Fenimore Woolson, *Two Women: 1862*

1878   Henry Wadsworth Longfellow, *Kéramos and Other Poems*

    Sarah Morgan Piatt, *A Woman's Poems*

1880   Census: 50,156,000

    Sidney Lanier, *The Science of English Verse*

1881   Bronson Alcott, *An Autobiographical Poem*

    Oliver Wendell Holmes, *Poetical Works*

Emily Dickinson, *Poems: Third Series*
Paul Laurence Dunbar, *Lyrics of a Lowly Life*
Edwin Arlington Robinson, *The Torrent and the Night Before*
1897   John James Piatt, *Odes in Ohio*
Edwin Arlington Robinson, *Children of the Night*
1898   John Jay Chapman, *Emerson and Other Essays*
George Cabot Lodge, *The Song of the Wave*
Edgar Lee Masters, *A Book of Verses*
1899   Stephen Crane, *War is Kind*
Paul Laurence Dunbar, *Lyrics of the Hearthside*
Louise Imogen Guiney, *The Martyrs' Idyl and Shorter Poems*
1900   Census: 76,304,000
Alice Fletcher, *Indian Story and Song from North America*
Edmund Clarence Stedman (editor), *An American Anthology, 1787–1899*
George Santayana, *Interpretations of Poetry and Religion*

ACKNOWLEDGMENTS

I wish to express my gratitude to Eliza Richards and Gregg Crane for their very useful feedback when the idea for this project first began to take shape. I am also grateful to each of the contributors, whose dedication and professionalism made the editing of this collection a genuine pleasure. Christa Vogelius and Nan Z. Da provided crucial assistance in the preparation of the manuscript which was especially timely. Finally, my thanks to Ray Ryan, Gillian Dadd, and the excellent staff at Cambridge University Press for their patience and expertise in shepherding this volume from its initial phases to final publication.

Introduction

It cannot be said of nineteenth-century American poetry that it needs no introduction. Shifting interests and new paradigms have substantially altered the ways in which we view and value a field that for some time has indeed seemed less like a field of study in its own right than the collected works of two writers of genius surrounded by a host of lesser lights. With many of the standards and methodological assumptions associated with a modernist aesthetic now called into question, older continuities have been challenged while new ones have emerged. In short, over the past two decades a growing body of scholarship has been engaged in reconceptualizing and reevaluating a largely neglected area of study in US literary history. Each of the essays commissioned for this collection reflects and helps advance this spirit of new directions and revisionism.

Of course, the recent surge of interest in verse written in the United States during the nineteenth century has not developed in isolation from trends that have marked literary criticism elsewhere. Among these, three seem worth singling out in particular: the waning importance assigned to distinctions between high or elite culture and popular or mass entertainment; the increased appreciation for women's contribution to poetry and the various traditions from which it proceeds; and the rewriting of literary history in ways that travel outside or beyond national demarcations. When applied to nineteenth-century verse written in the United States, each of these rubrics overlaps to a considerable extent, but not so much so that, for the purposes of this overview, they cannot be considered consecutively.

Although prose fiction has dominated the best-seller lists to the virtual exclusion of poetry for some time now, these positions were less fixed in the nineteenth century. From a commercial point of view, Lydia Sigourney was one of the country's most successful authors, in poetry or prose, through the 1820s and 1830s, a distinction that another poet, Henry Wadsworth Longfellow, would eventually claim as he rose to prominence. Those purchasing their volumes might be, moreover, just as likely to write poetry as read it; consolation verse and related modes of lyric representation like the ballad or hymn were especially favored and appeared in a remarkable variety of outlets such as diaries, letters, newspapers, periodicals, or gift books. A common idiom of middlebrow culture from the Jacksonian period onward, poetry, in the very conventionality of its cadences and the familiarity of its imagery, allowed unprecedented numbers of men and women to demonstrate a refinement and cultural literacy that prose alone did not provide. It accordingly emerged, in Kirsten Silva Gruesz's useful description, as "a kind of vernacular formation whose value lies in its openness of access to authorship." Whether the author in question was Longfellow or the local elegist, Sigourney or the untutored autodidact, this vernacular retained a heightened regard for poetry's prestige as elevated speech even as its uniformity of manner and message revealed what Gruesz calls "democratic and equalizing aspects."[1]

It's not enough to say, then, that the conventions of popular culture "influenced" poetry of the nineteenth century, as true as that may be. The more fundamental point is that the conventional as such became integral to perceptions of what poetry was or should be. (Even that great American original, Walt Whitman, built an entire aesthetic driven by a faith in the simple repeatability of experience – "what I assume, you shall assume" – and in the pleasures of surrogacy, vicarious performance, and ventriloquism that accompany it.) In addition to the standardizing effects of democratic culture, we should not overlook the pervasive influence of Christian humanism, with its faith in the universal accessibility of the Bible, its fondness for emblems, parables, and other homiletic devices, and its perception of sin as a predictable feature of human experience governing the rhythm of everyday life. Together such influences suggest why qualities such as imitativeness, transparency of meaning, and overt didacticism, far from being shunned, should be accepted as a kind of baseline or all-purpose template for poetic expression. Such influences also suggest why more modern interpretive approaches committed to drawing a firm line of separation between the original and the conventional are likely to be an encumbrance more than an aid when coming to terms with the vast majority of verse produced during this period.

The closely related distinction between the private and public so foundational to definitions of the modern lyric can prove to be problematic for the same reason. It seems telling that Poe, the proverbial odd man out of US literary history, should stand virtually alone among his contemporaries in stipulating that verse should have nothing whatever to do with social concerns. As many of the essays in this volume make clear, the alliance between poetry and political advocacy remained strong throughout the century. Topical social commentary was of course a staple of verse satire in the early colonial period as well, but given the bond that subsequently developed between sentimentality and reform poets could often be drawn to more personalized styles of expression when addressing the public sphere. With writers like John Stuart Mill codifying the view that poetry was a distinct mode of speech oblivious to all recipients, free of narrowly partisan purposes, and therefore describable as "feeling confessing itself to itself, in moments of solitude,"[2] the growing tendency to associate the lyric with spontaneity and pure disinterestedness paradoxically helped to make it an option of first resort when combating social injustice. To cite one among many possible examples, readers of *The Liberator*, *Freedom's Journal*, or *North Star* were apt to find embedded, among the editorials, essays, and reviews against slavery, short poems in the first person expressing the same sentiments but set forth in a manner that makes designations such as private or public seem more unsatisfactory than usual or even beside the point. In short, as with the distinction between the original and the conventional, the distinction between the personal and political can quickly become counter-productive when applied to conceptions and expectations surrounding poetry in this era.

Scholarly reconsiderations of women's verse in general and the cultural politics of sentimentalism more specifically constitute a second factor in the new wave of interest surrounding nineteenth-century American verse. Much more than attempts to recover non-canonical, forgotten voices, several studies appearing over the past ten years have broken new ground in uncovering literary histories quite different from previous narratives purporting to trace a dynastic line of succession from the Puritans through Emerson and Whitman down to moderns like Stevens and Ashbery. For example, in her account of shifting conceptions of female authorship, *From School to Salon: Reading Nineteenth-Century American Women's Poetry* (2004), Mary Loeffelholz documents the gradual waning of the domestic-pedagogical model exemplified by figures like Sigourney early in the century and its replacement by a more self-consciously aestheticized version of female creativity, while in *Poets in the Public Sphere* (2003), Paula Bennett identifies a body of sentimental verse whose gestures of dissent run counter to its genteel reputation and that has its roots in an eighteenth-century discourse of popular female protest and complaint. The special attention directed toward networks of publication, transmission, and circulation, whether formally institutionalized or more locally linked in reading communities of the kind documented in Mary Louise Kete's *Sentimental Collaborations* (2000), is also typical of this scholarship and its recognition of the various ways in which production and reception overlap and mutually influence one another.

The same broadly contextual approach to authorship extends as well to studies of the reception and influence of various dominant male poets of the time, as in Angela Sorby's account of the Fireside or Schoolroom Poets and Joan Shelley Rubin's history of the uses of poetry from the later nineteenth to the twentieth century.[3]

Theorizing and implementing new reading strategies sensitive to the poetics of convention is particularly critical when it comes to making sense of that much-derided phenomenon, the Poetess. Contributions by Loeffelholz, Bennett, and others who have been working in concert with parallel investigations among scholars of Romantic and Victorian literature, have considerably enriched our understanding of this ubiquitous figure. The product of two intersecting discourses, both of relatively recent vintage, the Poetess answers the demand for lyric transparency by foregrounding a self-effacing persona typically rooted in a secret sorrow or inexpressible loss thought to be quintessentially feminine. Something more than a term to identify women who write poetry and something less than a programmatic movement with a distinct ideology, the Poetess represents a beguiling combination of the personal and impersonal symptomatic of sentimental culture more generally. This is not to say that all women's poetry written in this tradition follows the pattern of a uniform type; to read a study like Eliza Richards's *Gender and the Poetics of Reception in Poe's Circle* is to come away with a vivid sense of the sheer diversity of styles possible under the title of Poetess – from the calculated ephemerality of Frances Osgood, the eerily self-absenting spiritualism of Sarah Helen Whitman, or the ambitious reformism of Elizabeth Oakes Smith.

A third and final development brings us to the internationalizing of American studies that has made the very designation "American" a necessarily contested concept. Gruesz's fine study, *Ambassadors of Culture: The Transamerican Origins of Latino Writing* (2002), remains a model of what a hemispheric approach can do for the poetry of the Americas by reconstructing shared interests and juxtaposing clashing agendas in figures like William Cullen Bryant or Walt Whitman and contemporaries such as José Heredia or José Quintero. Two recent collections of essays have performed the same service by exploring the many-sided transatlantic connections between the United States and Europe in ways that, going beyond a simple interest in literary influence or nationalist rivalry, have called attention to the significance of authorial exchange, overlapping readerships, and competing mythologies across continents.[4] Moreover, in addition to recognizing the importance of developments outside of national boundaries, we should note a growing interest in contextualizing the achievement of various writing communities within them. Robert Parker's edition of Ojibwe poet Jane Johnston Schoolcraft is a case in point, as are Ivy Wilson's selection from Albery Allson Whitman's extensive body of writings or new editions of other African-American poets such as George Moses Horton.[5]

To the extent that each of the developments I've been describing indicates a turn away from a Modernist poetics and its guiding principles, they also constitute a turn away from past attempts to define the field. One such attempt may be found in Roy Harvey Pearce's ambitious, influential, and still-rewarding study, *The Continuity of American Poetry* (1961), whose main thesis is succinctly stated in its opening pages: "the Americanness of American poetry is, quite simply, its compulsive 'modernism'."[6] Doing for American poetry what F. O. Matthiessen's *American Renaissance* had done for prose fiction twenty years before, Pearce's book sought to give the modern academy a canon it could respect. In this he largely succeeded, setting the terms for subsequent treatments by Albert Gelpi, Hyatt Waggoner, and Edwin Fussell that also linked the quest for poetic originality with national identity.[7] And yet to see to the modern lyric as the destined culmination of American poetry is, unavoidably, to see much of what went before as a series of dead ends, false leads, or flawed approximations. As Virginia Jackson has pointed out on a number of occasions, the irony of a project like Pearce's is that in order to save pre-twentieth-century poetry it was, in effect, forced to deny its existence as a source of interest in its own right.[8] (Whitman and Dickinson are of course the great exceptions here, though even their induction into the Modernist pantheon is not without its problems, if the general direction of commentary written on these two poets over the past twenty years is any indication.)

This is not to say that efforts to construct a new literary history do not face challenges of their own. For one thing, it is not always clear that the new approaches are all that new. It is still possible to encounter, despite many excellent readings to the contrary, studies that uphold the importance of a neglected poet on the grounds of historical significance while discounting formal concerns as de-politicizing, just as one still finds accounts that cannot seem to get beyond affirming the importance of discontinuity and dislocation and the need for multiple literary histories instead of simply going forward with the work of actually developing them. And if such examples would seem to betray an insufficient distance from previous models of interpretation, others suggest hardly any distance at all, as when High Romantic notions of originality and transcendence are scorned in one moment only to reappear in another, usually in the moralizing of social convention as an oppressive constraint whose overcoming is the only authentic mark of poetic agency. Then, too, from the opposite standpoint, we may ask whether reading practices associated with modern versions of formalism are always and necessarily anachronistic when applied to nineteenth-century verse. Definitions of the lyric that are recognizably modern in emphasis began to flourish, after all, in the early decades of the nineteenth century; Mill's landmark essay on poetry as overheard speech, for example, was published in 1833. Cautions about sensitivity to historical context can therefore cut both ways. Adjudicating such matters is expressly the challenge faced by any number of the essays collected here, whether the topic at hand is Longfellow or the Poetess, the conventions of reading as they developed through the century or the late verse of Herman Melville. Inasmuch as the choice between affirming a master narrative that endures across centuries and insisting upon the absolute singularity of the historical event is a false one, the ongoing critical negotiation among various continuities and discontinuities within nineteenth-century American poetry may indeed be less a challenge to overcome than a sign that the field has at last become a legitimate object of scholarly interest.

This volume is divided in two parts, the first containing chapters on topics of broad thematic or generic concern and the second treatments of individual authors. Mary Louise Kete surveys the multiple sites for the reception and circulation of verse as they evolved through the century, from the keepsake albums or homemade anthologies collected by individuals to the mass marketing of illustrated gift books, the production of school readers, and the emergence of major publishing houses. With a neo-classical aesthetic grounded in classical standards of learning and wit giving way to a more Romantic sensibility celebrating the natural language of the soul, the association between poetry and "the exchange of verbal tokens of sentiments" became increasingly prevalent. Coinciding with and complicating this shift in taste was the rapid growth of a literary marketplace, which did not eliminate so much as capitalize on newer ideas about poetry as a personal token or possession. As Kete emphasizes, the growing popularity of the anthology provides one example among many of the ways in which the transition was made from a private economy of exchange to the growth of mass marketing, the focus on individual authors, and the centralization of the publishing industry. Needless to say, the expanded distribution and circulation of poetry that accompanied this centralization did not necessarily benefit all reading communities; and in fact Robert Parker begins his chapter by pointing out that, as white poets took advantage of their newfound access to wider national audiences, American Indian poets were all the more confined to highly localized and comparatively obscure venues, a fact that helps explain why discovering the true extent of verse written by native peoples is still very much a work in progress. Drawing upon texts recently collected in an anthology of his own arranging, Parker brings to light the range and interests of one community of writers and readers that has been as yet largely invisible to the literary history of this period.

Virginia Jackson's "The poet as Poetess" explores the history of a construct that became increasingly prominent in the nineteenth century, and asks what was at stake in its rise and fall and why we should continue to care about it. Rather than a quaint relic from a bygone era, the Poetess emerges in Jackson's discussion as the product of a recognizably modern form of cultural overdetermination that occurs once the feminine is identified in terms of an erring or extravagant affect. Beginning with the polished couplets of Phillis Wheatley (memorialized in print as the "Ethiopian Poetess") and proceeding to the consolation verse of Sigourney and the more ambivalent example of Oakes Smith, Jackson makes a provocative case for the centrality of a figure who, by personifying the very spirit of lyric sensibility, anticipates the ascendancy of the lyric over other all other modes of poetic production that is still with us today. The same emphasis on imaginative excess and transport, combined with an apparent lack of interest in formal innovation, characterizes the verse of the transcendentalists, the subject of Stephen Cushman's chapter, which begins by revisiting the perennial mystery as to how this group could be such bold theoreticians of poetry while remaining such tame practitioners. Interpreting lyrics by Christopher Cranch, Ellery Channing, Margaret Fuller, and Thoreau in light of manifestoes such as Emerson's "The Poet," Cushman corrects common misperceptions about transcendental notions of organic form and describes the rationale behind their thinking about meter and rhyme. Auditory devices for putting us literally on the same wavelength as the divine, conventions of form such as meter and rhyme are, by virtue of their very impersonality, idealized in transcendentalist poetics to the point where the subject matter becomes secondary and the personality of the poet an encumbrance. For the transcendentalist as for the Poetess, the perfection of poetic or generic form and the de-individualizing or abstraction of experience go together.

The adaptation of poetic forms to new, changing, or damaged social environments constitutes the main topic of concern in the three chapters by Max Cavitch, Eliza Richards, and Elizabeth Renker. In a strikingly innovative approach, Cavitch explores slavery and related forms of enforced labor from the standpoint of the regimentation and disciplining of time that was central to the regimentation and disciplining of the laboring subject. If, as Cushman points out, someone like Emerson could glorify rhyme for its power to free us from an "imprisoning materialism," Cavitch is interested in the same power to emancipate, but with the crucial qualification that this occurs through and not despite the body. In calling attention to the ways in which meter not only replicates but may be seen to resist bodily compulsion, his wide-ranging essay includes discussion of plantation work songs, Bryant's thoughts on prosody, a poem by an unknown hand entitled "Jefferson's Daughter," the minstrel show, and contemporary theorizing about rhythm. Eliza Richards's chapter on the poetry of the Civil War examines the double challenge of imagining death on a mass scale and of responding to the rise of a mass media that gave an unprecedented but unreal immediacy to such sacrifice. Noting the peculiar prominence accorded to descriptions of the weather in dispatches from the front, Richards focuses on evocations of violence and battlefield carnage insinuated through tropes of the weather in the lyrics of Elizabeth Akers Allen, Emily Dickinson, and others. Richards's interest in the ways in which "earlier forms of poetic expression ... might be revised, and adapted to a new, dislocated, shocked sensibility" continues in Elizabeth Renker's discussion of verse in the postbellum era, long regarded as something of a blank page in American literary history. Part of the reason for this lacuna may be traced to the assumption that poetry and social realism are incompatible, an assumption that was first espoused systematically, as Renker shows, among arbiters of taste and highbrow literary periodicals of the time. Against this association of the poetic with the genteel, Renker calls attention to the considerable body of poems and songs produced in working-class circles from the end of the Civil War until the end of the century and offers interpretations of poems by Donn and Sarah Piatt that demonstrate why it is a mistake to think of treatment of matters such as class conflict and exploitation as an exclusively prose phenomenon. Her discussion concludes with Melville's later lyrics, which are taken to voice a withering critique of the identification of verse with an otherworldly idealism.

The chapters on Longfellow and Sarah Piatt profile two figures whose accomplishments have only recently been received with the critical seriousness they deserve. In addition to addressing their better-known texts, both chapters call attention to the more uncharted areas of their verse and suggest paths for further inquiry. Stephen Burt helps us appreciate how readily Longfellow could write against as much as within the role of national bard by reading the more celebrated lyrics against other, less prominent texts that show a different side of this author, while Jess Roberts finds a similar ambivalence in Piatt's relation to certain conventions of authorship during her time. In both poets the line between originality and whatever we care to call its opposite could not be less clear. Burt argues that the concept of translation in its most extended sense best captures Longfellow's talent not just as a polyglot collector who adapts an astonishing variety of traditions and poetic techniques but also in his role as "consoler, lay priest, [and] public example." For Roberts, the expectation of unconditional sincerity on the part of the Poetess and Piatt's own impulse toward irony and self-dramatization does not constitute a source of tension in her lyrics so much as an initiating framework that the poems variously negotiate. As attempts to rethink the place of convention in poetry, both chapters point to new ways of valuing these two undervalued figures.

Poe, on the other hand, has never been entirely abandoned by posterity, even if his radical formalism has made it difficult for critics to locate a place for him in literary history. In "Poe and Southern poetry" John D. Kerkering turns this difficulty to advantage by assessing the impact of Poe's aesthetic theories on subsequent Southern poets who were swayed by his preoccupation with the musicality and thus the ideality of verse but who also departed from his theories in crucial ways. Thus Kerkering demonstrates how Henry Timrod increasingly distanced himself from Poe's insistence that poetry was entirely reducible to the effects it produced on a hypothetical reader by conceiving the poet to be "ultimately a messenger of thematic content to those who cannot share his elevated experience." And if for Timrod that content is in the end linked to a nationalist concern with Southern or Confederate independence, in the case of Sidney Lanier the appreciation for the purity of poetic sound takes the further step of being tied to the purity of a racial essence that replaces the division between North and South with the division between white and black. In its attention to unsuspected connections among song, sound, nation, and race, Kerkering's account invites comparison with Ivy Wilson's chapter on James Monroe Whitfield and Albery Allson Whitman, two African-American poets whose careers span the second half of the nineteenth century and whose work assumes a special bond between poetry and cultural or national distinction, down to the cadences and rhythms of the former. Whitfield's friend and fellow emigrationist Martin Delany thought highly enough of Whitfield's work to appropriate it for dramatic effect in his novel, *Blake*, which showcases poetry as an oratorical performance in the service of revolutionary ferment and which, as Wilson shows, is responsive to certain themes and preoccupations in Whitfield's book of poems, *America* (1853). In Albery Whitman we discover a poet also "consumed with the aesthetics of sound" whose experimentation in a wide range of verse forms and techniques is accompanied by an abiding patriotism that can at times border on nativism. Readers interested in learning more about the shifting course of African-American poetry and poetics in the aftermath of slavery and of literary models such as the slave narrative will welcome Wilson's important chapter.

The place of Whitman and Dickinson in this collection deserves separate comment. It goes without saying that a volume like this cannot hope to do justice to the full breadth and creativity of commentary produced on these two figures in the recent past; for that the reader is referred to the excellent, full-length studies dedicated to each that have already appeared in the Cambridge Companion series. It does seem fitting, though, given the aim of this particular collection, to conclude with chapters that engage the two writers so long regarded as the source and inspiration for a truly national poetry from an international perspective. The alchemy through which the latter is reconstituted into the former is in fact the burden of Donald Pease's searching meditation, which explores the logic whereby colonial violence mediates poetic inspiration in "Song of Myself." The violence in question concerns, most immediately, the massacre at Goliad during the armed conflict between Texas and Mexico in 1836: Pease reviews the history of the event, Whitman's invocation of its memory in his role as editor of the *Brooklyn Daily Eagle* advocating war against Mexico in 1846, and his return to the tragedy nearly ten years after that in Section 34 of "Song of Myself." Emphasizing Goliad's importance as a site that, from the standpoint of state sovereignty, was unlocatable and whose true history was, from the standpoint of US mythology, subject to erasure, Pease calls attention to its curiously disruptive appearance in a poem otherwise known for celebrating the continuity of body, self, and nation. Because it can no more be forgotten than adequately remembered, colonial violence emerges in his reading as an uncontainable, ramifying force that not only touches other parts of the poem but that serves as the hidden catalyst for Whitman's utterance or what Pease calls "the site of the celebratory enunciation of his song."

Along with the Americas, the geography of the Far East and Asia captivated Whitman's imagination, a fascination shared by contemporaries like Henry David Thoreau, Lydia Maria Child, and John Greenleaf Whittier. In the final contribution, Cristanne Miller explores Dickinson's own imaginative investment in these regions, first by reviewing representations and discourses about the Orient the poet would have been familiar with, and next by analyzing the ways in which her poetry variously adopts and rejects these prevailing notions. Miller identifies an impressive range of texts for discussion and relates the frequency of their references to the East to the vogue of Orientalist enthusiasm prevalent among the New England intellectuals during the 1850s and 1860s. Especially informative are the connections drawn between articles on foreign lands from the *Springfield Republican* (delivered to the Dickinson household daily) and the poet's allusions to sites such as the "Circassian Land," "the World Cashmere," or the Ottoman Empire, where "fanciful description" is often accompanied by "an implied political stance." Somewhat neglected in commentary on this poet, race plays an important role here, all the more so because Dickinson's encounters with her swarthy pearl divers and dusky gypsies occur beyond the framework of US race relations. Miller does not overlook or minimize the exoticism evident in the poet's imaginings of the Far East, though she also points to moments of sympathetic identification that accompany preconceptions about its luxury, sensuality, or an inscrutable remoteness. Responsive to a continuing interest among scholars to situate this famous recluse in contexts outside the precincts of Amherst, her chapter makes vivid Dickinson's own responsiveness to peoples and cultures and issues outside the boundaries of her own country.

NOTES

1 Kirsten Silva Gruesz, *Ambassadors of Culture: The Transamerican Origins of Latino Writing* (Princeton University Press, 2002), pp. xiii, 26.
2 J.S. Mill, *Autobiography and Literary Essays*, ed. John M. Robson and Jack Stillinger (Toronto: University of Toronto Press, 1981), p. 349.
3 Angela Sorby, *Schoolroom Poets: Childhood, Performance, and the Place of American Poetry* (Durham: University of New Hampshire Press, 2005); Joan Shelley Rubin, *Songs of Ourselves: The Uses of Poetry in America* (Cambridge, MA: Harvard University Press, 2007).
4 Meredith McGill, ed., *The Traffic in Poems: Nineteenth-Century Poetry and Transatlantic Exchange* (New Brunswick, NJ: Rutgers University Press, 2008); Augusta Rohrbach, ed., *Special Issue: Poetry* (*Emerson Society Quarterly: A Journal of the American Renaissance*, 54 [2008].)
5 Robert Dale Parker, ed., *The Sound the Stars Make Rushing Through the Sky: The Writings of Jane Johnston Schoolcraft* (Philadelphia: University of Pennsylvania Press, 2007); Ivy Wilson, ed., *At the Dusk of Dawn: Selected Poetry and Prose of Albery Allson Whitman* (Boston: Northeastern University Press, 2009); Joan Sherman, ed., *The Black Bard of North Carolina: George Moses Horton and His Poetry* (Chapel Hill: University of North Carolina Press, 1997).
6 Roy Harvey Pearce, *The Continuity of American Poetry* (Princeton University Press, 1961), p. 5.
7 Hyatt Waggoner, *American Poets: From the Puritans to the Present* (New York: Harcourt Brace, 1968); Edwin Fussell, *Lucifer in Harness: American Meter, Metaphor, and Diction* (Princeton University Press, 1973); Albert Gelpi, *The Tenth Muse: The Psyche of the American Poet* (Cambridge, MA: Harvard University Press, 1975).
8 See for example Virginia Jackson, "'The Story of Boon': or, the Poetess," *ESQ*, 54 (2008), 241–43; "Bryant, or American Romanticism," in McGill, ed., *The Traffic in Poems*, p. 187; and Jackson's chapter in this volume.

PART I

Mandates, movements, and manifestoes

I

MARY LOUISE KETE

The reception of nineteenth-century American poetry

If the pursuit of what an author "really" intended to convey in the words of a particular poem is a fascinating though frustrating task, the pursuit of what was understood by readers from some past moment and time – such as nineteenth-century America – is even more intriguing. Recently, scholars have turned to the question of how nineteenth-century Americans responded to the genre of poetry in order to resolve what, in conventional accounts, has seemed like a paradox: nineteenth-century Americans wrote and read poetry extensively and valued it highly but most of the poetry they wrote was judged by the twentieth-century to be inconsequential at best and ugly at worst. The rise of modernist aesthetics in the early twentieth century had so totally displaced what had come before that by mid-century even the names of many formerly important poets of the nineteenth century – especially the names of women poets – were forgotten. Even more forgotten was a sense of what readers had appreciated in the work of once famous poets such as Henry Wadsworth Longfellow or Lydia Sigourney. The New Criticism of the early part of the century and then the poststructuralist criticism of the last part of the century contributed to this, as they asked questions that nineteenth-century American poetry didn't seem to answer. But as scholars in the emerging fields of critical race studies and feminist studies started to search for, as Alice Walker puts it, "our mothers' gardens," they inaugurated a broad-reaching reevaluation of nineteenth-century literary history.[1] Since the assumption that texts are part of a social process was central to this project, questions concerning the reader became more and more pressing: who was reading what, in what contexts, with what expectations, and to what ends?

There seem to be many resources for answering these questions, since nineteenth-century Americans eagerly documented their lives. There are publishing records detailing what was published, what was sold where, and for how much. There are wills that show what books certain people owned. There are reviews by critics in newspapers and magazines that express opinions about what readers should read and why. There are the published texts of poems. But the more evidence like this reveals about what was published, the more it begs the question of what poetry meant to the people who were reading it. For to study the reception of poetry is to study the dynamic relationships between people for whom poetry – the reading, writing, giving, selling and buying of poems – is part of a set of gestures and actions through which they act upon the world. Such bookkeeping records can be supplemented by other, more inferential, kinds of evidence such as the diaries and correspondence of published authors, detailing their opinions about what they were reading. But there are also fictional and non-fictional narrative accounts of scenes of reading that provide glimpses into the place of reading in everyday lives. And, then, there are poems that are about reading. There are also keepsake books, diaries, and albums in which ordinary readers copied the poems they most treasured. But the most direct, though most fragmentary and tantalizing traces of evidence are found in the margins of published books where a teardrop, dog-ear or an emphatic "yes!" or "OH! No!" remains of at least one reader's response.

That there is so much evidence makes the pursuit of the questions concerning the place of poetry in nineteenth-century America ever more intriguing. Such abundance allows us to imagine that we can better conceptualize the changing coordinates of what Hans Robert Jauss called the "horizon of expectations" set by the various cultural norms, assumptions, and criteria that shape the way readers understand and judge a literary work.[2] The following discussion summarizes the best of the recent scholarship that has drawn on this kind of material to revise our understanding of the trends and transformations in the reception of poetry in nineteenth-century America. There are two axes along which changes occur in the reception of poetry over the course of the century: aesthetics and circulation. The most important shift on the axis of aesthetics was away from the neo-classical standards of taste toward the new romantic aesthetic that would dominate the rest of the nineteenth century. If the axis of aesthetics describes *what* people liked to read and what kind of pleasures they expected from reading poetry, the axis of circulation describes *how* readers gained access to poetry. Were they given a hand-copied poem as an expression of thanks? Did they listen to a recitation of a poem at a party? Did they read a poem printed in a newspaper along with the news from the capital and advertisements for patent medicines? Did they buy an anthology to see what was newest in American poetry; or had they saved up to buy the latest publication by their favorite celebrity poet? Or, were they required to read, memorize, and perform a group recitation of certain poems for a school graduation exercise? For the nineteenth century saw dramatic changes in the ways in which poetry circulated and these changes profoundly affected the ways in which readers understood and valued it. The most important transformation along this axis was the development of a commercial literary marketplace that multiplied the amount and kinds of poetry that were available to readers. This development transformed readers in remarkable and various ways over the course of the century and reshaped the dimensions of the horizon within which nineteenth-century Americans experienced poetry.

Though the kind of poetry that was revered and the kind of experience that poetry fostered changed over time and between different groups of nineteenth-century Americans, the fact that it was highly valued and widely practiced did not. Only the German philosopher Georg Wilhelm Hegel (1770–1831) had anticipated, what would seem so obvious to twentieth-century literary historians and so impossible to imagine for most nineteenth-century readers, that the novel would be to the newly dominant, middling classes of the new nationalist states what the epic poem had been to aristocratic cultures. Though many now would argue that this was particularly true in America, nineteenth-century Americans would have been greatly surprised by this claim. Poetry was everywhere. Their poets experimented in a wide variety of forms, participating in transatlantic aesthetic movements as well as in the project of articulating a distinctively American language to express the exceptionality of their national experience. But more importantly, though few would describe themselves as "poets," poetry pervaded the lives of ordinary Americans who found solace and amusement in the writing, reading, creation, and performance of verse in the home, the workplace, and their churches. This is what supported Ralph Waldo Emerson's prediction that poetry would lead in the new age and that America would sing itself in meter-making arguments despite America's more obviously prosaic aspects.[3] Likewise, in 1855 Walt Whitman could argue that the new American cosmos and its language of common sense was best celebrated in verse and in the 1860s, disappointed by the reception of his novels, Herman Melville turned to poetry as the only and best medium for capturing the horror of the war. Later, as the frontier closed in the decades after the Civil War, public schools seeking to produce a relatively unified and homogenous American school experience turned first to poetry. Central to that experience was the memorization and oral performance of poetry that inculcated certain myths of America above others and certain standards of grammar and pronunciation above others. Toward the end of the century, poetry that had become associated with schooling began to lose its status as art as the newly defined distinction between high or elite culture and low or popular culture became more and more important.[4]

Throughout the nineteenth century poetry was a social act that was integral, not incidental, to work, play, and worship. Though for the most part lost upon modern readers, poetry remained a consistent domestic art that played differing yet key roles in the constitution and reproduction of relationships within communities in the nineteenth century. The traces of this remain in narrative accounts, fictional and otherwise, including diaries or memoirs which recount the importance of learning and reciting poetry as a part of home entertainment or which recount the excitement of attending poetry readings at the local lyceum or opera hall. Poetry had an instrumental purpose – as prayer, as consolation, as instruction, as amusement – for it was key to the formation and consolidation of relationships. This was as true for black communities under the codes that restricted or criminalized literacy for slaves and other blacks throughout the first half of the century as it was for free white communities with access to education.

While the set of nineteenth-century African-American poets who published is very small until after the Civil War, the evidence for the importance of poetry to African-American cultures is strong. Traces of verse traditions came to be collected and published by white editors under rubrics such as "Negro Spirituals," "work songs," and "humorous songs." The importance of poetry is also attested to in slave narratives, the memoirs of slave owners, and accounts of travelers to the slave owning regions. Attenuated as they were by time, distance, and the force of slave owners who consciously attempted to disrupt language and cultural affinities, the West African conventions of narrative and lyric verse remained prominent. Some of these include character types, tropes, and situations from various West African epic traditions, or the responsorial – call and response – form of elegy or the trope of verbal sparring – signifying – between two or more participants. Most importantly, perhaps, was the ability to draw on deep traditions of oral-formulaic verse to subvert the effect of being officially locked out of the flow of information through printed channels. The fundamental power of verse to refract what it represents allowed slaves to share information and to create and perpetuate traditions that coalesce as a distinctively African-American vernacular culture.

The medium of verse helped to define, protect, and reproduce community values under adversity, both during the time of slavery and after, as the conclusion of the Civil War and the passage of the 13th, 14th, and 15th Amendments to the US Constitution ostensibly removed the legal barriers to literacy.[5] Even during the war, one of the most pressing needs that both private and government agencies had attempted to address was the freed people's lack of literacy skills. Central to the pedagogy used to teach literacy to both adults and children was poetry. Rhymes, as had been conventional

18

in Anglo-American education for centuries, were used as mnemonics for the alphabet, arithmetic, and basic facts. But both sacred verse, in the form of hymns or Bible texts, and secular verse in the form of popular contemporary volumes by authors such as Whittier and classic poetry from the English tradition such as Shakespeare were fundamental to the curriculum of the newly formed "freedmen schools." While poetry had a much greater place in all nineteenth-century schoolrooms than it does today, the emphasis on the recitation of poetry as a key to literacy overlapped helpfully with the oral practices of the formerly enslaved. This was not a new or unique occurrence, for from the earliest days of European colonialism's exploitation of Africans, poetry or verse had been one of the key nodes for the syncretism of various European and African traditions that comes to yield certain definitively American cultural forms such as gospel, jazz and rock and roll. In the years after the Civil War, black-owned presses began to publish for the new black readerships and black writers began to find black audiences who had a sophisticated, strong appetite for printed poetry. This is the environment that lays the groundwork for the explosion of black poetry in the early twentieth century.

The axis of taste

Poetry remained a constant throughout nineteenth-century America, but what was read and why it was considered beautiful did not. There were two major transformations. The most important was the shift in taste away from the neo-classical aesthetic of the late eighteenth and early nineteenth centuries toward the new romantic aesthetic. For America joined the transnational embrace of the romantic aesthetic quite late relative to Britain. Before the 1830s, American readers most valued poetry that advertised its own artfulness and displayed the poet's mastery of elevated yet decorous diction in the expression of universal truths from an ironic or didactic distance within a limited set of classical genres. The reasons for the continued dominance of this neo-classical aesthetic in early America are complicated. Not least of these is what Americans of the early national period would have understood as the natural alliance between their political project of forming a republic inspired by their understanding of the model provided by the Roman Republic and a standard of taste modeled upon their idealized understanding of the art of ancient Rome and Greece. One of the most famous poets of the early national period, Joel Barlow (1754–1812), believed that the classical aesthetic would direct poetry, painting and the other fine arts in such a way that they would transmit ideas of glory into human minds and in particular into the minds of Americans.[6] For Barlow and others of his

Revolutionary generation, the neo-classical aesthetic promised access to the world as it should and could be.

But a volume of poems published in 1773 by an enslaved black woman, Phillis Wheatley, from Boston, provides two other kinds of insight into what readers valued in the neo-classic aesthetic. One kind of insight comes from the provocative testimonials that introduce her *Poems on Various Subjects, Religious and Moral*.[7] Conventional wisdom held that neither girls nor Africans were intellectually capable of the kind of learning, analytical thought, and creative talent needed to write poetry of this order, so John Wheatley (the poet's putative owner) and the British publishers attempted to preempt any accusations of fraud that could be expected given the quality and content of the book. John Wheatley provided a brief account of the life of this prodigy who "was brought from *Africa* to America" (p. 7) as a little girl and mastered speaking, reading, and writing in English upon her own initiative and in less than two years. But the publishers also attach a public "Attestation, from the most respectable Characters in *Boston*, that none might have the least Ground for disputing their *Original*" ("To the Publick," p. 8). Much has, appropriately, been made of the racist and sexist dimensions of this famous scene in which the young black girl is examined by the leading men of Boston to ascertain whether she had indeed the learning in the classical tradition that would have been necessary for the author of the masterful neo-classical poems that were to be published under her name. Though much later Thomas Jefferson would try to insist that Wheatley's poetry was merely religious and therefore not art, no one in the room that day seemed to have doubts about the value of her poetry.[8] Rather, Wheatley is being examined precisely because her poetry seemed too good to have been written by "a young Negro Girl" (*Poems*, p. 8). It is true that no one would have publicly examined the qualifications of Timothy Dwight or Joel Barlow to write and publish verse modeled on their understanding of classical Greek and Roman models; as educated white men, though their talent might be questioned, their qualifications were established. No one knows what the Doctors of Divinity, government officials, and other leading men actually required of this young girl in order to convince them she was "thought qualified to write them" (p. 8) and no one knows what she felt during this interrogation. But her poems indicate that, like Dwight or Barlow or Milton before her, she would have accepted the idea that one needed to earn and defend one's qualifications to compete for the title of poet. No one was naturally a poet; both poems and poets were the products of artful work. And the most important qualification for a poet was to be a good reader and to be a good reader required access to a difficult canon of texts plus the talent and ability to master it. Once mastered, however, this difficult reading allowed the reader access to experiences, feelings, and knowledge that would otherwise be alien. It is because neither the reading nor the writing of poetry was valued for its "naturalness" but rather as an art that Phillis Wheatley was able to transcend what was understood as her "natural" limitations of sex, race, and servitude.

Full of apt allusions to Latin and Greek authors, Wheatley's *Poems on Various Subjects* shows her mastery of the common neo-classic genres including odes, elegies, epigrams, ekphrases, and aubades. But Wheatley's opening poem, the ode "To Maecenas," is one of the fullest expressions of the difficult pleasures of reading in the neo-classical mode and perhaps the best testament to Phillis Wheatley's qualifications to be an author. To be an author, a poet, meant first having been an authoritative reader and, second, being able to address an authoritative reader whose recognition would seal one's authority. Excellent poetry – "what poets sung, and shepherds play'd" – depends upon having a reader whose "genius" is equal to receiving or recognizing the "noble strains" of poets (p. 9). Maecenas, the famous patron of Virgil and Horace in Augustan Rome, here stands in for all of Wheatley's patrons: John Wheatley but also the group of the "most respectable Characters in *Boston*" who so famously judged her as "qualified" to have written these poems (p. 9). "To Maecenas" details the experience of excellent reading that, the poem declares, she shares with those readers who have become her patrons. First, reading poets such as Homer causes a sensational response in the qualified reader: she feels the earth move, she sees lightning, she experiences horror and sympathy for characters who inhabit a very different world from colonial New England. Second, reading the classic writers leads the speaker to self-reflection as they provide a standard against which she can judge her own work. Lastly, reading the classics has given shape to the speaker's ambitions. Audaciously, for a "young Negro Girl ... under the Disadvantage of serving as a Slave," the speaker apparently seeks to be the second of "*Afric's* sable race" to find "first glory in the rolls of fame" (p. 10). "To Maecenas" demonstrates the liberating qualities of a rigorous aesthetic for it allows a young slave to transcend the contingencies of her everyday life, to feel with the aristocratic heroes of the *Iliad*, to stake a claim to challenge Virgil for the laurels which would mark one as deserving universally acknowledged and eternal fame. The pleasure offered by the neo-classical aesthetic is the pleasure of rules fulfilled, universal standards achieved, and objective truths prevailing through skill and wit on the part of reader and writer. It is the pleasure of the confrontation with difference, particularly the difference between one's ordinary, disappointing, and limited life and the extra-ordinary and un-limited because abstracted, perfections of a depicted world.

By the 1830s, however, American tastes had shifted dramatically as they began to articulate an American version of the Romantic aesthetic. Readers increasingly turned to poetry that operated in a very different mode, one that offered not escape from the particular contingencies of the self but a fuller expression of the unique subjectivity of the individual. This happens gradually, beginning in the second decade of the nineteenth century as poets such as William Cullen Bryant and Lydia Sigourney begin publishing poems influenced by their reading of the British Romantic poets. Bryant's "Thanatopsis" of 1817 and Sigourney's *Moral Pieces in Prose and Verse* of 1815 are two of the earliest indications that the horizon of expectations had begun to change along the axis of aesthetics. Americans began to value poetry that stressed the importance of emotions and that strove to express areas of experience neglected or invisible to the rational mind in a language and a style that was unique to the individual subject. For the individual became the source and standard of beauty; and nature, loss, children, and the pathos of everyday life became the favored topics. This shift seemed to many as a shift toward a more democratic aesthetics. As Emerson would explain in the 1830s, the experiences of the ordinary non-heroic person were as worthy of celebration as the extra-ordinary experiences of heroes.[9] To be a poet did not mean being first an excellent, practiced, and sophisticated reader of the art of others but to be an excellent reader of one's self and thus one's world; to be a poet meant being able to collaborate in the ongoing artistic creation of the world and to be one's most natural self. Good poetry, like good poets, was less the result of art than the triumph of nature. Good poetry, as Emerson puts it in "The American Scholar," makes the reader feel: "This is my music; this is myself."

Lydia Sigourney's popular poem, "The Unspoken Language" of 1849, explains this shift along the axis of aesthetic value as well or better than any essay from the era as it makes an argument for the superiority of spontaneous inspiration and the natural language of the soul. Verbal language, she begins, "is slow, the mastery of wants / Doth teach it to the infant, drop by drop." "Years of studious toil / Unfold its classic labyrinths to the boy" and "He who would acquire / The Speech of many lands, must make the lamp / His friend at midnight."[10] Sigourney then proposes that this course is incomplete if it does not recognize the prior and superior claims of the "unspoken language" of love, which is "Simple and sure, that asks no discipline / Of weary years." This love, "the language of the soul," is not learned from books or any rational practice. Instead it is "told through the eye" in an instantaneous moment of mutual identification between the beholder and the beheld that, as Sigourney depicts, every ordinary person could expect to have experienced (p. 35). Her models are not laurelled poets, but ordinary people at moments of emotional crisis: a mother and child, two young people in love, a woman at a friend's deathbed.

The supremacy of this non-verbal and extra-rational communication stems from its lack of artifice: it cannot be faked since it bears the "signet ring of truth" that is recognizable to any reader from personal experience (p. 35). Poetry written in this "language of the soul" as Sigourney would put it (or the "dialect of common sense" as Whitman called it,[11] or the "discourse of sentiment" as literary theorists call it) appealed to readers on very different grounds than had the neo-classical aesthetic and created a very different kind of experience. Henry Wadsworth Longfellow's "Dedication" to his masterwork of 1850, *The Seaside and the Fireside*, offers additional insight into the nature of this romantic reading experience that depends upon the ability of the poet to deploy the grammar and lexicon of shared emotion against what seems to be normative forces of alienation, in which individuals are otherwise separated by distance, death, or time. The poem begins with a depiction of the speaker:

> As one who, walking in the twilight gloom,
>   Hears round about him voices as it darkens,
> And seeing not the forms from which they come,
>   Pauses from time to time, and turns and hearkens.

This lonely figure walking on the shore is able to "hear" the voices of his friends (despite their absence) who have sent "words of friendship, comfort and assistance" in the language of sentiment. Not only does this language allow "kind messages" to "pass from land to land," but also and more importantly, it can convey the actual "pressure of a hand." Toward the ending of the poem, the reader of the poem is addressed in the second person and described in terms quite similar to the ones in which the speaker had described himself: walking by the seaside, "Saddened, and mostly silent, with emotion." Readers of this kind of poetry had the chance to, as Longfellow puts it, learn from the "silent tokens" that "when seeming most alone, / Friends are around us, though no word be spoken" aloud; the dead can continue to help the living and in fact can "live forever young" in the form of emotional memories encoded in verse. "Dedication" suggests that Longfellow understood that the exchange of verbal tokens of sentiments or emotions offered a way to bridge alienation, to collaborate with another in "endeavor[s] for the selfsame ends, / With the same hopes, and fears and aspirations."[12]

American readers responded strongly to the romantic valorization of strong emotions and the power of emotions to work upon the world. Many poems depict the power of emotional conversation to form communities as in the case of Longfellow's "Dedication," or to create gardens out of deserts as in the case of William Cullen Bryant's "The Prairies" of 1832. "The Prairies" models the kind of romantic reading that transforms the world (which Emerson would call "creative reading") into something created by and constitutive of the self. In contrast to the model of neo-classic reading offered by Wheatley, this one requires only a physical and emotional access to nature and it leads not to the reader aspiring to become something other than the self but to the speaker becoming more of the self. In reaction to his first sight of the prairies, something for "which the speech of England has no name," the speaker's "heart swells, while the dilated sight / Takes in the encircling vastness." The viewer and the viewed collapse in Bryant's word "sight," which encompasses both the speaker's organ of perception and the object of perception in its dilation. Fostering an emotional response to whatever is being perceived, in the case of the speaker of "The Prairies" the vastness of the western prairie, or in the case of the reader the poem "The Prairies" itself, encourages an American experience of sublimity. Having entered into an emotional sympathy with the prairie that allows the speaker to read more than he can see – to imagine the past and the future of the prairies – and to become a co-creator of what of he sees, the speaker ends with a newfound confirmation of his radical individuality: "in the wilderness alone."[13]

Like much American romantic poetry, Bryant's poetry invites the reader to appropriate the experience of "The Prairies" toward the reader's own task of self-making, not only in terms of the topic of the poem, but also in terms of the formal devices of the poem which work toward enhancing its accessibility and toward breaking down the difference between author and reader. Longfellow and Sigourney, like Bryant, worked in many of the conventional lyric and narrative verse forms, allowing the familiarity of the form (including conventional rhyme schemes and meters) to help foster an emotional connection with the material. Edgar Allan Poe, in fact, claimed that poems worked – elicited emotional sensory responses – primarily due to the formal elements of poems that could affect the reader on an extra-rational level.

The second major shift along the axis of taste comes quite late in the century and is much less dramatic than the shift from the neo-classical to romantic aesthetic, but it marks a significant transformation in the cultural poetics of poetry. Americans continued to value poetry that appealed primarily to feelings and which grounded its authority on the authenticity of the poet's voice. But increasingly over the last quarter of the century they began to appreciate greater formal experimentation as a way to achieve a more realistic expression of the world as it is perceived. Walt Whitman, for example, shared the American romantic desire to create poetry that appealed to, spoke for and with the emotional and sensational natures of an American audience. But his initial audiences were put off by what they saw not as formal innovations but as lapses from, or failures of, convention that got in the way of his achieving these goals. But by the closing decades of the nineteenth century more Americans began to appreciate poetry that was more innovative, that was more obviously about aesthetic concerns such as language and form, that was less anxious about being accessible to readers, and was more interested in displaying the originality of the author and the author's powers of perception. The early romantic and sentimental dictum of "make it work" had begun to be replaced by the modernist urge to "make it new."

The axis of circulation

So much changed in terms of the material conditions of reading poetry over the course of the nineteenth century and each of these changes affected the way readers understood, judged, and used poetry. Among other things, first oil, then gas, then electricity replaced candles and daylight for many; emancipation and the free public school movement radically expanded the percentage of readers; paper became cheaper, printing processes became faster, rail and canal transport made shipping published material faster. Each of these changes affected the poetics of reception as much as any changes of aesthetic standards. The most important transformations along the axis of circulation came with the proliferation of mass media venues for publication: the development of a commercial literary marketplace through which poetry circulated to readers in exchange for money. This supplemented the gift-oriented, non-commercial economy through which poetry had traditionally circulated within colonial America and that continued to operate through the nineteenth century. American readers became buyers of poetry.[14] Later, a second transformation on the axis of circulation came when poetry became institutionalized, not only within the new publishing industry, but also within the American educational system. Each of these stages along the axis of circulation – gift, commodity, imposition – shifts the expectations and the quality of the experience of reading poetry.

On the gift economy pole of the axis of circulation, authority tends to be vested in the reader, who serves as a patron whose judgment rests on whether a particular poem serves that reader's purpose. Beginning in the early part of the century, young Americans took up the habit of exchanging keepsake poetry among their friends and neighbors and keeping it in personal collections. These albums also provide insight into what the writers were reading and insight into what they valued to the degree of wanting to redeploy these as representations of themselves. The function or purpose of this long-standing trend was summarized in the dedication to one example of these:

> Should dearest friends some kind memento trace,
> Along the unwritten columns of this book
> When distance or the grave hides form and face
> Into this volume sweet 'twill be to look.
> Each fond remembrance oft will speak to you
> In language which may never be forgot
> Of those who ever constant were and true
> And gently whisper O forget me not.[15]

Throughout the first half of the century these albums tended to contain handwritten if not originally composed poetry. As repositories of "fond remembrances," the poetics of these albums is, above all, devoted to the function of bridging the distances of geography or death by allowing the writer to continue to speak to (or whisper to) the reader in a language, because shared, which will never be forgot.

In the early part of the century, the poems in these albums are drawn from the poetry columns of newspapers, from hymns or song lyrics shared in church or in choral groups such as shape note singing societies. The poems in these early albums are written by hand, carefully, in ink or pencil. One of their most interesting characteristics is the tendency for the writer or copier of the verse to make small personalizing changes in poems by published authors and then put their own names to them without anxiety as to the "ownership" of the poems. They might be adaptations of Shakespearean sonnets, copies of popularly reprinted mourning verse by an American author, or wholly original attempts to celebrate the bond felt between the writer and the reader of the poems. On the one hand, this reflects what I have called the instrumental or functional nature of the poetics of these books, since what is important in a given poem is its potential to continue the emotional and reciprocal bond between reader and writer. On the other, it reflects the difference between what later coalesces into a canon of British and American nineteenth-century poets under the attention of scholars and experts and the wider field of poetry from which this canon derived.

By the 1830s, as developments in print technology and the economy facilitated the expansion of the number of presses in America, publishers began to foster the habit of gift book keeping and exchange. Presses began to produce elaborately bound dedicated "blank books" containing illustrations and other "apparatus" designed to encourage the owner's practice of poetry. Before that, Americans would have turned any bound tablet of paper to this purpose or even sewn their own loose sheets of paper into a "book."

One of the most conventional things about Emily Dickinson's life was that she occasionally gave the poetry she wrote as gifts to her close friends and neighbors. Presses also began to market anthologies of verse, illustrations, and short prose in attractive, though relatively inexpensive, volumes designed to be given as presents. This trend started in the late 1820s with the production of many *Tokens, Garlands* and *Albums* organized thematically for specific markets: members of certain churches, reform groups, or the new holiday market that came into being as the celebration of Christmas began to become commercialized. Though some of these gift books might feature original verse by famous or familiar poets, which had been commissioned specifically, they also contained many reprints of non-attributed works or works by poets who were not protected by copyright until much later in the century. Commercially published gift books joined the world of the private gift economy of the ordinary reader to the public market economy of the commercial literary marketplace. Modeled upon earlier traditions of manuscript album keeping, these served, in turn, as models for how one might arrange one's own personal album – what should be included, what principles of taste, what principles of organization.

Whether a keepsake book was a collection of remembrances produced for or by the owner or a collection of poems produced by a publisher to target an imagined audience sharing particular values (such as abolition or Congregationalism), they share several important characteristics. First, they are anthologies – collections of disparate pieces organized in response to the perceived needs of the readers rather than as an expression of a particular author's coherent aesthetic. Second, they depend heavily on the practice of appropriating previously published (or produced) work to a new poetic context. In the first case, the critical point is that the keepsake book is reader-centric. In the second case, the critical point is that the poetics of keepsake books is essentially conservative in that it favors the redeployment of items into new forms in a manner similar to that followed by the quilter or, as the late Claude Lévi-Strauss put it, the *bricoleur* who recycles heterogeneous, found materials into something new.[16] From mid-century on, in fact, the owners of these albums tended to supplement handwritten verse entries with typeset poetry, news stories, or pictures cut from publications such as newspapers or magazines. But thirdly, these keepsake books were repositories of gifts the owner had received and could imagine, one day, passing on as a legacy of his or her emotional existence.

In the 1820s, when a young Bowdoin College student, Henry Wadsworth Longfellow, announced to his father his ambition to become a professional poet his father replied, "there is not wealth enough in this country to afford encouragement and patronage to merely literary men."[17] This less than enthusiastic response might seem painfully familiar to any number of English majors whose parents wonder, like Stephen Longfellow, why their bright child refuses to consider law school. However, in America of the 1820s as had been true in colonial America, there really was no way to make money – support oneself – as a poet. Poetry generally, as had been true of Phillis Wheatley's volume, was published by subscription, a process by which authors and booksellers would ask patrons for a gift of money to underwrite the printing of an edition. In exchange, the patron would receive a copy of the book as a kind of present. Of course, Phillis Wheatley could never have made money from the publication of her book in any case since as a slave and as a girl any profit would have gone to her master. But even had she not been a slave girl, she would not have expected to make more than a token profit. There would be no economic market in America for poetry *per se* despite a high demand for it on the part of readers until at least the 1840s. Early in the century, the logic of the gift governed not only the verse written by the many Americans who did not aspire to the title of poet (though they may have been assiduous writers of verse) but also to the work of those like Wheatley or Longfellow who did.

One reason why there was no commercial marketplace for poetry in the early part of the century had to do with copyright law. Through the early part of the nineteenth century, American presses were theoretically required by law to pay to reprint the work of American authors, but didn't have to pay to reprint the work of non-American authors. Early presses could easily give their readers as much poetry as they wanted – and they wanted a lot – without paying for it by reprinting works by British authors or by printing verse by local writers who felt honored just to see their work in print. This may also have had to do with the poetics of neo-classicalism, in which the cultural value of art was in inverse relation to its economic value: poetry was beyond a price.

In any case the rapid expansion of the publishing industry in the first half of the nineteenth century both depended on and fostered the appetite of Americans for poetry. To a degree, the "pricelessness" of poetry subsidized the proliferation of newspapers that could no more forgo the poetry column than twentieth-century local newspapers could forgo a comics section. Editors of these local papers chose their selections from various sources, including their readers, other newspapers, magazines, and books, without bothering themselves too much about paying or even accurately acknowledging the authors. Magazines like the famous *Godey's Lady's Book* sought large regional and later national audiences and competed aggressively with each other for a place in the kitchen or on the parlor tables, where they served as a common pantry of print for anyone in the family to draw on. In

America, these magazines and newspapers were often the only supplement a family might have to the Bible that also, with its variety of genres, served as a kind of general storehouse of culture for its readers. As a storehouse or pantry, the magazine or newspaper encouraged extensive but also instrumental reading. Like a dress pattern, the poetry in a magazine was there to be used, appropriated, and adapted by its readers.

Poetry from commercial sources like magazines often found its way, sometimes slightly changed, into non-commercial circulation as readers appropriated a poem for their own purposes. But magazines or journals were also crucial to the formation of self-conscious and non-geographically bound reading communities interested in shared aesthetic or cultural goals. One of the most important, though short-lived of these, was *The Dial*, but it did much to articulate and disseminate the values and work of the American transcendentalists far beyond the geographical limits of Concord and Boston. And readers from Vermont or Maine, for example, could agree or disagree with the aesthetic arguments made by Edgar Allan Poe in Virginia's *Southern Literary Messenger*. Abolitionists could read inspiring verse in Frederick Douglass's *North Star*. Editors such as Poe or Fuller or later William Dean Howells could use their power of deciding who and what to publish and, hence, who and what would be read. But they also began to articulate and argue for the principles of taste they used in making these decisions. Informal academies of taste and tastemakers began to coalesce around certain periodicals. Distinctions began to be made; and readers with money could endorse or reject these distinctions by buying particular magazines rather than others, hoping to read particular poets or kinds of poetry rather than others. The problem of patronage that Longfellow's father had worried about was solved, as poetry became a commodity that American readers, as consumers, could subsidize not only through giving and receiving but through buying. As consumers, readers could enter into an extended community with the poets they liked through buying their works.

The rise of a literary marketplace expanded the kinds of poetry that were available for readers to appropriate in their personal economies. But in mid-century, what Meredith McGill has described as the culture of the reprint gave way as the rights of authors to payment and to proper attribution gained currency and legal support.[18] Readers, too, began to more firmly associate the names of living authors with their poems, which makes sense as a shift toward the romantic aesthetic insisted that the value of a poem depends on the authenticity of its connection to the essential nature of the author's self. Beginning in the 1830s and 1840s, authors such as Lydia Sigourney began to recognize how much presses, in their publications of gift books, newspapers, and magazines, relied on poetry to make their money.

Recognizing and embracing the commodity value of poetry, Sigourney and others inaugurated a new professional possibility even as they shifted the taste of American readers toward the new romantic aesthetic that would thrive in a commercial literary marketplace. By demanding to be paid and to have their work published under their own names, poets were not only assuring their own property rights. They were also making the name of the poet part of the value of the poem: in other words, they were establishing a meaningful distinction or difference in value between poems written by oneself or one's neighbor and a poem written by Longfellow. Poets such as Longfellow and Sigourney thus helped to create a market for single-authored volumes of poems. Presses eagerly produced volumes at various price points based on the quality of the bindings and number of illustrations for audiences who began to make cult figures of certain American poets. For the rise of a commercial marketplace for poetry created a new relationship between readers and poetry. On the market pole of the axis of circulation, authority is vested outside the reader in the author and in institutionalized arbiters of taste such as editors, critics, and publishers. Now consumers rather than patrons, readers increasingly sought and enjoyed authoritative guidance to make sense of the proliferation of American poetry.

In the 1840s, magazines, newspapers, and commercial gift books were joined by a new kind of publication: the anthology. Gift books, newspapers, and magazines all share aspects of the anthology in that they are collections, but the new anthologies, pioneered by Rufus Griswold in 1842 with the publication of his *Poets and Poetry of America*, offered readers collections sorted by broad rubrics that apparently appealed strongly to his readers. Though it was and continues to be argued that by the term, "American Poet," Griswold meant poets born in America whom he knew or whom he thought he would benefit from, he offered a pragmatic baseline for what had been a somewhat abstract argument over the nature and possibility of a distinctively American poetry. *Poets and Poetry of America* keyed into an eager desire of American readers to read their selves in the form of poetry written by fellow Americans and marks the currency of antebellum America's concern with the problem of national identity. The poems provided a range of examples of how Americans were experiencing the world and a range of examples of how to express these American experiences for readers to learn from and for readers to judge themselves against. But Griswold's other anthology of 1842, *Gems of Female American Poets*, reflected America's interest in (or perhaps anxiety over) the question of gender. Griswold expanded his project in 1848 into an even more comprehensive *Female Poets of America* to meet an expanding audience of readers willing and eager not only to read the actual poetry of these authors but also to view the public display of what would otherwise be the private lives of women. For Griswold's anthologies introduced each poetess with a biographical note and often a picture that emphasized the characteristics of the "female poet" that he endorsed. These stylized portraits offered a particular model of femininity, one that diminished the challenge to conventional gender hierarchy otherwise posed by the concept of a woman participating in the public sphere of the literary marketplace.

Much of the contention that surrounded Griswold's publications came from fellow critics who realized how much was at stake in the establishment of a canon of approved poets and poetry. As the main way that poetry circulated in America had shifted by mid-century to the market, money was a not inconsiderable concern. But the success of anthologies and magazines speaks also to the desire of Americans to be taught through and about poetry. Early on, nineteenth-century educators such as Emma Willard, Lydia Sigourney, and Horace Mann had all included verse in the schoolbooks they designed for their own use. Verse had been a staple pedagogical tool for centuries. But in mid-century even adult readers were willing and eager to be taught what it meant to be an American or an American woman through poetry. Part of the appeal of the set of poets first known as the Fireside Poets (Longfellow, Whittier, Lowell, and Holmes) was not just their willingness to be accessible to a reader as a welcome friend at the fireside, but also to allow the reader to learn from what the poet shared. But the term "Fireside Poets" suggests that the readers and the authors are participating in a kind of educational collaboration – a conversation – if not between equals, then between parties who both have something to contribute.

Later in the nineteenth century, this same group of poets was renamed as the "School Room Poets" in acknowledgment of their having been enlisted in the frankly ideological work of serving the developing American public education system.[19] Poems such as Whittier's *Snow-bound* or Longfellow's "Paul Revere's Ride" supplied material for learning to read both silently and out loud. Students were required to memorize and to perform poetry, alone and in groups, as part of the curriculum on which they were officially judged and as part of organized entertainments. These poems helped students to internalize a shared sense of what it sounded like, felt like, and meant to be an American, whether one was a freed slave, a recent immigrant, a white settler of Nebraska, or a student at Boston Latin School. But this canonization had a deleterious effect on the aesthetic standing of these poets and of their aesthetic since they came to be so associated with children, pedagogy, and the enforced consumption of poetry. The dominant aesthetic mode would form in reaction against both everything that nineteenth-century Americans had thought beautiful and the main ways that nineteenth-century Americans had valued poetry.

Conclusion

Mary Wilkins Freeman's short story "The Poetess" of 1890 provides a dramatic description of the intersection of the aesthetic axis of the horizon of expectations with the axis of circulation. Freeman's story reminds us that the study of the reception of poetry involves the study of the dynamic relationships between people as it tells of the last days of "the very genius of gentle old-fashioned, sentimental poetry."[20] An atypical genius or muse, Freeman's protagonist Betsy is an older, impoverished, but genteel poetess who lives in an unnamed New England village where the vestiges of former prosperity struggle valiantly for dignity in an environment characterized by late-summer dust and poorly bearing bean-vines. Looking into the face of a bereaved mother who has asked her to write a poem commemorating a boy who has just died, the poetess's "face took on unconsciously lines of grief so like the other woman's that she looked like her for a minute" (p. 109), despite what Freeman describes as important differences. In stark contrast to her younger, plump, financially secure, and married friend, Betsy the poetess is poor to the point of starvation, unmarried, childless. Freeman spends quite a bit of effort to describe the operation of sentiment as it circulates through a gift economy. Translating the "unspoken language" of emotions into verse allows the poetess to sympathetically bridge these differences to produce a poem that does more than commemorate the dead boy. Betsy's poetry is the epitome of sentimentality as it depends upon her ability to enter into, and then express in words, the feelings of others rather than on any desire to express the uniqueness of her own limited, individual experience.

Freeman's story aptly describes the operation of the gift economy of sentiment that not only links individuals together into communities, but also helps to constitute the individual subjectivity of the participants. So moved is the mother by the poetess's ability to express her loss, she has the elegy professionally printed and presentation copies made so that she may share them with her friends and relatives, who, she assumes, share in her grief and will appreciate the gift of consolation that the poem offers. Having given her poem freely to her younger friend, the poetess enjoys the return of extensive recognition for her self – as the poetess – and her work as the poem circulates through the village. Giving the poem to her circle of neighbors is a way for the grieving mother to engage them in a collaborative task of reconstituting her self in the face of her loss. So elegant is the "appearance of this last" poem that it "was worth more to her [Betsy] than its words represented in so many dollars" (p. 115), for though she may have barely enough to eat, this kind of publication verifies her status as a poet, her status as a person whose existence matters. In Freeman's story, both women are confident that everyone will appreciate such a tasteful and touching testament to the lost boy, the mother's grief, and the poetess's gift. Both women are shocked to learn that their confidence is, tragically, misplaced.

Upon being told that the college-educated minister of the village, who has himself published poetry in commercial magazines, has deemed that the *"poetry you wrote was jest as poor as it could be, an' it was in dreadful bad taste to have it printed an' sent round that way,"* the poetess burns all her poetry, gathers its ashes in a china teacup, and succumbs to an illness that has been complicated by poverty (p. 115, author's italics). On her deathbed, the poetess asks the minister to remember her in verse – hoping that "if she never wrote poetry that was any good, she might make a good subject for good poetry" (p. 120). The sentimental form and practice of poetry, of which the poetess is the muse, is not just "old-fashioned," it is obsolete, supplanted, or (as in this story) killed by a shift in aesthetics and by a wholesale transformation of the expectations for how poetry should be distributed. In Freeman's story, the superiority of the minister's taste is signaled to the villagers by the fact that his poetry has a commodity value – it has been bought and sold, printed and distributed – in the public marketplace. Betsy's poetry, being a gift, is beyond and beneath price. Suddenly, since it has no price – no sign of material value having been ascribed by some kind of public standard – it has no value. Freeman's realist local color story is, perhaps, overly melodramatic. But it is generally true that at the beginning of the century the main way poetry circulated in America was predominantly through some version of gift exchange and by the end of the century the balance had shifted toward a commercial market. And it is true that this shift had a profound, though not necessarily mortal, effect on the horizon of expectations within which American readers experienced poetry. Freeman's story marks the tipping point on the axis of circulation as it attempts to describe the human and therefore aesthetic consequences of this shift.

NOTES

1 The title essay to Alice Walker's collection *In Search of Our Mothers' Gardens* (New York: Harcourt Brace Jovanovich, 1983) reminds us that we must sometimes search beyond the literary traditions to find the cultural legacy left to us by those whose circumstances limited their access to print.

2 Hans Robert Jauss's 1970 study *Towards an Aesthetic of Reception* (Minneapolis: University of Minnesota Press) was one of a set of important works from that period that laid the groundwork for the revisions in how scholars think about and construct literary history.

3 Poetry was of great concern to Ralph Waldo Emerson whether he was, as in "The American Scholar," investigating the challenges to an American culture or, in "The Poet," exploring what it would mean if individuals realized their actual potential as creators.

4 In an early example of the powerful new literary history, Lawrence Levine's *Highbrow/Lowbrow* (Cambridge, MA: Harvard University Press, 1990) explains the way that a hierarchy of culture displaces a more heterogeneous, eclectic, and protean sense of culture in the later nineteenth century.

5 The 13th Amendment (1865) abolishes slavery, the 14th (1868) grants citizenship to former slaves, and the 15th (1870) extends the right to vote to black men. Passed during Reconstruction, the privileges and rights granted by these Amendments were systematically subverted by local statutes, mores, and vigilante violence until reinforced by the Civil Rights Acts of 1964.

6 Barlow, in fact, tried to write an epic of America, called *The Columbiad*, that would deploy the power of the classical aesthetic.

7 As remained conventional for publications by African Americans up through the middle of the nineteenth century, Wheatley's volume is introduced by white authors. See Vincent Carretta's edition of *The Complete Poems of Phillis Wheatley* (New York: Penguin, 2001). Subsequent page references from this text will be cited in parentheses.

8 See Query XIV of Thomas Jefferson's *Notes on the State of Virginia*, ed. Frank Shuffleton (New York: Penguin, 1999), p. 147.

9 As Emerson put it in "The American Scholar" (1837), "the literature of the poor, the feelings of the child, the philosophy of the street, the meaning of household life, are the topics of the time" (*The Norton Edition of Emerson's Prose and Poetry*, ed. Joel Porte and Saundra Morris [New York: Norton, 2001], p. 67).

10 Lydia Sigourney, *Illustrated Poems by Mrs. L.H. Sigourney* (Philadelphia: Carey and Hart, 1849), pp. 34–39. Subsequent page references from this text will be cited in parentheses.

11 In the "Preface" to the 1855 edition of *Leaves of Grass*, Walt Whitman attempts to define the character of American English as "the powerful language of resistance ... it is the dialect of common sense." See Richard Bridgman's facsimile edition of the 1855 *Leaves of Grass* (San Francisco: Chandler Publishing, 1968).

12 *The Complete Works of Henry Wadsworth Longfellow*, 14 vols. (Boston: Houghton Mifflin, 1902), II: 123, 124.

13 *The Poetry of the American Renaissance*, ed. Paul Kane (New York: Braziller, 1995), pp. 35–38.

14 See Mary Louise Kete's *Sentimental Collaborations: Mourning and Middle-Class Identity in Nineteenth-Century America* (Durham, NC: Duke University Press, 2000) for a discussion of the way that anthropological models for understanding how gifts work in both traditional and contemporary cultures help us to understand literary poetics.

15 In 1837 Lois Gould wrote this on the first page of a blank book she was giving to her daughter-in-law, to be used as an album which she had titled *Harriet Gould's Book*. The texts of the poems from *Harriet Gould's Book* are copied in the appendix to Kete, *Sentimental Collaborations*.

16 The anthropologist and cultural theorist, Claude Lévi-Strauss, introduced a serious consideration of the way that do-it-yourselfers (*bricoleurs*) turn bits and

pieces of available materials into new, useful, and even beautiful things, in his *The Savage Mind* (University of Chicago Press, 1966).

17 Samuel Longfellow, *The Life of Henry Wadsworth Longfellow*, 2 vols. (Boston: Ticknor and Fields, 1886), II: 46.

18 Meredith McGill, *American Literature and the Culture of Reprinting, 1834–1853* (Philadelphia: University of Pennsylvania Press, 2003).

19 See Angela Sorby's *Schoolroom Poets: Childhood, Performance, and the Place of American Poetry, 1865–1917* (Hanover, NH: University of New Hampshire Press, 2005) and Mary Loeffelholz's *From School to Salon: Reading Nineteenth-Century American Women's Poetry* (Princeton University Press, 2004).

20 *A Mary Wilkins Freeman Reader*, ed. Mary Reichardt (Lincoln: University of Nebraska Press, 1997), p. 111. Subsequent references from this text are cited in parentheses.

2

ROBERT DALE PARKER

American Indian poetry in the nineteenth century

Scholarship and teaching about nineteenth-century American poetry usually shows no awareness of American Indian poetry. Often, when the concept of American Indian poetry is even mentioned, it comes up only to note the supposed absence of poetry by American Indians, even though white American poets wrote so much about Indians.[1] Rarely, scholars take note of two or three Indian poets, typically Jane Johnston Schoolcraft, John Rollin Ridge/ Yellow Bird, or Alex Posey, all writers known (when at all) more for their prose than for their poetry. Lamenting the absence of attention to early American Indian poetry, and suspecting that there must have been a good deal of it, I took up the not so extraordinary yet more or less unprecedented task of looking for it. When I looked, I found many poems, including far more poems by Schoolcraft, Ridge, and Posey than even the few scholars who attended to those writers had seen. I put together an anthology, *Changing is Not Vanishing: A Collection of American Indian Poetry to 1930* that showcases the work of 83 poets, including 39 from the nineteenth century, and provides a bibliography listing the work of almost 150 Indian poets up to 1930, 51 of them from the nineteenth century. Drawing on that anthology, this chapter takes up the modest but in some ways – for the history of nineteenth-century American poetry – revolutionary task of introducing the range and preoccupations of early American Indian poetry.[2]

For most Native American peoples, land – not conceived as ownable or alienable in the Euro-American sense – is central to their culture, belief, stories, and self-conception as a people. By contrast, Euro-American settlers, at least as a group, defined themselves partly by their determination to take Indian land from Indian peoples and drive Indians into the invisible distance of the western sunset. Much has been written about the American lust for land, especially from perspectives that admire the notion of manifest destiny or take it for granted, but most scholars of nineteenth-century American literature have read little about land from the perspective of writing Indians, still less from the perspective of Indians writing poetry. Indian poets wrote about the full range of topics that other poets wrote about – such as love, nature, and family – but they wrote often about land, and they often wrote in protest against colonialism and against the federal government that dedicated itself to taking Indian land. Indian-centered thinking about land thus merged with the more immediate concerns of contemporary Native politics. In such contexts, this review of nineteenth-century American Indian poetry will look at poems about colonialism, the federal government, and land, as well as more traditional topics such as nature and love. It will look, as well, at the more culturally specific topic of poems that suggest Indian writers internalizing the colonialist, anti-Indian attitudes of the colonizing culture around them. For Indians, like everyone else, are sometimes susceptible to the colonialist pressures that they also sometimes resist or show indifference to.

First, it may help to note a few additional contexts. Almost all the surviving poems by nineteenth-century American Indians were written in English. While many poets, notably Posey and poets from the early twentieth century, use words and phrases from their Native languages, the only known poet who left poems written in her Native language is Jane Johnston Schoolcraft. In the course of my research, I came across so many poems – and other writings – by Schoolcraft, most of them unknown to previous scholarship, that I put together a separate volume of her writings, which includes several poems in Anishinaabe. While Schoolcraft's poems remained unknown because she left them unpublished, most of the surviving work by other Indian poets was published in local newspapers and periodicals. Most nineteenth-century poetry by whites also appeared in newspapers and periodicals. Still, changes in the systems of production and distribution – that is, increasingly cheaper and larger-scale printing, more widespread and more efficient means of distribution (more and better roads and canals, the emergence of steamships and the railroad, the expanding postal system) – made it possible for many white poets to win wider, even national audiences, in part through book publication.[3] Indian poets, by contrast, stayed local. Schoolcraft and Posey passed up chances for wider publication.[4] As they wrote about the land, they also understood their writing in relation to the land they wrote about.

If there is one issue in Indian–white conflict that the poems speak to most often and most passionately, it is "removal," the conventional euphemism for the forced expulsion of Indian nations from their lands. Removal brings together into one issue the conflicts over land, colonialism, sovereignty, and the resentment of federal power. Many poems lament removal, not only the famous Cherokee Trail of Tears but also other expulsions, including repeated removals in the 1830s, 1840s, and beyond as the relentless white hunger for other peoples' land pushed Indian nations from one promised refuge to another. On the eve of removal, in 1838, an unnamed Cherokee – probably the much-admired Reverend Jesse Bushyhead – bids his homeland goodbye:

> Adieu ye scenes of early sports,
>   A last, long sad adieu;
> Ye hills and dales and groves and brooks,
>   This is our last review...
>
> Adieu the land that gave me birth,
>   Thou God that rules the sky,
> Protect that little spot of earth
>   In which our fathers lie.
>
> Tread lightly on the sleeping dead,
>   Proud millions that intrude,
> Lest, on your ashes be the tread
>   Of millions still more rude.
>   ("The Indian's Farewell," pp. 68–69)

In similar words, William Walker, forced with his people to leave Ohio in 1843, wrote the following lines in Wyandot (rendered here in his English translation – the original Wyandot has not survived) as he prepared to leave his home:

> Farewell, ye tall oaks, in whose pleasant green shade
> I've sported in childhood, in innocence played,
> My dog and my hatchet, my arrow and bow,
> Are still in remembrance, alas! I must go...
>
> Sandusky, Tyamochtee, and Broken Sword streams,
> No more shall I see you except in my dreams.
> Farewell to the marshes where cranberries grow,
> O'er the great Mississippi, alas! I must go...
>
> Let me go to the wildwood, my own native home.
> Where the wild deer and elk and buffalo roam,
> Where the tall cedars are and the bright waters flow,
> Far away from the pale-face, oh, there let me go.
>   ("The Wyandot's Farewell," p. 66)

Bushyhead and Walker associate their homeland with the personal past of their own childhood play and with its flora and fauna, its earth and its waters. While Walker wants to shun the white interlopers altogether, Bushyhead, forced to leave behind his ancestors' graves, pauses first to lay down something like a golden rule for invaders: they had better "tread lightly on the sleeping dead," literally as well as figuratively, he warns, or their own descendants and other interlopers will follow their model and do unto them as they have done to the Cherokees. The whites, he says, may think now that they own the land they have stolen, but he warns them not to abuse their tenure or take it for granted, for their supposed ownership is as transient as they have made his.

In yet another similar poem, Choctaw Israel Folsom asks – with sardonic incredulity at the hypocrisy of whites who promised that Indians could keep their land as long as the grass shall grow and the waters run –

> Have the waters ceased to flow?
> Have the forest[s] ceased to grow?
> Why do our brothers bid us go
>   From our native home?
>
> Here in infancy we played,
> Here our happy wigwam made,
> Here our fathers' graves are laid, –
>   Must we leave them all?
> ("Lo! The Poor Indian's Hope," p. 67)

As Bushyhead appeals to a larger justice in the universe that will eventually catch up with the invaders, so Folsom concludes:

> Whiteman, tell us, God on high –
> So pure and bright in yonder sky, –
> Will not then His searching eye
>   See the Indians' wrong?
>   (p. 67)

Folsom's poem was published in 1875, five years after his death and many years after removal, leaving it unclear whether he wrote the poem just before the Choctaw removal of 1831–35 or later as he recalled his anger as he was about to begin the long, forced journey. Indeed, poets continued to write about removal long after it ended (and they still write about it). Richard C. Adams, a Delaware, strikes many of the same notes as Bushyhead, Walker, and Folsom. Changing federal decisions forced the Delawares into repeated removals, and Adams calls attention to the series of broken promises as one removal and broken promise piled on top of another:

> With sorrow, grief and suffering, we were forced at last to go,
> From the graves of our forefathers to a land we did not know.
> But this was now guaranteed to us, "as long as water shall run,"
> Yet on they pushed us, on and on toward the setting sun!
>
> "And this will be the last move," they tell us, if we go,
> "You will hold the country this time as long as grass shall grow."
>   ("To the Delaware Indians," 1899, p. 197)

As James Harris Guy – a talented Chickasaw poet and a tribal police sergeant whose considerable poetic ambitions came to an early end when he was murdered while trying to arrest brutal criminals – summed up the dilemma four decades after Chickasaw removal,

> The white man wants the Indian's home,
>   He envies them their land;
> And with his sweetest words he comes
>   To get it, if he can.
>
> And if we will not give our lands,
>   And plainly tell him so,
> He then goes back, calls up his clans,
>   And says, "let's make them go."
>   ("The White Man Wants
>   the Indian's Home," 1878, p. 142)

Guy's curious choice of the word "clans," a category of identity central to the self-definition of many Indian peoples, ironically casts whites as not so different from Indians as the whites like to believe, though still far more presumptuous and greedy.

Such poems set out to lock in a cultural memory, to make it impossible to lose the recollection of the land and the lives that were lost and transformed during removal. In 1848, nine years after the Cherokee Trail of Tears, Te-con-ees-kee cannot even let go of the name of his homeland, Georgia: "Though far from thee Georgia in exile I roam, / My heart in thy mountain land still has its home."

> Georgia, O Georgia there is a stain on thy name!
> And ages to come will yet blush for thy shame,
> While the child of the Cherokee exile unborn,
> The results of thy violence deeply will mourn...
> For this comes the name of the land of my birth,
> On my ear as the sound of a curse on the earth.
>   ("Though far from thee
>   Georgia in exile I roam," p. 121)

The coupling of "curse" and "earth," bound by assonance and by the parallel syntax of linked prepositional phrases, rests on the bitter concession that the beloved land, now stained with violence, no longer belongs to the Cherokees whose heart still makes it their home.

In their new homes after removal, the removed nations soon felt pressured to realign their concepts of land along Euro-American models. In a poem read to Cherokee students in 1855, C. H. Campbell seems anxiously to suppose that whites are watching and that Cherokees had better internalize and impose on themselves the pressure they feel coming from white surveillance:

The *pale face* now are strong, and *we* are *free*;
As *they* have progress made, so *we* must do –
Must learn to cultivate the mind, the soil,
And reconcile ourselves to honored toil.
                    ("Our tribe could once of
                    many *warriors* boast," p. 129)

With an intense feeling of *we* the Cherokees versus *they* the whites, Campbell toes the line of typically white pleas for Indian progress. Such pleas defined progress through anti-Indian myths, calling for Indians to become farmers, as if Cherokees had not farmed for centuries, and calling for Indians to work hard, as if they had not worked hard before. Still, Campbell walks both sides of the cultural fence, for his remark that whites "have progress made" can look down on whites with a condescension not anticipated in the usual white ways of thinking.

Moreover, Campbell of course was right to see that whites' craving for Indian land would not let up after removal. In 1887, Congress passed the General Allotment Act, better known as the Dawes Act after its chief sponsor, Senator Henry L. Dawes. The Dawes Act called for redistributing communally owned reservation lands by "allotting" parcels of land to individual Indians, who would be made citizens once they received their allotments. The Act ended communal land ownership and "opened" "surplus" land – meaning unallotted Indian land – to settlers and speculators, that is, to white people. Even allotted lands could eventually be sold, and white people were usually best positioned to buy it. Troubled by such abuses, Alex Posey (Muskogee/Creek) resented the corrupt officials who administered the Dawes Act. "Ye men of Dawes," he wrote, "avaunt! / Return from whence ye came!" To Posey, federal officials might "strut majestically" but their talk was still "As sleek as ratpaths" ("Ye Men of Dawes," probably 1894, pp. 158–59). Posey was an unusual figure, alert to opposite perspectives on allotment. Much as he resented the "men of Dawes," he ended up working with them. Like many Indians who identified with what they were pressured to see as progress, Posey supported allotment, even while he poured scorn on the corruption that came with it.[5] The Dawes Act's advocates and defenders envisioned it as making Indians into citizens and bringing Indian people into the mainstream economy, but its actual effect was to devastate reservation communities and traditions, casting most reservation land into white hands.

Given the centrality of land to the self-conception of most Indian peoples, including the history of removal and the more conniving, indirect removal of the Dawes Act, it is hard to know how to read "A New Citizen," written in 1887, after the passage of the Dawes Act, by Elsie Fuller, a sixteen- or seventeen-year-old Omaha:

Now I am a citizen!
    They've given us new laws,
Just as were made
    By Senator Dawes.

We need not live on rations [promised by treaties],
    Why? there is no cause,
For "Indians are citizens,"
    Said Senator Dawes.

Just give us a chance,
    We never will pause.
Till we are good citizens
    Like Senator Dawes.

Now we are citizens,
    We all give him applause –
So three cheers, my friends,
    For Senator Dawes!

(p. 228)

Perhaps Fuller is taking what was called a "progressive" stance or, in more accurate terms, an assimilationist stance (matching the views in the Hampton Institute school newspaper that published her poem). Perhaps, that is, she is genuinely thanking Senator Dawes for disavowing treaty obligations, such as the commitment to provide rations as well as the commitment to respect Indian nations' ownership of Indian lands. Or perhaps, dripping with sarcasm and cleverly defying the views of her school newspaper, she scorns Senator Dawes and everything that he represents for Indian people. Though no one would call Fuller's effusion great poetry, by the usual meaning of such terms, whether we see it as naïve or as sly it showcases a culturally, historically resonant impasse between opposite meanings. In that way it evokes the intense debates about allotment across many Indian communities as, in the ensuing decades, the federal government imposed devastating allotment policies on one Indian nation after another. As Posey put the question in 1894, hoping that Indian Territory might achieve statehood and, with his characteristic humor, playing off Hamlet's famous soliloquy,

To allot, or not to allot, that is the
Question; whether 'tis nobler in the mind to
Suffer the country to lie in common as it is,
Or to divide it up and give each man
His share pro rata, and by dividing
End this sea of troubles? To allot, divide,
Perchance to end in statehood;
Ah, there's the rub!

("To allot, or not to allot")

The white craving "to divide it up," to pry Indian nations and individual Indians from their land and from each other, however corrupt the means, infected Indian–white relations across many other areas that overlapped with the struggle for land. James Harris Guy blames "the fearful fall" of once "honest and fearless" Indians on the dishonor and lies of "the whiteman" ("Lament of Tishomingo," 1879). Just as skeptically but with more humor, Tso-le-oh-woh (Cherokee), watching whites joust for appointment to federal offices that put them in position to abuse Indians, marvels at "How blest we are, we little *reds*," that such loving, "kind-hearted Christian whites" "Will sell their very purses ... to get to be our nurses," and all with no thought for "The magic of a dollar. *No indeed!*" ("A Red Man's Thoughts," 1853).

While the law might offer Indians protection, corrupt officials and speculators knew how to manipulate the law or break it with impunity. Thus lawyer poets Richard C. Adams and Too-qua-stee (DeWitt Clinton Duncan, Cherokee) give their outrage a legal turn. Adams explains the closed, circular logic of colonialist law:

> If the Indian seeks the Government, there his grievance to relate,
> He must first obtain permission from those who rule the State!
> If his rights are there denied him and an attorney he would seek,
> He is sternly then reminded he has no right to speak!
> "For under section so and so, which guides your legal move,
> "You see no attorneys can appear for you, except if we approve;
> "And if, in our opinion, your claim does not adhere
> "To the interests of the public, then your cause we cannot hear."
> ("To the Delaware Indians," 1899, p. 197)

Adams conveys how the Delawares, like many other Indian nations, were driven into a Kafkaesque house of bureaucratic mirrors, so that whatever they did to deserve their rights or get their rights recognized, the ground beneath them still shifted and the bureaucracy tilted against them. In "Cherokee Memories" (1900), Too-qua-stee recalls an idyllic interlude between the brutality of removal to Indian Territory and the later encroachment onto Indian Territory of white people and culture with their laws and statutes. He envisions an outraged Lord upbraiding white men for their misguided sense of legal entitlement:

> Go tell those white men, I, the Lord of Hosts,
> Have marked their high presumption, heard their boasts.
> Observe their laws; their government is might
> Enthroned to rule, instead of perfect right.
> Could I have taught them such gross heresy,
> As "Greatest good to greatest number" be? ...
> Should just minorities be made to yield

> That wrong majorities may be upheld?
> In nature, is this not the rule that brutes
> Observe in settling up their fierce disputes?
>
> (p. 200)

Too-qua-stee/Duncan sees whites as violating the larger principles of their own law and of legal and ethical principles too broad to belong to any one group.

In less legal domains, Duncan's Lord is no less stunned by white presumption and vanity:

> Go tell those white men not to be so proud;
> 'Twas I that hid the lightning in the cloud.
> That twice ten thousand years, or thereabout,
> Should pass ere they could find the secret out,
> Shows dullness quite enough to chill their pride
> And make their swelling vanity subside.
> Steam, too, I made; its power was nothing hid;
> From age to age it shook the kettle's lid
> Full in their view; but never could they see it,
> Till chance vouchsafed from mystery to free it.
> The art of printing, too, is all my own,
> Lo! every foot of living thing had shown,
> (I ordered so) as long as time had run,
> How easily the printing job was done.
>
> ("The White Man's Burden," 1899, p. 200)

In the guise of a sneering god, Too-qua-stee/Duncan dismisses whites on exactly their points of pride – verse, perhaps, included. In such ways, many Indian poets don't simply run outside white-imposed stereotype. They also run outside the possibility of being reduced to resisting stereotype. They look down on the presumptions that would confine Indians and Indian artistic production to derivative or second-class status, as if Indian poets were incapable of pronouncing on topics beyond their own Indian identity. Nineteenth-century American Indian poets thus speak not only to the local topics of tribal and Indian relations with whites. They also speak to international culture and controversies. Posey, Too-qua-stee/Duncan, and J. C. Duncan (Cherokee) allude to the wars in Cuba and the Philippines, with Posey proclaiming in 1896 that "Cuba shall be free" and with the others, later in the fighting, looking skeptically at the acceleration of American imperialism.

Indeed, in terms not always pointed to conflict between Indians and whites, the poems often take a broadly oppositional stance, protesting cultural habits and assumptions that came to dominate American culture, perhaps afflicting Indians especially, but also burdening the nation at large. In "In UNCLE SAM's dominion," from 1895, Posey laments that "A few own all the 'dust.' / They rule by combination / And trade by forming trusts" (p. 160). At the end of the century, in 1899, Too-qua-stee's "A Vision of the End" offers a scathing, almost Swiftian vision of catastrophe:

> I once beheld the end of time!
> Its stream has ceased to be.
> The drifting years, all soiled with crime,
> Lay in a filthy sea.
>
> (p. 204)

Rather than representing the end of time himself, as yet another in the long, stock series of terminal Mohicans vanishing into the western horizon, Too-qua-stee/Duncan looks down on the devastation of the world, especially the white world, and pronounces on it.

At the inverse of Duncan's filthy apocalypse of "reeking waste" where "all that men were wont to prize ... / In slimy undulations roiled," where "government, a monstrous form ... / On grimy billows rode," and where "all the monsters ever bred ... / Lay scattered, floating, dead" (p. 204), including "Greed – immortal Greed – ... / A monarch of the slime" (pp. 204–5), other Indian poets, especially Posey, wax lyrically over nature in the familiar tradition of Euro-American Romantic poetry. John Rollin Ridge's magnificent "Mount Shasta" (1853) echoes Percy Bysshe Shelley's "Mont Blanc," and Posey's stirring "Tulledega" echoes passages in Wordsworth's "The Prelude," such as "The Boy of Winander" episode. More generally, Schoolcraft, Ridge, Posey, and others continue the Romantic tradition as they write about flowers, birds, rivers, and the landscape. The land, as we have noted, often carries intense meaning for Indian poets who write out of traditions that see their cosmology wedded with the land of their origin and their ancestors. Ridge's California poems mark an exception, however, for Ridge, a Cherokee, grew up in Georgia before his family's removal to Arkansas and then his own flight to California. When he writes of the California landscape, therefore, he writes of a world that is not the world of his family or ancestors, though his attunement to the land may still owe to a Cherokee or more broadly Native heritage of thinking through landscape. It may also owe to the self-consciousness about landscape that forced exile can provoke, as, again, in the words of Ridge's fellow Cherokee Te-con-ees-kee: "Though far from thee Georgia in exile I roam, / My heart in thy mountain land still has its home." For many poets, such preoccupations merge Native traditions with the traditions of Euro-American Romanticism.

In Jane Johnston Schoolcraft's romantic nature poems, for example, the natural world speaks to her. She recalls that when she returned to her native land after a trip to Europe and saw her first pine trees, it dawned on her that she had seen no pine trees in Europe, and then suddenly she felt the pine tree welcoming her home:

> Mes ah nah, shi egwuh tah gwish en aung
> Sin da mik ke aum baun
> Kag ait suh, ne meen wain dum
> Me nah wau, wau bun dah maun
> Gi yut wi au, wau bun dah maun een
> Shing wauk, shing wauk nosa
> Shi e gwuh ke do dis an naun.
>
> Ah beauteous tree! ah happy sight!
> That greets me on my native strand
> And hails me, with a friend's delight,
> To my own dear bright mother land
> Oh 'tis to me a heart-sweet scene,
> The pine – the pine! that's ever green.
> ("To the Pine Tree," undated,
> first published in 2007, p. 56)

When she translates her poem into English, Schoolcraft revises it to fit English rhythm and rhyme. But first she imagines the Anishinaabe version by drawing on the model of English or Euro-American poetry, writing in what had been an oral language and shaping the words into rhyming lines that mix the syntactical patterns of Anishinaabemowin with the syntactical patterns of English.[6] Schoolcraft's Anishinaabe poems are the first known poems written in an American Indian language, in this case a language that centers on distinctions between animate and inanimate. "Zhingwaak" (Schoolcraft's "shing wauk") is animate, and even in Schoolcraft's English the pine tree emerges as animate. It "greets" her and "hails" her with a Romantic and with an Anishinaabe accent. The pattern of an animate, articulate natural world continues in some of Schoolcraft's other poems. In "The Miscodeed" (undated, first published in 2007), for example, the little pink flower (the miscodeed) is the "first to greet the eyes of men / In early spring," with its "pretty head / Oft peeping out" (p. 60).

When the poets turn to love, a fair number of poems imply a cross-racial attraction. Often, an Indian speaker romanticizes blue eyes or golden hair without a trace of self-questioning. Many of Ridge's poems fit that formula. "The Stolen White Girl" describes an Indian capturing a white, a popular genre in prose by whites, but Ridge's poem tells the tale of captivity from the Indian captor's perspective. Even so, it repeats white fantasies of an Indian man stealing away a blue-eyed damsel. Against the convention of captivity narratives, however, this blue-eyed damsel has earlier fallen in love with her dark captor. In "False, but Beautiful" (1868), the habit of imagining a conventionally white lover leads Ridge to give a "snowy arm" even to a lover introduced as "Dark as a demon's dream" (p. 102). But in another of his poems a dark man warns his implicitly white lover of "the coming storm": "my dark doom thou too must share – / ... And if my portion is despair, / Such too must be thy state" ("The Dark One to His Love," 1849, p. 82).

Ridge's "The Man of Memory" (1848) spins a remarkable variation on the history of love poems, describing an old man who cannot free himself from a torturing memory of having raped his sweetheart: "He madly used his conscious power / To make that trusting girl his passions' prey" (p. 78). While Ridge's poem seems partly like a young man's rape fantasy, defending against the fantasy by making the rapist wallow in guilt, the poem's reconsideration of patriarchal privilege can reverberate with later readers influenced by the way feminists have intensified the critique of rape.

In Ridge's remarkable poem love or violence can have to do with land and war. It seems an odd poem for a twenty-one-year-old to publish, and a newly married twenty-one-year-old at that, but even at that age Ridge felt haunted by his own memory of violence. For at the age of twelve he watched as twenty-five Cherokees from the anti-treaty John Ross party murdered his father, John Ridge, in an organized vendetta against the Ridge party for signing the 1835 Treaty of New Ochota. In that treaty, John Ridge and his allies – under enormous pressure – agreed to give up Cherokee lands and move the Cherokee people into exile in the west. As John Rollin Ridge later recalled in a letter included with his posthumous book of poems, the assassination "darkened my mind with an eternal shadow."[7]

Of course, there are many differences between the assassination and the poem. In one case, the elderly "man of memory" in Ridge's poem recalls an act of sexual violence that he himself committed. In the other case, Ridge witnessed others commit political violence on his father. Still, the political violence had to do with land, and land and love have much to do with each other. We sometimes love a particular land, and we often associate love with the land where we love. We also commonly eroticize landscape and conflate the theft and abuse of land, the rape of land, with the rape of women. In the same way, more broadly following the trail of violence and trauma, we might conflate one form or instance of violence with another or one violence-haunted memory with another. Drawing on Freud's insight in "Mourning and Melancholia" that when a loved one dies we feel – unconsciously and often in some ways consciously – somehow responsible, somehow at fault or guilty, it seems plausible to suppose that the young Ridge, witnessing the brutal murder of his father and living under the pall of its melodramatic notoriety, would wonder why *him*. What did he do to cause or deserve this violence? From there – admittedly at the risk of oversimplifying the poem, but without claiming that the poem reduces to this one skein of suggestiveness – it seems that Ridge's poem partly takes his own haunting by violence and projects it outward onto another, conflates the haunting memories of the rape of the land and the violence against his family with a rape of the beloved. He seems to project the burden of living under a haunting memory of witnessed violence onto the imagination of what it might be like to live a haunted life, not just for one decade but for many decades. More largely, the haunting memory is not only Ridge's. His personal and familial memory registers a larger memory and trauma of the Cherokee people and of all peoples forced into exile, forced into arguments with each other and within themselves over how to respond to the colonialist pressure to give up their lands and, more largely, to give up their culture and heritage. Thus Ridge's poem about men trying to reimagine their relations with women itself offers a haunting metaphor both of potentially reimagined gender relations and of a people trying to find ways to reimagine its relation to a history of trauma.

Beyond nature and love but not beyond politics, many of the poems can misguide or perplex later readers by falling prey to the stubborn cliché of the vanishing Indian, immortalized in James Fenimore Cooper's *The Last of the Mohicans*. An anonymous Cherokee poem from 1871 offers a typical example:

> Faster and fiercer rolls the tide
> That follows on our track...

> There is no hope; the red man's fate
> Is fixed beyond control,
> And soon above each hearth and home
> The mighty waves will roll.

> Why is it thus, are we accurst
> And will oblivion's gloom,
> Give back no ray to tell us why
> Extinction is our doom?
> ("Faster and fiercer rolls
> the tide," pp. 138–39)

To this poet, the Cherokee and Indian future looks hopeless: the Euro-American flood dooms Indian people to extinction. In a variety of ways, however, other poets see Indian people as disappearing but use the language of disappearance to describe what sometimes sounds more like change than like disappearance.

48

That vexed spot between opposite understandings of change spins poign-
antly through a more or less dactylic poem to the 1895 graduating class of
the Carlisle Indian School from the Cherokee Samuel Sixkiller, "the class
poet":

> Farewell to dear class, to friends and to strangers,
> Assembling here in our honor today,
> To help Nature's children – the wildflower rangers,
> And make pure Americans from ocean to bay...
>
> When shall the culture, the art and refinement
> Drive from our minds, roving thoughts of the past?
> Shall broad education, or savage confinement,
> Conquer the Red Man now fading so fast?
>
> (p. 229)

We might suppose that Sixkiller gives in to a demeaning view of Indians as
wholeheartedly as the anonymous poet of 1871, for Sixkiller's poem repeats
the full range of demeaning views that were drummed into the ears of students at Carlisle, the most famous and influential of the Indian boarding
schools.[8] But it is more striking when Sixkiller, combining two stereotypes,
conflates Indian people with nature and at the same time trades on the dominant culture's infantilizing of Indian people by referring to the Carlisle
graduating class – excitedly on the verge of adulthood and leadership – as
children. He sees Indians as Nature's wildflowers, versus the "art and refinement" offered by Carlisle. For Sixkiller, Indians are fit for nostalgia, figured
here, as so often, in sunsets and images of noble but vanishing masculinity
"when the sun in his glory, / Shall shine on the last of the noble Red Man"
(p. 230). The idea in *The Last of the Mohicans'* title was already a cliché when Cooper's novel came out in 1826, but somehow those hardy last
Indians were still busy dying in 1895 and, while supposedly still fading into
the sunset, have managed to stay around ever since.

And in some ways that ability to keep living by dying is Sixkiller's point,
whether he knows it or not. For when Sixkiller repeats the boilerplate stereotypes that demean him and his fellow students, he also uses stereotypes to
move beyond stereotypes. Maybe, in some ways, when an Indian student
repeats back what the Carlisle teachers and the dominant culture say about
Indians, it is mere repetition, but in some ways maybe it is also repetition
with a difference. To be sure, it can disturb us to see an Indian repeating the
clichés of a dominant culture that refuses to recognize contemporary Indian
people, if we think of Sixkiller and his fellow students – who may have
been the ones who chose him as their class poet – caught in the pressure
to parrot and perhaps to believe what their teachers tell them. But maybe

in some ways Sixkiller's poem veers toward – or at least invites us to ask whether it veers toward – survival skills and even mimicry, a strategy for living on instead of fading into the sunset and dying.[9] Sixkiller says what the Carlisle teachers and administrators want to hear, but that does not mean that he thinks what they want him to think. Nor does it mean that his fellow students believe that he thinks what the poem says. He might have given them reason to know better. They might have known better about how most of them thought. When Sixkiller asks "Shall broad education, or savage confinement, / Conquer the Red Man now fading so fast?" he might mean savage confinement as opposed to broad education, suggesting that before coming to Carlisle he and his fellow students were confined by savagery. Nevertheless, he might mean – or regardless of his intentions, his words can mean – that the arguably not so broad education he receives while confined at Carlisle is itself partly a new version of savage confinement. In that case, his poem would surreptitiously turn the colonialist language of Carlisle against itself.

A little more boldly, a poem the following year by Melinda Metoxen (Oneida), one of Sixkiller's classmates, refers to "Iceland's voyagers, so bold" who "First discovered ... America." But then, under the cover of her need to fill out the rhyme, she adds a dash and a few more words that sneak in an editorially ironic qualifier: " – so we're told" (p. 233). In such ways, school authorities sometimes seem to have slipped, publishing poems by their students that deliberately, as with Metoxen, or perhaps not so deliberately, as with Sixkiller, smuggle in sentiments that undermine the school's authority. Writing a poem to his teacher the year after he graduates, and not knowing that his teacher would publish the poem, Sixkiller worries that the promises of Carlisle aren't panning out back home in Indian Territory. He can't find a job, and instead he finds himself getting "down in the face" and "mighty tired" "[w]ith nothing 'tall to do." It is surprising that Carlisle printed such a poem, but Sixkiller surrounds his worries with praise for Carlisle and with sighs for its "big and cosy nest." Ironically, he feels homesick for school, so uncritically homesick that he can point out – without quite recognizing – how going away to school might have contributed to his worry that back home life now "goes pretty slow" ("My First Winter Out of School," 1896, p. 231).

The life of nineteenth-century American Indian poetry has continued to "go pretty slow," but we are ready to change that now. Perhaps the uncovering of nineteenth-century American Indian poetry can shift the way readers approach Indians and the thinking about Indians in poems by non-Indians, reminding us of what in some ways we might hope readers already know, that Indians are not the passive or fading objects they are often imagined to

50

be. Still, these poems hold their value not for what they show about non-Indians so much as for what they show about Indians themselves and about the imaginative work in Indian writing. In 1853, for example, the so-called Klinkerfues comet sailed across the American skies. In response, Tso-le-oh-woh published "What an Indian Thought When He Saw the Comet" in the *Cherokee Advocate*:

> Flaming wonderer! that dost leave vaunting, proud
> Ambition boasting its lightning fringed
> Immensity – cleaving wings, gaudy dipp'd
> In sunset's blossoming splendors bright and
> Tinsel fire, with puny flight fluttering
> Far behind! Thou that art cloth'd in mistery
> More startling and more glorious than thine own
> Encircling fires – profound as the oceans
> Of shoreless space through which now thou flyest!
> Art thou some erring world now deep engulph'd
> In hellish, Judgement fires, with phrenzied ire
> And fury hot, like some dread sky rocket
> Of Eternity, flaming, vast, plunging
> Thro' immensity, scatt'ring in thy track
> The wrathful fires of thine own damnation
> Or wingest thou with direful speed, the ear
> Of some flaming god of far off systems
> Within these skies unheard of and unknown?
> Ye Gods! How proud the thought to mount this orb
> Of fire – boom thro' the breathless oceans vast
> Of big immensity – quickly leaving
> Far behind all that for long ages gone
> Dull, gray headed dames have prated of –
> Travel far off mystic eternities –
> Then proudly, on this little twisting ball
> Returning once more set foot, glowing with
> The splendors of a vast intelligence –
> Frizzling little, puny humanity
> Into icy horrors – bursting the big
> Wide-spread eyeball of dismay – to recount
> Direful regions travers'd and wonders seen!
>
> (pp. 127–29)

Like the comet he wrote about, Tso-le-oh-woh remains "cloth'd in mystery." Apart from any history, written or oral, that I have not uncovered, for over a century and a half he, like other nineteenth-century American Indian poets, has stayed "within these skies unheard of and unknown." Perhaps once more, now that we are ready to read these poems, some of the nineteenth-century American Indian poets may "boom thro' the breathless oceans vast / Of big immensity," "Travel far off mystic eternities," and return to readers "glowing with / The splendors of" their "vast intelligence," their report from "the oceans / Of shoreless space" – indeed, from Indian lands – that often still go unreported. Returning thus, they will not likely meet the ominously confident, all-seeing transparent eyeball of Emerson's *Nature*. They might even burst "the big / Wide-spread eyeball of dismay" that little knows how a newly uncovered body of poetry might pass through its perception. Tso-le-oh-woh, who likely suffered through forced removal from his ancestral lands, wrote for a local audience, the English-language readers of the *Cherokee Advocate*, which published in Sequoyah's Cherokee syllabary as well as in English. And yet for all its local roots, as it spoke to a readership fresh from watching the comet light the skies above the newly acquired but still vulnerable lands of the Cherokee Nation, the "vaunting, proud ambition" of Tso-le-oh-woh's Miltonic, Romantic, and Cherokee poem calls out from "direful regions travers'd and wonders seen" and speaks to later generations about the transience and the recovery of memory, imagination, land, and the "mystic eternities" of poetic apprehension.

NOTES

1 Nineteenth-century African-American poets, including Ann Plato, Alfred Islay Walden, and especially Albery Allson Whitman, also wrote about American Indians. See Joan R. Sherman, ed., *African-American Poetry of the Nineteenth Century: An Anthology* (Urbana: University of Illinois Press, 1992).

2 All poems quoted from and referred to in this chapter can be found in *Changing is Not Vanishing: A Collection of American-Indian Poetry to 1930*, ed. Robert Dale Parker (Philadelphia: University of Pennsylvania Press, 2011). Subsequent page numbers will appear in parentheses. For Posey, see also Matthew Wynn Sivils's excellent new edition of all Posey's poems.

3 William Charvat, *The Profession of Authorship in America: 1800–1870*, ed. Matthew J. Bruccoli (Columbus: Ohio State University Press, 1968), pp. 29–48, 100–05.

4 Robert Dale Parker, introduction titled "The World and Writings of Jane Johnston Schoolcraft," in *The Sound the Stars Make Rushing Through the Sky: The Writings of Jane Johnston Schoolcraft*, ed. Robert Dale Parker (Philadelphia: University of Pennsylvania Press, 2007), pp. 35–36; and Daniel F. Littlefield, Jr., *Alex Posey: Creek Poet, Journalist, and Humorist* (Lincoln: University of Nebraska Press, 1992), pp. 118–19.

5 Littlefield, *Alex Posey*.

6 I owe this observation about Schoolcraft's syntax to Margaret Noori, who teaches Anishinaabe language and literature at the University of Michigan, and to John Nichols, who teaches Anishinaabe language and literature at the University of Minnesota.

7 John R. Ridge, *Poems* (San Francisco: Henry Payot, 1868), p. 7. On John Rollin Ridge's life, see James W. Parins, *John Rollin Ridge: His Life & Works* (Lincoln: University of Nebraska Press, 1991). Hard feelings between descendants of the Ross and Ridge parties sometimes continue today.

8 Amelia V. Katanski describes how the Carlisle Indian School used its printing press to discipline the thinking of Indian students. See Katanski's *Learning to Write "Indian": The Boarding-School Experience and American Indian Literature*, (Norman: University of Oklahoma Press, 2005), chs. 2–3. (Katanski does not discuss the poems by Indian students included in Carlisle publications.)

9 On anti-colonial mimicry, see the classic discussion by Homi K. Bhabha: "Of Mimicry and Man: The Ambivalence of Colonial Discourse," in *The Location of Culture* (London: Routledge, 1994).

3

VIRGINIA JACKSON

The poet as Poetess

The Poetess is one of those nineteenth-century social facts that make twentieth- and twenty-first-century literary historians uncomfortable. Like the horsehair sofa, the Poetess seems to us now a somewhat embarrassing commonplace of nineteenth-century culture we do well to live without. Eve Sedgwick's observation on the fortunes of "sentimentality" goes double for the Poetess:

> The strange career of "sentimentality," from the later eighteenth century when it was a term of high ethical and aesthetic praise, to the twentieth when it can be used to connote, beyond pathetic weakness, an actual principle of evil ... is a career that displays few easily articulable consistencies, and those are not ... consistencies of subject matter. Rather, they seem to inhere in the nature of the investment of a viewer *in* a subject matter.[1]

Like "sentimentality," the Poetess is difficult to define except as an occasion for shifting historical definitions of women and of poetry. Yet notions of the nineteenth-century Poetess have not only depended on changing understandings of gender or verse or poetics (histories to which we will return), but have consistently converged on a hermeneutics of suspicion. Is the Poetess just a fancy name for the woman poet? If so, then why not "drop the feminine termination," as the poet Elizabeth Oakes Smith suggested in the mid nineteenth century?[2] Perhaps it has proven difficult to follow Oakes Smith's sensible suggestion because what is at stake in the idea of the Poetess is overdetermined, in excess of subject or subject matter. The Poetess neither is nor was simply a poet. What you think a Poetess is may depend entirely on your investment in the idea – and certainly depended on very different nineteenth-century investments in the idea. Such a relativist definition of the Poetess as a hologram of readerly desire may fit twenty-first-century postmodern or poststructuralist tastes better than did the lace-collared portrait of the woman poet over the horsehair sofa, but the most interesting thing about the strange career of the Poetess since the eighteenth century is that the figure seems to have had this apparently modern indexical function all along.

In the preface to his 1848 edition of *The Female Poets of America*, Rufus Griswold began by warning his readers that

> It is less easy to be assured of the genuineness of literary ability in women than in men. The moral nature of women, in its finest and richest development, partakes of some of the qualities of genius; it assumes, at least, the similitude of that which in men is the characteristic or accompaniment of the highest grade of mental inspiration. We are in danger, therefore, of mistaking for the effervescent energy of creative intelligence, that which is only the exuberance of personal "feelings unemployed." We may confound the vivid dreamings of an unsatisfied heart, with the aspirations of a mind impatient of the fetters of time, and matter, and mortality. That may seem to us the abstract imagining of a soul rapt into sympathy with a purer beauty and a higher truth than earth and space exhibit, which in fact shall be only the natural craving of the affections, undefined and wandering. The most exquisite susceptibility of the spirit, and the capacity to mirror in dazzling variety the effects which circumstances or surrounding minds work upon it, may be accompanied by no power to originate, or even, in any proper sense, to reproduce.[3]

Even in the context of the 1840s, Griswold was a reactionary, but his tortured apprehension that what would merit high ethical and aesthetic praise in a composition by a man may "be only the natural craving of affections, undefined and wandering" in a poem by a woman managed to collapse into one nineteenth-century moment the trajectory that it took "sentimentality" two centuries to accomplish. Further, the problem for Griswold is precisely the difficulty of distinguishing aesthetic accomplishment from pathetic weakness, since the reader's investment in a subject matter may so easily be in error. The "danger … of mistaking for the effervescent energy of creative intelligence, that which is only the exuberance of personal 'feelings unemployed'" is the danger of not knowing what one is reading. The fact that the phrase "we are in danger of mistaking for genius" was penned by Lord Byron further complicates matters.[4] Certainly the valuation of male genius and the devaluation of female affection is the most striking and offensive subject matter in Griswold's prose, but the indeterminate relation between the two may be the passage's more pressing concern. How can one tell (male) mental originality from (female) affective imitation? The impossibility of doing so is the real subject of the passage, and that excess, that pathos of indeterminacy, is also the subject matter of the Poetess. The nineteenth-century Poetess may be best defined as the feminized figure of extravagant feeling that emerges when you are not sure what kind of poet or poem you are reading, a definition that makes the Poetess central to any historical understanding of the last three centuries of American poetics.

Given the duck-rabbit, now-you-see-her-now-you-don't character of the nineteenth-century Poetess, it is perhaps unsurprising that the very feminist critics who have been appalled by such caricatures as Griswold's have tended to disagree about what a nineteenth-century Poetess is or was. Those disagreements have brought the specter of the Poetess back into visibility in recent years. As Paula Bennett wrote in 2007, "after a century or more in history's dustbin, the Poetess has made a stunning comeback" in the early twenty-first century:

> Not only is there an entire website, The Poetess Archive [http://unixgen.muo-hio.edu/~poetess/], devoted to this figure, but an ever-increasing number of articles and books, including some by the most prominent scholars in the field, are given over wholly or in part to discussing her ... As a result of this inquiry, scholarly interest in nineteenth-century women's poetry, including Poetess poetry, has shifted from addressing it as the stable object of a massive recovery project to understanding it as a discursively-produced set of reading effects fractured along the same lines as the poets themselves.

Bennett herself both celebrates and laments the recent boom in and critical direction of Poetess studies, not only because she has been personally responsible for a substantial portion of the recovery of nineteenth-century American women's verse, but because she thinks that to characterize all nineteenth-century women poets as Poetesses is to forget how many different kinds of poems "nineteenth-century U.S. women wrote. Writing for a popular literary market ... these poets wrote hymns and psalms, parodies and satire, odes and elegies, erotic verse and lullabies, work songs and protest poems, screeds and memorials, epics and epyllions, and jingles and riddles ... Might it not be more accurate as well as less confusing, to speak of Poetess poems or Poetess thematics, rather than Poetesses *per se*, especially since these poets did not apply the label to themselves?"[5]

It is a good question. If we define a nineteenth-century Poetess as a nineteenth-century woman poet, then the answer would have to be no. On the other hand, if we define the Poetess as a figure detachable from the work of the woman poet, a figure defined by this very detachability, then the answer would also have to be no. Over a decade ago, Yopie Prins and I proposed a performative, generic definition of the nineteenth-century Poetess, claiming that

> As a type, the Poetess exemplifies the theory of her own apparent historical obscurity ... One reason for the perpetual disappearance and reappearance of the Poetess is that she is not the content of her own generic representation: not

a speaker, not an "I," not a consciousness, not a subjectivity, not a voice, not a persona, not a self. [6]

The nineteenth-century Poetess, we suggested, was a trope in a rather pure sense, as definite and slippery as a turn of phrase. For this reason, it is difficult "to speak of Poetess poems or Poetess thematics," since to do so would imply that the figure is consistent. It isn't. Further, what Prins and I did not emphasize then but would stress now is that of course the trope of the Poetess worked differently at different moments over the course of the nineteenth century. How could the Poetess of 1821 be the Poetess of 1891, when everything else about poetry (including the definition of the word itself) had changed in those seventy years?

If, as I have argued elsewhere, the nineteenth century saw the historical transformation of many varied verse genres into the single abstraction of what critics now refer to as the post-romantic lyric, then it makes sense that it is as difficult to define the Poetess of the nineteenth century as it is to define the lyric of the nineteenth century.[7] The notion that poetry is or ever was one genre (like the notion that the Poetess is or ever was one generic figure or theme) is the primary symptom of the lyricization of poetry: the songs, riddles, epigrams, sonnets, epitaphs, *blasons*, lieder, elegies, marches, dialogues, conceits, ballads, epistles, hymns, odes, eclogues, and monodramas considered lyric in the Western tradition before the early nineteenth century were not lyric in the same sense as the poetry we now think of as lyric. The fact that after the nineteenth century we came to think of almost all poetry as lyric is the secondary symptom of lyricization. As we have progressively idealized poetry-as-lyric and lyric-as-poetry (an idealization that especially characterizes avant-garde poetry communities that define themselves as post- or anti-lyrical), the fewer actual verse genres have addressed readers in specific ways. The nineteenth century was the period in which the shift from many verse cultures articulated through various social relations gave way to an idea of poetry devoted to the transcendence of those relations (via beauty, say, or truth, or Literature, or Culture, or Poetry). The stipulative function of the hymn or the elegy or the ode or the epistle or even the satire tends to dissolve when we think of all of these genres as "poetry," which by definition cannot have a pragmatic cultural function but must represent the receding horizon of an ideal.[8] At the beginning of the nineteenth century, the process of lyricization was just underway (think *Lyrical Ballads*), so Bennett is quite right to point out that women poets wrote all kinds of poems and not just "Poetess poems." In fact, as the passage from Griswold suggests, the nineteenth-century transformation of poetry from a set of verse genres to an aesthetic ideal that transcended genre may entail a transformation of the woman poet from a writer of various verse genres into the figure of the Poetess that exceeded conventions of gender and genre and thus came to represent Poetry.

This is to say that it is difficult to think about the history of the nineteenth-century American Poetess without thinking about the history of eighteenth- and nineteenth-century American poetics. The two most important attempts to think both histories together in recent nineteenth-century American literary studies are Mary Loeffelholz's *From School to Salon: Reading Nineteenth-Century American Women's Poetry* (2004) and Eliza Richards's *Gender and the Poetics of Reception in Poe's Circle* (also 2004). These books have advanced the conversation about the nineteenth-century American Poetess by identifying the figure with larger cultural economies of verse in the period. As Loeffelholz writes, during the course of the nineteenth century, there was "a broad shift from reading, reciting, writing, and publishing poetry in the didactic context of primary and secondary schooling to reading, reciting, and publishing poetry in the emergent later nineteenth-century venues of autonomous high culture, like the salon." According to Loeffelholz, that meant "a broad shift" over the course of the century "in the social locations in which American women gained access to authorship in the genre of poetry."[9] Because of her focus on "access to authorship," Loeffelholz prefers to write about women poets than about Poetesses, but the very historical transition she traces makes the idea of "*the* genre of poetry" women could author harder to imagine. Because poetry was not one but many genres in the nineteenth century, what Loeffelholz actually shows is that the definition of authorship changed as various verse genres collapsed into a lyricized notion of poetry as such. With that collapse (a process that occupied the course of the century) the specter of the Poetess emerged – or one could also say that as an idealized figure of the Poetess emerged, an idealized genre of poetry progressively replaced most social (including didactic or pedagogical) uses of verse.[10] As Eliza Richards argues, the dialectical relation between ideas of the Poetess and uses of poetry meant that much nineteenth-century women's poetry might seem to us (as to contemporaries like Griswold) derivative, since so much popular women's verse depended on what Richards calls "lyric mimicry," on the Poetesses' intimate mirroring of various popular ideas of poetry as such. To read nineteenth-century women's poetry, according to Richards, is to discover "a cultural field in which genius is a product of mimicry and poetesses continue to influence the structures that repudiate their importance. They show us the range of ways that persons become personifications of poetic media."[11] If, as Richards rightly suggests, the nineteenth-century Poetess came to be a personification of poetry, and if, as Loeffelholz rightly suggests, the social locations of what we now call poetry shifted over the course of the nineteenth century, then it follows that the Poetess was such a charged figure in the nineteenth century because she became the index of the historical transformation that eventuated in modern poetics. While Richards assumes that poetesses indulged in "lyric mimicry" throughout the century, and Loeffelholz suggests that women poets' relation to "the genre of poetry" changed significantly in the course of the century, perhaps what really happened was that the modern (or post-nineteenth-century) lyric emerged as the genre we now call poetry by means of the figure of the Poetess. In order to understand the fortunes of the nineteenth-century figure of the Poetess, then, we need to first understand the figure's emergence at the end of the eighteenth century.

Certainly when in 1593 Gabriel Harvey wrote of "the heauenly deuises of the delitious Poetesse Sappho" he did not mean to imply that Sappho made ancient song into modern lyric (especially since, as Yopie Prins has shown, that transformation was accomplished much later, in the nineteenth century), but when in 1748 Lady Luxborough wrote to William Shenstone "I am no *Poetess*; which reproachful name I would avoid, even if I were capable of acquiring it," she did imply that by the mid eighteenth century a Poetess was not simply "a female poet; a woman who composes poetry" (though that is the definition still given by the *OED*, from which both of these historical instances are drawn).[12] If at some point in the eighteenth century the Poetess became more or other than a woman who composes poetry, perhaps that is because eighteenth-century verse for the most part adhered to neo-classical protocols of genre. As Paula Backscheider has so amply demonstrated, women did not just write "poetry" in the eighteenth century; they wrote circuit-of-Apollo poems and imitations of Tibullus's elegies, *apologeia*, thankful or hopeful or regretful or devotional hymns, sonnet cycles, fragments, friendship poems, devout soliloquies, locodescriptive about particular places, and odes to particular friends or lovers or patrons. As Backscheider writes, in eighteenth-century verse by British women poets, "the choice of genre reveals a great deal about the woman, her education, her aims and purposes, and her aspirations. Women were, after all, working within genres and poetic conventions shaped by men."[13] But what about poetic genres that did not reveal very much about the woman poet, or genres in which what was revealed put the poetic conventions shaped by British men under new forms of stress? At those moments, "the reproachful name" of the Poetess began to overshadow the work of the woman poet.

Consider the late eighteenth-century American woman poet most often read by students of American literature today. Phillis Wheatley was kidnapped as a small child from the coast of Gambia, brought to Boston and sold to a genteel family who gave her a literate education, their last name, and the first name of the boat that brought the captive child through the Middle Passage. By her early teens, Wheatley was composing with great facility in various verse genres in the language and idiom in which her captors educated her. Those genres were shaped by white British men, so it stands to reason that for over two centuries readers have looked to Wheatley's choice of genre in order to learn more "about the woman, her education, her aims and purposes, and her aspirations," that is, more about an enslaved African woman in a British colony on the verge of revolution. Modern readers have of course wanted see signs of resistance in Wheatley's forms; her contemporaries at first scrutinized her genres to judge whether a slave girl could have written them in the first place.

As Henry Louis Gates and many others have pointed out, eighteenth-century skepticism about the poet's race gave way to twentieth-century skepticism about the poet's racism; while Wheatley's first sponsors may have wanted to prove that the black female poet behind the poems could have written them, modern readers have lamented that the first African-American woman poet wrote poems that conformed to rather than resisted the racial typing those sponsors imposed.[14] What neither Gates nor many other scholars go on to point out is that the typing at stake in Wheatley's poems also involved poetic types, and that in New England in the last decades of the eighteenth century there was a complex relation between neo-classical protocols of verse genres and changing protocols of race and gender. *POEMS ON VARIOUS SUBJECTS, RELIGIOUS AND MORAL. BY PHILLIS WHEATLEY*, Negro Servant to Mr. John Wheatley, of Boston, in New England, was published in London in 1773, prefaced by the poet's disclaimer, by an "attestation" signed by eighteen of "the most respectable Characters in *Boston*," by a biographical note and endorsement by John Wheatley, and by a dedication to the Countess of Huntingdon, whose patronage made the publication possible.[15] It has often been noticed that these paratexts index the social relations that conditioned all of the poems in the volume (the Boston social hierarchy, Wheatley's enslavement by a "good" master, her enlistment into the transatlantic tension over manumission and into pre-Revolutionary discourses of rights via the Countess of Huntingdon's politics, the economic necessity of patronage), but perhaps it is less obvious that the verse genres in the volume also index those relations. The elegies, odes, hymns, dedications, poems of consolation, epistles, and rebuses that make up the volume each negotiate an elaborate local and transatlantic, pre-Revolutionary and post-neo-classical logic of address. Many of the poems are occasional and thus address not only a specific moment but a specific audience that may have commissioned a given poem or would have circulated the poems as part of the occasion. Of the

thirty-eight poems in Wheatley's volume, thirteen were elegies for members
of families Wheatley knew and that knew her as the Wheatleys' slave.[16]
As Eric Slauter has argued, even the epyllion "Niobe in Distress for her
Children slain by Apollo, from *Ovid's* Metamorphoses, Book VI. and from
a View of the Painting of Mr. *Richard Wilson*" (the thirty-fourth poem in the
volume), while one of the few poems not dedicated to a particular historical
person, makes a petition at "a point where neoclassicism and contemporary
slavery intersect":[17]

> APOLLO's wrath to man the dreadful spring
> Of ills innum'rous, tunefull goddess, sing!
> Thou who did'st first th' ideal pencil give,
> And taught'st the painter in his works to live,
> Inspire with glowing energy of thought,
> What *Wilson* painted, and what *Ovid* wrote.
> Muse! Lend thy aid, nor let me sue in vain,
> Tho' last and meanest of the rhyming train!
> (*Collected Works*, p. 101)

As Slauter notes, in these lines Wheatley formally "imitates Pope and
Milton," but thematically, "her imitation resonates with the contemporary
petitions that argued for freedom based on the emancipatory rhetoric of
colonial rebellion." By using one genre to do the work of another Wheatley
was of course also imitating Pope and Milton, but as Slauter suggests, "by
sympathizing with both Niobe and her subjects, Wheatley's imitation of
Ovid's conservative poem ultimately allowed white colonial readers to see
themselves within the context of their own rhetoric – as slaves to British
tyranny – but it may also have prompted them to reflect on their status
as tyrants themselves."[18] "What *Wilson* painted, and what *Ovid* wrote"
together provided a generic occasion for Wheatley's petition to the Muse to
be the patron of even the "last and meanest of the rhyming train" – that is,
to be, like the Countess of Huntingdon, the patron of enslaved or formerly
enslaved Africans with only natural and not legal rights. But were natural
rights not what colonial readers claimed themselves? The question is left
hanging fire in this as in all of Wheatley's poems, prompting many modern
readers to complain that Wheatley's verse lacked the courage of its convic-
tions, or imitated its sources too closely to ideologically diverge from them.[19]
Indeed, while it is possible to read Wheatley's petition to the Muse as a suit
for abolition or recognition, it is also possible to read it as a submission to
the logic that placed the slave girl "last and meanest." The weight that a
white colonial reader or any reader gives to the implication of the natural
rights discourse that conditioned that petition will depend on the reader's

desire for that implication. If what colonial or later readers had were only Wheatley's texts, the question of that desire would remain (as it has in much Wheatley scholarship) the pathos of reading Wheatley, the double bind of her historical and hermeneutic predicament. But of course Wheatley's texts never did or could stand alone; neither her contemporary readers nor our contemporaries did or do read Wheatley without knowing that the effect of her performance as skilled versifier always already exceeded what she actually wrote, that whatever genre she wrote *in* she always wrote *as* a Poetess.

Five years after the publication of her book, in the same year that (upon the death of John Wheatley) Phillis Wheatley finally managed to be freed, Jupiter Hammon published "An ADDRESS to Miss PHILLIS WHEATLY, Ethiopian Poetess, in Boston, who came from Africa at eight years of age, and soon became acquainted with the gospel of Jesus Christ." As in Wheatley's volume, the prefatory data in Hammon's title index Hammon's relation to Wheatley: like him she is African, and since she has printed her poems, he can address her in verse in print. But the broadside printed in Hartford which Hammon began "Miss Wheatly, pray give me leave to express as follows," casts the "Ethiopian Poetess" in one of the few verse genres she did not "express," the seventeenth-century broadside in hymnal meter, each quatrain keyed to a specific Biblical verse. The first quatrain gives some idea of the whole:

> O come you pious youth! Adore
> The wisdom of thy God,
> In bringing thee from distant shore,
> To learn his holy word.
> *Eccles. xii.*[20]

The elaborate seventeenth-century verse protocols of the Puritan quatrains literalize the sentiment in one of Wheatley's earliest poems, "On being brought from AFRICA to AMERICA," which infamously begins, "'Twas mercy brought me from my *Pagan* land" (*Collected Works*, p.18). That line and the seven that follow it have made so many modern readers wince that Gates has resorted to suggesting that someone *might* suggest that they are an anagram for a more explicit abolitionist message, but in Hammon's broadside, the late eighteenth-century tension between revolutionary and anti-slavery discourses is not resolved in favor of a post-eighteenth-century call for racial equality or individual freedom but is instead smoothed over or covered up by a regression to Puritan providential promise.[21] But is that regression really a cover? If the question her contemporaries sensed in Wheatley's genres fell between their own anti-colonial sympathies and their practice of slaveholding, then Hammon's quatrains make Wheatley more

American than most of her American readers, since her aesthetic genealogy
goes back to the verse style of Wigglesworth. I would read Hammon's poem
to Wheatley not only as a foundational moment in African-American verse
history (as it is most often read) but as a foundational moment in the history of the modern Poetess (as it is never read). By addressing Wheatley as
the "Ethiopian Poetess" Hammon emphasized her modernity at the same
time that his hymnal, scripturally allusive quatrains gave her a pre-modern
pedigree. By the end of the eighteenth century, perhaps the *only* figure that
could be all of these things at once – revolutionary and slave, Puritan and
Ethiopian – was the figure of the Poetess.

This is not to say that Wheatley herself was the prototype of the nineteenth-
century American Poetess, but I do mean to suggest that her historical situation was so radically overdetermined that it allows us to see the emergence
of the category that would be so central to nineteenth-century American
poetics. It also allows us to see how ideologically and generically malleable
that categorical figure could be, and thus how the figure became part and
parcel of the post-eighteenth-century process of lyricization. When in the
New York Magazine in 1796 (twelve years after Wheatley's death in poverty
at thirty-one) one "Matilda" published his/her verse reflections "On Reading
the Poems of Phillis Wheatly, African Poetess," he or she turned the figure of
the Poetess toward a very late eighteenth-century, post-Revolutionary form
of racism:

> The unfavor'd race in shade are meant to be
> The link between the brutal world and we.
>
> ...
>
> A PHILLIS rises, and the world no more
> Denies the sacred right to mental pow'r;
> While, Heav'n-inspir'd, she proves *her Country's* claim
> To Freedom, and her own to deathless Fame.[22]

In heroic couplets far inferior to Wheatley's, Matilda makes the "African
Poetess" an American in a very different way than did Hammon. If Hammon's
solution to the problem of extending legal rights to those admitted to have
natural rights was to give Wheatley an aesthetic birthright to American identity via an antiquated Puritan genre, Matilda rationalizes unequal rights by
converting natural rights discourse into the discourse of the Great Chain of
Being in an earlier eighteenth-century Popean or Augustan genre. According
to the latter logic, divine authority can replace revolutionary violence as
the agent of social change, and that change can maintain the trope of race
as social hierarchy: the African Poetess "rises," and thus the entire Chain
is improved. While still closer to "the brutal world" than white Americans,

the African Poetess "proves *her Country's* claim / To Freedom" by exemplifying the improvement of even the lower links in the Chain when British tyranny has been overthrown and national identity realized.[23] For her fellow Poetess Matilda as for her fellow slave Hammon, print fame as Poetess gave Wheatley's work a metapragmatic function in excess of the stipulative functions of the genres in which she and they wrote, but that excess did not amount to *the* theme of the Poetess. Indeed, the lesson of Wheatley's emergence as Poetess is that as she came to represent an idealized notion of what it meant to write poetry, that ideal was open to definition.

In an essay entitled "Our Phillis, Ourselves," Joanna Brooks has recently suggested that the history of Wheatley's poems is a history of their use and abuse by white readers. Brooks argues that Wheatley made her own transatlantic success as African Poetess possible "not by securing a single endorsement by powerful men [Gates's now-famous "trial of Phillis Wheatley" by the eighteen Boston grandees who signed her "attestation"], but by cultivating an intricate network of relationships among white women."[24] Brooks produces an impressive body of evidence to prove her point, and if she is right, then yet another metapragmatic function of Wheatley's verse was as medium for an emerging white bourgeois culture of feminized collective affect.[25] According to Brooks, "white women circulated Wheatley's manuscript poems [especially the elegies] in Boston and beyond as a currency of friendship, familial relationship, education, and consolation." If that circulation promoted a career that came at Wheatley's expense (including the expense of her second manuscript collection, now lost, which her white female patrons failed to have published), then "the story of Wheatley and her white female patrons in Boston makes plain the evasions, irresponsibilities, and betrayals at the heart of white sentimentalism and its racialized divisions of emotional labor."[26] That story may very well be the tragedy of Wheatley, but it is also a fair description of the figurative economy of the nineteenth-century Poetess, a figure made to order for the emerging culture of vicarious experience in the nineteenth century.

Another name for the culture of vicarious experience might be "romanticism" – or, of course, "sentimentalism" – but the story of Phillis Wheatley makes visible the tricky ways in which the figure of the Poetess could both represent Poetry and come to represent shifting sets of values attached to poetry. Those values were neither simply sentimental nor romantic, though the complex historical changes that took place under those large rubrics are also visible in Wheatley's story. The collective affect that characterized the history of sentimentalism to which Segwick alluded as well as the discourses of natural rights that characterized the advent of Romanticism took many forms as Wheatley gained recognition as Poetess. Those forms had everything to do with the consequences of Middle Passage modernity, and with the Atlantic as a "beginning" of modernity, as Édouard Glissant has put it, a beginning "whose time is marked by ... balls and chains gone green."[27] Glissant's metaphor suggests not only the obscurity of the origins of modernity in slavery and terror, but the naturalization of those origins, their transformation in post-eighteenth-century intellectual history – and in post-eighteenth-century poetics – into a second nature too "green" to appear as the violent effect of culture. I am suggesting that the story of Phillis Wheatley helps us to see the Poetess as an aesthetic category forged in the crucible of Black Atlantic "double consciousness," of the history of post-Middle Passage modernity to which Paul Gilroy has attributed the central philosophical categories of Hegel, Marx, and Nietzsche.[28] To put the Poetess is such highbrow company may seem a long way from my opening invocation of the figure as the domestic furniture of nineteenth-century culture, and my choice of a pre-nineteenth-century enslaved woman poet may seem a strange place from which to trace the emergence of the popular nineteenth-century, typically white Poetess.[29] My point is that the figure that could be cast by the time that Griswold wrote in 1848 as nature mistaken for culture had its beginnings in cultural genres – specifically, and of all things, verse genres – that, precisely through the mediating figure of the Poetess, came to be mistaken for nature.

In the case of the canonical early nineteenth-century American Poetess, Lydia Sigourney, that mistake was literal indeed. As Nina Baym has so memorably written, "if Lydia Howard Huntley Sigourney had not existed, it would have been necessary to invent her. In fact, she *was* invented." What Baym means is that "as American women writers published in ever larger numbers before the Civil War, one of them was bound to be construed as an epitome of the specifically *female* author in her range of allowed achievements and inadequacies," but it is also true that Sigourney was invented as the category of the nineteenth-century Poetess was consolidated.[30] Since Baym's influential essay was published in 1990, a number of critics have pointed out that Sigourney's popular image as sentimental elegist in her time and our own is "a partial and reductive creation," as Loeffelholz has put it.[31] In fact, Baym calculates that no more than 32 percent of Sigourney's poetic production consisted of the elegies for dead children and poems of consolation for which she became so famous as "the Sweet Singer of Hartford"; most of Sigourney's prolific career was devoted to the composition of deeply political, historical narrative verse in all sorts of genres (from monodies to epics), verse actively engaged in the causes of Indian rights and abolition – that is, in the terrible consequences of Atlantic modernity. Why, then, have

Sigourney's poems come down to us as anthologized gems like "Death of an Infant" (1827)?:

Death found strange beauty on that cherub brow,
And dash'd it out. There was a tint of rose
On cheek and lip; – he touch'd the veins with ice,
And the rose faded. – Forth from those blue eyes
There spoke a wishful tenderness, – a doubt
Whether to grieve or sleep, which Innocence
Alone can wear. With ruthless haste he bound
The silken fringes of the curtaining lids
For ever. There had been a murmuring sound
With which the babe would claim its mother's ear,
Charming her even to tears. The spoiler set
His seal of silence. But there beam'd a smile
So fix'd and holy from that marble brow, –
Death gazed and left it there; – he dared not steal
The signet-ring of Heaven.[32]

As a reader, I am rather partial to this little sonnet with a stump tail, this angry *memento mori* that has come to seem "the signet-ring" of sentimental nineteenth-century American Poetess verse. But perhaps my partiality is informed not only by the number of times I have encountered (and by now, taught) Sigourney's much-anthologized poem, but by the mode of reading that prompted the making of all of those anthologies in the first place. As Leah Price has argued, the nineteenth century saw a shift in reading practices realized in and made possible by anthologization, a shift in which "how one reads became more important than what," in which "the conservative hierarchy of genres gave way to a reactionary hierarchy of readers."[33] By "reactionary" Price means to signal the emergence of professions of reading (criticism, edition, scholarship) in the nineteenth century, professions that came to displace the common or general or everyday reader. Certainly Sigourney's sonnet is not addressed to professional readers (though it has now been taken up by them), but it is also not addressed to any particular reader. Baym suggests that the popularity of Sigourney's infant elegies may be traced to their availability to a range of readers, since "a generic elegy, like a greeting card, is available to the large number of people whose circumstances it suits at the moment."[34] "Death of *an* Infant" certainly qualifies as a generic elegy, but it is "generic" in a specifically nineteenth-century sense. Wheatley's elegy "On the Death of the Rev. MR. GEORGE WHITEFIELD. 1770," the broadside that made Wheatley famous on both sides of the Atlantic before the publication of her 1773 volume, is certainly a "generic" elegy, as it adheres to neo-classical elegiac conventions of address, of praise, of heroic comparison, classical allusion, and national exaltation (not to mention to near-perfect heroic couplets); the fourteen other elegies in Wheatley's first volume are all similarly "generic," but also all similarly composed on the occasion of the death of a specific, named individual, either a famous public person like Whitefield or a particular member of a family ("On the Death of J. C., an Infant" may be said to be a "generic" elegy, though the name of the infant fits the very particular circumstances of his parents).[35] Wheatley's elegies for specific historical people were made available to a range of unspecific readers – that is, were made for a print public – but Sigourney's "generic" elegies for a public type were made for private consumption. The level of abstraction in Sigourney's sonnet allows each reader to make of it what she will: the pathos of Death's attack on the white, blue-eyed, rose-tinted baby is not in the mother's helplessness but in the reader's helpless witness. In "Death of an Infant," the personified Death apparently has absolute agency and the reader has no agency at all – but that appearance is deceptive, since so much about this poem depends upon a way of reading rather than, as in Wheatley's elegies, on hierarchies of genre. As Kerry Larson has written so aptly of Sigourney's consolation verse,

> It's not the withdrawal of an external context that's notable but the way in which the poem is drawn to totalize this idea. "I love everybody": Sigourney's reported last words, so often taken as a parody of sentimental fatuity, may also be taken as a token of the nearness of the social whole, where everybody has become a somebody that is more real and more important than anybody who might figure in the poem.[36]

Whether the dead baby's transformation into Heaven's jewelry seems triumph or loss will depend on the white Christian reader's desire to be consoled. If Phillis Wheatley was made a Poetess by readers who used her for their own purposes, Lydia Sigourney became a Poetess by making poems that any reader could use and repurpose.

This is to say that the forty years that separate Wheatley's and Sigourney's poems not only mark an expansion of the category of the Poetess but mark an expansion or abstraction of poetic genres. These two histories were mutually enabling. In "Death of an Infant," how one reads is indeed more important than what, since the content of the poem will be a matter of each reader's construction: the "strange beauty" of infant nature is an ideal – like the white, blue-eyed genderless innocent itself – on which any content could be projected. In this sense the infant is, as figure, a literal analogue to the poem, a pentameter quasi-sonnet neither Shakespearean nor Italian, with an extra half-line that does not qualify as a Miltonic six-line "tail." It has all the features of an ideal, anglicized poem, but it is not actually any particular kind of poem. As the rose-cheeked babe is no particular child but an ideal-ized doll, the text is a pretty but "generic" poem. We could read the half-line as the scene-stealer here, the turn that upsets Death's authority in the previous fourteen lines, but to read in this way would be to engage in an elevation of a way of reading dependent on the interpretive skill of the reader, a way of reading more important to the poem than would be the social relations supposed by a particular verse genre. By privileging a way of reading over a protocol of genre, Sigourney's poem contributes to the history of lyricization at the same time that it gave broader scope to the figure of the nineteenth-century American Poetess.

Certainly scholars have been right to point out that "Death of an Infant" is not representative of Sigourney's *oeuvre*; as Paula Bennett has suggested, "treating Sigourney as a Poetess would require passing over" not only aspects of her many political and historical poems that could "not be more time-, place- and text-specific, but [ignoring] everything else that is various and challenging in her poetry, putting an 'empty figure' in their place."[37] But to say that Sigourney's reputation (which Bennett herself has characterized as "the foremother of an entire century of Emmeline Grangerfords") did not match her actual practice does not mean that Sigourney's work did not mark an important moment in the rise of the nineteenth-century American Poetess.[38] Neither Sigourney nor Wheatley (nor any other historical person) could actually *be* a Poetess anymore than any writer before the late nineteenth century could be a lyric poet. Both the category of the Poetess and the abstract generic category of the lyric were representations of messier historical realities, empty figures (like the dead, white, blue-eyed infant in generic poetic form) that could be filled at will. As the century progressed, both abstractions were indeed filled any number of times in any number of ways. In the middle of the century, the poet Elizabeth Oakes Smith wrote in her autobiography that

> In our country of general knowledge amongst the people, the grades of culture are unnoticed, and our differences are known to exist more in the power to express ourselves, than by claim to rank either by wealth or learning. Hence it is that we turn to poetry for expression, and in this find a recognition other-wise denied us, and this is natural and instinctive with us.[39]

By the mid nineteenth century, a personally expressive "natural and instinctive" poetry could be invoked as a cultural, very American ideal. I have focused this chapter on the emergence of the figure of the idealized nineteenth-century Poetess rather than on the figure's later career and per-mutations in order to suggest some ways in which the Poetess became iden-tified with a lyricized notion of poetry as such and to suggest what that lyricized notion of poetry owed to other cultural ideals. The reason that successful antebellum poets like Oakes Smith "could not avoid inhabiting" the figure of the Poetess (as Richards has suggested) was that the figure allowed readers to personify a way of reading poetry that replaced hierarchies of genre with hierarchies of expression, a way of reading that could, like race, appear deceptively natural.[40] Oakes Smith's successful personification of that lyricized notion of poetry may be measured not only by the rather beautiful way in which her prose counters Griswold's, but by the portability of the most famous figure in her poetry across genres. *The Sinless Child*, a long narrative, Wordsworthian, Schilleresque – which is to say, canonically Romantic – poem first published in the *Southern Literary Messenger* in 1842 became (to her chagrin) Oakes Smith's most influential creation, its child heroine Eva transformed into the title character in Longfellow's smash hit dactylic hexameter verse epic *Evangeline* in 1847, and into Stowe's iconic Little Eva in her best-selling, world-changing sentimental novel of 1852.[41] As even this brief invocation of the fortunes of the figure suggests, Eva became such a successful literary commodity in exactly the same way that the Poetess rose to prominence: both were empty, idealized figures that could be turned toward different economies of value across rather than in the service of a range of highly charged literary genres, but those economies themselves were of course not historically relative but were emphatically historically determined. The controversy over the classical meter of Longfellow's verse epic of modern diaspora was one symptom of the abstraction of verse genres that accelerated in the mid nineteenth century; the fact that Stowe could count on her mid-century readers to recognize her abolitionist novel's doomed heroine as a poetic ideal was another. The race politics that made an innocent white female child seem an ideal vehicle for "natural and instinctive" vicarious personal expression depended on abstraction. The gender politics that made the Poetess seem an ideal figure for such expression also depended on abstraction. The ideological freight of those abstractions has been weighed by literary historians for some time, but what literary history has not yet understood is the way in which those figures participated in the history of the nineteenth-century lyricization of American poetry, a process in which ways of reading became more important than what one read, in which the social relations indexed by genre became the social relations transcended by Poetry. It is difficult to imagine social relations more in need of transcendence than those present to the readers of the 1842 *Southern Literary Messenger* or the 1847 *Evangeline* or the 1852 *Uncle Tom's Cabin*, unless they were the relations negotiated by Wheatley in the 1770s or protested by Sigourney in her 1820s and 1830s poems on colonial history and Indian rights. For most of the nineteenth century, the Poetess represented that transcendental potential, but the figure waned in importance and visibility after the 1880s, as the collapse of verse genres into Poetry was accomplished and there was little tension between genres for the Poetess to transcend or represent. The generic excess that the Poetess personified came to be personified after the end of the nineteenth century by the abstract lyric "speaker" of modern lyric reading. That is why in the 1840s Poe and Longfellow could still so effectively exploit the figure of the Poetess, why Whitman could draw on it in the 1850s while keeping his distance from it in the 1870s and 1880s, and why Frances Ellen Watkins Harper, as an eminent black orator immersed in print address, had such an awkward relation to the figure in her antebellum career and why she could not revive it at the end of the century.[42] It is why newspapers and magazines and anthologies and gift books and scrapbooks were full of anonymous and pseudonymous Poetess poems throughout the century. It is why Emily Dickinson could write as a Poetess in the 1860s but could only be published as a lyric poet in the 1890s. And it is why the history of the Poetess is so hard to tell, since, like the history of nineteenth-century American poetry, it has been hidden all along in plain sight behind the very ways of reading that the rise and fall of the Poetess made possible.

NOTES

1 Eve Kosofsky Sedgwick, "Wilde, Nietzsche, and the Sentimental Relations of the Male Body," in *Epistemology of the Closet* (Berkeley: University of California Press, 1990), p. 150. Sedgwick's aim is to distinguish "the feminocentric Victorian version" of sentimentalism from "the twentieth-century one with its complex and distinctive relation to the male body," but I would maintain that Sedgwick's argument that the latter is the highly charged "glass closet" or "empty secret" at the center of modern culture also applies to the widely circulated open secret of the Poetess within nineteenth century culture – and if it can so apply, then the nineteenth century and indeed the Poetess herself must form more than a feminized bridge between the eighteenth-century honorific and the twentieth-century damning senses of the "sentimental."

2 Elizabeth Oakes Smith, "To Mary Forrest," *Evening Mirror*, around March 1855; cited by Eliza Richards from a clipping in the Special Collections of the University of Virginia Library in *Gender and the Poetics of Reception in Poe's Circle* (Cambridge University Press, 2004), p. 180.

3 Rufus W. Griswold, ed., *The Female Poets of America* (Philadelphia: Carey and Hart, Publishers, 1848), p. 3.

4 George Gordon Lord Byron, *The Giaour: A Fragment of a Turkish Tale* (London: Printed by Thomas Davison for John Murray, 1814), line 957.

5 Paula Bernat Bennett, "Was Sigourney a Poetess? The Aesthetics of Victorian Plenitude in Lydia Sigourney's Poetry," *Comparative American Studies*, 5.3 (2007), 267, 270.

6 Virginia Jackson and Yopie Prins, "Lyrical Studies," *Victorian Literature and Culture* 27.2 (1999), 523.

7 For other examples of my argument on lyricization, see *Dickinson's Misery: A Theory of Lyric Reading* (Princeton University Press, 2005), and "Who Reads Poetry?" *PMLA*, 123.2 (January 2008), 181–87.

8 The classic definition of poetry as so ideally lyric that no actual poet can write it is of course John Stuart Mill's essay "Thoughts on Poetry and Its Varieties" (1839). In *Autobiography and Literary Essays*, vol. 1 of *The Collected Works of John Stuart Mill* (University of Toronto Press, 1981). Given its unrealizability in Mill's essay, it is somewhat ironic that Mill's definition of the lyric as "overheard" speech became the norm for the term in twentieth-century literary criticism (see, for example, Northrop Frye, *Anatomy of Criticism: Four Essays* [Princeton University Press, 1957]).

9 Mary Loeffelholz, *From School to Salon: Reading Nineteenth-Century American Women's Poetry* (Princeton University Press, 2004), p. 4.

10 The implications of Loeffelholz's argument about the historical shift "from school to salon" are far-reaching, and would entail a longer consideration of the "field of production" in which the Poetess emerges than it is possible to pursue here, but of which her book offers the best possible view. See also Angela Sorby, *Schoolroom Poets: Childhood, Performance, and the Place of American Poetry, 1865–1917* (Hanover, NH: University Press of New England, 2005). The danger of misinterpreting the importance of nineteenth-century American poetry to educational practices as the "cultural work" of poetry *tout court* is evident in Joan Shelley Rubin's *Songs of Ourselves: The Uses of Poetry in America* (Cambridge, MA: Harvard University Press, 2007) and in Stephen Burt's essay on *Schoolroom Poets*, "When Poets Ruled the School," *American Literary History*, 20.3 (Summer 2008), 508–20.

11 Eliza Richards, *Gender and the Poetics of Reception in Poe's Circle* (Cambridge University Press, 2004), pp. 25, 198.

12 For an account of the transmutation of Sappho from ancient to nineteenth-century poet and of ancient poems into modern lyrics see Yopie Prins, *Victorian Sappho* (Princeton University Press, 1999). The *Oxford English Dictionary* is itself of course a creation of the middle of the nineteenth century, and it is telling that even the current edition's definition of list of instances of the term stops with a passage by Arthur Symonds from 1873.

13 Paula Backscheider, *Eighteenth-Century Women Poets and Their Poetry: Inventing Agency, Inventing Genre* (Baltimore: Johns Hopkins University Press, 2005), p. 19. Backscheider's book is exemplary both for the range of eighteenth-century verse genres practiced by women poets it makes visible and for the strain of reconciling those genres with modern critical notions of lyric voice and personal agency.

14 See Henry Louis Gates, *The Trials of Phillis Wheatley* (New York: Basic Books, 2003), for a somewhat simplified version of the history of racist readings to which Wheatley's poems have been subjected.

15 A facsimile publication of the 1773 *Poems* is available in John C. Shields, ed., *The Collected Works of Phillis Wheatley* (Oxford University Press, 1988),

pp. 1–127. Further references to the *Collected Works* are cited parenthetically in the text.

16 The circumstances of the composition and circulation of each of Wheatley's extant poems could each occupy an article in themselves, but it should also be noted that in addition to the elaborate social networks on which the familiar elegies depended, Wheatley cultivated a print public recognition in her elegies for famous men, first and foremost in the poem that first made her famous, her elegy for the celebrated evangelical minister George Whitefield. As Max Cavitch has written, "not recognized as a mourner, perhaps not even by herself, Wheatley set about acquiring the means of recognizing and managing the mourning of others. She identified the expressions of grief that were intelligible to those around her, and she used them to create a conscious community of memory in which, though a socially dead person herself, she could nevertheless relate to the living with a measure of authority." See "Mourning of the Disprized: African Americans and Elegy from Wheatley to Lincoln," in Max Cavitch, *American Elegy: The Poetry of Mourning from the Puritans to Whitman* (Minneapolis: University of Minnesota Press, 2007), p. 187.

17 Eric Slauter, *The State as a Work of Art: The Cultural Origins of the Constitution* (University of Chicago Press, 2009), p. 199. Slauter's longer argument that Wheatley's book appeared at a particular moment of cultural transition ("the beginning of the romantic movement against neoclassicism [190–91]") would be interesting to consider in relation to the particular moment of transition that has come to be understood as the construction of the Romantic lyric.

18 *Ibid.*, pp. 113, 117.

19 See, for example, Amiri Baraka's complaint in 1962 that Wheatley's "pleasant imitations of eighteenth-century English poetry are far and, finally, ludicrous departures from the huge black voices that splintered southern nights with their *hollers, chants, arwhoolies,* and *ballits*" (cited by Gates in *The Trials of Phillis Wheatley*, p. 76). Note the very un-British and non-white genres Baraka opposes to Wheatley's neo-classical elegies, odes, and hymns.

20 Jupiter Hammon, "An ADDRESS to Miss PHILLIS WHEATLY, Ethiopian Poetess ..." first appeared as a broadside in Hartford, Connecticut in August, 1778. An open-access, legible electronic transcription of that broadside is available through the University of Virginia Library at http://virgobeta.lib.virginia.edu/ catalog. Most editions of Hammon's poem available to modern readers delete the scriptural references, thus deleting the genre of Hammon's address.

21 At the end of *The Trials of Phillis Wheatley*, Gates performatively claims (pp. 87–88) that "just a few days after a recent Fourth of July," he received a fax from a man named Walter Grigo, "sent from a public fax machine in Madison, Connecticut. Mr. Grigo – a freelance writer – had evidently become fascinated with anagrams, and wished to alert me to quite a stunning anagram indeed. 'On Being Brought from Africa to America,' this eight-line poem, was in its entirety, an anagram, he pointed out. If you simply rearranged the letters, you got" an explicitly abolitionist poem that ends with the plea "America, manumit our race."

I thank the Lord," a line in a meter Wheatley never wrote and would not have recognized.

22 Matilda's poem appeared in the *New York Magazine* 1 [n.s.] (1796), 549–50, and is reproduced in its entirety in Eugene L. Huddleston, "*Matilda's* 'On Reading the Poems of Phillis Wheatley, African Poetess', " *Early American Literature*, 5:3 (Winter 1970/1971), 57–67. Huddleston's article is especially interesting for its understanding of the Poetess "Matilda": "If Matilda's poetry reflects his experiences, he was a New Yorker, a Revolutionary, a Western traveler, a patrician, and a sentimentalist" (57).

23 Matilda's version of racism supports Slauter's argument that "in ways we are only beginning to appreciate, the Age of Revolutions gave rise simultaneously to a modern language of rights and to modern forms of racism" (*The State as a Work of Art*, p. 177).

24 Joanna Brooks, "Our Phillis, Ourselves," *American Literature*, 82.1 (March 2010), 7–8. Brooks's essay effectively dismantles the sensational fiction of Wheatley's "trial" on which Gates's account depends and that (as Brooks shows) others have adopted as historical fact, putting in its place a suggestive account of Wheatley's agency in assembling her own prefatory documents to achieve the London publication.

25 The model of collective affective community Brooks invokes is deeply indebted to Lauren Berlant's theorization of "the *Uncle Tom* form" of female, bourgeois, sentimental culture in the later nineteenth and twentieth centuries. See Lauren Berlant, "Poor Eliza," *American Literature*, 70 (1998), 635–66. The difference between the late eighteenth century and the forms of sentimental culture Berlant describes is a good measure of the difference between Wheatley's genres and the personally expressive, lyricized genres of the nineteenth and twentieth centuries.

26 Brooks, "Our Phillis, Ourselves," 18, 17.

27 Édouard Glissant, *Poetics of Relation*, trans. Betsy Wing (Ann Arbor: University of Michigan Press, 1997), p. 6.

28 See Paul Gilroy, *The Black Atlantic: Modernity and Modern Consciousness* (Cambridge, MA: Harvard University Press, 1993). I do not pretend to summarize Gilroy's argument by merely invoking its broadest outlines.

29 Tricia Lootens has consistently called attention to the importance of thinking about race when thinking about the nineteenth-century Poetess. See especially her essay "Hemans and Her American Heirs: Nineteenth-Century Women's Poetry and National Identity," in Isobel Armstrong and Virginia Blain, eds., *Women's Poetry, Late Romantic to Late Victorian: Gender and Genre, 1830–1900* (Basingstoke and New York: Macmillan, St. Martin's, 1999) pp. 243–60.

30 Nina Baym, "Reinventing Lydia Sigourney" originally appeared in *American Literature*, 62 (1990), 385–404, and is included in Baym's *Feminism and American Literary History: Essays* (New Brunswick: Rutgers University Press, 1992), p. 151.

31 Loeffelholz, *From School to Salon*, p. 34. Loeffelholz's chapter on Sigourney, "The School of Lydia Sigourney," represents an important extension of Baym's argument.

32 Lydia Sigourney, *Poems; by the Author of "Moral Pieces in Prose and Verse"* (Boston and Hartford, 1827). Though my argument here is informed by recent debates over the status of Sigourney as Author as Poetess, it is worth noting that many of her poems were published anonymously or pseudonymously.

33 Leah Price, *The Anthology and the Rise of the Novel: From Richardson to George Eliot* (Cambridge University Press, 2000), p. 156. Although the titular subject of Price's book is the novel, its point about what Bakhtin called "the novelization of genre" is crucial for what we might (but don't often) call the rise of the lyric. See Mikhail Bakhtin, *Speech Genres and Other Late Essays*, trans. Vern W. McGee, ed. Caryl Emerson and Michael Holquist (Austin: University of Texas Press, 1986).

34 Baym, *Feminism and American Literary History*, p. 153.

35 On the importance of the print history of Wheatley's broadside elegy for Whitefield, see Patricia Willis, "Phillis Wheatley, George Whitefield, and the Countess of Huntingdon in the Beinecke Library," *Yale University Library Gazette* (April 2006), 161–77.

36 Although Larson's argument is about Sigourney's abstraction of the social whole and my argument stresses her abstraction of verse genres, the two forms of abstraction of course come to the same thing. See Kerry Larson, *Imagining Equality in Nineteenth-Century American Literature* (Cambridge University Press, 2008), p. 96.

37 Bennett, "Was Sigourney a Poetess?" p. 283. Much of Bennett's essay is taken up with an argument against the definition of the Poetess in "Lyrical Studies"; Bennett ends her essay with an answer to "Lyrical Studies" and to the question in her title: "Sometimes witty, sometimes heavy-handed, sometimes passionate with outrage, sometimes irritatingly didactic or excessively sentimental, Sigourney's play with the poetic conventions of her period and place *was* her 'voice,' it was her 'consciousness,' it was her 'self.' She was a poet. She was not a Poetess" (283).

38 Bennett makes this remark in her head note for the Sigourney selections in Bennett's excellent anthology, *Nineteenth-Century American Women Poets: An Anthology* (London: Blackwell Publishers, 1998), p. 3. The reference is of course to the parodic Poetess figure in Twain's *Huckleberry Finn*, who composes elegies for dead children on commission.

39 *A Human Life: Being the Autobiography of Elizabeth Oakes Smith. A Critical Edition and Introduction*, ed. Leigh Kirkland, Ph.D. Diss., Georgia State University, 1994, p. 314. Cited by Richards in *Gender and the Poetics of Reception in Poe's Circle*.

40 My curtailed reading of Oakes Smith in these pages is deeply indebted to Eliza Richards' chapter "Elizabeth Oakes Smith's 'unspeakable eloquence'" in *Gender and the Poetics of Reception in Poe's Circle*, pp. 149–90. See also "'The Poetess' and Nineteenth-Century American Women Poets," the essay that Richards and I co-wrote for the inaugural issue of the *Poetess Archive Journal*, 1.1 (12 April 2007), www.poetessarchive.com/

41 Reprinted in *The Sinless Child and Other Poems*, ed. John Keese (New York: Wiley and Putnam, 1843), a feminized, gilt-edged portable "pocket" book four and a half inches long by three inches wide.

42 On Harper's vexed relation to the category of the Poetess and to modern lyric reading, see Meredith McGill, "Frances Ellen Watkins Harper and the Circuits of Abolitionist Poetry" (paper presented at the McNeil Center for Early American Studies, Philadelphia, PA, July 15, 2010; forthcoming in *Early African American Print Culture*, ed. Laura Cohen and Jordan Stein).

4

STEPHEN CUSHMAN

Transcendentalist poetics

In the opening paragraph of his essay "The Transcendentalist," first delivered as a lecture on December 23, 1841, as part of a series on "The Times,"
Ralph Waldo Emerson offers this helpful formulation: "What is popularly
called Transcendentalism among us, is Idealism; Idealism as it appears in
1842." But what is idealism? Unsystematic in his use of the term, which
titles the sixth section of his *Nature* (1836) and which he associated at various moments in various moods with, among others, Plato, Plotinus, George
Berkeley, Emanuel Swedenborg, Immanuel Kant (whose 1781 *Critique of
Pure Reason* uses the term "transcendental" to describe knowledge that
transcends what he called Understanding [*Verstand*], or knowledge provided by sense experience), Johann Gottlieb Fichte, Friedrich von Schelling,
Samuel Taylor Coleridge, Thomas Carlyle, Hinduism, Buddhism, and Sufism,
Emerson continues in the next sentence of "The Transcendentalist" with a
straightforward distinction:

> As thinkers, mankind have ever divided into two sects, Materialists and
> Idealists; the first class founding on experience, the second on consciousness;
> the first class beginning to think from the data of the senses, the second class
> perceive that the senses are not final, and say, The senses give us representations
> of things, but what are the things themselves, they cannot tell. The materialist
> insists on facts, on history, on the force of circumstances and the animal wants
> of man; the idealist on the power of Thought and of Will, on inspiration, on
> miracle, on individual culture. These two modes of thinking are both natural,
> but the idealist contends that his way of thinking is in higher nature.[1]

This passage contains statements and oppositions to question (where, for
example, does the boundary between experience and consciousness lie?), but
it serves to establish two important and necessary points. First, in the history
of ideas Emerson's description of transcendentalism continues the response
to and reaction against John Locke's insistence, in *An Essay Concerning
Human Understanding* (1689), on the senses as gatekeepers of all human
knowledge, the response and reaction that began with Berkeley's *A Treatise*

Concerning the Principles of Human Knowledge (1710). Second, in trying to make transcendental idealism accessible to a non-specialist lecture audience, Emerson describes it in such a way that it becomes a very large category indeed. Emerson's rhetorically shrewd, enlarging move has some of the same effect as that of this sentence in "The Poet" (originally delivered in the same lecture series as "The Transcendentalist"): "The people fancy they hate poetry, and they are all poets and mystics!"[2] The people fancy they do not understand transcendental idealism, and they are all – or, at least in Emerson's lecture hall, mostly – transcendental idealists! When he asserts in the same essay that the transcendentalist "believes in miracle, in the perpetual openness of the human mind to new influx of light and power; he believes in inspirations, and in ecstasy,"[3] Emerson moves beyond the rigors of epistemological philosophy to project an attractive image of a radiant sensibility with which few of his educated listeners would have wanted to deny all connection.

Emerson's strategic inclusiveness makes good sense for his lecture, but it poses some problems, too. If one takes "transcendentalist" to include anyone open to a new influx of light and power from a source not immediately verifiable by the senses, one has many, many people to consider. Likewise, if one allows the term "poetics" to dilate far enough to include such usages as Gaston Bachelard's *La poétique de l'espace* (*The Poetics of Space*, 1958), in which "poetics" functions as shorthand for something like "general principles governing the way a subject experiences a particular phenomenon," then the possible instances of transcendentalist poetics would swiftly exceed our grasp. A quick check of book titles built around the phrase "the poetics of X" – and none of these books is classified under "poetry" or "literary criticism" – fills in the blank with cities, cinema, social work, transubstantiation, punishment, culture, political economy, perspective, belief, knowledge, violent death, gender, manhood, movement, ascent. Given the elasticity of the two terms, we could not automatically rule out, for example, some kinds of meditative or therapeutic practices, whether nineteenth-century or twenty-first, from consideration under the heading "transcendentalist poetics."

The eye of the needle will be small here. The term "transcendentalist" will limit itself primarily to the people who began meeting in Massachussetts in the fall of 1836 – the first meeting consisted of four youthful Unitarian ministers, Emerson, Frederic Henry Hedge, George Ripley, and George Putnam – and, increasing in number, continued meeting through the 1840s. Often referring to themselves as "Hedge's Club," because they met when Hedge could leave his pastoral duties as minister of the Unitarian church in Bangor, Maine, and travel to Boston, sixteen of these people, described as regular attenders, appear by name in the diary of Bronson Alcott, who calls them "The Symposium Club": in addition to those already named and Alcott himself, Convers Francis, James Freeman Clarke, Cyrus A. Bartol, Margaret Fuller, Elizabeth P. Peabody, Theodore Parker, William H. Channing, John S. Dwight, Jones Very, Henry David Thoreau, Robert Bartlett, and Caleb Stetson. To this core George Willis Cooke suggests adding, as "occasional attendants," "Dr. [William Ellery] Channing, [Orestes Augustus] Brownson, Charles Follen, Samuel J. May, William Russell, George Bancroft, Christopher Cranch, S[amuel] G. Ward, Mrs. Samuel (Sarah) Ripley, Miss Elizabeth Hoar, Thomas T. Stone, George P. Bradford, Le Baron Russell, and William D. Wilson," commenting that probably "several of these names should be added to the sixteen mentioned by Alcott as those of regular members."[4] Not all these people wrote and published poems, but Emerson, Fuller, Thoreau, Channing, Very, Hedge, Cranch, Clarke, Dwight, and Ward did, and some of them will contribute to the sampling here.

As for the term "poetics," again the usage will be narrow, expanding only to encompass general discussions of poetry and, especially important for the members of this extraordinary club, the poet, while much of the time it will refer to and include consideration of small details or features of poetic form and prosody in specific poems, which appeared in the short-lived organ of the transcendentalists, *The Dial: A Magazine for Literature, Philosophy, and Religion*, published in sixteen numbers, four volumes, from July 1840 through April 1844. Subsequently, Emerson selected many of these poems for inclusion in his eccentric but revealing anthology *Parnassus*, published in Boston by James R. Osgood in 1875. In focusing on poems published in *The Dial* and often reprinted in *Parnassus*, we add to our potential sample the work of William Ellery Channing, nephew of Dr. William Ellery Channing and usually referred to as "the younger," and of the Sturgis sisters, Ellen Sturgis Hooper and Caroline Sturgis Tappan, both of whom were friends of most of those who wrote for *The Dial* and moved in the orbit of the club, even if their names do not appear among those of the regulars.

Bold, inspiring, quirky, Emerson's famous lecture-turned-essay "The Poet," eventually published in *Essays: Second Series* (1844), offers many memorable statements and formulations that characterize transcendentalist poetics. In this sentence, for example, Emerson makes his Platonic-idealist-transcendentalist leanings clear: "For poetry was all written before time was, and whenever we are so finely organized that we can penetrate into that region where the air is music, we hear those primal warblings, and attempt to write them down, but we lose ever and anon a word, or a verse and substitute something of our own, and thus miswrite the poem."[5] For Emerson, as for many of the people around him in Hedge's Club, poetry exists before, apart from, and, one could even say, above individual poems, which in turn are the imperfect efforts of poets to transcribe into language the rhythmic pulsations of the supernatural they can sometimes overhear: "The men of more delicate ear write down these cadences more faithfully, and these transcripts, though imperfect, become the songs of nations."[6]

So principle number one of transcendentalist poetics, at least according to Emerson, is that poetry, which comes from a Greek verb meaning "to make," does not come solely from the mind of a poet making things up in the privacy of his or her room; it broadcasts continually as an exquisitely organized transmission of divine beauty or soul or spirit, which the poet, by means of faculties and sensibilities most of us lack or have lost, manages to receive and turn into language the rest of us can read. Two other principles follow from this one in Emerson's thinking. The first is that the language a poet uses to transcribe these transmissions of divine beauty or soul is necessarily figurative – Emerson calls it symbolic and often speaks of emblems or tropes – because the most powerful, most memorable language is that which represents or manifests the correspondence between things we can know with our senses and things we cannot. According to Emerson, we need symbols, emblems, and tropes because these are what enable us to talk about and apprehend realities beyond our senses, supernatural or spiritual realities. Without figurative language and its symbolic functions we would be confined to the immediate world of sense experience and have no access to the supernatural or spiritual.

The second principle that follows is that nature, by which Emerson means not just the green world but also "art, all other men and my own body,"[7] as he explains in his earlier *Nature*, plays a crucial role in mediating between the eternal and supernatural realm of poetry, on the one hand, and, on the other, the time-bound and mundane realm of the poet trying to transcribe the divine broadcasts. Nature must play the role of go-between because "Nature is the symbol of spirit," as Emerson declares in the "Language" section of *Nature*, and "nature is a symbol ... certifying the supernatural," as he adds in "The Poet."[8] This designation of nature as supernatural symbol leads Emerson to the assertion that "poems are a corrupt version of some text in nature with which they ought to be made to tally," an assertion he follows with one of the many exhilarating passages in "The Poet":

> A rhyme in one of our sonnets should not be less pleasing than the iterated nodes of a seashell, or the resembling difference of a group of flowers. The pairing of the birds is an idyl, not tedious as our idyls are; a tempest is a rough ode, without falsehood or rant: a summer, with its harvest sown, reaped, and stored, is an epic song, subordinating how many admirably executed parts. Why should not the symmetry and truth that modulate these, glide into our spirits, and we participate the invention of nature?[9]

The transitive use of "participate" to mean "share in" or "partake of" is rare, but the rarity of Emerson's usage, and the unfamiliar relationship among subject, action, and object, which this transitive use of "participate" suggests, leads usefully to some reflection on the paradoxes of transcendentalist poetics. To put it simply, in the relationship among poet, poem, nature, and the supernatural, who does what to whom? Who participates (in) the inventing? In asserting an analogy between the poem and nature, an analogy that prescribes that the form of a poem should be like a form in nature, Emerson affirms the theory of organic form developed by August Wilhelm von Schlegel and subsequently transmitted to Emerson by Coleridge, who in defense of Shakespeare distinguishes between "mechanic" form and "organic" form, arguing that the latter "is innate; it shapes as it develops itself from within, and the fullness of its development is one and the same with the perfection of its outward form."[10] As others have pointed out, most notably Walter Pater in an essay on Coleridge, the organic metaphor offers a pleasing image of how we experience many good poems – they seem to take the shapes they do "naturally" and do not distract us with the creakings of their artificiality – but that same metaphor erases the role of the poet, as inventor, craftsman, student of literary history and convention, from the process altogether. Once again, he or she is nothing but an impersonal transmitter, albeit one of higher quality than would operate in a non-poet. In defense of Emerson and other organicists, we could argue that they use the natural metaphor simply as an analogy and that Coleridge, Emerson, and other writers knew very well how hard a poet has to work to produce the appearance of naturalness. In speaking of the organic naturalness of poem, this argument would go, Emerson is merely trying to distinguish what he sees as the greater range and flexibility of the contemporary poetry of the 1840s when compared to the eighteenth-century neoclassicism of Dryden, Pope, and Swift, whom he represents very sparingly in *Parnassus*.

In transcendentalist poetics, then, the myth is that nature is in charge of the poet's poem, and like any myth this one tells a story about something real, in this case the real shift in the second half of the eighteenth century and first half of the nineteenth toward a poetics of greater variation, whether on the macro-level of subject matter (including, in the poems of Wordsworth for example, the points of view and concerns of uneducated people in rural settings) or on the mid-level of mode and genre (as imitations of classical poems, usually in heroic couplets, made way for representations of individual subjectivity in sonnets, ballads, meditative poems in blank verse) or on the micro-level of prosody (as, for example, accentual verse and tri-syllabic substitutions in iambic lines became more frequent).

This myth-making is neither hard to understand nor hard to accept. What gets trickier in transcendentalist poetics is the implied relationship between nature and the supernatural. If nature is a symbol of the supernatural, or the spiritual, as Emerson often calls it, it is so because the supernatural is greater than or exceeds or transcends the natural, as the symbolized always is greater than or exceeds or transcends the symbol. In other words, the supernatural should be in charge of or determine or invent the natural. But in insisting on the doctrine or principle of correspondence, adapted from the writings of Swedenborg – that everything in nature corresponds to something supernatural and vice versa (did the detractors of John Locke read far enough in his massive *Essay* to find this remarkably similar assertion in his argument for the existence of God: "For I judge it as certain and clear a Truth, as can any where be delivered, That *the invisible Things of* GOD *are clearly seen from the Creation of the World, being understood by the Things that are made, even his Eternal Power, and God-head*"?[11]) – transcendentalist poetics paradoxically limits the supernatural to what we know of nature, so that nature ends up controlling and determining and inventing the supernatural, or at least our ideas of it. Even with his qualification that by "nature" he does not mean only the green world, but means instead everything outside his own mind, reading Emerson and the other transcendentalists soon makes it clear that for the members of Hedge's Club nature is mostly a matter of sunsets, seasons, fields, ponds, seashores, and mountaintops, or in the language of the passage about rhyme from "The Poet," seashells, mating birds, storms, and agrarian summers. Presumably – although we may not understand how – in its abundant omnipresence the supernatural would also invent and irradiate technology, industry, business, economic depression, politics, immigration, urbanization, ghettos and slums, prostitution, war against Mexico, potato famine, native American removal and genocide, tuberculosis, alcoholism, mania and mental illness, clear-cutting of forests, extermination of buffalo. But despite a few rather rose-colored and unconvincing paragraphs about the new encroachments of the railroad – Emerson's in "The Poet," Thoreau's in *Walden* (1854) – the transcendentalists, who often placed themselves at the forefront of social and political reform movements, kept these aspects of "nature," or the material world, out of their poems. In doing so, they appear to forget the wisdom of one of their own, Bronson Alcott, who in his "Orphic Sayings," published in the first number of *The Dial* (July 1840), declares of God, "Nature does not contain, but is contained in him."[12]

One of the large paradoxes of transcendentalist poetics, then, is that such a progressive group of radical protesters should confine the subject matter of their verse to a relatively narrow bandwidth of the supernatural broadcast. In many instances the neo-classical Augustan poets, against whom they reacted, showed a greater willingness to range more widely, at least within the gritty contexts of political intrigue, social scandal, bawdy sexuality, and imperfect sanitation characteristic of eighteenth-century London. But another paradox, and in some ways the more puzzling one (since one could argue that the high-thinking transcendentalists made up on the vertical axis of vision what they forfeited on the horizontal), has to do with the formal schemes and designs of their verse: how could people so deeply committed to protest, reform, inspiration, ecstasy, experiment, innovation, naturalness, and unconventionality settle for writing verse so mildly metered and rhymed as this little proto-imagist poem, entitled "The Morning Breeze" and printed on the penultimate page of the first number of *The Dial*, by Margaret Fuller, first editor of the magazine and subsequently associated in many minds with the early history of feminism in the United States:

> Ocean, that lay
> Like a sick child, spiritless, well nigh death,
> Now curls and ripples in eternal play
> Beneath thy breath.
> (*The Dial*, 1:135)

This poem, with its pair of iambic pentameter lines sandwiched between two iambic dimeters, includes features to appraise and ponder appreciatively, such as the rhyming of lines of different lengths or Fuller's treatment of the conventional etymological connection of "spirit" with wind and breath or the uncanny relation of this marine meditation to her own subsequent death by drowning at sea in 1850, but it also includes features that might cause some to wince, such as the "death–breath" rhyme, which by 1840 had already become one of the most predictable in English.

The beginnings of an answer to this question about the formal temperateness of transcendentalist poetry return us to Emerson's version of organic theory and a well-known sentence in "The Poet," usually quoted out of context: "For it is not metres, but a metre-making argument that makes a poem, – a thought so passionate and alive, that, like the spirit of a plant or an animal, it has an architecture of its own, and adorns nature with a new thing." This sentence subsequently became an authorizing dictum for many a writer of free verse in the United States during the twentieth century, but read closely and in context, Emerson's statement in fact endorses nothing like free verse, although it does not explicitly rule it out. In the paragraph immediately preceding, he takes pains to distinguish between "men of poetical talents, or of industry and skill in meter," on the one hand, and "the true poet," on the other. He then closes the paragraph with a disparaging assessment of contemporary poets who are "men of talent who sing, and not the children of music." For such second-raters, the "argument is secondary, the finish of the verses is primary."[13]

The word "argument" comes from a Latin verb meaning to make clear, assert, prove, and claims kinship through its Indo-European root with a clan of words meaning to shine, such as "argent." By "argument" Emerson does not mean only debate; he also means subject, topic, or theme, and his use of the phrases "children of music" and "a thought so passionate and alive" suggests that for him the true poet is one whose thoughts and subjects shine with supernatural or spiritual radiance, whether or not he or she is as skillful as others in deploying various metrical forms. But nowhere in this section of "The Poet" does he urge the true poet to abandon conventional metrical forms. He merely asserts that, in themselves, metrical forms are not sufficient for the production of true poems, a relatively modest assertion with which Dryden, Pope, and Swift certainly would have agreed.

As the history of twentieth-century verse demonstrates, one can be an organicist poet without being a transcendentalist, and as a small sampling of poems published in *The Dial* (with one exception) will demonstrate, one can be a transcendentalist poet without doing anything particularly innovative with meter, rhyme, caesura, or enjambment, as Walt Whitman or Emily Dickinson would be doing within ten or twenty years. In fact, as the poems themselves show, the transcendentalist poets, including Emerson, for good reasons generally considered the best among them, apparently took for granted that poems should be regularly metrical without much variation; that they should rhyme (although there are occasional examples of unrhyming verse, most often blank verse) with rhymes that are predominantly exact, monosyllabic, and masculine; and that the ends of lines should correspond with major syntactic junctions (the most daring uses of enjambment mostly appear in some of the poems of Emerson and Ellery Channing, who gave *The Dial* more poems than any other person, and even their enjambments are relatively tame compared to instances in Donne or Milton, both liberally represented in *Parnassus*), while the interiors of lines make moderate, if any, use of caesuras and rarely contain a period ending a sentence. Emerson's blank-verse poem "The Snow-Storm," published in *The Dial* in the third number of the first volume (January 1841), contains two exceptions that confirm these general rules, both the mimetic enjambment "the courier's feet / Delayed" and this deeply cut caesura: "For number or proportion. Mockingly / On coop or kennel he hangs Parian wreaths" (1:339). But in rhyming poems such moves are not common among the *Dial* poets, and they are virtually unknown, for example, in the sonnets of the much admired and often singled-out Jones Very, such as "The Barberry Bush," published in the first number of volume II (July 1841), though Very could write Miltonic blank verse, as he shows in "The Evening Choir," published in the first number of volume III (July 1842).[14]

As further examples of prevailing formal norms in transcendentalist poetics, consider the first two stanzas from each of three poems, each titled "The Poet," the first by Ellen Sturgis Hooper (second number of first volume of *The Dial*, October 1840), the second by her sister Caroline Sturgis Tappan (published by Emerson in *Parnassus* but not one of the twenty-six poems she contributed to *The Dial*), and the third, consisting of only the two stanzas, by Ellery Channing (second number of third volume of *The Dial*, October 1842):

> He touched the earth, a soul of flame,
> His bearing proud, his spirit high,
> Filled with the heavens from whence he came,
> He smiled upon man's destiny.
>
> Yet smiled as one who knew no fear,
> And felt a secret strength within,
> Who wondered at the pitying tear
> Shed over human loss and sin.
>
> (*The Dial*, I:194)

> Thou hast learned the woes of all the world
> From thine own longings and lone tears,
> And now thy broad sails are unfurled
> And all men hail thee with loud cheers.
>
> The flowing sunlight is thy home,
> The billows of the sea are thine,
> To all the nations shalt thou roam,
> Through every heart thy love shall shine.[15]

> No narrow field the poet has,
> The world before him spreading,
> But he must write his honest thought,
> No critic's cold eye dreading.
>
> His range is over everything,
> The air, the sea, the earth, the mind,
> And with his verses murmurs sing,
> And joyous notes float down the wind.
>
> (*The Dial*, III:264)

The homogeneity among these examples is impressive. Congruence of subject matter aside, and we shall return to it later, these examples enable us to construct something like a prosodic baseline or backdrop for *The Dial* and transcendentalist poetics: iambic meter, here tetrameter in all three instances; exact rhymes ("high"–"destiny" and "mind"–"wind" are the only exceptions, aside from the unrhyming first and third lines of Channing's first stanza); masculine rhymes ("spreading"–"dreading" in two trimeter lines the only exception); endstopped lines ("pitying tear / Shed" a very mild enjambment); few caesuras and those occurring between parallel phrases or items in a series; and complete alignment of stanza and sentence.

With the stylistic norms implicit in these three poems – not only prosodic norms but also norms of tone, rhetoric, and subject matter – we can compare fruitfully other poems printed in *The Dial*. By contrast with the three treatments of the poet, none of which rises tonally above lukewarm earnestness, Fuller's "A Dialogue" (first number of first volume, July 1840) hums with an erotic current that anticipates Dickinson's many racy treatments of her flowers. The eponymous dialogue is one between a dahlia, who speaks this first stanza, and the sun: "My cup already doth with light o'errun. / Descend, fair sun; / I am all crimsoned for the bridal hour, / Come to thy flower." To this invitation, the hard-working sun (perhaps Fuller's image for the emotionally remote Emerson?) replies, in sublimating solar self-denial enforced by a strong, get-thee-behind-me caesura in the penultimate line:

> Ah, if I pause, my work will not be done,
>   On I must run,
> The mountains wait. – I love thee, lustrous flower,
>   But give to love no hour.
>   (*The Dial*, 1:134)

Even without the possible biographical resonances – Emerson's five-line "Silence," published in the next number (October 1840), sounds like his response to Fuller's "Dialogue" ("They put their finger on their lip, – / The Powers above; / … They love but name not love" [*The Dial*, 1:158]) – Fuller's frisky come-hither stands out as a lively exception among poems in the first number, which includes Cranch's "To the Aurora Borealis" (apostrophe to the northern lights in headless iambic tetrameter couplets, the same metrical form as "Twinkle, Twinkle, Little Star"); Thoreau's "Sympathy" (remorseful elegy for his brother John, cast in the same iambic pentameter quatrains as Gray's "Elegy Written in a Country Churchyard" and subsequently reprinted, without a title but now with Gray's elegiac indentation pattern, in the "Wednesday" chapter of *A Week on the Concord and Merrimack Rivers* [1849]); Emerson's "The Problem" (ambivalence toward priests and clergy in forcefully regular iambic tetrameter couplets broken up by a few inexact rhymes, "cowl"–"soul", "Parthenon"–"zone", "date"–"Ararat", "wind"–"mind"); and Ellen Hooper's untitled poem beginning "I slept, and dreamed that life was Beauty" (stoic resignation to opposition between beauty and duty in iambic tetrameter couplets), subsequently "translated into Italian and attributed to Kant," according to Cooke.[16]

After the first number of *The Dial*, which contains slighter productions as well, including poems by both Emerson's late brother Edward ("The Last Farewell" in rhyming eight-line stanzas of iambic trimeter and a refrain; reprinted by Emerson in *Parnassus*) and late wife Ellen ("Lines" in rhyming quatrains of iambic dimeter with liberal use of anapestic substitution), notable exceptions to the prevailing formal norms of transcendentalist poetics do appear and suggest not only that some of these poets had other kinds of poems in them but also that they did not merely default into a formally tame, rhetorically earnest style because they could not imagine anything else; they chose that style as the one they thought best suited to the poetry of transcendentalism. Two examples of these exceptions will serve, one coming from Thoreau, the other from Cranch.

First published in the fourth number of volume III of *The Dial* (April 1843) and subsequently reprinted in the "Tuesday" chapter of *A Week on the Concord and Merrimack Rivers*, Thoreau's eleven translations of short poems he attributes incorrectly to Anacreon, rather than to the later authors of the *Anacreontea* composing in imitation of the earlier poet, show him working in a mode and style that seventy years later will characterize a distinct strain of transatlantic poetic modernism. Here is "Cupid Wounded," the last of the eleven translations:

> Love once among roses
> Saw not
> A sleeping bee, but was stung;
> And being wounded in the finger
> Of his hand cried for pain.
> Running as well as flying
> To the beautiful Venus,
> I am killed, mother, said he,
> I am killed, and I die.
> A little serpent has stung me,
> Winged, which they call
> A bee – the husbandmen.
> And she said, If the sting
> Of a bee afflicts you,
> How, think you, are they afflicted,
> Love, whom you smite?
> (*The Dial*, III:489–90)

One of the paradoxes of Thoreau's choosing to rhyme in his own original poems is that he was such an accomplished reader of ancient Greek poetry, and ancient Greek poetry tends to avoid rhyme, as Milton reminds us correctively in the note that introduces the second edition of *Paradise Lost* (1674). In translating the original meter (so-called Anacreontics, each line consisting of two feet and, because of allowable variations, seven or eight syllables), Thoreau avoids end rhyme ("he"–"me" the only exception, as it prepares the ear for "bee"), avoids metrical regularity (the line "And being wounded in the finger" could be scanned iambically, but it does not represent a rigid norm), uses mid-line caesuras effectively, uses enjambment effectively, and varies the lengths of lines irregularly. The result is an attractively fresh, conversational naturalness that the translator himself, in his introductory remarks about Anacreon, identifies as "modern": "There is something strangely modern about him."[17] And indeed there is, since it would not be astonishing to find this poem among the works of Ezra Pound or H. D. or some others of classical sensibility among that generation.

Much as he admires and enjoys Anacreon, however, Thoreau also takes care to distance himself from the Greek poet with this sentence, which concludes the introduction: "True, our nerves are never strung by them [Anacreon's poems]; – it is too constantly the sound of the lyre, and never the note of the trumpet; but they are not gross, as has been presumed, but always elevated above the sensual."[18] In other words, for Thoreau, and for the readership of *The Dial* he addresses, these poems are too light for a steady diet; real transcendentalists require poems that trumpet their thinking and their rhetoric more earnestly. Thoreau's final phrase, "but always elevated above the sensual," speaks volumes about the tendencies of transcendentalist poetics. It also makes it hard not to smile in anticipation of Thoreau's admiration for Whitman's *Leaves of Grass* twelve years later.

"Correspondences," the example from Cranch, published in the third number of volume I of *The Dial* (January 1841) does not depart from the transcendentalist norm with respect to subject matter. In fact, it takes as its title and subject one of the cherished principles of transcendentalism, as Cranch obliquely acknowledges in the final sentence of his introduction to the poem: "I am no Swedenborgian, nor must the following lines be bound down to a dogmatic meaning; yet I will confess they were written after rising from an hour or two spent over the attractive writings of the great Seer of Sweden."[19] What distinguishes this poem as an exception, as it lays out in a few lines many of the same ideas that animate Emerson's "The Poet," are the long unrhyming lines, printed in the conventional indentation pattern used for printing poems in classical elegiac meter and which Cranch uses, as he adapts the classical meter we tend to hear as dactylic (as in the original meter, Cranch's shorter indented lines end with a stress), to experiment with prose rhythms and syntax uncharacteristic of his regular iambic poems. Here are the opening four lines:

> All things in Nature are beautiful types to the soul that will read them;
> Nothing exists upon earth, but for unspeakable ends.
> Every object that speaks to the senses was meant for the spirit.
> Nature is but a scroll, – God's hand-writing thereon.
>
> (*The Dial*, 1:381)

Cranch's poem is not the first one printed in *The Dial* to experiment with adaptations of classical elegiac meter. In the previous number (October 1840), James Freeman Clarke published "First Crossing the Alleghanies," which uses the same meter and which immediately follows, and contrasts sharply with, Emerson's "Silence," but although metrically admirable, Clarke's poem feels more self-consciously labored than Cranch's, which, in its experimentation with longer, more syntactically supple lines, anticipates Whitman's innovations in bringing the patterns of Hebrew poetry into cooperation with the syntax of English sentences. With a few minor adjustments Cranch's four lines could be dropped into Whitman's "Song of Myself," which brims with lines in triple meter, and escape detection by many readers.

With all the possibilities suggested by these two exceptions available to them, why did the transcendentalist poets decide that regular meter and rhyme suited most of their poetry best? Again the clue comes from Emerson. In two journal entries, written three years apart and later both incorporated into the essay "Poetry and Imagination" (much of it delivered as a lecture in 1854 but published in *Letters and Social Aims*, dated 1876), he muses on rhyme and meter. An 1851 entry is headed "Rhyme" in pencil:

> We are lovers of rhyme & return & period & reflection. Metre begins with pulsebeat. Young people like rhyme, drum, tune, things in pairs, and in alternation. Then they like to transfer the rhyme to life, & to see a melody as coarse as "April June & November" [/] "Thirty days hath September" in their life … By & by when they see real rhymes, man & maid, Nature & art, Nature & mind, Character & History, they do not value any longer these rattles & dingdongs [,] rudest barbaric rhymes of Superstition.[20]

An entry from 1854, headed "Metres" and blended into the same paragraph of "Poetry and Imagination" with this entry, continues the meditation:

> I amuse myself often, as I walk, with humming the rhythm of the decasyllabic quatrain, or of the octosyllabic with alternate sexsyllabic or other rhythms, & believe these metres to be organic, or derived from our human pulse, and to be therefore not proper to one nation, but to mankind. But I find a wonderful charm, heroic, & especially deeply pathetic or plaintive in the cadence,

& say to myself, Ah happy! if one could fill these small measures with words approaching to the power of these beats.[21]

Emerson's account of meter has some problems, since he wants to derive the accentual-syllabic meters of English verse, which resulted from linguistic change brought about by the Norman Conquest and did not come into the history of English poetry until the fourteenth century, from the human pulse and then to generalize those meters to all the world, despite the fact that, for example, ancient Greek, classical Chinese, and early Germanic meters are not accentual-syllabic. But his accounts of both rhyme and meter reveal why he and other transcendentalist poets deliberately made these formal features of prosody a cornerstone of their poetics. In the case of meter, Emerson is explicit: meter is organic, meter is natural, and since for a transcendentalist what is natural symbolizes the supernatural, the power of meter, as Emerson experiences it, humming to himself the ballad stanzas that begot the common meter of hymnody (what he means by octosyllabics alternating with sexsyllabics), which Dickinson will wield like no one before or since, has its part to play in symbolizing the power of spirit or soul. Never mind that someone who wishes for words to fill the small measures of meter is putting the meter before the argument, in contradiction to the sentiment expressed in "The Poet"; never mind that Emerson ignores the role convention and association play in generating the pathos he feels in the meters of poems he has read all his life and of hymns that connect him to the earliest sources of his own radical Protestantism. For Emerson and the transcendentalist poets in sympathy with him, meter comes physiologically from the heart, and a poem without meter would be a corpse without a pulse. For any poet who experiences meter as Emerson does, to write in meter is not to defer weakly to tradition; it is to affirm and proclaim vitality against the encroachments of soul-killing materialism.

A few pages later in "Poetry and Imagination" Emerson clinches the connection between writing in meter and a religious poetics of prayer, worship, liturgy:

> Outside of the nursery the beginning of literature is the prayers of a people, and they are always hymns, poetic, – the mind allowing itself range, and therewith is ever a corresponding freedom in the style, which becomes lyrical. The prayers of nations are rhythmic, have iterations and alliterations like the marriage-service and burial-service in our liturgies.[22]

Although one does not have to have been a Unitarian minister to associate the rhythmic and metrical patterns of prayers and other liturgical forms used in worship with the rhythms and meters of poetry, it cannot be pure coincidence that so many of the members of Hedge's

Club were saturated by these rhythms and meters, a circumstance that distinguished them from many who happen to have beating pulses. Even Thoreau, who stoutly refused church membership, shared in the transcendentalist association of meter with scriptural or liturgical language, as he demonstrates in a journal entry dated June 24, 1840, subsequently revised and used in the "Sunday" chapter of *A Week on the Concord and Merrimack Rivers*: "There is no doubt but the highest morality in the books is rhymed or measured, – is, in form as well as substance, poetry. Such is the scripture of all nations. If I were to compile a volume to contain the condensed wisdom of mankind, I should quote no rhythmless line."[23] In the case of Emerson's entry on rhyme, which for him often slides into synonymity with verse or poetry in general, his remarks join with his poem "Merlin" (1846) and other moments in "Poetry and Imagination" to show that for him rhyme is not simply a matter of phonemic likeness between two words after their final accented vowels; it is an image of pairing writ large, and the auditory pairings of words in poems come to stand for increasingly general and abstract pairings. The one between male and female hints at the potentially erotic valences of rhyme (the alliteration of "man & maid" pairing the words that refer to this potentially procreative pairing), and Emerson is not the first to recognize or exploit those. But unique to transcendentalism is the pairing of "Nature & mind," a pairing that suggests another version of the correspondence between nature and spirit, the defining correspondence asserted by the members of Hedge's Club. For them, or for the poetry-loving among them, rhyme is the most suggestive verbal image of correspondence, and as such it plays a crucial role in representing the ultimate correspondence, the ultimate connection reflected in the etymology of the word "religion," meaning "to reconnect" or "to re-bind": rhyme binds words as religion, in the many expansive senses in which the transcendentalists thought of religion, binds the natural to the spiritual. For this reason off-rhyme plays a drastically limited role in the poetics of transcendentalism; too much of it transposes a poem from the major key of correspondence, pairing, alignment, balance, harmony, concord, and affirmation to the minor key of more complicated, qualified, and provisional connections, as Dickinson knew better than anyone.

One last paradox remains to be considered: why do the transcendentalists put so much emphasis on the poet and yet so carefully circumscribe the operations of a poet's personality in their poems? In addition to the essay and three poems titled "The Poet," many moments in transcendentalist writing focus on the poet, among them the "Prospects" section of Emerson's *Nature*; his *Dial* poems "Woodnotes" (October 1840), "Woodnotes II"

(October 1841), and "Saadi" (October 1842); Fuller's "A Dialogue: Poet, Critic" (April 1841); Thoreau's "The Poet's Delay" (October 1842) and the dialogue between Hermit and Poet that opens the "Brute Neighbors" chapter of *Walden*; and Ellery Channing's epistolary series "The Youth of the Poet and the Painter" (beginning July 1843) and "To the Poets" (April 1844).[24] But for all the attention lavished on poets, the poetics of transcendentalism is not a poetics of representing an individual personality, of personalizing an "I" beyond the unavoidable intimacies inherent in the use of the first-person singular pronoun, and statements such as Whitman's in "A Backward Glance O'er Travel'd Roads" (1888), even though he had staunch admirers among the members of Hedge's Club, would be unthinkable in the pages of *The Dial*: " 'Leaves of Grass' indeed (I cannot too often reiterate) has mainly been the outcropping of my own emotional and other personal nature – an attempt, from first to last, to put *a Person*, a human being (myself, in the latter half of the Nineteenth Century, in America,) freely, fully and truly on record."[25] Regardless of his persistent celebrations of spirit in the material world, this simple yet revolutionary sentence effectively divides Whitman from the transcendentalists, as clearly and as sharply as Dickinson's poetics of personal drama, with all the urgencies, crises, breakings, and skewings impending behind her off-rhymes, divides her.

It is not that the transcendentalist poets had no personalities; some of them had quite colorful ones. Nor is it that the transcendentalist poets were too humble and self-effacing to talk about themselves; many were not. Instead, to return to the language of Emerson's "The Poet," the paradox for a transcendentalist poet, who in setting himself or herself up as would-be transcriber of the divine broadcast would seem to be an egotist every bit as colossal as many a reader's image of Whitman, is that to personalize one's transcriptions would be to "substitute something of our own, and thus miswrite the poem"; it would be to realize imperfectly the ideal nature of one's own material circumstances, to fail to transcend the understandings of one's little self and one's limited senses, to cloud the divine broadcast with idiosyncratic static.

For all its exaltations of individual perception and intuition, a basic self-denial lies at the heart of transcendentalist poetics and confirms the rootedness of that poetics in a Christian ethos, no matter how liberal or unorthodox. The poet denies him- or herself the representation of his or her personality in order to function more efficiently and effectively as a representer of what transcends the personality. It is no wonder that the transcendentalists so idealized the poet as someone who could accomplish such an arduous feat of self-denial. It also makes perfect sense that Emerson and those who took their cues from him would idealize poets into "liberating gods" – he uses the phrase twice in "The Poet" – that is, into people who could deny themselves thoroughly enough to reveal to the rest of us, by means of vision, by means of figurative language, by means of pulse-beating meter, by means of corresponding rhyme, the way to emancipation from imprisoning materialism. In idealizing the poet as emancipator, even savior, the transcendentalists extend the Romantic valuation of the poet as secular priest and would seem to be founding their poetics on a persistent wistfulness for someone to assume a new version of the messianic role at the center of the same religion in which so many of them began and from which so many of them dissented.

NOTES

1 Ralph Waldo Emerson, *Essays and Lectures* (New York: Library of America, 1983), p. 193.
2 *Ibid.*, p. 454.
3 *Ibid.*, p. 196.
4 George Willis Cooke, *An Historical and Biographical Introduction to Accompany "The Dial"* (New York: Russell and Russell, 1961), 1:47–53; see also 1:158–69.
5 Emerson, *Essays*, p. 449.
6 *Ibid.*
7 *Ibid.*, p. 8.
8 *Ibid.*, pp. 20, 452–54.
9 *Ibid.*, p. 459.
10 Samuel Taylor Coleridge, *Shakespearean Criticism*, ed. Thomas Middleton Raysor, 2nd edn (London: Dent, 1960), 1:198.
11 John Locke, *An Essay Concerning Human Understanding*, ed. Peter H. Nidditch (Oxford: Clarendon Press, 1975), p. 622. Emphasis original.
12 *The Dial: A Magazine for Literature, Philosophy, and Religion* (New York: Russell and Russell, 1961), 1:93. Subsequent quotations from poetry published in *The Dial* are cited parenthetically in the text.
13 Emerson, *Essays*, p. 450.
14 *The Dial*, II:131; III:97–98.
15 Ralph Waldo Emerson, ed., *Parnassus* (Boston: James R. Osgood, 1875), p. 95.
16 Cooke, *Introduction*, II:55.
17 *The Dial*, III:485.
18 *Ibid.*
19 *Ibid.*, 1:381.
20 *The Journals and Miscellaneous Notebooks of Ralph Waldo Emerson*, vol. XI, 1848–51, ed. A. W. Plumstead and William H. Gilman (Cambridge, MA: Belknap Press, 1975), pp. 418–19; Emerson's cancellations omitted.
21 *Ibid.*, vol. XIII, 1852–55, ed. Ralph H. Orth and Alfred R. Ferguson (Cambridge, MA: Belknap Press, 1977), pp. 284–85; Emerson's cancellations omitted.
22 *Letters and Social Aims*, vol. VIII of *Complete Works of Ralph Waldo Emerson*, ed. Edward W. Emerson (Boston: Houghton Mifflin, 1903), pp. 53–54.

23 *Journal of Henry David Thoreau*, ed. Bradford Torrey and Francis H. Allen, vol. I, 1837–46 (Salt Lake City: Peregrine Smith, 1984; originally published Boston: Houghton Mifflin, 1906), p. 151.

24 Works appear in *The Dial* as follows: I:242–45; II:207–214; III:265–69; I:494–96; III:200; IV:48; IV:473.

25 Walt Whitman, *Complete Poetry and Collected Prose*, ed. Justin Kaplan (New York: Library of America, 1982), p. 671.

5

MAX CAVITCH

Slavery and its metrics

Lucy Terry (*c.* 1730–1821) has long been credited – not without good reason – as the first known African-American author, and her one surviving work, the poem "Bars Fight" (*c.* 1746), is widely anthologized as the earliest surviving poem by an American slave. The story of the poem's survival – composed by Terry shortly after an Indian raid on Deerfield, Massachusetts, in 1746, and preserved and transmitted through memorization and recitation until its first known publication in 1855, over thirty years after her death – is a highly plausible, but by no means indisputable, combination of legend and painstaking scholarship. The relation of the 1855 text to the original composition and its subsequent iterations is not definitively known. Readers of "Bars Fight" have continued to pursue the poem back to its likely but obscure origins in the versifying practice of a teenaged slave who had been kidnapped from Africa to New England as a young child and who was remembered and praised down the generations as a witty storyteller and skilled poet.[1] It is the poem's pursuit of Terry that interests me here.

I say "pursuit of" rather than "attribution to" because the latter term conventionalizes a relation between verse and subject that, in the history of the poetry of slavery (though not only there), exceeds and problematizes such typifications. For the most part, while there have of course been numerous controversies over the author-attribution of certain texts (Shakespeare's plays, for example, and the Federalist Papers), as well as over specific stylometric methods for making such attributions, the propriety of author-attribution itself is rarely questioned. If authorship can be known, it should be known. This imperative seems especially well-founded in relation to author-groups historically denied access to literacy, or to means of publication, or upon whom the requirement of anonymity or pseudonymity has been imposed. That the names of hitherto uncredited women and minority authors continue to be added to the canons of literature and the histories of culture is a triumph of modern scholarship.

94

Yet these hard-won attributions are also affirmations of a poetics of individuated authorship that many of us are inclined to look at with some skepticism – not only because we may want to distinguish between the producer of a text and the producers of the text's meaning, but also because of what tracking down and naming an author may facilitate: for example, narcissistic forms of readerly identification that often go unexamined; underestimating or forgetting the racialization of authorship's entitlements; misapprehension of individuation and self-possession as invariably empowering; and, not least, the fabulation of poetic language as personal voice.

Thus one reader might overlook or discount the fact that the personalization of poetic achievement through the attribution of an author's name also renders that author open to charges of personal insufficiency or blameworthy inauthenticity. Such charges have pursued Phillis Wheatley from her day to ours. Another reader, straining to hear the author's "own" voice, may engage in a powerfully motivated pursuit of what Herbert Tucker calls "intersubjective confirmation of the self" to the neglect of the poem's highly conditional subjectivity – as figured, for example, in the normative pietism and complex citational practice of Jupiter Hammon's "Address to Miss Phillis Wheatly" and in many other poems of slave addressivity.[2] Another reader, by stipulating individual authorship and practicing silent reading, may disable recognition of a history and ethos of strategic generality and collective performance. The reception history of Frances Ellen Watkins Harper's poetry has tended to chase it away from the complex and often depersonalizing contexts of both print and political action.

To challenge and denaturalize such affirmations of individual authorship need not mean carelessly risking, as Meredith McGill puts it in relation to Harper, "the hard-won visibility of this African American woman poet."[3] One needn't condemn any poet to subjectlessness, or deny subjectivity to any and all enactments of voice in poetry, in order to turn a less personalizing gaze – and ear – toward the figures of subjectivation in the poetry of slavery. McGill's focus on the bibliographic concept of format as one such figure of subjectivation, for example, doesn't mean she rejects the meaningfulness of biographical coherence and authorial intention. But she does seek to raise our reading practices up out of the valley of the shadow of complacently dematerialized and dematerializing ways of reading.

In her work on Harper, McGill adapts the bibliographic concept of format in order to provide new leverage on authorship as well as readership. Here, I attempt something similar by adapting the phenomenological concept of rhythm for a reading of the poetry of slavery – by which I mean not just poetry by slaves and former slaves, such as Terry, Hammon, Wheatley, Albery Allson Whitman, and George Moses Horton, but also poems of slave subjectivity by whites and other freeborns – as a history of subjectivation through rhythm, that is, as a continuing history of both the subject's formation (agency) and its subordination (deprivation of agency).

This history of subjectivation through rhythm has been prone to caricature by sympathetic and unsympathetic readers alike. The crux is pretty obvious. To talk about the sophistication and ubiquity of slave rhythm's triumph over mindless kinesthesia is to veer toward one of slavery's most enduring racist caricatures – what the Jamaican-American critic Joel Rogers, writing in Alain Leroy Locke's foundational anthology *The New Negro*, himself referred to as "That elusive something, [that] for lack of a better name, I'll call Negro rhythm."4 From Rogers to recent critics including Houston Baker, Eric Sundquist, and Jack Kerkering – who are more likely to speak of an "African" or "African-American" or "Pan-African" *sound* – the tension between the particularizing force of cultural and regional specificity and the generalizing, even transcendentalizing force of racial identity is perhaps an unresolvable tension.5 But just how that tension gets performed and analyzed metrically has never been a prominent feature in the critical history of African-American poetry or of American poetry more broadly construed – even in twentieth- and twenty-first-century studies. That is, the poetic history of subjectivation through rhythm has rarely if ever been told in relation to the prosodic history of the slavery era, in relation to the ways in which rhythm in poetry was understood, performed, and theorized during the seventeenth, eighteenth, and nineteenth centuries. The history and criticism of nineteenth-century American poetry in particular – the focus of this volume – remain largely uninformed by this prosodic history.

By the late seventeenth century, England had joined several other, more precocious European powers as a major player in the transatlantic slave trade. Not only direct involvement, but also general interest in and knowledge of slavery spread rapidly through the English-speaking world, just as the English language became more and more widely known among slave populations. For most of the eighteenth century, Great Britain was the world's biggest trader in slaves, and slavery was practiced throughout its colonies. Britain formally abolished the slave trade in 1807 and the practice of slavery in 1833; the USA followed with its own ban on the trade in 1808, but would not formally abolish slavery until 1865. For the first century of its existence, the USA ensured that slavery was a fundamental condition of the global economy and thus also a fundamental condition of cultural production and consumption.

The presence of Africa in the English poetic imagination, which had hitherto been negligible, by the late seventeenth century reached a kind of critical mass that prompted a literary chain reaction, which in turn has recently prompted James Basker, in the Introduction to his monumental anthology of seventeenth- and eighteenth-century English poems about slavery, to call for renewed attention to "an Afrocentric poetics of the Enlightenment."[6] The thousands of lines of poetry Basker collects help initiate a reconstruction of that poetics. Yet while the prosodic theories and principles informing poetic practice are often implicit and sometimes manifest in the poems themselves, the vast prosodic literature of the period remains unrecuperated.

Fair enough, for a commercial anthology of poetry that already has to work hard to overcome twenty-first-century prejudices against pre-romantic conventions of meter and poetic form. Anthologies of nineteenth-century poetry, too, tend to rely on poems themselves to manifest the prosodic theory behind the practice, which they sometimes do, or often seem to do, in ways that could nevertheless benefit from being read in the context of the now much less familiar discourse of nineteenth-century prosody.[7]

One of the poets excerpted in Basker's anthology is the British anti-slavery radical John Thelwall, who, Basker notes, was a leader in the critique of household consumption of West Indian sugar. Basker excerpts a passage from one of the many untitled poems in Thelwall's massive, polygeneric work *The Peripatetic* (1793), a passage that mocks the tea-drinking "Daughters of Albion," who "At morn, at eve, your sweeten'd beverage sup, / Nor see the blood of thousands in the cup."[8] The excerpt is powerful, but it omits the poem's narrative context as well as its opening fourteen lines, which are richly suggestive of the link between prosody and slavery, a link that defined the course of Thelwall's career.

The poem both emerges from and finds itself enclosed within the prose narration of the capture of a songbird witnessed by the narrator. It is a versified extension of his critique of the "powers of sympathy":

> to what cruelty or injustice will not some men submit to obtain the bread of idleness! What cruelty or injustice will not Pride and Luxury thoughtlessly encourage, if their senses may but be gratified with the fruits of inhumanity! Go,
>
> > Daughters of Albion's gay enlighten'd hour!
> > Hail the sweet strains your captive warblers pour;
> > Their graceful forms and downy plumage prize,
> > And the gay luster of their varied dyes:
> > Nor ever think, while tremulous they sing,
> > Or flutt'ring spread the glossy-tinctur'd wing,
> > That fluttering wing, that tremulated strain
> > Of lingering griefs, and cruel bonds complain:

Nor ever think – that, for a sordid joy,
Their hopes, their rights, affections ye destroy;
Doom them the air's unbounded space to change,
For the dull cage's loath'd, contracted range;
There, every social throb condemn'd to mourn
Which each sad summer bids in vain return.[9]

The poem takes form and takes flight in the course of an elaborate figuration of the slaves of the sugar islands as songbirds that have been trapped and caged in order to produce revenue for the trappers and music for Albion's tea-swilling ladies. There is, in the narrator's shift from prose to verse, a hint of his identification with the songbird's and thus with the slave's "tremulated strain" and more than a hint of his ambivalence toward "the heroic couplet of the smoothe, but cold and formal school of Pope."[10] As Michael Scrivener has noted, "the political repression he struggled against in the 1790s can be renamed as a speech impediment or the condition of speechlessness, two problems Thelwall approached after 1801 as a speech therapist and scientist of language."[11]

Indeed, Thelwall's career as a renowned speech therapist and theorist of rhetoric, elocution, and prosody is a fully politicized extension of his anti-slavery activism and his reaction to the sometimes violent suppression of his own speech (Thelwall was tried unsuccessfully for high treason in 1794). What is particularly striking in Thelwall's work and thought is the conjunction of the physiology of speech and its political/rhetorical uses. He opens his critique of previous English prosodists by faulting them for their reliance on formal rules, "instead of appealing to physical analysis, the primary principles of nature, and the physiological necessities resulting from the organization of vocal beings."[12] And these "vocal beings" are absolutely fundamental to Thelwall's conception of democratic society – not just vocal beings like poets (such as himself and his friends Samuel Taylor Coleridge and William Wordsworth), or elite polemicists (such as his antagonists Edmund Burke and William Godwin), but also, and especially, "the oppressed and injured labourer," whether in the English factory or on the American or Antillean plantation.[13]

With John Thelwall, nineteenth-century Anglo-American prosody began its agonized and fascinating inquiry into the relation between sound and work, and the poetry of slavery continued to be at the center of that inquiry. Paying closer, phenomenologically informed attention to this prosodic discourse should help us better appreciate what was going on when English-speakers sat down (or stood up) to read and write and sing and recite the poetry of slavery.

Take, for example, the age-old question as to whether verse is a fetter to expression, like Thelwall's cage or the silken gyve on a songbird's leg, or whether it is, conversely, an enabling resistance, like the resistance of the air that makes possible the freed bird's flight. This question takes many different forms in different eras and suggests many different stakes for different questioners. But for a wide range of nineteenth-century prosodists, the question seemed especially to require a more fully developed, objective theory than it had hitherto generated: a new "science of English verse," as Johns Hopkins professor and ex-Confederate soldier Sidney Lanier called it.[14] There was a broadly felt dilemma. On one hand, there was keen desire for comprehensiveness, quantification, precision, and, certainly not least, the prestige of a scientific discipline. Could there be a single system for marking rhythmic patterning based in quantifiable principles of what Coventry Patmore called "English metrical law"?[15] On the other hand, there was grave concern for the perceived degradation and possible loss of individual agency and purpose, of what Matthew Campbell has called "the rhythm of will."[16] The literal mechanization of poetic creation itself, in an age of rapid industrialization and the depersonalization of the laboring subject, was a very worrisome prospect.[17] Was this the way the science of verse would tend?

As Yopie Prins has observed, the "formalization of metrical theory coincides with a general nineteenth-century tendency toward the codification of numerical modes of analysis."[18] This included the precise and broadly synchronized measurement of time, which has its foundation not only in the design and proliferation of increasingly accurate mechanical clocks from the late seventeenth century onwards, but also – and anything but coincidentally – in the growing need for the precise measurement, control, and temporal coordination, on a massive scale, of the periodicity of labor. Slavery, and the rapid industrialization and imperial expansion of the English-speaking world that slavery helped enable, made this need both acute and extremely profitable. There is nowhere, perhaps, where this is better seen than in the plantation system of the antebellum South and in the Northern mills and factories where free-wage laborers kept time with their enslaved counterparts.[19]

Thus it should come as no surprise that nineteenth-century prosodic discourse is broadly inflected by the language of slavery. For example, according to Ralph Waldo Emerson, the poet is a "liberating god" who "unlocks our chains."[20] And Patmore writes of the necessary "shackles of artistic form," insisting that "language should always seem to *feel*, though not to *suffer from* the bonds of verse."[21] Indeed no one in the nineteenth century could have failed to perceive, whether consciously or unconsciously, that slavery continued to transform the relation of time-keeping to sound. It mediated and confounded pre-industrial and industrial work-places and time-sensibilities. It reinforced the connections between time, sound, and pain, with its bells, with its whips and, not least, with its songs. Sounds both lyrical and unlyrical facilitated new and prodigious rhythms of work, and they also helped locate and keep track of ever-expanding populations of American slaves. Overseers were often great promoters of the singing and chanting of slaves; if you could hear them, you knew where they were. And this singing and chanting, long before its verses started to be systematically transcribed and published, had a perva-sive influence on American popular song, particularly through blackface performance and minstrelsy.

Moreover, poetry – sung, chanted, or spoken – was perhaps the most important, often the only, resource slaves had for the palliation of monot-ony – the monotony of physical work – through cognitions and sensations of melody and harmony and the assertion of rhythmic complexity and forms of dissonance against the mechanistic regularity of repetitive coerced labor: a rhythmic protest, one could say, against the mechanization of time and movement, or a slave dysprosody – disturbances of intonation, stress, pause, etc. – to oppose slavery's violently enforced periodicity.[22]

The psychoanalyst Nicolas Abraham lends some phenomenological support to this notion of slave dysprosody. He writes in his essay on "Rhythmizing Intentionality," not about the figure of the slave explicitly, but about the later, analogous figure of the assembly-line worker and his relation to the "object" or machine:

His effort to adhere to the object makes him a stranger to himself, an "alien." Yet, this occurs precisely because he does not have a rhythmic experience of periodicity. Nonetheless, there is one condition that may sometimes enable the mechanized laborer to overcome this "alienation" and to affirm himself in the face of the machine: if he sings while working. Transported into the imagi-nary, he makes his gestures the incantatory rite of his demiurgic power. We are presented here with two distinct and irreducible phenomena: first, the execu-tion of movements made in time with a perceived periodicity, and second, the rhythmization of this kinesthesia.

What does the rhythmizing act consist of? Objectively, nothing has changed: the same movements are executed with the same efficacy. The difference is that for the singer, the movements have received a new signification: no longer a means of adapting to the machine or of executing a task, they are now sighted with a view to something unreal and transcendent, whose imaginary presence they must represent. This something, which is nothing other than rhythm, is not itself the totality of these movements, but what, by means of these movements, we are able to intend beyond them: expectations, surprises, fulfillments – in short, a specific structure of temporality.[23]

Does slave dysprosody make of its harmonies and melodies and melismas and syncopations a kind of enabling resistance to enforced labor's soul-killing periodicity? Or does it merely reinforce that periodicity as yet another one of slavery's dehumanizing technologies – bodies, like the brains of Robert Browning's slavish poet, "beat into rhythm"?[24]

If we accept rhythm, as Abraham asks us to, as the object of phenomenological intentionality, then what of the assembly-line worker or the chattel-slave himself or herself being sighted (objectified) as a body "in respect to which ethical behavior has been suspended"?[25] This is a question for all revisions of Husserlian phenomenology, including Abraham's psychoanalytic revision. More specifically, we could ask: How does the phenomenological critique of scientific rationalism work in relation to the historical conditions of nineteenth-century slavery (and of nineteenth-century scientific prosody) as an outcome of such rationalism? Is the meaningfulness of the "rhythmizing intentionality" of the singing laborer as described by Abraham strictly limited to individual consciousness in and of a world in which, "[o]bjectively, nothing has changed"? Does "rhythmizing intentionality," to paraphrase W. H. Auden, make nothing happen?

The antebellum American poet and prosodist, William Cullen Bryant, arguing against imitation of the school of Pope, wrote of the need for a more liberal, variegated style of versification in American poetry that would keep pace with and do justice to contemporary American life.[26] Bryant's own experiments with a looser sort of blank verse were important but tentative. Far more exciting, noted James Kennard, Jr. (with a sarcastic edge), was the improvisatory syncretism of slaves, animadverting at the end of an essay called "Who Are Our National Poets?" that Bryant's own name – along with those of Henry Wadsworth Longfellow, Fitz-Greene Halleck, and John Greenleaf Whittier – would be a better answer to that question if he were to "consult the taste of your fair countrywomen; write no more English poems; write negro songs, and Yankee songs in Negro style; take lessons in dancing of the celebrated Thomas Rice..."[27]

The popularity of Thomas Rice and many other white antebellum minstrel performers helped ensure cultural saturation by the rhythms of the black vernacular, as did many black performers themselves. One of the first and most famous African Americans to perform regularly both for and with whites, William Henry Lane, was known as Master Juba or, after the publication of Charles Dickens's sketch of him in *American Notes for General Circulation* (1842), as Boz's Juba. The novelty and complexity of the rhythms of Juba's performance not only spurred the emergence of later styles of American dance and music but also quickly appealed to the era's poets and prosodists in relation to their own efforts to measure and to modify the pace of nineteenth-century poetry. In 1835, author and Virginian Nathaniel Beverly Tucker wrote to Edgar Allan Poe of his efforts as a poet to cultivate the beauty, not of faultless versification, but of "rugged" rhythms that would be "the more graceful for a little awkwardness":

> I do not know to what to liken those occasional departures from regular metre which are so fascinating. They are more to my ear like that marvelous performance – "clapping Juba," than any thing else. The beat is capriciously irregular; there is no attempt to keep time to all the notes, but then it comes so pat & so distinct that the cadence is never lost.[28]

Thus an aspiring white poet writing to the United States' first major poetic theorist comparing his struggle to reconcile accentual and syllabic imperatives with the more successful rhythms of minstrel dance steps, derived in part from the rhythmic accompaniments of plantation labor and slave-quarter recreation.

Rhythms also worked their way back from parlor to field. Sometimes this seems to have happened directly, as when Poe's friend, the Georgia poet Thomas Holley Chivers, wrote a song "to be sung by my father's Negroes at a Corn Shucking."[29] More often, these rhythms moved promiscuously among sites of slave- and wage-labor, public entertainment, collective composition and performance, and private reading and writing – as when the so-called Negro Spirituals were, beginning in the 1860s, transcribed, printed, and thus not only disseminated among white readers but also "returned" in a more durable and conventionally literary form to African Americans. The topos or sub-genre of the corn-song itself reverberates through nineteenth-century American poetry, in a multiplicity of rhythms and at all levels of cultural prestige: in the anonymizing profusion and variation of plantation songs;[30] in relatively straightforward imitations like Chivers's; in their countless minstrel-show adaptations and lampoons by both black and white artists; in popular adaptations by white authors including Joel Chandler Harris's "Corn-Shucking Song" and by African-American performers like the Fisk Jubilee Singers; in African-American dialect poems such as James Edwin Campbell's "Song of the Corn" and Paul Laurence Dunbar's "A Corn-Song"; and in standard English lyrics such as Dunbar's "The Corn-Stalk Fiddle," John Greenleaf Whittier's "The Corn Song," S. C. Cromwell's "Corn-Shucking Song," Constance Fenimore Woolson's "Corn Fields," William T. Dumas's "Corn-Shucking," and Sidney Lanier's "Corn."

As in "Corn" and his other experimental verses, so too in his prosodic theory did Lanier draw on the common faculty he calls, anticipating Nicolas Abraham, "rhythmic intention," in order to underscore his point that the most complex rhythms in English poetry are to be found as much if not more in "the rhythmic perceptions of the people" as in elite poets and composers. His chief examples are Mother Goose nursery songs and the "patting Juba" of the Southern plantation, both in his view fully qualifying as expressions of a type of freedom whose moral justification is the same enlarged perception and exalted love of the beautiful cultivated in the rhythmic perception of Shakespeare, or Milton, or Hayden.[31]

In both Milton and Master Juba, Lanier implies, there is a meaningful relation between unorthodox or experimental prosody and political liberty – not a direct analogy, in which the slave's chains would be exactly "like" the constraints of conventional meter, but an overdetermined relation whose excess of context includes the more recent theories of the rhythmic foundation of subjectivity to be found in the work of phenomenologists like Maurice Merleau-Ponty and Abraham and in the work of literary theorists such as Philippe Lacoue-Labarthe and Henri Meschonnic, as well as in the work of other nineteenth-century prosodists who, like Lanier, were directly confronted with the rhythmic conditioning of slave subjectivity.

Among these other prosodists, Haverford professor Francis Gummere insisted that rhythm was "the essential fact of poetry." Nor were he and Lanier alone in drawing from their understanding of the rhythmizing collectives of Southern plantation life the conclusion that rhythm, as Gummere put it, "is an affair of instinctive perception transformed into a social act as the expression of social consent."[32] Gummere himself launches broad imperatives from his ethnography of rhythm: "Poetry, like music, is social; like its main factor, rhythm, it is the outcome of communal consent, a *faculté d'ensemble*; and this should be writ large over every treatise on poetry, in order to draw the mind of the reader from that warped and baffling habit which looks upon all poetry as a solitary performance." He abhors what he takes to be the passivity of contemporary readers and auditors of poetry, and urges a reeducation of listening, in which the "muscular sense" would take precedence over the "sense of hearing."[33] Listening itself is, in other words, a type of physical labor, not just something you do passively while others are (singing and) laboring.

Around the same time, W. E. B. Du Bois, too, was writing about having derived a sense of the possible cultural outcome of communal consent in a context of labor from what he called the Sorrow Songs. And, as John Kerkering has observed, Du Bois imagined this outcome as being based in a rhythmic consent to a post-national, Pan-Negroist racial identification.[34] "If," Du Bois wrote in his essay "The Conservation of Races," "among the gaily-colored banners that deck the broad ramparts of civilizations is to hang one uncompromising black, then it must be placed there by black hands, fashioned by black heads and hallowed by the travail of 200,000,000 black hearts beating in one glad song of jubilee."[35] In a way that is phenomenologically compelling, Du Bois here resists the temptation to draw sharp distinctions between physical and intellectual labor. He does so, for example, by attributing the work of "fashion[ing]" to "black heads" rather than "black hands," and by characterizing song as the synchronized "travail" of hearts. Performed in the awful shadow cast by the phrase "to hang one uncompromising black," Du Bois's unsettlement of dualism hails something beyond a transcendental, Husserlian phenomenology of rhythm (i.e. rhythm as something external to consciousness and therefore subject to pure description) to one that is existential (pace Martin Heidegger) in the manner of Merleau-Ponty – that is, with an orientation toward the body and its experience in the concrete world. The poetry of slavery gives special point to Merleau-Ponty's characterization of rhythm as a "body schema" [*schéma corporel*][36] – that is, as a kind of habit that we acquire precognitively, but that we may also learn, at least partially, to understand in relation to both the formation and the subordination of subjectivity and to its bodily structures of perception.

In other words, Merleau-Ponty's emphasis on corporeity – on *being* rather than *having* a body – pushes past Husserl's stickier attachment to a conceptual dualism in which the consciousness of perception has a clear inside (Husserl's "consciousness") and outside (Husserl's "reality"). But it also harkens back to the much earlier anthropologies of rhythm through and with which Romantic prosody emerged, for example in August Wilhelm von Schlegel's writings on the primordial and ongoing linguistic enterprise of the constitution of consciousness through rhythm. Along with many others, Emerson drew from Schlegel the idea that conventional language was a fossilization – a Pompeian freezing – of the dynamic human interactions that give rise to metaphor: "language is the archives of history, and, if we must say it, a sort of tomb of the muses. For, though the origin of most of our words is forgotten, each word was at first a stroke of genius, and obtained currency, because for the moment it symbolized the world to the first speaker and to the hearer."[37] The relation between "speaker" and "hearer," in Emerson as in Schlegel, is not merely or necessarily that of an active speaker and a passive hearer. "One must," as Emerson puts it elsewhere, "be an inventor to read well."[38] Thus his "first speaker" and "hearer" exist to one another in a dynamic structure of balanced reciprocation rather than a relationship of dominance and submission – less like the Hegelian relationship between master and slave and more like the freely associative activity of Novalis's "first signifier" and "second signifier."[39]

The relation of anthropology and linguistics is strained in romantic poetics precisely because, while the general tendency is to understand language as a relational semiotics, the nature of that relation – its structure, its temporality, its phenomenology – remained in dispute, and would continue to do so, latently or manifestly, throughout the nineteenth and most of the twentieth centuries. Is it a relation of authority imposed by one upon another – by father upon child, by institutionalized tradition upon subsequent generations, by master upon slave? Or is it a freely willed and reciprocally renewed relation between equal subjects? These questions frame not only the poetry of slavery, but also the broader history of poetic rhythm, and the attempts at its theorization, from the late eighteenth century to the early twentieth.

But the poetry of slavery dramatically underscores and amplifies these questions. Its thematizations include the acquisition of literacy and ownership of cultural heritage as forms of liberation – but liberation, one wants to ask, into what regulatory mechanisms of rhythmic experience? Its techniques incorporate neo-classical precision, romantic variation, and folk improvisation – but with what degrees of authority and submission? Its circulation and publication as poetry help objectify and disseminate the pulse of experiences often horrifying and sometimes seemingly ineffable – but, in doing so, do they also compound and advertise a structuring attachment to subjection? It encompasses a brutal history of forced labor – but whose work do poems themselves objectify?

No single poem can provide all the answers. But in the remainder of this chapter I'd like to demonstrate how the reading of a particular poem can engage these questions in the context of the prosodic history I've begun to open up.

"Jefferson's Daughter" (1839) is a short poem on a hot topic: the sale of a female slave supposed to be the illegitimate daughter of Thomas Jefferson. The poem represents the latest episode in a history of rumors about Jefferson's sexual relationship with his slave Sally Hemings – rumors that began circulating widely and provocatively in the transatlantic press in 1802, often in the form of poems by such well-known American and British authors as Joseph Dennie, John Quincy Adams, Thomas Fessenden, and Thomas Moore. The identity of the author of "Jefferson's Daughter" is less certain. It may be the work of William Wells Brown, as Marcus Wood asserts.[40] It was, in any case, one of the poems that Brown, a fugitive slave, compiled in his 1848 anthology of anti-slavery poetry, and he later spun the incident into his well-known novel, *Clotel; or, The President's Daughter: A Narrative of Slave Life in the United States* (1853). Here is the poem as it initially appeared in *Tait's Edinburgh Magazine*, where it is signed only "E.":

JEFFERSON'S DAUGHTER.
"It is asserted, on the authority of an American newspaper, that the daughter of Thomas Jefferson, late President of the United States, was sold at New Orleans *for 1000 dollars.*" – *Morning Chronicle.*

> Can the blood that at Lexington poured o'er the plain,
>   When thy sons warred with tyrants their rights to uphold –
> Can the tide of Niagara wipe out the stain ?
>   No! Jefferson's child has been bartered for gold!
>
> Do ye boast of your freedom? Peace, babblers, be still!
>   Prate not of the goddess who scarce deigns to hear.
> Have ye *power* to unbind? Are ye wanting in *will*?
>   Must the groan of your bondsmen still torture the ear?
>
> The daughter of Jefferson sold for a slave!
>   The child of a freeman, for dollars and francs!
> The roar of applause when your orators rave
>   Is lost in the sound of her chain as it clanks.
>
> Peace, then, ye blasphemers of Liberty's name!
>   Though red was the blood by your forefathers spilt;
> Still redder your cheeks should be mantled with shame,
>   Till the spirit of freedom shall cancel the guilt.
>
> But the brand of the slave is the tint of his skin,
>   Though his heart may beat loyal and true underneath;
> While the soul of the tyrant is rotten within,
>   And his white the mere cloak to the blackness of death.
>
> Are ye deaf to the plaints that each moment arise?
>   Is it thus ye forget the mild precepts of Penn –
> Unheeding the clamour that "maddens the skies,"
>   As ye trample the rights of your dark fellow-men?
>
> When the incense that glows before Liberty's shrine
>   Is unmix'd with the blood of the gall'd and oppress'd –
> Oh! then, and *then* only, the boast may be thine,
>   That the stripes and stars wave o'er a land of the blest.
>
> E.[41]

Many readers of nineteenth-century poetry will associate these rhymed anapestic tetrameter quatrains with memorable popular verses such as Byron's "The Destruction of Sennacherib" (1815) and Clement Clarke Moore's "A Visit from St. Nicholas" (1823) and, more broadly, with the genre of the limerick. But how would readers *in* the nineteenth century have experienced the poem's anapestic meter?

According to the author of the first major American statement on prosody written after the Revolution, they would, or at least should, have experienced it as an accentual rhythm and not as a quantitative one. That is, according to Thomas Jefferson (the very same) they would ideally already have developed a conscious sense of English-language poetry, pace Samuel Johnson, as being organized and experienced chiefly as patterns of stressed and unstressed syllables – not, as in classical prosody, by the perceived duration of those syllables. For Jefferson, the modernization and simplification of prosody for the study and appreciation of poetry in English is a matter of political significance, occupying his attention during long walks in the Bois de Boulogne in 1786 when he might have been thinking instead about establishing a lasting peace with England, quashing North African piracy, or repaying America's debt to France. Prosody matters to Jefferson because of the linguistic and cultural authority to which it gives access. The English language and the canon of English poetry are the birthright of native speakers of English, regardless of nationality. Moreover, he insists, democratically, that the rules of prosody do not exhaust the limits of rhythmic variation. There is a liberty that co-exists with formal constraint – a political principle of which Jefferson was one of the great exponents. "No two persons," he wrote, "will accent the same passage alike. No person but a real adept would accent it twice alike. Perhaps two real adepts who should utter the same passage with infinite perfection yet by throwing the energy into different words might produce very different effects."[42] In other words, equality is not monotony.

Thus, at least some nineteenth-century readers of the poem "Jefferson's Daughter" would have appreciated and undertaken the challenge, not to submit unthinkingly and unquestioningly to its anapestic meter, but rather to pursue meaningful rhythmic variation through multiple, experimental readings. The poem lays down many gauntlets simultaneously, asking hard questions about the history and nature of American freedom while also refusing to let the lines scan too neatly, as in line 5, where the anapestic meter, which plots "Peace" as an unaccented syllable, jars with the heavy accent that sense, as well as the strong medial caesura, would place on that word. One might well feel like a bit of a "babbler" here, temporarily caught up in the rhythmic turbulence of such a line.

In nineteenth-century poetics, the anapest is frequently associated with shifting, accelerating movement. Bryant argues that the insertion of an anapest in a line of iambic measure "quickens the numbers, and gives additional liveliness."[43] And Poe's use of anapestic meter in the poem "Annabel Lee" prompted the great historian of English prosody, George Saintsbury, to write archly that "the miraculous power of the anapaest [has] gathered itself into something superhuman here ... the swiftness rises, and doubles right through the poem, till, in the last stanza, you cannot keep up with it. It leaves you panting far behind."[44] More soberly, Saintsbury dates the "tragicalising" of the anapest (i.e. its use in poems on serious subjects) only a generation or two earlier than "Jefferson's Daughter."[45] Many contemporary readers of that poem would have noted, as Saintsbury did half a century later, that anapestic meter still carried with it a ready if not exclusive association with song and other light verse. In other words, the poem's anapestic meter would have generated conceptual and tonal as well as rhythmic turbulence.

The choice of anapestic meter for such a vehement poem on such a grave topic could be deliberately ironic or merely untutored – possibilities that contribute to the general ambiguity of authorship and voice. The passive voice of the epigraph ("It is asserted") immediately alerts us to the potential difficulty of tracing speech back to an identifiable speaker, even as the authority of newsprint (of "an American newspaper," of the London *Morning Chronicle* that cites it, and of *Tait's Edinburgh Magazine* which publishes the poem along with its epigraph) lends an air of credibility and objectivity to what otherwise might be dismissed as groundless partisan rumor. The poem is signed by a mere cipher, though the authorial voice that one is tempted by the conventions of lyric reading to infer is aggressively insistent, judgmental, hortatory; is at least somewhat familiar with American history, geography, and iconography; alludes to the Psalms; and seeks to differentiate himself or herself sharply from a nevertheless indeterminate cohort of Americans. To whom is this poem addressed? To slaveholding Americans? To white Americans? To women as well as men? To recent immigrants as well as to the descendants of the Revolutionary generation? And by whom is this audience being addressed? A slave? A former or escaped slave, like William Wells Brown? A free African American? A white abolitionist?

If it can be determined that this poem is by William Wells Brown, or by any other known author, students of American poetry will rightly applaud the attribution. But what if the poem's ability to elude conventional attribution is one of its most meaningful features? Perhaps that is why Brown and William Lloyd Garrison both chose to reprint it. They both omit the signature "E." in their reprintings, suggesting perhaps an inclination to move away from personal attribution, away from treating such a poem as an objectification of the labor of a particular individual – not because that person is not known (perhaps it *was* written by Brown), but because they want to interfere with, rather than reinforce, what readers think they can know about an author's work (that is, both the activity and the artifact of labor) and about their own work of reading.

One can read "Jefferson's Daughter" as the rhythmizing intentionality of an inferred speaker that emanates from a place of inaccessibility the poem itself only vaguely approximates. It is not exactly "the plain" at Lexington, or the falls of Niagara, or the lecture hall where the "orators rave," or the auction block in New Orleans, or even the fantasmatic national space "before Liberty's shrine" over which "the stripes and stars wave." It could be the speaker's psyche, or perhaps a physical hiding place, such as Brown and many others occupied as fugitive slaves. In other words, the inaccessibility of place in the poem could represent the trauma of slavery as yet to be coordinated with conscious experience ("Oh! then, and *then* only"). Or it could represent the illocality of slave subjectivity – the displacement of expressive agency from the site of the slave's subjugation to the products of the mechanized rhythms of coerced labor.

It's no accident that "Jefferson's Daughter" shares its page in *Tait's* with a poem entitled "Ode to Labour," a poem that was reprinted a few months later in Glasgow's *Chartist Circular*. The transatlantic working-class labor movement initiated by the Chartists inspired many with the conviction that the relation between chattel slavery and wage slavery transcended analogy. And it made absolutely untenable, once and for all, the notion that the industrialized economies of Great Britain and the Northern USA weren't fully complicit with and in many ways themselves modeled on the slave economies of the Southern USA, the Caribbean, and Latin America. Wherever you are, as Emerson put it, "there is complicity."[46]

It is there in the poetry of slavery, if the rhythms proper to capital can be said to have anything at all in common with the rhythms proper to poetry. In his book on rhythm, Henri Lefebvre writes that capital "constructs and erects itself on a contempt for life and from this foundation: the body, the time of living. Which does not cease to amaze: that a society, a *civilisation*, a culture is able to construct itself from such disdain [*dédain*]."[47] This disdain is by no means inherent in conventional meters such as the anapestic tetrameter of "Jefferson's Daughter." But disdain can marshal the capacity of writers and readers alike to accept as natural or inevitable somatic registrations of alienation akin to that of Abraham's "mechanized laborer," and to steer clear of sensations of profound disturbance that would exceed the consoling but hardly revolutionary dysprosody of that laborer's "rhythmizing intentionality." In a sense, the authors of both "Jefferson's Daughter" and "Ode to Labour" are poets of a revolution they can't imagine taking place. Both poems end not in violent upheaval but with images of peaceful transition, forgiveness, and mercy – in the former, "the mild precepts of Penn" brought back into practice in a post-slavery society under the same billowing national flag, and in the latter an exhortation to peaceful regime change. Metrical conventions don't in and of themselves inhibit revolutionary struggle. But they can sometimes lend the inhibition itself an air of artfulness and invention. By the same token, metrical iconoclasm can't take the place of revolutionary action, but it can sometimes lend the revolutionary imagination a somatic experience of lasting estrangement. It's to these extremes of inhibition and estrangement that a fuller prosodic history of the poetry of slavery, and the subjects it dogs, might turn.

NOTES

1 For the most recent and reliable account of Terry's life, see Gretchen Holbrook Gerzina, *Mr. and Mrs. Prince: How an Extraordinary Eighteenth-Century Family Move out of Slavery and into Legend* (New York: Amistad/Harper Collins, 2008).
2 Herbert F. Tucker, "Dramatic Monologue and the Overhearing of Lyric," in Chaviva Hosek and Patricia Parker, eds., *Lyric Poetry: Beyond New Criticism* (Ithaca, NY: Cornell University Press, 1985), p. 242.
3 Meredith L. McGill, "Frances Ellen Watkins Harper and the Circuits of Abolitionist Poetry" (paper presented at the McNeil Center for Early American Studies, Philadelphia, PA, July 15, 2010).
4 J. A. Rogers, "Jazz at Home," in Alain Locke, ed., *The New Negro* (1925; New York: Atheneum, 1968), p. 220.
5 For an historical atlas of African-American rhythm, see Ronald Radano, *Lying Up a Nation: Race and Black Music* (University of Chicago Press, 2003), esp. pp. 230–77.
6 James G. Basker, ed., *Amazing Grace: An Anthology of Poems about Slavery, 1660–1810* (New Haven: Yale University Press, 2002), pp. xlv–xlvii.
7 See, for example, Marcus Wood, ed., *The Poetry of Slavery: An Anglo-American Anthology, 1764–1865* (Oxford University Press, 2003).
8 Basker, *Amazing Grace*, p. 482.
9 John Thelwall, *The Peripatetic*, ed. Judith Thompson (Detroit: Wayne State University Press, 2001), p. 91.
10 John Thelwall, *Selections for the Illustration of a Course of Instructions on the Rhythmus and Utterance of the English Language* (London: J. M'Creery, 1812), p. xviii.
11 Michael Scrivener, *Seditious Allegories: John Thelwall and Jacobin Writing* (University Park: Pennsylvania State University Press, 2001), pp. 191–92.
12 Thelwall, *Selections*, pp. i–ii.
13 John Thelwall, *Sober Reflections on the Seditious and Inflammatory Letter of the Right Hon. Edmund Burke, to a Noble Lord, Addresses to the Serious Consideration of His Fellow Citizens* (London: H. D. Symonds, 1796), p. 32.
14 Sidney Lanier, *The Science of English Verse* (New York: Scribners, 1880).
15 Coventry Patmore, *Essay on English Metrical Law: A Critical Edition with a Commentary*, ed. Mary Augustine Roth (Washington: Catholic University of America Press, 1961).
16 See Matthew Campbell, *Rhythm and Will in Victorian Poetry* (Cambridge University Press, 1999).
17 See Jason Hall's essay on John Clark's *Eureka* machine, a mid-century mechanical device for producing Latin hexameters ("Popular Prosody: Spectacle and the Politics of Victorian Versification," *Nineteenth-Century Literature*, 62.2 [2007], 222–29).

18 Yopie Prins, "Victorian Meters," in Joseph Bristow, ed., *The Cambridge Companion to Victorian Poetry* (Cambridge University Press, 2000), p. 106.

19 See Mark M. Smith, *Mastered by the Clock: Time, Slavery, and Freedom in the American South* (Chapel Hill: University of North Carolina Press, 1997).

20 Ralph Waldo Emerson, "The Poet," in *Essays and Poems*, ed. Joel Porte, Harold Bloom, and Paul Kane (New York: Library of America, 1996), pp. 462, 463.

21 Patmore, *Essay*, p. 8.

22 For the literary-critical riff on the medical term "dysprosody," see Yopie Prins, "Historical Poetics, Dysprosody, and *The Science of English Verse*," *PMLA*, 123.1 (January 2008), 229–34.

23 Nicolas Abraham, *Rhythms: On the Work, Translation, and Psychoanalysis*, trans. Benjamin Thigpen and Nicholas T. Rand (Stanford University Press, 1995), 76.

24 Robert Browning, "The Last Ride Together," in *Robert Browning: The Poems*, 2 vols., ed. John Pettigrew (New Haven: Yale University Press, 1981), 1:610.

25 Nelson Maldonado-Torres, *Against War: Views from the Underside of Modernity* (Durham, NC: Duke University Press, 2008), p. 226.

26 William Cullen Bryant, "On Trisyllabic Feet in Iambic Measure" (1819), in *Prose Writings of William Cullen Bryant*, vol. I, ed. Parke Godwin (New York: Russell and Russell, 1964), pp. 57–67.

27 [James K. Kennard, Jr.], "Who Are Our National Poets?" *The Knickerbocker; or New York Monthly Magazine* (October 1845), 341.

28 [Nathaniel Beverly Tucker], letter to Edgar Allan Poe, in *The Complete Works of Edgar Allan Poe*, vol. XVII, ed. James A. Harrison (New York: Thomas Y. Crowell, 1902), p. 22.

29 Emma Lester Chase and Lois Ferry Parks, eds., *The Complete Works of Thomas Holley Chivers*, vol. I (Providence: Brown University Press, 1957), p. 197.

30 A selection of these songs appears in the corn-shucking accounts and ex-slave interviews appended to Roger D. Abrahams's *Singing the Master: The Emergence of African American Culture in the Plantation South* (New York: Penguin, 1992), pp. 203–328.

31 Lanier, *Science of English Verse*, pp. 186, 315.

32 Francis B. Gummere, *The Beginnings of Poetry* (New York: Macmillan, 1901), p. 99.

33 *Ibid.*, p. 101.

34 John D. Kerkering, *The Poetics of National and Racial Identity in Nineteenth-Century American Literature* (Cambridge University Press, 2003), pp. 134–38.

35 W. E. B. Du Bois, "The Conservation of Races," in *Writings*, ed. Nathan Huggins (New York: Library of America, 1986), p. 820.

36 Maurice Merleau-Ponty, *Phenomenology of Perception*, trans. Colin Smith (London: Routledge, 2002). Smith translates "*schéma corporel*" as "body image" rather than "body schema."

37 Emerson, "The Poet," p. 457.

38 Emerson, "The American Scholar," in *Essays and Poems*, p. 59.

39 Novalis, "Fichte Studies," in Jochen Schulte-Sasse, ed., *Theory as Practice: A Critical Anthology of Early German Romantic Writings* (Minneapolis: University of Minnesota Press, 1997), pp. 93–95.

40 Wood, ed., *Poetry of Slavery*, p. 571.

41 The poem is reproduced in William Wells Brown, ed., *The Anti-Slavery Harp; A Collection of Songs for Anti-Slavery Meetings* (Boston: Bela Marsh, 1848), pp. 23–24. It also appeared that year, without the epigraph from the London *Morning Chronicle*, in *The Liberator*, 18.21 (May 26, 1848), 84.

42 Thomas Jefferson, *Writings*, ed. Merrill D. Peterson (New York: Library of America, 1984), pp. 611–12.

43 Bryant, "On Trisyllabic Feet," p. 66.

44 George Saintsbury, *A History of English Prosody from the Twelfth Century to the Present Day*, 3 vols. (1906–1910; New York: Russell and Russell, 1961), III: 485.

45 *Ibid.*, p. 67.

46 Emerson, "Fate," in *Essays and Poems*, p. 771.

47 Henri Lefebvre, *Rhythmanalysis: Space, Time and Everyday Life*, trans. Stuart Elden and Gerald Moore (London: Continuum, 2004), pp. 51–52.

6

ELIZA RICHARDS

Weathering the news in US Civil War poetry

The outpouring of poetry in newspapers and magazines, North and South, during the Civil War period, served the wartime work of calling men to arms, offering solace for those who lost loved ones in battle, and justifying blood sacrifice in the name of patriotism. Precisely when the constitution of nations was at stake, writers and readers believed that poetry's communicative powers could both express and shape national beliefs and sentiments.[1] Poetry's communicative powers depended not just on its internal formal and rhetorical properties, but also on the vast informational network that served the conflict and helped determine its outcomes; especially in the North, telegraph, railroad, newspapers, and magazines consolidated into a mass media system that drew its energy from the war. The hunger for information fueled a new profession: the eyewitness reporter sent in sketches or stories composed at the site of events unfolding. Railroad and telegraph transmission enabled people far away from the action to receive reports with an astonishing rapidity that caused a newly intense addiction to the news; people needed only "bread and newspaper," according to Oliver Wendell Holmes, Sr. Newspapers like *Harper's Illustrated Weekly*, *Frank Leslie's Illustrated Weekly*, and *Southern Illustrated Weekly* fed that addiction, carrying poetry alongside journalistic reportage and illustrations. These communicative modes or genres were by no means separate; each informed the other.[2]

Poetry adapted to this new environment by responding rapidly to war events gleaned from newspaper coverage and finding ways to shape, motivate, rationalize, and analyze war efforts. Many poets of the period – John Greenleaf Whittier, Walt Whitman, Herman Melville, and Julia Ward Howe among them – expressed an urgent need to remake poetry in a way that gave it relevance in a period of national crisis.[3] If they were not going to trade their pens for guns, as many of their peers were doing, then they needed to make poetry more than an indulgent form of entertainment and self-expression, which is how their earlier efforts seemed to them once the war broke out. Some poets, particularly at the beginning of the conflict, chose to address themselves directly to the task of inciting action. Countless poems appeared calling men to enlist, for example; Walt Whitman's "Beat Beat Drums," later included in *Drum-Taps*, was among them, appearing in *Harper's Weekly* on September 21, 1861. Julia Ward Howe's "Battle-Hymn of the Republic," written as alternative lyrics for the popular Northern song "John Brown's Body," was published on the first page of the *Atlantic Monthly* in February of 1862; its militant Christian rationale for Northern violence became so popular that it was soon on everyone's lips; she heard reports that it was "sung in chorus" by Union soldiers.[4]

But other poets took a less practical, more philosophical or meditational approach to the problem of imagining a place for poetry in a time of war, and I want to focus on their work in this chapter. Especially in the second year of the conflict, when it became clear that the South would not easily give up its fight to establish a new nation, and when the death tolls mounted to unprecedented highs, poetry was used increasingly as a way of thinking through the aesthetics and ethics of distant violence. For it was a paradoxical effect of the rapid, nearly immediate transmission of information from the battle fronts that it made people on the home front acutely aware that they were not present, that others were fighting and dying for them. On a daily basis, the lists of the dead published in local newspapers, along with images and reports of battles in a range of local and national periodicals, confronted civilians with their own relative safety, their remove from danger, gained at the cost of the lives of others. What to make of this situation – how to feel when strangers die for you, how to imagine mass death at a distance, how to visualize invisible suffering – these are some of the pressing topics in much Civil War poetry. These questions have come to be such a part of American everyday lives in the late twentieth and twenty-first centuries, perhaps, that we take the situation for granted, for the United States has long been involved in highly lethal wars in foreign lands that we at home learn about with a highly mediated immediacy; but the mass scale of death in conjunction with a newly forged mass media network made this state of affairs obvious and deeply perplexing in the mid nineteenth-century United States. Taking up antebellum topics and tropes, Civil War poets demonstrate the ways that war troubles earlier forms of poetic expression; they further demonstrate how these forms might be revised and adapted to a new, dislocated, shocked sensibility.

A number of critics have taken up the question of the ways wartime poetry draws upon and revises the pastoral tradition.[5] No one, however, has noted the persistent tendency of poetry in the period to look to the sky rather than the land for the meanings of war. Studies of *Battle-Pieces* have noted Melville's complex ways of retrospectively prophesying military and political outcomes of the war by offering weather forecasts; and studies of individual poems by Emily Dickinson have argued that she figures particular atmospheric occurrences as wartime events (she describes the morning sky as if it were a confrontation between blue and gray forces, for example).[6] But they have not generalized from those particular observations to note and explore what is clearly a tradition, or a culture-wide way of thinking about war via figures of the weather. Mary Favret has traced such a tradition in English poetry of the eighteenth and early nineteenth century, demonstrating that poets like William Cowper, Anna Barbauld, and Samuel Taylor Coleridge think through the question of "war at a distance" via meterological figures. England's empire-building, Favret argues, inspires poets to read the weather as a way of thinking through what it means to be a citizen of a nation perpetually at war abroad. Remote wars pressure English poets to find a way of relating distant events with present experiences, especially in sensory terms; the weather provides a medium for such meditations.[7] Favret's insights hold true for US Civil War poetry, which recognizes and refers to an English tradition of speaking about war in terms of the weather; even more particularly, Civil War poetry of all kinds – Northern and Southern, popular and experimental, broadly or narrowly circulated – draws sustained parallels between weather and the circulation and reception of news in wartime. Something is in the air during the Civil War, and the only way to address this amorphous, elusive, ever-changing, and semi-tangible subject is to talk about the air directly.

The weather mattered on both literal and figurative levels of signification, and those levels were inextricably linked in Civil War journalism and the poetry inspired by it. Weather was first of all an important condition of battle. As a writer remarked in an essay entitled "Weather in War," published in the *Atlantic Monthly* in 1862, "It is not very flattering to that glory-loving, battle-seeking creature, Man, that his best-arranged schemes for the destruction of his fellows should often be made to fail by the condition of the weather."[8] In a war fought primarily in Southern climates that differ starkly from those of the North, unpredictable weather more than once contributed to the Union army's difficulties in unknown terrain: heavy rains, extreme heat, sudden shifts from hot to freezing temperatures caused problems with overexposure and the recovery of the wounded from battlefields, for example. The vast differences in weather between the North and South – extreme cold versus extreme heat, snowstorms versus torrential rains – were ripe for interpretation in terms of the political and cultural character of the people, especially when scientific theories of the time attributed a people's character to the climate they lived in: Southerners were hot-blooded and emotional, Northerners more temperate and rational.[9] As much as climate separates and differentiates, however, observing the weather allows those differences to be physically imagined at a distance, at least according to Civil War poets. Watching autumn leaves fall in Massachusetts evokes blood spilling onto warmer Southern battlefields, for example.[10] Science of the period had recently come to understand weather as a global system, moreover, which meant that what goes around, comes around: what is elsewhere will eventually arrive here, perhaps in altered form.[11] For this reason, probably, poetry about the migration of birds figured prominently in the Civil War period.[12] The US Civil War was external and internal simultaneously, because one nation threatened to become two. What was far away for Northern civilians could be in the backyard of their Southern counterparts, so that proximity and distance are held in a complex, ever-shifting relation, and the weather reports in newspapers and poetry of the period tried to chart and make sense of these dynamics.

I will begin to develop these ideas by examining a cluster of Northern and Southern poems that take up the figure of snow. Favret traces a poetic tradition from the *Iliad*, through Milton's *Paradise Lost*, James Thomson's *The Seasons*, William Cowper's *The Task*, and then the Romantic poets, in which winter's weather serves as a figure for war.[13] All the poets I discuss here are cognizant of this tradition, and comment on and adapt it to the particular circumstances of a civil war with massive death tolls in a mass media age. My first section, "An Even Face," traces the transfiguration of snow from Emerson's "The Snow-Storm" (1835) to Elizabeth Akers Allen's "Snow" (1864) and Emily Dickinson's "It sifts from Leaden Sieves – " (about late 1862, according to Dickinson's editor, Ralph W. Franklin; revised, sometimes radically, in 1863, 1865, 1871, and 1873). These poems (along with many others that I will not have time to discuss) suggest that there is a New England tradition of thinking about aesthetic practices via the figure of snow. Working within the romantic tradition of imbuing empirical observations about the natural world with symbolic, revelatory significance, poets find an analogue for imaginative processes of creation in the way snow transforms the world. The Civil War radically changes the ways that writers think about both snow and the functions and possibilities of poetry. Allen and Dickinson offer major transformations of the antecedent, antebellum poem by Emerson, adapting their inheritance to new conditions. In the second section, I will turn to the poems of Henry Timrod, "The Poet Laureate of the South," to think about the ways his closer yet still distant relation to the battle (he lived in Charleston and Columbia, South Carolina during the war, fleeing Columbia when it was set on fire during one of Sherman's final marches) is expressed through his figurations of cotton in summertime (the "SNOW OF SOUTHERN SUMMERS!").[14] The comparison begins to track the complex relations between war, news, and weather, North and South, as they intermix both physically and symbolically. I hope to indicate the intricate web of associations that poets of the time worked within and thought through, transforming poetic practice and aesthetic understanding in the process.

"An Even Face"

In "The Snow-Storm," Emerson casts the north wind as a barbaric artist that, through the medium of snow, transforms the world into a whimsical architectural wonderland while people huddle together inside a farmhouse:

> Announced by all the trumpets of the sky,
> Arrives the snow, and, driving o'er the fields,
> Seems nowhere to alight: the whited air
> Hides hill and woods, the river, and the heaven,
> And veils the farmhouse at the garden's end.
> The sled and traveller stopped, the courier's feet
> Delayed, all friends shut out, the housemates sit
> Around the radiant fireplace, enclosed
> In a tumultuous privacy of storm.
>
> Come see the north wind's masonry.
> Out of an unseen quarry evermore
> Furnished with tile, the fierce artificer
> Curves his white bastions with projected roof
> Round every windward stake, or tree, or door.
> Speeding, the myriad-handed, his wild work
> So fanciful, so savage, nought cares he
> For number or proportion. Mockingly,
> On coop or kennel he hangs Parian wreaths;
> A swan-like form invests the hidden thorn;
> Fills up the farmer's lane from wall to wall,
> Maugre the farmer's sighs; and at the gate
> A tapering turret overtops the work.
> And when his hours are numbered, and the world
> Is all his own, retiring, as he were not,
> Leaves, when the sun appears, astonished Art
> To mimic in slow structures, stone by stone,
> Built in an age, the mad wind's night-work,
> The frolic architecture of the snow.[15]

The wind's transformation of the landscape is cast in militaristic terms: "trumpets of the sky" herald its arrival, and it quickly wrests the land from its human inhabitants, imprisons them indoors, occupies the territory, and lays waste, albeit temporarily and playfully, to the competitors' territory. The "fierce artificer" from another world mockingly replaces man-made structures with outlandish parodies that invert human perspectives and values: it decorates animal cages rather than human homes with wreaths, turns thorns into swan shapes, and erases the "farmer's lane" by filling up its "walls." Replacing practicality and symmetry with a "frolic architecture" lacking "number and proportion," the "myriad-handed" artist quickly overrides cherished structures that were long in the making. It is left to the human artist to "mimic" painfully, slowly, and inadequately the "mad wind's night work" once he withdraws.

Mimesis is strangely doubled here. If we are familiar with Romantic poets taking nature as their model, and seeking to create, in Emerson's formulation, "a metre-making argument … a thought so passionate and alive, that, like the spirit of a plant or animal, it has an architecture of its own, and adorns nature with a new thing," here nature mimics people in a way that is secondary and dependent.[16] The wind is inspired by human endeavor, and his recreation only makes sense as a commentary on the original; his "wild work" is described in distinctly Grecian terms, evoking ancient architectural ruins. The wreaths are "Parian," an adjective derived from the Greek island of Paros, known for its fine white marble, and "swan-like" evokes numerous Greek myths, such as the rape of Leda by Zeus in the body of a swan, or figures, such as Apollo, the god of poetry, for whom the swan was sacred. So when Emerson says that it is left to Art to "mimic in slow structures, stone by stone, the frolic architecture of the snow," we might pause in perplexity, wondering exactly what he means. Would a human architect seek to design a functionless building, especially if he created the blueprint on which the whimsical parody was based? What sort of artist would want to mimic the distinctly dysfunctional snow sculptures of the wind? And now that we think about it, if the night wind is so inhuman, why does Emerson personify it as an artist and artisan, give it hands, creative inspiration, and competitive impulses? After all we have to conclude either that Emerson was unsuccessful in getting away from the idea that art is a human endeavor, or that he is suggesting that, by placing one's self imaginatively in the place of the wind, which works in the medium of snow, the poet can take a verbal walk on the wild side. For snow both makes and unmakes the world in this poem, erasing physical work, marks of ownership, human communication networks, and social codes, creating a blank page for antic expression. By covering the physical world in white, "the mad wind's night work" encourages the poet, in a "tumultuous privacy of storm," to write all over it. Far from nature inspiring the poet, here the poet inspires nature, taking the occasion of a storm to project mental imaginings onto the outside world.

This is Elizabeth Akers Allen's starting point in "Snow," published in the *Atlantic Monthly*, one of the leading pro-Union periodicals, in February 1864, after the battles of Shiloh, Antietam, Gettysburg, Chickamauga, and others had claimed tens of thousands of lives.[17] A prolific and popular poet, generally recognized for her graceful nature poetry (and, under the name of Florence Percy, as the author of "Rock Me to Sleep," one of the most popular poems to emerge from the war years), Allen contributed poems throughout the war, marking the temperature of the conflict through the changing seasons in poems like "Spring at the Capital," in which she imagines seeing blood on white spring flowers after looking at a "white encampment" in the distance, outside of Washington, DC.[18] Explicitly working from formally experimental predecessors, both Emerson's "Snow-Storm" and Longfellow's "Snow-Flakes" of 1858, in "Snow" Allen smooths, tames, and shapes their work into tetrameter lines, balanced between iambs and trochees, with an unbroken abaab rhyme scheme. She revises Emerson's depicted scenario as well, putting things in their place:

> Lo, what wonders the day hath brought,
> Born of the soft and slumberous snow!
> Gradual, silent, slowly wrought; –
> Even as an artist, thought by thought,
> Writes expression on lip and brow.
>
> Hanging garlands the eaves o'erbrim,
> Deep drifts smother the paths below;
> The elms are shrouded, trunk and limb,
> And all the air is dizzy and dim
> With a whirl of dancing, dazzling snow.
>
> ("Snow," stanzas 1–2)

So much for Emerson's mad wind's unruly disruption; we seem to have a highly conservative poet here, one who seeks to make her own poem a proper antecedent of Emerson's that offers a tidied version of the farm scene that his night wind messed up. Allen's "soft and slumberous" snow hangs "garlands," not on chicken coops and dog kennels, but appropriately, on the eaves of a house. Her snow etches its mimetic double of the human gradually, silently, and slowly, "Even as an artist, thought by thought, / Writes expression on lip and brow." Less wildly ambivalent and unsettling than Emerson's poem, Allen's first stanzas personify nature so fully that it only knows how to sculpt the human form just as a human artist would. Harnessing and stabilizing Emerson's night wind's myriad-handed work, Allen sucks all the air out of her depiction, seemingly arriving at a conclusion by the end of the second stanza of a six-stanza poem.

But the poem takes a dark turn from there, beyond stasis to death and even killing. A poem that seemed to be bent on escaping current events becomes gripped by them; the whimsical scene of exterior decoration, fully evocative of Emerson's earlier poem, warps into a nightmare vision of disorientation and mass death in the next three stanzas:

> Dimly out of the baffled sight
> Houses and church-spires stretch away;
> The trees, all spectral and still and white,
> Stand up like ghosts in the failing light,
> And fade and faint with the blinded day.
>
> Down from the roofs in gusts are hurled
> The eddying drifts to the waste below;
> And still is the banner of storm unfurled,
> Till all the drowned and desolate world
> Lies dumb and white in a trance of snow.
>
> Slowly the shadows gather and fall,
> Still the whispering snow-flakes beat;
> Night and darkness are over all:
> Rest, pale city, beneath their pall!
> Sleep, white world, in thy winding-sheet!
>
> (stanzas 3–5)

Now that we have read further, the second stanza does not seem so cheery after all: the "dancing, dazzling snow" recedes, and Allen sketches a much starker picture. The "deep drifts smother the paths," "the elms are shrouded, trunk and limb," and even the air, "dizzy and dim," seems unable to breathe. Apocalyptic, depopulated poetic landscapes have taken the place of Emerson's animating personifications. The violence continues "Till all the drowned and desolate world / Lies dumb and white in a trance of snow." Rather than covering to recreate, like Emerson's night wind, this windless snow smothers to kill, hurls downward to make and join "waste." Allen depicts a total annihilation that telescopes civilization until it disappears entirely: "Dimly out of the baffled sight / Houses and church-spires stretch away." Even the trees "fade and faint with the blinded day."

The Civil War is the not-so-hidden subtext, disrupting the Emersonian nature aesthetic in which the imagination is free to remake the world in its own image without damage or cost. If we need more evidence, beyond the snow, weighty as lead, "hurled" down like missiles and laying "waste," we might notice the corpse-like description of the elms whose articulated parts, "trunk and limb," summon the amputation and dismemberment so ubiquitous during the war. The "banner of storm unfurled," stridently patriotic in its unrelenting demands, insists on continuing its siege until the entire "pale city" is buried in a mass grave, a single "winding-sheet" (the Civil War dead, especially regular infantry, were frequently buried in mass graves if they weren't left to the elements, if only because there wasn't the manpower to spend on the dead).[19]

If we are wondering how the speaker can still talk if the whole world has been destroyed, we learn that, like Emerson's "housemates," she has sought shelter out of the storm in a room, and – quite strangely – stares at a picture of Rome and an olive-wreath on her wall, rather than looking out the window. Here the war surfaces fully as the subject of the poem, and the weather metaphor recedes:

> Clouds may thicken, and storm-winds breathe:
> On my wall is a glimpse of Rome, –
> Land of my longing! – and underneath
> Swings and trembles my olive-wreath;
> Peace and I are at home, at home!
> ("Snow," final stanza)

Shut in, a lone survivor, her view intolerable if there even are windows, she can only look at the history of civilization to imagine an ancient place "at home, at home" with peace. Even that radical disjunction from the natural world, however, does not keep the threat of destruction at bay, for the very place she looks to reassure herself of the rise of civilization has fallen, as a result of war. The late eighteenth-century English historian Edward Gibbons famously attributed the "decline and fall of the Roman Empire" to barbarian invasions that were possible due to the loss of civic virtue. Allen's snow actively recalls Emerson's frolic savagery in order to suggest that poets, or at least this poem, can no longer use the natural world as a playground where the imagination is free to roam. The snow imposes a vision of mass death upon the speaker in spite of herself, one she seeks to escape. Bunkered in her home, she assembles pieces into a collage-like figure of a shrine – a picture of Rome in place of the world outside her window, an olive-wreath beneath – shoring up fragments in a vain attempt to look elsewhere and see something different. The weather brings the news home to the speaker, who invokes peace as a desperate plea in response.

To distill a difference between the antebellum aesthetics of Emerson and the "bellum" aesthetics of Allen, we might say that a creative imagination working on and transforming the world has been replaced by the grimmer task of picking up the pieces and trying to reconstruct something out of what seems like nothing. Emily Dickinson's poem "It sifts from Leaden Sieves – " both validates and develops this distinction. Though recent critics continue to add to the index of Dickinson poems that can be interpreted as oblique (Dickinson's word) commentaries on the war, this poem is not among them.[20] Implicitly, I am suggesting that many if not most poems written from 1861 to 1865 can be read as Civil War poems not, or not only, because they are thematically "about" the war, but because they were written during that period and are part of a media network that cannot seal itself off from an event it is dependent upon. This poem was first sent to Susan Dickinson in 1862, then revised and included in a fascicle about the spring of 1863, according to Dickinson's editor R. W. Franklin. I quote the fascicle version below, noting variants.

> It sifts from Leaden Sieves –
> It powders all the Field –
> It fills with Alabaster Wool
> The Wrinkles of the Road –
>
> It makes an Even Face
> Of Mountain – and of Plain –
> Unbroken Forehead from the East
> Unto the East – again –
>
> It reaches to the Fence –
> It wraps it, Rail by Rail,
> Till it is lost in Fleeces –
> It flings a Crystal Vail
> On Stump, and Stack – and Stem –
> A Summer's empty Room –
> Acres of Joints, where Harvests were,
> Recordless – but for them –
>
> It Ruffles Wrists of Posts –
> As Ancles of a Queen –
> Then stills it's Artisans – like Swans –
> Denying they have been – [21]

Rather than remaking the world in a fantastic jumble (Emerson), or burying it in a winding sheet (Allen), Dickinson's "It" – at first the snow, then something more mysterious – gives the world a sinister facelift, covering up signs of devastation. Like a cosmetician, it "powders all the Field" and "fills with Alabaster Wool / The Wrinkles of the Road." Fixing up the landscape might not seem so bad, until we hear that "It makes an Even Face" and an "Unbroken Forehead" of the entire world, "from the East, / Unto the East – again." That leaves us to wonder, if the globe is a head, where the rest of the body is; it might also suggest that this face is being made up for posthumous viewing. In *This Republic of Suffering*, Drew Gilpin Faust discusses the advances in embalming during the Civil War. If families had the money, they hired embalmers near the front to prepare bodies for shipment home – often a long way by train, for Union soldiers – so that loved ones could be seen one last time and given a proper burial.[22] Embalmers and other middlemen in this process quickly realized that there was money to be made identifying and preserving the dead for distant burial; Dickinson's image of filling wrinkles with wool on a bodiless face begins to suggest the detached, clinical gaze that would accompany such engagements with the Civil War dead.

The poem foregrounds the fragmentation not only of poetic understanding and worldview, as Allen's "Snow" does, but of the human body. "It sifts" through images of body parts, vainly trying to reassemble the human, the inevitable aesthetic task, Dickinson indicates, that accompanies modern warfare. Countless Civil War reports of battlefields (Dickinson replaces the first version's "Wood" with "Field" in this second version, strengthening the military association) covered with wounded and dead soldiers used metaphors of autumn harvest, underscoring the gruesome yield of war. The Battle of Antietam, for example, which took place in a cornfield on September 17, 1862, could not help but evoke comparisons between harvests of grain and of men, for they literally mingled; the corn was flattened and covered with blood by the thousands of soldiers who died there.[23] In Dickinson's poem, the snow "flings a Crystal Vail / On Stump, and Stack – and Stem – / A Summer's Empty Room – / Acres of Joints, where Harvests were." Dickinson buries the amputated limbs in the snow of amnesia: the stumps, stacks, stems, and acres of joints are left to memorialize themselves; they have no other record. As if covering wounds that have no possibility of healing, "It flings a Crystal Vail"; or, in variant form, "It deals celestial Vail" – doling out forgetfulness or numbness. Simultaneously closing and opening the distance between Southern battlefields and the Northern homefronts, the snow of winter covers the summer's field, where the remains of harvest evoke amputation.

More than Emerson and Allen, Dickinson makes plain her participation in a poetic tradition of identifying winter and war. The variant for "Artisans" is "Myrmidons," the war-like people that Achilles led to battle against Troy. This single word foregrounds the martial metaphor implicit in Emerson's "Snow-Storm" by summoning the story of the Trojan War, as depicted in Homer's *Iliad*, in the language of Alexander Pope's translation (that translation was in her family library, as were volumes by Milton, Thomson, and Cowper).[24] The association is confirmed and extended with the simile "like

Swans," which recalls Emerson's swan-like thorn, but also, in conjunction with "Myrmidons," points more clearly to the story of Zeus's rape of Leda in the guise of a swan. The child of that union was Helen of Troy, the face that launched a thousand ships.

An extended passage in the *Iliad* compares in detail a warlike snowstorm with the Greeks' blizzard-like bombardment of Troy with stones:

> And now the Stones descend in heavier Show'rs.
> As when high Jove his sharp Artill'ry forms,
> And opes his cloudy Magazine of Storms.[25]

This excerpt suggests that Dickinson's poem is steeped in the metaphoric logic of the *Iliad*: the heaviness and minerality, for lack of a better word, of her snow metaphors – lead, alabaster – summons the storm of rocks in the epic. Her sifting and powdering "It" summons Jove's godly impersonality; both are busy in the sky delivering lethal messages to humans without concern for the consequences, but Dickinson's "It" is so far removed that it doesn't have a name or a place in a belief system as Jove does. Even so, in one way "It" is more intimate, for it is engaged in domestic activities that are suitable for a war at home. The poems also share "fleeces" as an evocation of snow:

> The circling seas, alone absorbing all,
> Drink the dissolving fleeces as they fall;
> So from each side increased the stony rain,
> And the white ruin rises o'er the plain.

Dickinson's synonym for fleeces, "alabaster wool," further underscores the connection: alabaster is a word derived from Greek for a fine white stone, originally mined in Egypt, from which ornamental vessels and sculptures were carved.[26] Dickinson inverts the earlier metaphoric valence: if in the *Iliad*, battle is described as a snowstorm, in Dickinson's poem, a snowstorm is described as a battle ... or is it? By the end of the poem, "It" is also "lost in fleeces," and it is unclear which is the tenor and which is the vehicle. Dickinson underscores the remoteness of present violence by referring to even more elusive and remote past violence, historical, but also mythical and beautiful, inspiration for an enduring poetic tradition which, she suggests, might come to an end if sense can't be made of the present violence.

Out of supposedly "recordless" carnage, a new body of poetry arises, albeit in parts, parts that recall those just-buried pieces. The harvest of the dead may be "recordless" (Drew Gilpin Faust notes that many, many bodies were buried without record during the war[27]) or their records may be resurrected in altered and denied form. The speaker sees body parts everywhere.

Like Allen, Dickinson aligns the botanical world with human anatomy; Allen's tree trunks and limbs evoke their human counterparts, and Dickinson extends this logic. "Stump" can refer to both botanical and human portions; once that association is established, we can read "stem" as a metaphor for human dismemberment as well, and "stack" as human corpses piled like so much hay. The phrase "Acres of Joints" inverts the metaphoric valence, so that now human dismemberment signifies agricultural harvest; we do not commonly refer to a mowed field as full of "joints." If "Acres of Joints" are where "Harvests were," then we can understand that, rather than metaphoric equivalence, Dickinson has moved to a literal description of substitution: where grain was harvested now lie countless human bodies and their dismembered parts.

In a last gesture that gruesomely recalls Emerson's "frolic architecture," Dickinson's "It" "Ruffles Wrists of Posts – / As Ancles of a Queen – / Then stills it's Artisans – like Ghosts – / Denying they have been." The ruffling of the posts' wrists suggests that the speaker has difficult discerning between body parts and other things, so that her simile is oddly doubled and broken: ruffling the posts' wrists is like ruffling the Queen's "Ancles." That doesn't tell us much, beyond the certainty that corporeal disaggregation haunts the poem, disrupts a more conventional form of troping, and records the ramifications of the recordless dead the poem, on the face of it – the artificially composed face – denies.

Elizabeth Akers Allen, among others, clearly shares the critical impulse that scholars are ever more willing to attribute to Dickinson in contradistinction to her more popular peers and contemporaries (only Melville is more often credited with a savvy insight and resistance to injustices that others blindly promote).[28] The more I read Allen's poetry, the more it is unclear to me how anyone can think she is an inoffensive recorder of nature's moods, and the less I think her work should be relegated to the dustbins of history. After the "Bloody Autumn" of 1862, "Snow" is typical of her despondent commentary on the ways that ethics and aesthetics have been thrown into chaos and uncertainty. Though many critics and historians have found nature poetry of the period to work in the service of naturalizing and rationalizing state-sanctioned violence, both Dickinson and Allen offer a thoughtful meditation on mass violence; more to the point, they seek to forge connections between remote scenes of suffering, largely in the South, and the Union home front.[29] The weather is not only a metaphor for war; it is also a metaphor for news. The "simple news that nature told," as Faith Barrett has suggested, is not that simple once the war begins, but not just for Dickinson.[30]

"The Snow of Southern Summers"

American literary tradition as it is studied, taught, and transmitted bears a complex inheritance of the war. Studies of Civil War literature have tended, at least until recently, to take the victor's viewpoint; the pro-secession and pro-slavery sentiments of most Southern literature written before 1865 have made it easier to forget about or morally condemn than to incorporate in American literature surveys anchored by progressive democratic ideals. But in ignoring such a crucial part of the literary field, we give up understanding the ways American literature operates as a networked web (I don't believe it is a closed system) across sectional differences. "Northern" literature, I suggested in the previous section, is highly influenced by events in the South. I will go on to show that "Southern" literature is highly responsive to the literature of the North, which responds in turn. There may be sectional and political differences, but there is also substantial exchange. What will most clearly emerge in the brief chronological study of Timrod's poetry of the war years is that the differences collapse and become conflated and confused as the war wears on and the death tolls mount. Timrod's cotton, which he portrays as "the snow of Southern summers," the ideal counterpoint for the North's winter crop of frozen water crystals, disappears from his later poems, which are haunted by the dead, undifferentiated by region or political outlook. The dead speak to both sides, begging to be understood and incorporated in an aesthetic meditation on the cost of war.

Timrod's "Ethnogenesis" inaugurated the birth of a new nation and a new people on the occasion of "the meeting of the Southern Congress, at Montgomery, February, 1861," as the extended title tells us. Published in the *Charleston Daily Courier* on February 23, 1861, it was reprinted not only in Southern papers, but also in *Littel's Living Age*, a weekly Boston publication. Timrod's nature poetry had been popular enough in the North before the war that he published a volume of poems in the prestigious Ticknor and Fields series in 1860.[31] Northern readers were probably curious how secession would change the poet's outlook. They would see that he was quite familiar with the poetic tradition that associates winter with war even if, as a lifelong resident of South Carolina, he did not have much direct contact with winter weather. Working both within and against that tradition, Timrod broadcasts a new kind of snow that he promotes as far superior to the Northern sort. This kinder, gentler snow will help the South, along with the rest of a more amenable, milder climate, win the war:

> Beneath so kind a sky – the very sun
> Takes part with us; and on our errands run

All breezes of the ocean; dew and rain
Do noiseless battle for us; and the Year,
And all the gentle daughters in her train,
March in our ranks, and in our service wield
Long spears of golden grain!
A yellow blossom as her fairy shield,
June flings her azure banner to the wind,
While in the order of their birth
Her sisters pass, and many an ample field
Grows white beneath their steps, till now, behold,
Its endless sheets unfold
THE SNOW OF SOUTHERN SUMMERS! Let the earth
Rejoice! beneath those fleeces soft and warm
Our happy land shall sleep
In a repose as deep
As if we lay intrenched behind
Whole leagues of Russian ice and Arctic storm!
(*Poems*, pp. 92–93)

Rather than compete against those living in its atmosphere, alienating, isolating, and confusing the human population, Timrod's personified summer weather "takes part with us." Personification is far less ambiguous and far more persistent in "Ethnogenesis" than in the poems of Emerson, Allen, and Dickinson: the sky, the sun, the breezes, the year, the months ("all the gentle daughters"), all take human shapes so they can take up arms – fanciful arms – a "fairy shield," a "spear" of grain – in the name of cotton. Cotton, the thing not named, and one of the few things not personified in the passage, behaves atmospherically, like Southern snow, rather than like a plant. It blankets the earth in "fleeces," like Dickinson's (and the *Iliad*'s) snow, only more hospitably, nurturing the earth and keeping it warm. Its whiteness becomes the very atmosphere of moral purity that Timrod hopes will inspire the new Southern nation; at the same time, he associates the color of cotton with racial superiority. Timrod thus posits an alternative to Northern snow that appeals to the slaveholding South, one that makes weaknesses out of its counterpart's strengths. There is one strange ambivalence worth noting, however. The cotton stretches out in "sheets" like clouds, or like Allen's "winding sheets," but rather than wrapping the dead, it cultivates an opiate "sleep" that Timrod casts positively. He seems to suggest that cotton inures white Southern populations to Northern criticism as effectively as Russian ice and Arctic storm would deter travel; yet "lay intrenched" conflicts defensively with the "deep" "repose" of a sleeping "happy land," suggesting that the white Southern conscience that Timrod constructs and

bolsters here might require anesthesia in order for its dream of perfect whiteness to operate properly. "Ethnogenesis" very self-consciously works within
a Northern tradition in order to oppose it, but in responding to Northern
criticisms of Southern slavocracy, Timrod's poem betrays influences of the
positions he opposes.

It is clear that Timrod hopes his readership will extend beyond his region,
and that he can sway foreign viewers to a Southern viewpoint of the conflict. In the same way that Dickinson's "Even Face" stretches grimly around
the world from east to east, Timrod imagines that markets for cotton, like
ocean currents, will bring the warmth of Southern hospitality far and wide,
convincing the world that there is a kinder, gentler alternative to the capitalism of the North:

> The hour perchance is not yet wholly ripe
> When all shall own it, but the type
> Whereby we shall be known in every land
> Is that vast gulf which lips our Southern strand,
> And through the cold, untempered ocean pours
> Its genial streams, that far off Arctic shores
> May sometimes catch upon the softened breeze
> Strange tropic warmth and hints of summer seas!
>
> (p. 95)

Ocean currents, like news, weather, and desirable commodities, circulate
widely; Timrod's snowy cotton evokes all these currents in its appeal for
global acceptance for the new nation, which he promises will be superior to
the former United States and its remnant, the Northern States.

A companion piece to "Ethnogenesis," "The Cotton Boll" (published in
the *Charleston Mercury* on September 3, 1861) underscores the inevitability
that Southern cotton trumps Northern snow. Its infinitude rivals its com-
petitor's only as God's heaven rivals Satan's wasteland:

> To the remotest point of sight,
> Although I gaze upon no waste of snow,
> The endless field is white;
> And the whole landscape glows,
> For many a shining league away,
> With such accumulated light
> As Polar lands would flash beneath a tropic day!
>
> (p. 96)

The "waste of snow" is countered by an "endless" white field that glows
with holy light. Timrod could not be more adamant about the righteousness of the Southern cause, which he articulates by turning an inherited

tradition of winter war poetry back against itself. In order to accomplish this rhetorical feat, however, he must turn cotton into weather, vaporize its materiality so that it may become a medium of illumination, a means of communication, rather than a substance.

In "The Cotton Boll," even more than in "Ethnogenesis," Timrod registers awareness of his evaporation of materiality, rendering his own poetic logic suspect. The poem begins by drawing attention to the very figure he seems to want to erase: the slave.

> While I recline
> At ease beneath
> This immemorial pine,
> Small sphere!
> (By dusky fingers brought this morning here
> And shown with boastful smiles) ...
>
> (p. 96)

The poem presents a rhetorical problem from the outset; the white speaker's "ease" depends upon the labor of the "dusky" other; the cotton he claims as a pure, ethereal symbol – of global interconnectedness ("small sphere!"), of white superiority, of magical, mystical climatic harmony – only underscores the presence of a slave system that removes the speaker from the very thing he claims perfect union with and possession of. If leisured white superiority and black servitude were so natural, the slave would either be more fully present – an entire body rather than fingers and smiles – or totally absent, as he is in "Ethnogenesis," where the sister "months" plant, cultivate, and grow the cotton into an endless white sheet without visible help or effort. Here the slave peeks in, only partially materialized, and partially dematerialized. In a poem where white is light, holy illumination, it is not surprising that the slave is the absence of light, but he is not fully turned to night; his "dusky fingers" and his "boastful smiles" linger, as a reminder that the dream of the South hinges on a mythology of "the little boll," "a spell" like that "in the ocean shell" (p. 96). Timrod draws attention to the fantastic element of his reverie even as he seeks to naturalize it, suggesting that the material conditions of slavery are more present and contrary to the vision than he or his readers might longingly wish. In choosing cotton as his ideal mode of disseminating the good news of the South, Timrod seems to acknowledge a tangle in his "trembling line[s]" that he stops short of accounting for (p. 95). What he does not admit verbally is that he knows there is a difference between snow and cotton, between metaphors of weather, and the Civil War climate of the South.

By 1863, endless fields of glowing, snowy cotton have disappeared from Timrod's poetry, and spring replaces summer as his preferred season.

"Spring," published in the *Southern Illustrated News* on April 4, tries to celebrate the beauty of the South in springtime, but like its Northern counterparts during that time, thoughts of the dead and the wounded keep seeping into the images, until the war finally takes over the poem. As in Allen's poem "Snow," the process is gradual; it seems unconscious or accidental at first, and then gains momentum. At the outset, only "pathos" indicates the darker, advancing vision:

> Spring, with that nameless pathos in the air
> Which dwells with all things fair,
> Spring, with her golden suns and silver rain,
> Is with us once again.
>
> (p. 122)

Soon, blood seeps into the picture, at first in a way that could be overlooked as part of a playful personification – "In the deep heart of every forest tree / The blood is all aglee." The images accumulate, however, until the metaphor overwhelms the natural scene, and the tree seems to bleed, along with the sky: "the maple reddens on the lawn, / Flushed by the season's dawn." Then the seeds working their way towards the sun start to resemble war dead who rush to be resurrected en masse, or who refuse to stay dead and haunt the living:

> As yet the turf is dark, although you know
> That, not a span below,
> A thousand germs are groping through the gloom,
> And soon will burst their tomb.
>
> (p. 123)

The unsettling undertone is confirmed when the buds are described as abortions: "Still there's a sense of blossoms yet unborn." Just before the speaker faces the submerged topic of violence directly, he seems to be overwhelmed with a vision of a flood of blood, which he evokes inadvertently while trying to suggest an imminent profusion of flowers:

> In the sweet airs of morn;
> One almost looks to see the very street
> Grow purple at his feet.
>
> (p. 123)

This line of interpretation might seem more of a stretch, if the poem did not then turn directly to the topic of "war and crime" and "the call of Death" in "the west-wind's aromatic breath." Spring may awaken the blood in trees and the song of birds, but she will also "rouse, for all her tranquil charms, / A million men to arms" (p. 124). Then, the fields will run with real blood rather than the flushed hues of dawn and the dark red of just-unfolded maple leaves: metaphors will become material truths.

> There shall be deeper hues upon her plains
> Than all her sunlit rains,
> And every gladdening influence around,
> Can summon from the ground.

> Oh! standing on this desecrated mould,
> Methinks that I behold,
> Lifting her bloody daisies up to God,
> Spring kneeling on the sod,

> And calling, with the voice of all her rills,
> Upon the ancient hills
> To fall and crush the tyrants and the slaves
> Who turn her meads to graves.

> (p. 124)

Even the daisies will be spattered with blood, and the personifications of nature which so blithely populated Timrod's earlier poems will pray to God for an end to slaughter (and perhaps an end to his previous rhetorical strategies).

Though it may seem at first reading that Timrod blames the North alone for the bloodshed in the final stanza, his ambiguity matches that of his Northern counterparts Dickinson and Allen. Conventionally the Civil War-era rhetoric of the South depicts Northerners as tyrants and white Southerners as slaves; a Georgia secessionist, for example, proclaimed "we are either slaves in the Union or freemen out of it."[32] If Timrod means to suggest that Northerners, along with actual Southern slaves, are responsible for the carnage, he has mixed that conventional metaphoric use of "slave" with its literal meaning. The slippage leaves the phrase open to overlapping interpretations, the most obvious being that the Northern "tyrants" and the white Southerners they "enslave" are equally responsible for turning the earth into a repository of death, destroying the animating cycle of death and birth in balance. If Timrod is blaming Northerners and the literal slaves who populate the Southern region, then he is explicitly admitting servitude in his tribute to Southern purity when he very clearly avoided the topic in "Ethnogenesis" and "The Cotton Boll." And if the slaves are literal slaves, then the fact that their graves are overwhelming Spring's meads suggests that white Southerners, again, have blood on their hands. There's no way around it; death and injustice have infiltrated Timrod's vision of Southern righteousness. He cannot, no matter how hard he tries, make the Confederate cause as pure as the driven snow, or as the cultivated cotton.

ELIZA RICHARDS

The beginning of a complex pattern emerges that offers insight into the aesthetics and ethics of violence in US Civil War poetry, North and South. When confronted with the fact of violent, divisive conflict, Allen, Dickinson, and Timrod all look to the sky for explanation. Early in the war, Timrod, like Emerson before him, asserts the transformative power of the imagination; Emerson's night wind and Timrod's seasons both create a fleecy substance that covers the existing world and remakes it into an idealized wonderland. For Emerson, writing more than two decades before the war, that wonderland is created by a force described in militaristic terms that are clearly whimsical; Timrod, in 1861, more seriously enlists nature to fight for the Confederacy. There's a substantive difference between them, however. Emerson aestheticizes the weather in order to give shape to an abstract idea, while Timrod summons aesthetic power to vaporize commodities – cotton and slaves – and turn them into ethereal symbols. Cotton becomes a mode of communication analogous to the North's mass media networks; Timrod imagines cotton traveling far and wide, like tropical winds, touching people in foreign lands and converting them to the Southern cause. In 1861, Timrod in South Carolina, surrounded by the unspoken (unspeakable?) violence of slavery, which he seeks to justify without mentioning, turns slave labor into twilight in order to make present violence remote. He fails; dusky fingers and boastful smiles, however idealized, return us to the material subjects he begins to erase. Dickinson and Allen, at a distance from the war, conversely draw upon the weather to materialize the news of the battle front at home; winter's freezing temperatures and frozen precipitation bring the war home, in all its remoteness. By 1863, Timrod comes closer to their understanding of the ethical relation between materiality and metaphor. All three wartime poets, as distinguished from Emerson's earlier practice, show the ways that events shape perception as much as perception shapes events. Involuntarily, perhaps, the Civil War poets must leave themselves open to the elements and whatever they carry with them through the air.

NOTES

1 On the wartime functions of popular poetry see Alice Fahs, *The Imagined Civil War: Popular Literature of the North and South, 1861–1865* (Chapel Hill: University of North Carolina Press, 2001), Introduction through chapter 4. See also the "Introduction" to "*Words for the Hour*": *A New Anthology of Civil War Poetry*, ed. Faith Barrett and Cristanne Miller (Amherst: University of Massachusetts Press, 2005), pp. 1–16; and Faith Barrett, "Dickinson's War Poems in Discursive Context," in Mary Loeffelholz and Martha Nell Smith, eds., *A Companion to Emily Dickinson* (Malden, MA: Blackwell, 2008), pp. 107–32.

2 Oliver Wendell Holmes, "Bread and the Newspaper," *Atlantic Monthly* (September 1861), 346–52. On US Civil War media, see Menahem Blondheim. *News over the Wires: The Telegraph and the Flow of Public Information in America, 1844 to 1897* (Cambridge, MA: Harvard University Press, 1994); Joshua Brown, *Beyond the Lines: Pictorial Reporting, Everyday Life, and the Crisis of Gilded Age America* (Berkeley: University of California Press, 2002); Brayton Harris, *Blue and Gray in Black and White: Newspapers in the Civil War* (Washington: Brassey's, 1999); and W. Fletcher Thompson, Jr., *The Image of War: the Pictorial Reporting of the American Civil War* (New York: A. S. Barnes & Co., 1960). On poetry's relation to journalism in the period, see Eliza Richards, "Correspondent Lines: Poetry, Journalism, and the U. S. Civil War," *ESQ: A Journal of the American Renaissance*, 54.1–4 (2008), 145–70.

3 On this topic see Eliza Richards, " 'How News Must Feel When Traveling': Dickinson and Civil War Media," in Loeffelholz and Smith, eds., *A Companion to Emily Dickinson*, pp. 156–60.

4 Julia Ward Howe, "Battle Hymn of the Republic," *Atlantic Monthly* (February 1862),145; Julia Ward Howe, *Reminiscences, 1819–1899* (Boston: Houghton Mifflin, 1899), pp. 275–76.

5 In his book-length treatment of the subject, Timothy Sweet finds that Walt Whitman's work naturalizes Civil War violence through pastoral rhetoric; Herman Melville, in contrast, exposes and critiques the conversion of bodies into symbols of patriotic sacrifice via the pastoral. *Traces of War: Poetry, Photography, and the Crisis of the Union* (Baltimore: Johns Hopkins University Press, 1990). See also Faith Barrett, "Addresses to a Divided Nation: Images of War in Emily Dickinson and Walt Whitman," *Arizona Quarterly*, 61.4 (2005), 67–99.

6 Lawrence I. Berkove, " 'A Slash of Blue!': An Unrecognized Emily Dickinson War Poem," *The Emily Dickinson Journal*, 10.1 (2001), 1–8. J. D. McClatchy includes Dickinson's "aurora borealis" poem "Of Bronze – and Blaze –" in a collection of Civil War poetry, *Poets of the Civil War* (Library of America, 2005), p. 158.

7 Mary A. Favret, *War at a Distance: Romanticism and the Making of Modern Warfare* (Princeton University Press, 2010).

8 Anon., "Weather in War," *Atlantic Monthly* (May 1862), 593.

9 George Frederickson, "Uncle Tom and the Anglo-Saxons: Romantic Racialism in the North," in Elizabeth Ammons, ed., *Uncle Tom's Cabin: A Norton Critical Edition* (New York: Norton, 2010), pp. 464–73.

10 See David Cody, "Blood in the Basin: The Civil War in Emily Dickinson's 'The name – of it – is "Autumn" – '," *The Emily Dickinson Journal*, 12.1 (2003), 25–52. Also Barrett, "Addresses," 77–84.

11 Favret, *War at a Distance*, chapter 3.

12 See, for example, William Cullen Bryant, "The Return of the Birds," *Atlantic Monthly* (July 1864), 37.

13 Mary A. Favret, "Still Winter Falls," *PMLA* (October 2009), 1548–61.

14 "Introduction," in *The Collected Poems of Henry Timrod: A Variorum Edition*, ed. Edd Winfield Parks and Aileen Wells Parks (Athens: University of Georgia Press, 1965), pp. 1–14. "Ethnogenesis," line 24.

15 Ralph Waldo Emerson, "Snow-Storm," in *Collected Poems and Translations* (New York: Library of America, 1994), p. 34.

16 Ralph Waldo Emerson, "The Poet," in *Essays and Lectures* (New York: Library of America, 1983), p. 450.

17 Elizabeth Akers Allen, "Snow," *Atlantic Monthly* (February 1864), 200–01. Subsequent references appear in parentheses in the text.

18 Mrs. Paul Akers, "Spring at the Capital," *Atlantic Monthly* (June 1863), 766–67.

19 Drew Gilpin Faust, *This Republic of Suffering: Death and the Civil War* (New York: Knopf, 2008), chapter 3, "Burying."

20 Emily Dickinson, letter no.280 to T.W. Higginson, February 1863: "War feels to me an oblique place." *The Letters of Emily Dickinson*, ed. Thomas Johnson (Cambridge, MA: Belknap Press of Harvard University Press, 1958), p. 423.

21 Poem no.291, *The Poems of Emily Dickinson. Variorum Edition.* vol. 1, ed. R. W. Franklin (Cambridge, MA: Belknap Press of Harvard University Press, 1998), pp. 311–12.

22 Faust, *This Republic of Suffering*, pp. 82–98.

23 For a discussion of this trope, see Richards, "Correspondent Lines," 144–69.

24 Jack Capps, *Emily Dickinson's Reading, 1836 to 1886* (Cambridge, MA: Harvard University Press, 1966). Pope's *Homer*, Milton's *Paradise Lost*, and Cowper's *Poems* were in her father's library (p. 12); Capps lists Thomson's *The Seasons* in Appendix A, his annotated bibliography of Emily Dickinson's reading (p. 187).

25 *The Iliad of Homer*, trans. Alexander Pope, with notes by the Reverend Theodor Alois Buckley (1899), Book 12, lines 330–32. Accessed through Project Gutenberg www.gutenberg.org/files/6130/6130.txt

26 http://en.wikipedia.org/wiki/Alabaster

27 Faust, *This Republic of Suffering*, pp. 70–74.

28 "Dickinson's gory but decorative battlefield landscapes satirically undermine the idea that women writers lack the authority or perspectives to represent combat. At the same time, these poems suggest that the romantic lexicon – widely used by American poets during the Civil War – is inadequate to the task of representing battlefield suffering." Barrett, "Dickinson's War Poems in Discursive Context," p. 109.

29 Timothy Sweet offers the most sustained critique of pastoral rhetoric in Civil War literary and photographic representations: "Where Whitman and the photographers draw a pastoral or picturesque frame around the war, and thereby enlist nature in the service of legitimating its violence, Melville's battle-pieces reflect critically on any such attempt to naturalize the war or its ideological implications." Sweet, *Traces of War*, p. 7.

30 "If we choose to read Dickinson's 'This Is My Letter to the World' as a commentary on the difficulties of being a woman writer during a time of war, then the speaker's insistence that her work conveys nothing but 'the simple news that nature told' takes on a particular irony in light of some of Dickinson's Civil War poems." Barrett, "Addresses to a Divided Nation," 79.

31 Henry Timrod, *Poems* (Boston: Ticknor and Fields, 1860), pp. 92, 180. All subsequent quotations from Timrod's poetry are from this edition.

32 Quoted in James M. McPherson, *Battle Cry of Freedom: The Civil War Era* (New York: Ballantine Books, 1988), p. 241.

7

ELIZABETH RENKER

The "Twilight of the Poets" in the era of American realism, 1875–1900

The terms "poetry" and "realism" have a complex and mostly oppositional relationship in American literary histories of the post-Civil War era. The conventional account holds that realism, the major literary "movement" of the era, developed apace in prose fiction, while poetry, stuck in a hopelessly idealist late-Romantic mode, languished and stagnated. By this all-too-familiar account, American poetry produced little of value between Whitman and Dickinson and the modernists. Poetry is thus almost entirely absent from scholarship on American realism except as the emblem of realism's opposite: a desiccated genteel tradition. The long life of this tale in twentieth-century criticism has afforded it, until very recently, factual status, but its core elements did not in fact arise retrospectively from an impartial scholarly distance. Rather, the twentieth-century critics who promulgated this account reproduced the elements of a story already circulating during the last quarter of the nineteenth century. In the pages that follow, I will trace the narrative that poetry was in its "twilight" as it emerged in the last quarter of the nineteenth century, serving a particular ideology of poetry among elite poets and in highbrow literary periodicals; I will also argue that poetic counter-discourses in the era itself invalidate the standard narratives about postbellum poetry and its relation to realism.[1]

Nancy Glazener has penetratingly argued that "realism" was an institutional product of a cluster of highbrow periodicals she calls "the *Atlantic* Group."[2] The "twilight of the poets" also became a lively topic circulating in this elite literary sphere.[3] After Edmund Clarence Stedman published the term in 1885, it spread rapidly through literary culture and became an almost instant catchphrase, a sensationalist coin that writers enjoyed trading amidst their broader discussions about the degraded literary status, or status in general, of the modern era. It is crucial to my argument that we distinguish between the social role this concept played and actual poetic practices, including poetic practices that Stedman and his literary sphere did not and could not recognize as "poetry."

The twilight simulacrum that Stedman created from his highbrow perch in fact bore little relation to the lively life of poetry in other spheres of literacy. As Joan Shelley Rubin has shown, the genre of poetry was vital to American culture at all social levels during this era.[4] This was also the quarter-century during which, to cite only the three instances I will discuss, workers from across the broad terrain of American labor wrote, sang, recited, printed, and distributed thousands of original poems and songs advocating the cause of workers against capital; Sarah Piatt published scores of periodical poems as well as more than a dozen volumes of poetry; and Herman Melville published three of his four published poetry volumes (*Clarel* in 1876; *John Marr and Other Sailors* in 1888; and *Timoleon* in 1891). (Melville and Piatt both knew Stedman personally and would have been aware of his well-known views about poetry.)[5] Lifting this handful of examples out of a much more extensive literary field, I will argue that they represent an array of kinds of poetic production that show "realism" arising not exclusively in prose fiction, but within the genre of poetry itself. Thus, the twilight of the poets was not the twilight of the genre, but the twilight of a particular elite definition of the genre. The poets I discuss were not part of a formally recognizable "realist poetics" movement or a realist "war" of the kind Howells launched on behalf of realist fiction. Their divergent practices demonstrate that an array of poets was writing across social classes and levels of literacy, sometimes publishing in popular venues, sometimes in elite publications, and other times only in coterie fashion or not at all. The larger point is that poetry had an active and vital social life in this period that literary history has only recently begun to explore, one that specifically points to a new history of American realist poetry.

One "problem of definition," to invoke Michael Davitt Bell's formulation,[6] is that the term "realism" itself, however foundational to Americanist literary narratives, is so slippery as to be verging on incoherence. It is nevertheless clear that advocates of "realism" in the postbellum period used the term to situate their artistic ethos against a competing aesthetic variously signified by the terms "romance," "ideality" and "Truth." This idealist "Truth" designated not the truth of fact – the realists often claimed "fact," or had it attributed (often derogatorily) to them – but a form of transcendent truth that derived its meaning from beyond the world of material circumstance. Literary discourse in the period often simply assumed that the genre of poetry was inherently idealist. Since it presumably operated instead with reference to the better, higher, superior world of eternal and transcendent spirit rather than to material or actual fact, poetry was construed to be, by definition, antithetical to realism. The force of this assumption is one we can also hear in the era's use of the adjective "poetic," which did not always mean the genre of poetry *per se*. It described any form of writing that was imaginative and romantic, "romantic" in the sense of counterfactual or, as Nathaniel Hawthorne famously defined the genre of romance, as outside the world of everyday reality.[7] Like the "poetic," "poetry," in its more specific generic sense of measured verse, was expected to express ideal standards of perfection and excellence. What was to become of poetry, then, in an age of realists?

One of the locations in literary culture where we can anchor the genre debate in the last quarter of the nineteenth century is in Stedman's writings. A banker who ran a brokerage firm in New York, he was also one of the most distinguished men of letters of the era, a poet as well as the author of a series of influential anthologies and histories of British and American poetry.[8] In 1898, Theodore Dreiser reviewed his career in *The New York Times* and called him "the foremost of American critics."[9] Stedman published the term "twilight of the poets" in 1885, both in an essay by that title in *Century Illustrated Magazine* and in his book *Poets of America*, which appeared the same year. In 1875, his book *Victorian Poets* had already characterized the state of poetry with metaphors of "sunset," but it was the term "twilight" as he used it in 1885 that would then run rampant through literary discourse of the era and persist throughout Americanist literary criticism of the next century.[10]

Stedman's lament clearly bears no relation to the quantity of poetry the era produced and consumed, which was in fact prodigious.[11] Washington Gladden's article "The Poetic Outlook" commented in 1885, "Never before was there a time when so many people of both sexes had the knack of garnishing some sort of measure with some sort of rhymes."[12] Edmund Gosse argued that the problem modern poetry faced was that too many poets, including all the dead poets who "have forfeited their copyright," were flooding the market. Since new poets expected publication rights and royalties, while the dead poets were free, the new poets stood to lose in the marketplace contest. For Stedman, the twilight problem was not one of quantity, but of kind. He defines the "poetic" as "ideal literature"[13] and defines "the ideal" as that which, "though not made with hands of artificers, is eternal on the earth as in the heavens, because it is inherent in the soul."[14] A subtitle to his 1875 book *Victorian Poets* put it succinctly. Stedman called the contemporary phenomenon the "Embarrassment of the idealists."[15] He named the primary threats to poetry emerging both outside and inside the world of literature: science and realism.

The term "science" has its own complex discursive history; for present purposes it is important to note that the word was on all lips at this time as a rough synonym for modern knowledge. The term appears across the spectrum of American discourse, along with endless questions and claims about the implications of science for the age.[16] Stedman assessed the clash between science and poetry as a clash between kinds of mental activity. The rise of science led people to know things in a new way, in consequence of which they could no longer receive poetry as they had in the past. As Stedman put it, now "they KNOW better."[17] In other words, discourses other than poetry now met the desire for knowledge as the age conceived it, and it was unclear what need poetry would meet – if any – in this new order of things.

"Realism" was Stedman's term for poetry's primary opponent within the literary field. He noted that, until recently, "the imagination, paradoxical as it may seem, has been most heightened and sustained by the contemplation of natural objects, rather as they seem to be than as we know they are. For to the pure and absorbed spirit it is the ideal only that seems real; as a lover adores the image and simulacrum of his mistress, pictured to his inner consciousness, more than the very self and substance of her being."[18] (We will have cause to return to his metaphor of woman presently.) John Tomsich points out that the genteel writers were dedicated to expressing "the beautiful" – not "the real."[19] Indeed, Stedman hoped that "the phase of minute realism and analysis through which modern literature is passing" would come to its end, so that poetry could rebound after the realist mode had passed.[20] Practically speaking, of course, this ethos of idealist poetry was one that powerful literary figures like Stedman had the means to enforce. As Tomsich points out, "The genteel authors used their positions on the pre-eminent Eastern literary magazines – *Harper's*, *The Atlantic Monthly*, *Scribner's*, and *The Century* – to dominate the literary audience."[21] Stedman's friend Thomas Bailey Aldrich, for example, also a well-known poet, succeeded William Dean Howells as editor of *The Atlantic Monthly* in 1881. Stedman upheld Aldrich among contemporary poets "at the head of the younger art-school ... a poet of inborn taste, a votary of the beautiful."[22] Upon assuming the editorship at *The Atlantic*, Aldrich wrote to Stedman about their mutual views about poetry:

> I find it devilish difficult to get good poems for the *maga*. Our old singers have pretty much lost their voices, and the new singers are so few! My ear has not caught any new note since 1860. By Jove! I wish there were a nest of young birds in full song now! I don't call *you* a young bird. You are the only one of our day and generation who is doing anything at present. In your letter you speak of having written two poems. I wish you'd sent them to me. I am slowly making up my mind to publish none but incontestably fine poems in the *Atlantic* – which means only about four poems per year. What do you

think of that plan? If you could see the files of bosh sent to this office, you'd be sick at heart.[23]

Aldrich's metaphors of "singers," "birds," and "song" is the language of idealist romantic poetry that both he and Stedman spoke. Later, his own poem "At the Funeral of a Minor Poet" would imagine the late nineteenth century as a funereal era "where every nest / Is emptied of its music and its wings."[24]

Stedman's lament that poetry had lost its spirit of ideality in an age of science and realism received impassioned support in the culture of letters. His essay and its title rapidly suffused literary culture. Within weeks of its publication, a reviewer in *The Christian Union* wrote: "The poet is to lift men into his own atmosphere … to disclose the imperishable Ideal for the revelation of which the need is all the greater when the frost of materialism is blasting the finest growths of purpose and character."[25] James Herbert Morse also reviewed Stedman's essay, noting that "Realism has come to stay … and poetry has passed into its twilight."[26] An array of periodical essays responded to Stedman directly; poets wrote poems called "The Twilight of the Poets" dedicated to him. Edgar Fawcett's 1886 poem "The Twilight of the Poets," written for *The Literary World* "on reading his *Poets of America*," addressed Stedman as "Poet, though twilight, as your clear gaze marks";[27] Charles S. Greene's sonnet by the same title, published the next month in *Overland Monthly*, addressed Stedman as "gentle critic," holding up Stedman's poetic voice even "as from our sight / The great bards go, or cease to sing the tales / Of magic beauty."[28] (The word "gentle" here relates etymologically to "genteel," both of which, as Tomsich's excellent study of gentility demonstrates, designated an elevated class position, and in American usage denoted politeness, good breeding, and refined manners.)[29] Hamilton Wright Mabie agreed with Stedman's assessment of the twilight interval, arguing that the realist fiction of the era denied the "spiritual facts" and "spiritual laws" that lie behind the actual conditions upon which realists narrowly focused. Realism, Mabie writes, "does more than ignore these things; it denies them," and, in so doing, it "empties the world of the Ideal."[30]

The "twilight" sensation took on a life of its own as a general description of the era, routinely popping up in references that no longer explicitly connected the term to Stedman. The month after Stedman's essay hit print, an article in *The Nassau Literary Magazine* entitled "American Poetry" passively referred to "an epoch which has been called the Twilight of the Poets."[31] In June 1885, a review of recent verse in *Overland Monthly* similarly cited "this 'twilight of the poets' " without mentioning Stedman's names as did an 1887 review of James Russell Lowell.[32] While serving as President in 1905, Theodore Roosevelt reviewed Edwin Arlington Robinson's volume *The Children of the Night* and opened with the claim, "The 'twilight of the poets' has been especially gray in America."[33] Thus a term that began with a particular elite poet with a particular definition of the genre had assumed the status of fact. One of the most peculiar ironies of the twilight is that poets like Robinson who explicitly used twilight language, and who were hailed both then (as by Roosevelt) and later (as in the long history of twentieth-century Americanist scholarship, for example) as its saviors, themselves derived part of their credibility from addressing the poetic era in Stedman's terms.

Years later, cartoons ran with the headline "The Twilight of the Poets," mocking poets as antiquated or as more generally irritating and unwelcome, a hostility specifically connected to the poets' alleged disconnect from modern life.[34] A cartoon in *Puck* depicts a young man who courts a woman by quoting Horace, and then provides what he pedantically calls an inadequate translation of his own flirtation. She remarks that he would better suit her grandmother. This particular joke plays on one of the questions hovering over poetry's putative twilight: whether it was, at this modern time, simply a form of expression that had become obsolete.[35] A cartoon in the 1893 edition of *Life* depicts a conversation between an "Editor" and a "Canvasser." The latter is selling a "Spring Poet Ejector," which the Editor declines to buy. He says he's quite happy to do the job manually – that is, of throwing poets out of his office. The pun here – on "spring poets" who write romantically about the idyllic season of the year, and on a modern machine that works via a spring mechanism to eject those same poets – is especially apt in the period's discourse about whether poems can keep up with modernity. When a 1900 article in *Colman's Rural World* entitled "Agriculture" announced, "In America the last quarter of a century has been called the twilight of the poets and the high noon of practical men. Great accomplishments in agricultural production and stock breeding are not the result of chance or accident,"[36] it showed the broad currency of Stedman's phrase. In this case, Stedman was used against himself, not to rejuvenate the ideal poetry that is "not made with hands of artificers"[37] but to support the enterprises of the "practical men" of the world of work who might be more interested in inventing spring poet ejectors.

The charges that realism and science had thrown poetry into its twilight still preoccupied Aldrich in his poem, "Realism":

> Romance beside his unstrung lute
> Lies stricken mute.
> The old-time fire, the antique grace,

You will not find them anywhere.
To-day we breathe a commonplace,
Polemic, scientific air:
We strip Illusion of her veil;
We vivisect the nightingale
To probe the secret of his note.
The Muse in alien ways remote
Goes wandering.[38]

Aldrich presents a portrait of the Muse wandering amidst the "alien ways" of a realist era that has left "Romance" stricken. Aldrich's poem is formally perfect, right down to its perfect invocation of imperfection. An aabcbcddee rhyme scheme breaks only in the final, odd-numbered, unrhymed line, and the pattern of iambic tetrameter breaks only in two strategic places: mute romance lies stricken in line 2 and the poetic muse "Goes wandering" in line 11, both in metrically truncated lines of iambic dimeter.

Aldrich envisioned a death scene for the "twilight poet" in his 1891 poem, "At the Funeral of a Minor Poet." The title character, although "minor," "had at least ideals" (line 24), Aldrich laments, contrary to the reigning aesthetic of the age:

The mighty Zolaistic Movement now
Engrosses us – a miasmatic breath
Blown from the slums. We paint life as it is,
The hideous side of it, with careful pains,
Making a god of the dull Commonplace.

(lines 27–31)

Aldrich's disgust with the "Zolaistic Movement" of realism and its focus on the "dull Commonplace" echoes through other contemporary critiques of realism. In 1885, Mabie complained that "Realism is crowding the world of fiction with commonplace people; people whom one would positively avoid coming in contact with in real life."[39] Defining the genre of poetry as he did, Aldrich would not have engaged the sphere of society he derided as "slums."

Yet the sphere of society that made Aldrich shudder was in fact producing its own vernacular form of poetry. The labor song-poets, working entirely outside Aldrich's and Stedman's institutional sphere, might themselves have served as "hideous" realist subjects of the kind Aldrich derided. Certainly their social kin figured as subjects for Theodore Dreiser, for example, when both Carrie and Hurstwood navigate the world of work and labor strife, and of Edith Wharton, when Lily Bart faces the prospect of making hats for a living rather than wearing them. Surveying working-class culture in the

postbellum era, historian Clark D. Halker chronicles the extensive production and circulation of what he calls "song-poems," a genre of labor songs
and labor poems that were "written, composed, sung, recited, declaimed,
printed, and distributed throughout the country."[40] Between 1865 and 1895,
"the apex of indigenous worker song-poetry in the United States," forty-
three publications printed nearly 2,600 original song-poems in the English
language.[41] Labor historian Philip S. Foner's foundational *American Labor
Songs of the Nineteenth Century*, a collection of more than 550 examples
of the songs published by the nineteenth-century labor press, comments,
"There is no way of knowing just how many of the songs written for the
labor press were actually sung. The chances are that many never got off
the printed page and entered oral tradition. But from evidence in reports of
meetings, conventions, strikes, and political demonstrations, enough did to
warrant the conclusion that a fairly large number were sung by the workers of the time."[42] Well-known folk songs, hymns, and minstrel tunes often
provided the tunes to which workers sang the labor song-poems.[43] Perhaps
printed as poems in one place and as songs in another, or printed as poems
and later turned into songs, and commonly published anonymously or under
a pseudonym, the song-poems were generically versatile texts that served a
multiplicity of social functions.

Sorting through this complex archive, Halker identifies ninety-three
labor song-poets, the majority of whom were white men who "earned their
livelihoods in working-class occupations," primarily as skilled workers.[44]
Although exhaustive data on these individuals remains elusive, Halker concludes that many were immigrants, especially Irish, Scottish, and German
workers. He argues that the Gilded-Age labor movement was more international in nature than labor history has typically understood, speaking across nationalities in the USA and in a language that recalled ties to
European labor markets.[45] A network of cultural institutions and activities
for workers, including regular meetings, concerts, picnics, dinners, parades,
balls, dramas, lectures, debates, workers' libraries, and study groups, grew
along with steady protests by, and progress for, workers in the 1880s.[46] The
song-poems were a vital and ready part of this culture of labor.

Indeed, 1885 – the year Stedman's phrase took fire – was what Halker
calls "a banner year" for American labor. "Twenty years of resentment
found an outlet as workers went on the offensive. Strikes erupted throughout the country and workers joined organized labor by the hundreds of
thousands."[47] While serially publishing William Dean Howells's *The Rise of
Silas Lapham* this same year, *The Century* stopped the presses because of a
passage in the novel about labor trouble that used the word "dynamite."[48] It
might have been twilight for Stedman's poets, but one song-poem saw signs

of morning light. "The Light is Breaking," published in the *Denver Labor Enquirer* in 1887 (to be set to the tune of "The Morning Light is Breaking") announced:

> The glorious light is breaking.
> The darkness flights away,
> The people are awak'ning
> To see a brighter day,
> From ev'ry hill and valley
> Thro'out earth's wide domain,
> The friends of Labor rally
> To break the tyrant's chain.
>
> The freedman's tramp is sounding,
> Its echoes roll along,
> By hundreds and by thousands
> The people join the song.
> Now joyous acclamations
> Come rising on the gale;
> No more with lamentations
> The people will prevail.[49]

The culture that spawned the labor song-poems was to confront its own twilight. Workers challenged industrial capitalism with some success until the defeat of the American Railway Union at Pullman in 1894.[50] While we now see this history from the standpoint of its ultimate defeat, in the 1880s it might have looked as if light were breaking – or night were falling, depending on your stance.

Despite their invisibility in literary history, workers and their song-poems were not entirely insulated in their own time from poets in other class positions. For example, Halker cites Ohioian Donn Piatt as one of only two unequivocally upper-class labor song-poets of the era.[51] Operating from a vantage opposite Mabie and Aldrich, Donn called upon literature to embrace contact with subjects and people these others rejected. Donn was a lawyer, judge, Civil War veteran, publisher of the Washington, DC newspaper *The Capital* (which a contemporary called "the furthest extreme of free-lance criticism" of the federal government[52]), and relative by marriage to Sarah Piatt, whose portrait is painted on the ceiling of his home in West Liberty, Ohio. He was cousin to her husband, J. J. Piatt, a well-known genteel poet of the era.[53] He published his labor poem, "The Rich and Proud they Pass Me By," in the radical labor publication *John Swinton's Paper* in 1885.[54] Swinton had resigned from a lucrative position as managing editor at the *New York Sun* in 1883 to found his four-page weekly, whose goal was "to raise the social question, and to induce the working people to bring their interests in politics."⁵⁵ The paper flagged Piatt's poem as an "original" offering; in the lingo of the era, this indicated that he wrote it for Swinton's paper, rather than that the paper had clipped and copied it from another publication:

The rich and proud they pass me by,
　　For I am poorly born,
A workman rough, but naught care I
　　For all their lofty scorn.
I feel my manhood in me stir
　　No envy of their greed,
For Christ was bred a carpenter,
　　And God our work decreed.

My humble home is by the road,
　　Where my dear ones abide;
I care not for the rich abode,
　　Where dwells dishonest pride;
For peace and love breathe o'er us all,
　　And we can spurn the scorn
That looked down on the humble stall
　　Where Christ himself was born.

I know that from our dreary toil
　　They steal their silks and lace;
Their very break, wrought from the soil,
　　We give them, with their grace;
And man must sweat where fraud prevails,
　　And theft holds high command,
For cunning wins, while labor fails,
　　Throughout the freest land.

Let not despair our souls enthrall,
　　For God is with the right,
And we who feed and foster all
　　As readily can smite,
When gaunt privation haunts the den
　　And children cry for bread,
We wait the painted vermin then,
　　When labor strikes them dead.

We patient beasts, with human hearts,
　　Can bear the burden long,
But comes a time when nature starts
　　To right the cruel wrong,
As when miasma fills the air,

With fever's fearful train,
The thunder's roll, the lightning's glare
And storms come on amain.

In Donn's poetic vision, the "miasma," a word that Aldrich would use a few years later to deride the underclass, is nature's warning to the greedy rich, the "painted vermin" who have called upon themselves a coming storm of retribution. Donn's non-fiction also advocated social change on behalf of the working class.[56]

Sarah Piatt's poems occupy a similarly fascinating and layered position in the literary marketplace. The Piatt archive includes eighteen published volumes and at least 500 poems in over thirty periodicals and newspapers.[57] Paula Bennett exactingly traces her complex relation to genteel poetry by observing which poems appear in genteel publications and which poems, often political ones, appear in periodicals with a distinct market position, such as Donn's *The Capital* (Sarah published seventy-two poems here) or *The Independent* (a New York City weekly whose subtitle, "Devoted to the Consideration of Politics, Social and Economic Tendencies, History, Literature, and the Arts," indicates its socially progressive agenda on issues such as slavery and women's suffrage; here she published sixty-nine poems).[58]

Sarah's corpus includes a body of poems about labor, poverty, and class positions, both at home and internationally, with particular focus on Ireland and France. Matthew Giordano trenchantly assesses the way that her awareness of her periodical venues lies at the heart of "The Palace-Burner: A Picture in a Newspaper" (published in *The Independent*, 1872),[59] which Bennett rightfully identifies as her signature poem at this first stage of her entry into the canon.[60] Indeed, just as the labor song-poets trace lines of affiliation with the transatlantic contexts of European labor markets and immigration, here we find Sarah tensely aware of a class revolt across the sea, when urban workers in Paris established an insurrectionary government that came to be known as the Paris Commune. The Commune lasted from March 18 to May 28, 1871; when it was over, government forces executed over 17,000 people, including women and children.[61] Sarah's American peers energetically discussed the uprising, whether from positive, negative, or ambivalent stances, as a "revolution, made in the name and for the interests of the working-men," an "emancipation of the lower classes with which the hearts of the populace have been fired."[62]

Bennett has identified the illustration to which Sarah's subtitle for "The Palace-Burner" refers. Appearing in the 8 July 1871 issue of *Harper's Weekly*, it accompanied an article entitled "La Pétroleuse,"[63] the newly coined term for the figure of the female "petroleum-thrower" who had set fire to the city.[64] Other articles also obsessed over the revolutionary women in particular, describing them as "warrior-women," "fighting women," and "Amazons" of "courage and ferocity."[65] The anonymous author of "La Pétroleuse" tried to imagine the situation that had led the woman in the illustration to "crimes" that in turn resulted in her execution:

> Can we not imagine that such a poor creature, demoralized by want of work, and with her brain weakened by slow starvation, would hail the establishment of the Commune as a sort of millennium which would cure all her troubles, and would therefore burst into a fury of uncontrollable mania upon its violent suppression? Though the hand of this woman lighted the flame which burned some of the finest buildings of Paris, she is possibly not the most guilty author of the conflagration. Whose were the miserable jealousies and ambitions which within twelve months have converted her from a respectable woman into a Pétroleuse? Other people, who are among the loudest in condemning her, may have to answer this question some day before a tribunal at which all secrets will be made known.[66]

Bennett points out that both this article and Sarah's poem exhibit "ambivalent sympathy" for the palace-burner.[67] In Sarah's poem, a dramatic dialogue, a mother and son discuss the illustration, which fascinates the boy. The mother's initial horror at her son's attraction to this "fierce creature of the Commune" (line 34) opens into her admiration for this woman as "A being finer than my soul, I fear" (line 36). As Bennett points out, the poem breaches "the wall that presumably insulates the private from the public sphere," insisting that domestic virtue is not coterminous with social virtue and thus overturning a core principle of sentimental literature in the nineteenth-century United States.[68] Recall that Stedman had imagined poetry's opposition to realism by way of a heavily charged metaphor of the woman: "For to the pure and absorbed spirit it is the ideal only that seems real; as a lover adores the image and simulacrum of his mistress, pictured to his inner consciousness, more than the very self and substance of her being." Sarah juxtaposes the palace-burner with the domestic, genteel woman who discovers, with increasing agitation, that her vision of herself as "Languid and worldly, with a dainty need / For light and music" (lines 19–20) is probably a fiction. The poem ends with a scene of double anxiety: that her son now believes the "fierce creature of the Commune here / So bright with bitterness and so serene" (lines 35–36) to be "finer" than she is – and that his assessment is accurate.

The Paris Commune remained a point of reference in the United States. In 1887, the Denver *Labor Enquirer* published "The Song of the Workers: Remembering the Martyrs of Paris in 1871," by Charles E. Markham of San

Francisco, whose opening stanza imagines the "martyrs of Paris" to be operating in silent communion with American workers:

> We drift along the streets and hear our masters in their mirth;
> They've slain our friends – our martyrs – but their spirits walk the Earth.
> They're moving in a silent realm of service for the race;
> Their voices now are sounding from a hush! And awful place.

Markham's song-poem concludes by imagining the "final battle" to right the "ancient wrong" against which the Paris "martyrs" fought.[69]

From an entirely different vantage, the poems of the still-neglected Melville constitute an active and searing counter-discourse to the poetic idealism of the era. Melville's relation to the public sphere differed from that of the labor song-poets and Donn and Sarah Piatt. While the labor song-poets wrote explicitly for public circulation, consumption, and performance, and Donn and Sarah Piatt published tactically in a range of venues, Melville moved over the course of his career from writing for a large public following to publishing his final two volumes of poetry in editions of only twenty-five copies. Giordano describes Melville's stance with respect to his career as poet as one that moved to a coterie model.[70] Although Roland Hagenbüchle, who still accepted the twilight narrative in 1984, argues that the "verbal self-awareness" characteristic of Emily Dickinson is the poetic quality "almost totally absent from the work of the 'interregnum' poets,"[71] this statement is only true if one has already delimited the archive according to the twilight narrative. Certainly Melville's "verbal self-awareness" equals, and possibly exceeds, that of Dickinson. Melville eviscerated the foundation of idealist verse as an art of deception. Whereas William Dean Howells approvingly quoted a British critic who lauded American realism as "the real Realism," presenting an "almost photographic delineation of actual life, with its motives, its impulses, its springs of action laid bare,"[72] for Melville, the real was not nearly this simple an ontological category. On these grounds, Melville's realism demolished the heart of idealism itself. In his metapoem, "The Aeolian Harp," he positions himself explicitly against the culturally powerful definition of poetry as "a strain ideal" and proposes instead that the music of poetry engage the domain of what he calls, by emphatic contrast, "the Real."[73] Melville's Aeolian harp, a central trope in the tradition of romantic poetry, shrieks and wails "the Real" rather than providing the soothing music of communion with nature.

This evisceration of poetry as "a strain ideal" in fact animates many of Melville's late and unpublished poems. One such undated, unpublished poem, "Fruit and Flower Painter," was earlier titled "Ashes of Roses."[74] The phrase "ashes of roses" was familiar in his day, originating from a scene in

Romeo and Juliet.[75] It became the title of numerous poems of the era, including one by Elaine Goodale Eastman published in Stedman's 1900 *An American Anthology.*[76] Imagining the "ashes of roses," or the powdery residue that remains after burning, in "Fruit and Flower Painter" Melville immolates the poetry of "ideality," one of whose central tropes was the image of the rose. (Indeed, at his death Melville left an entire unpublished volume meditating largely upon poetic roses. *Weeds and Wildings with a Rose or Two* figures Melville's own poems as "weeds and wildings" in stark contrast to the more highly cultivated poetry of roses.) My transcription indicates his revised version of "Fruit and Flower Painter" as it stands on the page:

> She dens in a garret
>   As void as a drum;
> In lieu of plum-pudding –
>   She paints the plum!
>
>   No use in one's grieving,
>   The shops you must suit:
>   Broken hearts are but potsherds –
>   Paint flowers and fruit!
>
> How whistles her garret,
>   A seine for the snows:
> She hums *Si fortuna*
>   And – paints the rose!
>
>   December is howling,
>   But feign it a flute:
>   Help on the deceiving –
>   Paint flowers and fruit![77]

This "fruit and flower painter" is, by trade, an artist of the beautiful, a beauty of mode and of subject matter that Melville polemically contrasts with her impoverished conditions. As a musical instrument, the drum in the second line works metapoetically; this instrument is a hollow one, void like the garret in which she "dens," "dens" denoting a cave hollowed out of the earth. The idea of a drumbeat resonates in the sound of the poem's two-beat lines.

In a poem about the empty physical spaces of drum, garret, and den, we also encounter an implied blank space, the artist's canvas. This representational surface is a blankness that the poem construes as a place, as the phrase "in lieu of" or literally "in place, room, or stead of" reminds us. While, on his blank page, Melville represents the artist's hollow spaces, on her empty canvas she paints "the plum" instead of the plum-pudding for which she yearns in the void of her hunger. She serves the deceptive function of art, converting the whistles and howls of a bitingly cold world into a pretense of rosy beauty.

Although the canvas in question depicts flowers and fruit, the drum, whistles, hum, howling, and flute all function by contrast at the level of the metapoetic. Webster tells us that the transitive verb "hum" means "to sing in a low voice."[78] Her singing implicitly compares her artistic enterprise to Melville's as poet. (He used voice terms in other poems in a tactically metapoetic manner as well; in the last line of "A Utilitarian View of the Monitor's Fight," for example, he converts "sing" to "singe," a highly strategic poetic immolation of the concept that beautiful poetry could be apt for "grimed" subjects.[79]) The song she hums – "O fortuna" – is itself a thirteenth-century medieval Latin complaint poem about fate. She sings one theme but paints another, pretending that the sound of the howling December is instead the beautiful sound of a flute. Therein lies, according to the poem, "the deceiving." The ambiguity of the imperative constructions "feign it a flute" and "Help on the deceiving" suggests both that the artist participates in the commonplace deceptions of commercial art, and, at the same time, that she deceives herself and is thus drawn into the economy of deception that she serves. The distance the poem finally establishes between her artistic enterprise and Melville's own, between the deceptive aesthetic of idealism, even with respect to nominally real subjects like fruit and flowers, is one way of accounting for Melville's shift in revision from a poem originally in the first person to a female third person.

The putative twilight interval, arising from a particular class- and institution-bound ideology of poetry, has operated hegemonically to distort the history of the genre in the United States. Even as Stedman was lamenting the dusk in the last quarter of the century, and well before Santayana scathingly critiqued "the Genteel Tradition" in 1911, the era itself had already generated a counter-poetics of realism. The twilight narrative has simply kept it in the shadows.

NOTES

1 In the past decade in particular, scholars have at last begun to rewrite the history of postbellum poetry. See, for example, Joan Shelley Rubin, *Songs of Ourselves: The Uses of Poetry in America* (Cambridge, MA: Harvard University Press, 2007); Paula Bennett, *Poets in the Public Sphere: The Emancipatory Project of American Women's Poetry 1800–1900* (Princeton Unversity Press, 2003); Paula Bennett, Karen L. Kilcup, and Philip Schweighauser, eds., *Teaching Nineteenth-Century American Poetry* (New York: Modern Language Association, 2007); *Palace-Burner: The Selected Poetry of Sarah Piatt*, ed. Paula Bennett (Urbana: University of Illinois Press, 2001); Angela Sorby, *Schoolroom Poets: Childhood, Performance, and the Place of American Poetry, 1865–1917* (Durham, NH: University of New Hampshire Press, 2005).

2 Nancy Glazener, *Reading for Realism: The History of a U.S. Literary Institution, 1850–1910* (Durham, NC: Duke University Press, 1997), p. 5.
3 Glazener focuses exclusively on fiction.
4 Rubin, *Songs of Ourselves*.
5 He included poems by both in his 1900 *An American Anthology, 1787–1900: Selections Illustrating the Editor's Critical Review of American Poetry in the Nineteenth Century* (New York: Greenwood, 1968). Stedman mentions Melville once, as one of a group of poets who show "native fire." See Edmund Clarence Stedman, *Poets of America* (Boston: Houghton, Mifflin, 1898), p. 49.
6 See Michael Davitt Bell, *The Problem of American Realism* (University of Chicago Press, 1993).
7 Hershel Parker, *Melville: The Making of the Poet* (Evanston, IL: Northwestern University Press, 2008), p. 12.
8 John Tomsich, *A Genteel Endeavor: American Culture and Politics in the Gilded Age* (Stanford University Press, 1971), p. 114.
9 "Edmund Clarence Stedman," *New York Times*, September 11, 1898, accessed March 14, 2010, www.nytimes.com.
10 The last chapter of *Poets of America*, there called "The Outlook," appeared in *Century Illustrated Magazine* under the title, "The Twilight of the Poets." His 1875 book *Victorian Poets* (Boston: Houghton, Mifflin, 1889), invokes the "sunset" metaphor, p. 27. Other related terms in *Poets of America* include "dusk," p. 436 and "interregnum," p. 457. The cultural appeal, at the ends or beginning of centuries, of "twilights" as a mark of historical consciousness is resonant again now, with Stephenie Meyer's *Twilight* series at the forefront of popular culture. Meyer's concept, she reports, came to her in a dream in 2003. http://en.wikipedia.org/wiki/Stephenie_Meyer.
11 See Rubin, *Songs of Ourselves* and Carlin T. Kindilien, *American Poetry in the Eighteen Nineties* (Providence, RI: Brown University Press, 1956), p. 5.
12 Washington Gladden, "The Poetic Outlook," *Century Illustrated Magazine*, December 1, 1885, accessed February 29, 2010, American Periodicals Series Online, ProQuest. http://search.proquest.com.proxy.lib.ohio-state.edu. This URL pertains to all further references to this online series.
13 Edmund Gosse, "Is Verse in Danger?" *Forum* (January 1891), accessed February 19, 2010, American Periodicals Series Online, ProQuest. Stedman, *Poets of America*, p. 471.
14 Stedman, *Poets of America*, p. 471.
15 Stedman, *Victorian Poets*, p. 16.
16 For example, Donn Piatt, to whom I turn later in this chapter, wrote, "The Christian mind of to-day, as it has been in the immediate past, is much disturbed by the claim of so-called science." He goes on to conclude, "They cannot be reconciled." Donn Piatt, *Sunday Meditations and Selected Prose Sketches* (Cincinnati: Robert Clarke & Co., Publishers, 1893), p. v. On the discursive history of the term "science" in this period, see Elizabeth Renker, *The Origins of American Literature Studies: An Institutional History* (Cambridge University Press, 2007).
17 Stedman, *Victorian Poets*, p. 17.
18 *Ibid.*, p. 18.
19 Tomsich, *Genteel Endeavor*, p. 130.
20 Stedman, *Poets of America*, p. xiii.

21 Tomsich, *Genteel Endeavor*, p. 120.
22 Stedman, *Poets of America*, p. 440.
23 Thomas Bailey Aldrich to Edmund Clarence Stedman, October 1881; MMS (Misc Mss), Box 8, MMS.169 ("My dear Edmund," and signed "Ever affectionately yours, T.B.A."), Rare Books and Manuscripts Library, The Ohio State University Libraries, Columbus, OH. See also Ferris Greenslet, *The Life of Thomas Bailey Aldrich* (Boston: Houghton Mifflin, 1908), p. 141.
24 Thomas Bailey Aldrich, "At the Funeral of a Minor Poet," in *The Sisters' Tragedy: with Other Poems, Lyrical and Dramatic* (Boston: Houghton Mifflin, 1891), pp. 27–30. Further quotations from this poem are in the form of parenthetical line references in the text.
25 "The Twilight of the Poets," *Christian Union*, September 17, 1885, accessed February 19, 2010, American Periodicals Series Online, ProQuest.
26 James Herbert Morse, "'The Twilight of the Poets'," *The Critic: A Literary Weekly, Critical and Eclectic*, October 10, 1885, accessed February 19, 2010, American Periodicals Series Online, ProQuest.
27 Edgar Fawcett, "'The Twilight of the Poets,'" line 1, *The Literary World: A Monthly Review of Current Literature*, April 3, 1886, accessed February 19, 2010, American Periodicals Series Online, ProQuest.
28 Charles S. Greene, "The Twilight of the Poets: To E. C. Stedman," lines 13, 7–9, *Overland Monthly and Out West Magazine*, May 1886, accessed February 19, 2010, American Periodicals Series Online, ProQuest.
29 Tomsich, *Genteel Endeavour*, p. 2.
30 Hamilton Wright Mabie, "A Typical Novel," *The Andover Review: A Religious and Theological Monthly*, November 1885, accessed February 19, 2010, American Periodicals Series Online, ProQuest.
31 Anonymous, "American Poetry," *The Nassau Literary Magazine*, October 1, 1885, accessed February 19, 2010, American Periodicals Series Online, ProQuest.
32 Anonymous, "Mr. Lowell at Sixty-nine," *The Critic: a Weekly Review of Literature and the Arts*, February 18, 1887 and "Recent Verse. – II," *Overland Monthly and Out West Magazine*, June 1886, accessed February 19, 2010, American Periodicals Series Online, ProQuest.
33 Theodore Roosevelt, "The Children of the Night," *Outlook*, August 12, 1905, accessed February 19, 2010, American Periodicals Series Online, ProQuest.
34 "The Twilight of the Poets," *Life*, June 15, 1893 (cartoon); "The Twilight of the Poets," *Puck*, December 22, 1886 (cartoon), both accessed February 19, 2010, American Periodicals Series Online, ProQuest.
35 Edmund Gosse, "Is Verse In Danger?" *Forum*, January 1, 1891, accessed February 19, 2010, American Periodicals Series Online, ProQuest.
36 "Agriculture," *Colman's Rural World*, July 4, 1900, accessed February 19, 2010, American Periodicals Series Online, ProQuest.
37 Stedman, *Poets of America*, p. 471.
38 Thomas Bailey Aldrich, "Realism," in *Later Lyrics* (Boston: Houghton Mifflin, 1896).
39 Hamilton Wright Mabie, "A Typical Novel," http://search.proquest.com.proxy.lib.ohio-state.edu
40 Clark D. Halker, *For Democracy, Workers, and God: Labor Song-Poems and Labor Protest, 1865–95* (Urbana: University of Illinois Press, 1991), p. 31.

41 *Ibid.*, pp. 2, 32.
42 Philip S. Foner, *American Labor Songs of the Nineteenth Century* (Urbana: University of Illinois Press, 1975), pp. xii; xiv.
43 Halker, *For Democracy*, p. 78.
44 *Ibid.*, pp. 48–49, 60–61.
45 *Ibid.*, pp. 60–61. He notes that black and female workers are "conspicuously absent" from his sample, indicating the exclusion of black workers from organized labor and the subordinate function of women in industry, p. 60.
46 *Ibid.*, p. 28.
47 *Ibid.*, p. 47.
48 Robert E. Spiller, *et al.*, *Literary History of the United States: History*, 3rd rev. edn. (New York: Macmillan, 1963), p. 953.
49 Quoted in Foner, *American Labor Songs*, p. 304.
50 Halker, *For Democracy*, p. 28.
51 In this section, I refer to Donn Piatt as "Donn" to avoid confusion with Sarah Piatt. See *ibid.*, p. 49, p. 63 note 3. Halker believes Donn's sympathies with workers to have been limited by his class position; see p. 49.
52 Charles Grant Miller, *Donn Piatt: His Work and His Ways* (Cincinnati: Robert Clarke & Co., 1893), p. 228.
53 Bennett, ed., *Palace-Burner*, p. 169 note 45.
54 Donn Piatt, "The Rich and Proud they Pass Me By," in *John Swinton's Paper*, October 18, 1885.
55 Quoted in Foner, *American Labor Songs*, p. 235.
56 Donn Piatt, *Sunday Meditations*.
57 Bennett, ed., *Palace-Burner*, pp. xvii–xviii; Bennett, *Poets in the Public Sphere*, p. 139.
58 Miller, *Donn Piatt*, p. 228; Bennett, ed., *Palace-Burner*, p. lv note 18; Bennett, *Poets*, p. 136.
59 Matthew Giordano, "'A Lesson From' the Magazines: Sarah Piatt and the Postbellum Periodical Poet," *American Periodicals*, 16.1 (2006), 23–51.
60 Bennett, ed., *Palace-Burner*, p. xli; Bennett, *Poets*, p. 137.
61 Bennett, ed., *Palace-Burner*, p. 167 note 28.
62 "The Second Siege of Paris: Described by an Eye-Witness," *Harper's Weekly*, July 15, 1871, accessed March 12, 2010, *HarpWeek*, The Ohio State University Libraries, Columbus, Ohio, http://app.harpweek.com.proxy.lib.ohio-state.edu.
63 "La Pétroleuse," *Harper's Weekly*, July 8, 1871, accessed March 12, 2010, *HarpWeek*, The Ohio State University Libraries, Columbus, Ohio, http://app.harpweek.com.proxy.lib.ohio-state.edu.
64 Bennett, ed., *Palace-Burner*, p. 167 note 28. Quotations from the poem "The Palace-Burner" are in the form of parenthetical line references in the text.
65 "Women of Montmartre and 'La Pétroleuse'," *Harper's Weekly*, July 8,1871, accessed March 12, 2010, *HarpWeek*, The Ohio State University Libraries, Columbus, Ohio, 2010. http://app.harpweek.com.proxy.lib.ohio-state.edu.
66 "La Pétroleuse."
67 Bennett, *Poets*, p. 136.
68 *Ibid.*, p. 138.
69 Foner, *American Labor Songs*, pp. 303–04.

70 Matthew Giordano, "Melville's Coterie Authorship in *John Marr and Other Sailors*," *Leviathan*, 9.3 (2007), 65–78.

71 Roland Hagenbüchle, ed., *American Poetry Between Tradition and Modernism, 1865–1914* (Regensburg: Pustet, 1984), p. 14.

72 William Dean Howells, *Editor's Study by William Dean Howells*, ed. J. W. Simpson (Troy, NY: Whitson Publishing Co., 1983), p. 266.

73 Elizabeth Renker, "Melville the Realist Poet," in Wyn Kelley, ed., *A Companion to Herman Melville* (Malden, MA: Blackwell, 2006), pp. 482–96.

74 "Fruit and Flower Painter" has been converted from the MS version in which it stood during Melville's life into print in three editions: *The Works of Herman Melville* (London: Constable, 1924), vol. XVI; *Collected Poems of Herman Melville*, Howard P. Vincent, ed. (Chicago: Packard and Company, 1947); *Herman Melville: Tales, Poems, and Other Writings*, John Bryant, ed. (New York: Modern Library, 2001). Each printing interprets Melville's handwriting and revisions differently.

75 *Herman Melville: Tales, Poems, and Other Writings*, p. 584.

76 *An American Anthology*, p. 701.

77 MS Am 188 (369.1 [5]). By permission of the Houghton Library, Harvard University.

78 Noah Webster, *An American Dictionary of the English Language*, rev. Chauncey A. Goodrich (New York: Harper & Brothers, 1847).

79 "A Utilitarian View of the Monitor's Fight," lines 30,3, in Bryant, ed., *Tales, Poems, and Other Writings*.

PART II

Individual authors

8

STEPHEN BURT

Longfellow's ambivalence

In 1837 Henry Wadsworth Longfellow was a professor of modern languages at Harvard, a hardworking teacher still growing into his new job. Three years later, after *Voices of the Night* (1839) and *Ballads and Other Poems* (1841), he was famous: after *Evangeline* (1847) and *The Song of Hiawatha* (1855), he would become and remain for decades (to quote his preeminent modern critic, Christoph Irmscher) "America's, if not the world's, most widely recognized poet," admired by Queen Victoria and by her servants, and in his own country "so famous ... that he was asked [to name] a new state in the Union."[1] Schoolchildren all over the USA, for almost a century, memorized his poems in schools that bore his name.

Longfellow's broad and lasting popularity has become the most salient fact about him. "Not whole poems but memorable snatches" of his poetry, Dana Gioia wrote in 1994, survive even now in "American oral culture": "I shot an arrow into the air," "like ships that pass in the night," "Into each life a little rain must fall."[2] Americans wanted to hear what Longfellow wanted to say, and to buy what he wanted to sell: "a gentry-class poet in a democratic land," as Matthew Gartner put it, he showed how educated Cambridge and aristocratic Boston could speak to – could even unify – the American multitudes.[3] He has been seen and admired, recently, as a teacher, a literary journalist, a multiculturalist *avant la lettre*, a master of verse technique, a stay-at-home father (all qualities Irmscher has emphasized), and most of all as a translator: from his first publications (meant for US students of Romance languages) through *The Poets and Poetry of Europe* (1844), a celebrated translation of Dante (1865–67), *Poems of Places* (31 vols., 1876–79), and other poems rendered from at least eleven languages, Longfellow demonstrated, in Jose Martí's words, "el don raro de asir la música y el espiritú de las lenguas, de lenguas de Europa, y letra de ellas."[4]

Longfellow's international, polyglot reading, along with the travel in Europe that helped him sustain it, produced his unusual range of verse technique, including "Greek meters in English" (as James Russell Lowell complained): the well-known trochaic tetrameter of *Hiawatha*; the "Locksley Hall" couplet, in "The Belfry of Bruges," written not long after Alfred, Lord Tennyson's own "Locksley Hall"; and the mixed meter of the late masterpiece "Kéramos," whose stanzaic refrain and tetrameter couplets approximate an American *Rubaiyat*. Longfellow used a wide range of genres too: "psalms" (his own name for his early, popular, hymnlike poems), scenic descriptions, songs, moral fables, epics, sonnets, chants. Translated, adapted, or with no known source, there are (as J. D. McClatchy's recent edition emphasizes) many *sorts* of poems in Longfellow's *oeuvre* – indeed, one of the pleasures in reading Longfellow, especially if we are willling to skip around, is just how many kinds of poems we find.

Longfellow as popular poet, as public figure, as translator, and as craftsman, expert maker of applied art: how did these roles interact, in Longfellow's own sense of his career? How should they intersect, if we return to him now? Daniel Aaron warns us not to "separate the subtle artist from the household message-bringer," but the two Longfellows were not always on the same page: we can see them working together in, say, *Hiawatha*, but we can also see (especially after *Hiawatha*'s success) moments when Longfellow cannot bring himself the kind of uncomplicated messages he gave the rest of the world.[5] To survey all Longfellow's variety would take another book. Instead I will take up two kinds of poems that held Longfellow's interest for decades, kinds that include both some of his most popular works, some of those most responsive to the tastes of his own age, and some of the least, some poems written, as it were, for himself. In each case the more private, more conflicted poem reflects on the challenges and the expectations created by the more public, more famous, simpler work. The first case is the relatively short narrative poem, fit for a periodical or for a compilation, such as Longfellow gathered in *Tales of a Wayside Inn* (1863; expanded edition 1873); the second case is the sonnet, a form to which he returned throughout his writing life.

Tales of a Wayside Inn is a cyclopedia, a collection of verse tales in various kinds and forms, with a frame (they are told at an inn by New England travelers) and a self-presentation (a general prologue, and a generous Host) that recalls Chaucer's *Canterbury Tales*: it was almost entitled *The Sudbury Tales* (Charles Sumner convinced the poet to change the title). The first of the Tales, the Landlord's, remains the most famous: it is "The Midnight Ride of Paul Revere." None of Longfellow's poems anticipates its own communal and national uses more than this one; in particular, it anticipates recitation – "Listen, my children, and you shall hear."[6] When Jose Martí, in his posthumous tribute to Longfellow, writes of 5,000 children in Atlanta reciting "Excelsior," it is no figure of speech: by 1860 Longfellow might have expected it – several thousand had already assembled in Boston to hear the famous actress Fanny Kemble recite "The Building of the Ship."[7] Tetrameter with exact rhymes and a couplet norm, irregular meter with prominent ana-pests, make "Paul Revere" move fast and forcefully; it even describes its own meter, moving from the silversmith's "heavy stride" into the further speed of horseback ("He springs to the saddle, the bridle he turns") (*POW*, p. 364). Longfellow might have picked up such effects (as Paul Morin says) from Robert Browning's "How They Brought the Good News from Ghent to Aix" – there is nothing uniquely American about them.[8] There is, however, something oral, communal, ceremonial, not only in the measures (which are meant to be said out loud, not sung), but in how the poem concludes – with a national martyr, an unknown soldier ("one was safe and asleep in his bed / Who at the bridge would be first to fall"), and then with Revere himself as a resonant ghost: "A voice in the darkness, a knock at the door" means liter-ally the Bostonian messenger, but also the "midnight message" of American unity against an aggressor, a message "borne on the night-wind of the Past," which "The people will waken and listen to hear" (*POW*, p. 365).

That message has changed over time. On its initial appearances in peri-odicals (1860–61) and again in *Tales of a Wayside Inn*, "Paul Revere," as Angela Sorby writes, "was understood as … invoking the founding fathers to support the Union cause" in the Civil War, the current "hour of darkness and peril and need."[9] In its postbellum contexts, in amphitheaters and class-rooms, the poem lost its Union sentiments and became instead an almost contentless cue to American belonging: it could "teach children how to be Americans," incorporating "the forms and functions of an oral culture" – a record of history that could be recited, with its own symbolic chronology ("It was one by the village clock," "It was two," and so on) and its reso-nant places (the Old North Church). That public use, too, seems implicit, even anticipated, in the thumpingly speakable patriotic tale, whose "orality effects" (Maureen McLane's term) differ from the Celtic and English nation-alist poetry that McLane and others discuss in that there is no American primary oral tradition (no illiterate bardic poetry) to which they can pretend to belong.[10] Instead, Longfellow creates an American, synthetic, secondary orality, appropriate to a nation created by literate actors responding to writ-ten texts. Indeed, Longfellow emphasizes the Host's and guests' learning and their libraries – the Student owns "many a rare and sumptuous tome"; the Spanish Jew is "well versed in Hebrew books" and can recite "The Parables of Sandabar, / And all the Fables of Pilpay" (*POW*, pp. 357, 359).

All but one of the *Tales* have traceable soures, and all the tellers have real originals.[11] They appear in the poem, however, as composites, professional types (as in Chaucer) and also as ethnic types: a "Spanish Jew" and a theologian, a "young Sicilian" and an Anglophile landowner get along. That comity, too, is American. *Tales* makes explicit attacks on religious intolerance (as in the Theologian's tale, about Torquemada) even as it takes care to show that Catholic Europe and its denizens have much to offer a Protestant-dominated United States.[12] Near the end of the 1873 *Tales* the Student objects to demands for a wholly American story:

> Bread and ale, home-baked, home-brewed,
> Are wholesome and nutritious food,
> But not enough for all our needs;
> Poets – the best of them – are birds
> Of passage; where their instinct leads
> They range abroad for thoughts and words,
> And from all climes bring home the seeds
> That germinate in flowers or weeds.
>
> (*CPW*, p. 252)

Longfellow entitled an earlier volume *Birds of Passage;* the Student here seems to speak with Longfellow's voice.

The problem of making American poetry – of making the sort of poetry Longfellow wanted – was (as Irmscher suggests) a problem of how to "bring home" appropriately varied materials into a model where "translation becomes creation": almost as soon as Longfellow's name became widely known, he was accused (wrongly) of plagiarism by Poe, and (with more justice) of being "artificial and imitative" by, among others, Margaret Fuller.[13] Kirsten Silva Gruesz writes that Longfellow "staked his career on the belief in a universally intelligible poetic center, and on translation as the common route to it."[14] Most of his works have *something* to do with translation, even when they have no original in another tongue. Thus *Tales of a Wayside Inn* is a kind of translation into American of the *Canterbury Tales*, the "psalms" in *Voices of the Night* ecumenical latter-day answers to metrical psalms, and *Hiawatha* a very free adaptation of Henry Rowe Schoolcraft's transcriptions of Ojibwe stories, fashioned after a Finnish model into a romance itself concerned with "picture-writing," with intelligibility across cultures.

Indeed, these syncretic goals explain the sense – articulated by many of Longfellow's critics – that the poems lend themselves to translation all too well. Thomas McFarland writes that "translations of poems … are attenuated by their very nature," that work in one language can "never reach the essence" of poems in another, but he does not dismiss poetic translation thereby; instead he concludes that it represents, in a particular obtrusive form, the efforts and the failures inherent to art. For McFarland, "all cultural activity is a kind of translation," trying and never wholly succeeding to represent one person, one experience, one meaning, in terms of another.[15] McFarland's sentence (if not the theory behind it) describes Longfellow's body of work better than it describes any other American; Longfellow's poetry exists at every point along the continuum described by translators, and their detractors, from Dryden to this day, from literal translation, to "foreignizing" or intentionally unidiomatic translation, to free adaptation and "metaphrase," to the production for one language and culture of near equivalents to sources in another. Longfellow in his most popular hortatory poems ("A Psalm of Life," "Excelsior") also "translates" the melancholy sentiments we find in his letters and journals – he was a man often over-worked, and full of doubt – into terms fit for a large reading public; it is for this reason that we may find his language compromised, or "attenuated" (in McFarland's terms) when we read his best-known poems.

In other poems, other translations, we may not. No actors, so far as I know, have ever recited "The Saga of King Olaf" to a packed house: it is not one of Longfellow's most public poems. It is, instead, one of his most intricate tech-nical experiments: almost every one of its twenty-two segments uses a new stanza form. With "Paul Revere" it was the first of the *Tales* to be written (completed, apparently, in 1860); if he wrote "Paul Revere" for his national public, we might say he wrote "King Olaf" for himself – it represents an apex of his achievement as polyglot, adapter, technician, and "translator" in an extended sense. Longfellow took its characters and events from the prose (with short verse interpolations) of Snorri Sturluson or Sturlason, the author of the *Heimskringla* or Olaf Sagas (part of the Icelandic Younger or Prose Edda), which he read in the original, in Swedish and German versions, and in Samuel Laing's English.[16] Longfellow took cues, as to form, from *Fritjof's Saga*, the last and most highly esteemed long poem by the Swedish poet Esias Tegnér; Tegnér, like Longfellow, uses a different verse form for each canto. Longfellow assigns "King Olaf" to the Norwegian musician Ole Bull, a friend and a successful violinist whose large public admired his technique. To the virtuosic immigrant musician Longfellow assigns his virtuoso narra-tive poem, the one most devoted to technical variety and to conflicts within the poet, within his roles.

Those conflicts were severe. The historical king Olaf Trygvesson converted much of Scandinavia to Christianity, but they were forced conversions, often at the point of a sword. King Olaf in Laing declares "all Norway should be Christian, or die" and does his best to bring it about: at one point he burns down a barn full of pagan magicians.[17] Depicting (like Snorri) mar-riage, diplomacy, rivalry, ghosts, hauntings, intradiegetic verse composition, and honorable combat, Longfellow (unlike Snorri) confines the action to Scandinavia. He also gives "orality effects," with a stark Northern flavor:

> The mariners shout,
> The ships swing about,
> The yards are all hoisted,
> The sails flutter out.
>
> The war-horns are played,
> The anchors are weighed,
> Like moths in the distance
> The sails flit and fade.
> (*POW*, p. 422)

As prose about a culture whose court poets composed intricate verse, the sagas gave Longfellow (as they had given Tegnér) a story that lent itself to diverse songs, and a way to think about secondary or synthetic orality, about the role of the national bard. This particular saga also let Longfellow think about the contradictions of any attempt to improve a society, to make it more moral, through military force – contradictions that in 1859–60 would have been on his, and many other, minds.

Almost all written between October and December 1860, the poem shows not only mixed feelings about the coming war, but Longfellow's mixed feelings about his status as de facto national bard. The abolitionist senator Charles Sumner seems to have asked Longfellow in 1859 for a war poem: Longfellow responded, "You say to me as King Olaf said to his Scald, 'Write me a song with a *Sword* in every line!' But how write War-songs, if there is to be no war? And how would it all rhyme with the 'Arsenal at Springfield,' and your discourse on the brass-cannon" – Longfellow's already famous poem, and Sumner's remarks to Longfellow, deploring war?[18] By the time of that exchange, as "Paul Revere" shows, Longfellow was already – at least to the Northern states, and whether or not he wanted the role – something like a skald, a court poet, himself, writing the songs of the nation for the nation.

Introducing an English translation of *Fritjof's Saga* in 1867, Longfellow's friend Bayard Taylor praised Tegnér as, in effect, the Swedish Longfellow: "the central [poet] of the period," whose work implies "a calm, earnest, beautiful life, in which the fire and enthusiasm of the poet, the sedate strength of the scholar, the tender and solemn humanity of the preacher and the social and domestic affections … are blended."[19] Longfellow seems to have seen himself in Tegnér too, writing on *Fritjof's Saga* in 1837, and incorporating some of Tegnér's writing into *Evangeline*. When Tegnér died in 1847 Longfellow responded with "Tegnér's Drapa" (a drapa is a Norse funeral song): the last stanza of the memorial poem urges "bards of the North" who describe "the days of Eld," "Preserve the freedom only / Not the deeds of blood!" (*CPW*, p. 111).

It is an impossible request – so "The Saga of King Olaf" would show – and it is, in a way, a request for another translation: the results highlight, as Erik Thurin says, "the ironic discrepancy between the teaching of the gospel and the weapons wielded by Olaf ... as Christ's champion."[20] "King Olaf" also translates, of course, European stories for the New World, keeping distant and slightly alien (as theorists of translation recommend) the language of that source: that distance comes through the sometimes elliptical multiple narrators and through the unusual variety of stanza forms and genres: love song, lament, prayer, lyrical interlude. The stanzas' shapes themselves do allusive work: sailors enter battle, in "King Svend of the Forked Beard," to the metrical shape of "The Charge of the Light Brigade."[21]

Above all the poem translates – its King Olaf tries to translate – Christian precepts into national practice, with the mixed success, and the overtone of hypocrisy, that we might expect when religion arrives in a wash of blood. King Olaf resolves to "Preach the Gospel with my sword, / Or be brought back in my shroud!" (*POW*, p. 405). To the pagan magician and "Sea-King" Raud, Olaf simply says "Be baptized! or thou shalt die!" (*POW*, p. 407). To the laconic narrative force of the sagas Longfellow adds scenes and songs, including a Christmas feast with appropriate weather:

> Then over the waste of snows
> The noonday sun uprose,
> > Through the driving mists revealed,
> Like the lifting of the Host,
> By incense-clouds almost
> > Concealed.
>
> > > (*POW*, p. 410)

Embedded in a recently pagan culture where glory comes through violence, the Christian message itself is "almost" (but not quite) "concealed" (*POW*, 410). As Andrew Hilen says (quoting earlier critics) "the very nature of the subject compelled Longfellow to [a] show of force and violence" that worked against his irenic temperament.[22] It also allowed for beautiful juxtapositions, transitions from story to song, from event to refrain, that sound less like the Longfellow of "Paul Revere" than like the young Yeats:

> It is published in hamlet and hall,
> > It roars like a flame that is fanned!
> The King – yes, Olaf the King –
> Has wedded her with his ring,

And Thyri is Queen in the land!
Hoist up your sails of silk
And flee away from each other.
(*POW*, p. 416)

Olaf *does* conquer – as the Union would. However propelled by
Longfellow's ambivalence, the poem is what Sumner had asked him to
write. Song XII, "King Olaf's Christmas," repeats Sumner's request: "Sing
me a song divine / With a sword in every line, / And this shall be thy reward"
(*POW* 83).[23] Longfellow endorsed abolition in *Poems on Slavery* (1842),
dismaying his Southern admirers, and his letters to Sumner (along with his
donations to black churches) show his continued commitments.[24] But abolitionists in the late 1850s faced their own problem of translation, one almost
analogous to the task that faced a newly Christian king: how to translate a
deep, and in most instances a religious, conviction into public policy? Would
such a "translation" require praise for war? This vexing twenty-two-part
poem, with its multiple speakers and singers, its feuds and its carnage, its
ambiguous hero with his ambiguous ending (as in the Edda, the heroic king
simply vanishes under the sea), says both yes and no.

"King Olaf" includes, as we might expect, battle songs, and martial glory,
and skalds and rival families; it also includes a rare, successful caricature,
the priest Thangbrand, who goes to Iceland in order to make that land
Christian. Instead, he makes enemies, and flies into a rage when he sees
himself, "a figure in shovel hat, / Drawn in charcoal on the wall," with the
caption "This is Thangbrand, Olaf's Priest":

> Hardly knowing what he did,
>   Then he smote them might and main,
> Thorvald Veile and Veterlid
>   Lay there in the alehouse slain.
>   "Today we are gold, to-morrow mold!"
> Muttered Thangbrand, Olaf's Priest.
> Much in fear of axe and rope,
>   Back to Norway sailed he then.
> "O King Olaf! Little hope
>   Is there of these Iceland men!"
>   Meekly said,
>   With bending head,
> Pious Thangbrand, Olaf's Priest.
>   (*POW*, pp. 403–04)

Thangbrand may not be a hypocrite – he believes what he says, but he is a bad
"translator" of Christianity into Iceland, and an unsuccesful proselytizer as
well. King Olaf himself does better (he does make his nation Christian) but his

last battle prompts no triumphal ode. Instead, Longfellow concludes with the song of a nun, "Astrid the Abbess." The song is not in the Eddas, and it uses the same meter Longfellow used to translate St. Teresa's famous prayer ("All things are passing / God never changeth" [POW, p. 694]), the same meter as "The Challenge of Thor," with which the twenty-two-part work began:

> Thou art a God too,
> O Galilean!
> And thus single-handed
> Unto the combat,
> Gauntlet or Gospel,
> Here I defy thee!
> (POW, p. 387)

Theodore Roosevelt, who read and admired "The Saga of King Olaf" in his youth, appears to have had the experience but missed the meaning, regarding it as martial celebration; TR later encouraged his eldest son to "memorize … all the most stirring parts."[25] Longfellow's nun, "entreating / The Virgin and Mother," and invoking St. John the Baptist, accepts Thor's "challenge of battle" in a more felicitous way, refusing to take up "the weapons / Of war." Instead, the Christians of days to come will triumph with "Peace cry for war-cry! / Patience is powerful; / He that o'ercometh / Hath power o'er the nations!" (POW pp. 429–30). It must have been, in the fall of 1860, a melancholy conclusion, and (as the poem says) a difficult hope to sustain.

Though his most famous poems, by 1860, were narrative, Longfellow first gained national attention as a lyric poet, for "A Psalm of Life" and other poems collected in *Voices of the Night* (1839). Its "success," writes Colonel Higginson, "was regarded as signal, because the publisher had sold 850 copies in three weeks." Another Bowdoin alumnus, Nathaniel Hawthorne, admired them unreservedly ("Nothing equal to some of them was ever written in this world"). Higginson almost predicts the eclipse into which these poems would understandably fall when he writes that some critics disliked "the very simplicity which made [the poems of 1839] so near to the popular heart."[26] Indeed, Longfellow from the start of his career was self-conscious about that very quality, telling his readers, in effect, that he himself craved the simple reassurances that his poems could offer them: "Come, read to me some poem," he implored in "The Day Is Done," "some simple and heartfelt lay, / That will soothe this restless feeling, / And banish the thoughts of day" (POW, p. 48).

The "psalms" and "hymns" are public poems, as their churchly titles imply, even as they speak to inward doubts, questions, or grief: their stanzas end up "bonding speaker to reader," as Lawrence Buell writes, "in a credal affirmation that will be clear and publicly acceptable," and fit for both sexes in an age of sentiment.[27] Longfellow's implicit desire not to disappoint readers, his apparent desire to help them live their lives – part of what the nineteenth century liked – explains why the lyric poems can disappoint readers today.

Yet we have seen a more reflective, and a more disturbing, Longfellow in "King Olaf" among the narrative poems, and among the lyric poems we can see him in some of Longfellow's eighty-three sonnets. Here, too, his achievement begins with the work of translation: his first published sonnets were versions of Lope de Vega and other poets from the Spanish Golden Age. Longfellow's first sonnet with no European original, written in 1842, was "Mezzo Cammin," propelled by allusion to Dante and Milton: most of the rest come from the last ten years of his life.[28] Longfellow knew some of his poems would be recited; sometimes he wrote with recitation in mind. But the sonnet has been since its invention in Sicily a quintessentially *written* form, one whose asymmetrical parts segregate it from measures for song, and from public recitation too: Longfellow's sonnets are poems we may read to ourselves.

Yet even in them, he sometimes pursued the roles of consoler, lay priest, public example. Indeed, he wrote sonnets recommending that role to himself. Poetry, a sonnet called "The Poets" says, can (and should) "assuage the bitterness of wrong" (*CPW*, p. 66). "The Descent of the Muses" portrays the Nine and their arts as delightful or practical, never confounding, or frustrating, or sublime: "Proud were these sisters, but were not too proud / To teach in schools, of little country towns / Science and song, and all the arts that please" (*CPW*, pp. 319). Both these sonnets come from *Kéramos and Other Poems* (1878); the latter may commemorate the teachers and women's-college graduates who moved South to teach black children during Reconstruction, in what W. E. B. Du Bois lauded as "the crusade of the New England schoolma'am."[29]

We can find in such sonnets the use of poetry as an anodyne substitute for religion, the insistence (as Gartner says) on "useful answers to the largest human questions," that led "respectable" American poetry into a corner, or a dead end, by the time of Longfellow's death – so American critics in the 1880s and 1890s complained.[30] Agnieszka Salska goes so far as to say that Longfellow "did not think self-expression a legitimate function of poetry" – which may be too far; we can, though, see how in his non-narrative poems "experience gets generalized into comforting, didactic paradigms."[31] That generalization takes place most obviously in the poems that became most popular in his lifetime.

In other poems it does not take place at all: the contrast shows the difference between the side of him most important to his public, and the side that we have yet to recover now. We can see that contrast not just among poems, but within them: in the sonnet "Nature," for example (also from *Kéramos*), we get an eloquent, slippery play with sound, and an introspection balked at the last moment, by the professional poet's obligation to reassure. Nature is to adults, Longfellow says, as a mother to a "little child":

> So Nature deals with us, and takes away
>   Our playthings one by one, and by the hand
>   Leads us to rest so gently, that we go
> Scarce knowing if we wish to go or stay,
>   Being too full of sleep to understand
>   How far the unknown transcends the what we know.
>
> (POW, p. 649)

Indeed we cannot know "how far"; perhaps "Nature" is merely earthly, with no afterlife. Yet the last line implies that we can know after all, that nature (like mothers) should have our best interests in mind. The distance between the weariness of the Tennysonian main clause ("So Nature ... go or stay") and the dry admonition of the last two lines is the distance between the introspective Longfellow and the Longfellow conscious that what he published, tens of thousands of people (or more) would soon read – whether or not they themselves would "understand" the consolation he could give.

Other sonnets consider craft, and vocation, with little thought of a public role, and no consolation at all. "The Broken Oar" (again from *Kéramos*) endorses, as a symbol for the professional poet's career, a (real) Icelandic inscription on a (real) oar: "Oft was I weary, when I toiled at thee" (*POW*, p. 651). Unmoralized weariness, exhaustion simply depicted rather than made to do good, comes to Longfellow as yet another translation. Another sonnet stands even farther apart from, or above, the reassurance that made Longfellow so popular: it is a sonnet his biographers quote whole, because it was (what early biographers so prized) part of his literary "remains," a work unpublished during the poet's lifetime. They prized it, too, for its powers – harsh and unconsoling by the standards of his day, and unconsoling even by our own. It is "The Cross of Snow," his sonnet about the death of his second wife, by fire, in their home, written eighteen years after the event:

> In the long, sleepless watches of the night
>   A gentle face – the face of one long dead –
>   Looks at me from the wall, where round its head
>   The night-lamp casts its halo of pale light.
> Here in this room she died; and soul more white
>   Never through martyrdom of fire was led
>   To its repose; nor can in books be read

The legend of a life more benedight.
There is a mountain in the distant West
That, sun-defying in its deep ravines
Displays a cross of snow upon its side.
Such is the cross I wear upon my breast
These eighteen years, through all the changing scenes
And seasons, changeless since the day she died.

(*POW*, p. 671)

Here are the technical virtues of the other sonnets, and here, too, the inter-nationalism that marks almost everything Longfellow wrote, his determination to make American counterparts for European (and not only English) achievements: here, overwhelmingly, though, is his unassuaged grief. The late Fanny Longfellow and the cross in the mountains (the Mountain of the Holy Cross, in Colorado, the state that Sumner asked Longfellow to name) are American counters to the landmarks, the saints, and the saints' legends of Catholic southern Europe. They are monuments and examples of lasting virtue on a North American continent with endurance but no resurrection, no credible belief in a life after death, where (as Longfellow put it in "The Jewish Cemetery at Newport") "the dead nations never rise again" (*POW*, p. 335); nor do dead individuals. The poem becomes, as it were, an ironic translation of the pious sonnets by Lope and others with which Longfellow began his translating career.

Twentieth- and twenty-first-century readers may admire the sonnet for the same reasons that Longfellow chose not to print it. Higginson explains that "it was true to Longfellow's temperament to write frankly his sorrow in exquisite verse; but it became Longfellow's habit … to withhold his profoundest feelings from spoken or written utterance," that is, not to publish them once he had written them down. Even before Fanny's death, in the same 1859 letter to Sumner that seems to have prompted "King Olaf," Longfellow complains that he must play the paterfamilias, compelled to weep only in secret, as well as the "Oncle d'Amerique" for the rest of the world. After her death, he wept a great deal: "I cannot speak of the desolation of this house," he wrote in 1862, "and the sorrow which overwhelms and crushes me. I must be patient and silent … It is very difficult to built up again such a shattered life. It crumbles away like sand."[32] It took him eighteen years to get such sentiments – persistent, if not constant, for all that time – into a poem.

We may imagine that Longfellow did not publish the poem in his lifetime simply because he did not want to air such private grief; but we may think, as well, that he would not have wanted to make public an admission that he could not console himself. The "deep world-weariness" that Eric

Haralson finds all over Longfellow's non-narrative poetry finds, in some of the popular poems, a supposed remedy, even when the stated remedy (as in "Nature") seems inadequate; what is unusual in "The Cross of Snow" is that there is no remedy anywhere.[33]

Longfellow was indeed, as Irmscher put it, "a consummate literary professional who became the most popular poet America has ever had."[34] Yet depiction of Longfellow as a purely professional writer, a man who had only the goals of his public in mind, does justice neither to the quality of his translations, nor to his original work, nor (most of all) to the way in which Longfellow's whole life addresses, and often vexes, distinctions between translation and original, public declaration and private sentiment, poetry as object for commercial exchange and topical debate and poetry as what the poet writes for himself. We have to read *Hiawatha* and *Evangeline*, and "Paul Revere," and *Voices of the Night*, with an eye to Longfellow's projected and real, public and professional, roles. We can also see Longfellow addressing himself, before he addresses his public, and thinking *about* the ways in which he addressed his public, about the kind of translation that address involved, if we look at the right poems, "King Olaf" perhaps most of all. It is an argument familiar to students of Robert Frost, who himself invoked Longfellow's example with the title of his first book: Longfellow is more like Frost, in this way, than we think. To the Longfellow whose *Hiawatha* gave its name to streets and schools; to the good father, the translator, the fascinating man of letters who did not only make poems; to the Longfellow of recitations and consolations, of "I shot an arrow into the air," we might add a Longfellow that modernist readers might have liked, had they not been so averse to the others: a maker of strange, remarkably international, virtuosically crafted, and unconsoling poems.

NOTES

1 Christoph Irmscher, *Longfellow Redux* (Urbana: University of Illinois Press, 2007), p. 11.

2 Dana Gioia, *Disappearing Ink* (St. Paul, MN: Graywolf, 2004), p. 56; Henry Wadsworth Longfellow, *Poems and Other Writings*, ed. J. D. McClatchy (New York: Library of America 2000), p. 53; Henry Wadsworth Longfellow, *Complete Poetical Works*, ed. Horace Scudder (Boston: Houghton Mifflin, 1893), p. 274, cited hereafter in text as *CPW*; Longfellow, *Poems and Other Writings*, p. 18, cited hereafter in text as *POW*. Because *POW* is both textually reliable and widely available, and because it contains most (by no means all) of the most important poems, I cite *POW* when quoting work included there, *CPW* for poems not included in *POW*.

3 Matthew Gartner, "Becoming Longfellow: Work, Manhood and Poetry," *American Literature*, 72. 1 (2000), 61.

4 Jose Martí, *Poetas angélicos* (Havana: Editorial Letras Cubanas, 1993), p. 47. The Spanish quotation may be rendered in English as: "the rare gift of grasping the music and spirit of language, of European languages, and their literatures."

5 Daniel Aaron, "Longfellow's Legacy," *Maine Historical Society Quarterly*, 27.4 (1987), 56.

6 On "Paul Revere" as a poem designed for recitation, see esp. Angela Sorby, *Schoolroom Poets* (Lebanon: University of New Hampshire, 2005).

7 Martí, *Poetas angélicos*, p. 45; T. W. Higginson, *Henry Wadsworth Longfellow* (Boston: Houghton Mifflin, 1902), p. 200.

8 Paul Morin, *Les sources de l'oeuvre de Henry Wadsworth Longfellow* (Paris: Emile Larose, 1913), p. 163.

9 Sorby, *Schoolroom Poets*, p. 16.

10 See Maureen McLane, "Ballads and Bards: British Romantic Orality," *Modern Philology*, 98.3 (2001), 423–43.

11 See Higginson, *Henry Wadsworth Longfellow*, p. 214; for more, see discussions of each tale in Morin, *Les sources*, and also John van Schaick, *Characters in "Tales of a Wayside Inn"* (Boston: Universalist Publishing House, 1939).

12 One priest in 1928 even called Longfellow "the first American Protestant to make serious effort to enter fully into the spirit ... of Catholicism." R. P. Hickey, *Catholic Influence on Longfellow* (Kirkwood, MO: Maryhurst Normal Press, 1928), p. 17.

13 Irmscher, *Longfellow Redux*, p. 273; Margaret Fuller quoted in Aaron, "Longfellow's Legacy," p. 45.

14 Kirsten Silva Gruesz, *Ambassadors of Culture: The Transamerican Origins of Latino Writing* (Princeton University Press, 2002), p. 78.

15 Thomas McFarland, *Shapes of Culture* (Iowa City: University of Iowa Press, 1987), p. 82.

16 Andrew Hilen, *Longfellow and Scandinavia* (New Haven: Yale University Press, 1947), p. 99.

17 Snorri Sturlason, *Heimskringla: the Olaf Sagas*, trans. Samuel Laing (1844; New York: Dutton, 1933), pp. 53, 68, 58–59.

18 Henry Wadsworth Longfellow, *Letters*, vol. IV (1857–65), ed. Andrew Hilen (Cambridge, MA: Harvard University Press, 1972), pp. 129–30.

19 Esias Tegnér, *Fritjof's Saga*, trans. W. L. Blackley, with preface by Bayard Taylor (New York: Leypoldt and Holt, 1867), p. vi.

20 Erik Thurin, *The American Discovery of the Norse* (Lewisburg, PA: Bucknell University Press, 1999), p. 106.

21 For a comparison of each canto and stanza form with Icelandic, Danish or Swedish originals, see Morin, *Les sources*, pp. 338–62.

22 Hilen, *Longfellow and Scandinavia*, p. 102.

23 This segment went through a great deal of revision: for the deleted passages, see *ibid.*, pp. 98–102.

24 See Christoph Irmscher, *Public Poet, Private Man: Henry Wadsworth Longfellow at 200* (Amherst: University of Massachusetts Press, 2009), p. 115.

25 Theodore Roosevelt, *An Autobiography* (New York: Macmillan, 1913), p. 21; Theodore Roosevelt, Jr., "Average Americans in Olive Drab: The War as Seen by Lt. Col. Theodore Roosevelt," www.theodoreroosevelt.org/life/tedsrecollections.htm

26 Higginson, *Henry Wadsworth Longfellow*, pp. 140–42.
27 Lawrence Buell, *New England Literary Culture* (Cambridge University Press, 1986), p. 116.
28 For concise comment on the sequence and dates of the sonnets, see *The Sonnets of Henry Wadsworth Longfellow*, ed. Ferris Greenslet (Boston: Houghton Mifflin, 1907), pp. xi–xii.
29 W. E. B. Du Bois, *The Souls of Black Folk* (New York: Bantam, 1989), p. 18.
30 Gartner, "Becoming Longfellow," p. 78; Sorby, *Schoolroom Poets*, pp. 77–79, and see John Timberman Newcomb, *Would Poetry Disappear?* (Columbus: Ohio State University Press, 2004).
31 Agnieszka Salska, "From National to Supranational Conception of Literature: The Case of Henry Wadsworth Longfellow," *American Transcendental Quarterly*, 20.4 (2006), 617.
32 Higginson, *Henry Wadsworth Longfellow*, p. 211; Longfellow, *Letters*, vol. IV, p. 130; Higginson, *Henry Wadsworth Longfellow*, pp. 280–81.
33 Eric Haralson, "Mars in Petticoats: Longfellow and Sentimental Masculinity," *Nineteenth-Century Literature*, 51.2 (1996), 329.
34 Irmscher, *Public Poet*, p. 5.

9

JESS ROBERTS

Sarah Piatt's grammar of convention and the conditions of authorship

Writing to Edmund Clarence Stedman sometime in the late 1880s or early 1890s, poet Sarah Piatt expresses no small irritation at his or his "friends'" apparent rejection of her verse.[1] While the details are unclear, her tone is not. Following a tensely polite salutation and words of customary modesty, she goes on to insist that whatever time Stedman had spent "discussing" her verse was ill spent: "I am sorry that you took the trouble to speak of me at all. I do not belong to the animals that go in herds. Whether my place be on the height or elsewhere, I choose to stand alone."[2] Implying that whatever venue he was considering her poems for, likely a magazine or anthology, was the domain of the "herds," Piatt implicitly likens her contemporaries to literary sheep and positions herself in opposition to them. Sounding out from what has long been considered the female choir of submission, the defiance in Piatt's letter appeals to a deep desire I recognize in both myself and my students, one that is likely shared by many twenty-first-century readers of nineteenth-century women's poetry: the desire to hear women declare openly their deep frustration with the powers that restricted their range of lived experience and expression.

For all of this defiance, though, much of Piatt's life in print conformed to, cultivated, and maintained a version of female authorship often associated with "the herds" of male and female writers whose poetry filled the pages of newspapers and periodicals and whose books lined the shelves of nineteenth-century parlors. Despite her criticism of "the magazines" – to be excluded from them, she wrote to Stedman, was "the interposition of a merciful providence that saves one … from very poor company" – well over one hundred of Piatt's poems appeared in the *Atlantic Monthly* and *Scribner's*, in *Harper's* and the *Galaxy*, in the *Century* and the *Independent*, among others. The books of verse that, according to her letter to Stedman, she "piteously" "begged" her husband not to publish numbered eighteen by the time of her death.[3] Her poems were anthologized in numerous collections during her lifetime, including R. H. Stoddard's expanded edition of Rufus

Griswold's *The Female Poets of America* (1873) and Stedman's later *An American Anthology* (1900).⁴ Furthermore, the poems that we might think of as challenging most openly the poetic and social conventions of the time often appeared alongside poems, her own and others', that seem unabashedly to employ those conventions and within print contexts that affirmed their value and virtue.⁵ Though contemporary reviews of her poetry frequently register discomfort at her "obscurity" and "difficulty," and though some assert that she needed "more heart" and "less art," reviewers also celebrate with striking regularity her "womanliness" and "feeling."⁶

While Piatt's letter to Stedman distinguishes those who go in "herds" from those who do not, a survey of her poetry indicates the limitations of just such an approach. Piatt wrote a considerable number of poems that resemble those we might associate with "the herds" (i.e. poems that make consistent use of popular poetic conventions) and a considerable number that do not (i.e. poems that overtly trouble or challenge those conventions). For example, her highly conventional sentimental infant elegy "His Share and Mine," written in the vein of Maria Lowell's "The Alpine Sheep" and republished several times during her life, stands beside "Her Blindness in Grief" and "No Help," poems that appear to rage against the futility of the conventions of mourning. Throughout her career, Piatt makes seemingly unambivalent use of conventions in some poems while in others openly questioning or critiquing those very conventions in subtle and sophisticated ways. Despite Piatt's claims in her letter to Stedman, her own poems give the lie to the tidy opposition between the poets who go in "herds" and the single poet who "stands alone." In the pages of her books and the lines of her poems, the strands of defiance and convention are not so easily disentangled.

To my mind, Piatt's use of convention exemplifies her canny understanding of language and has much to teach us about nineteenth-century poetry and our recovery of it. Absent an overt interest in subjectivity and/or formal experimentation, women's poetry in the nineteenth century, with the notable exception of Emily Dickinson, has long confounded a literary critical tradition that deeply values Emersonian and Whitmanian forms of originality which define themselves in explicit opposition to convention. This overtly conventional poetry resists subversive political readings and demands an attention to form even as it yields little to New Critical methods. By writing poems that both embrace and reject well-worn tropes and images, Piatt makes visible and confronts the limitations and possibilities of convention. And by illuminating the complex work of convention in the print world of postbellum America, Piatt's poetry troubles the dichotomies between authenticity and inauthenicity, originality and conventionality, protest and submission that continue to undergird and limit the study of nineteenth-century poetry. More than merely defying or subverting convention, Piatt anatomizes particular conventions – disassembles them, scrutinizes their logic, plays out their implications, and clarifies their place in the multifaceted and dynamic print culture that took shape in the wake of the Civil War.

For good reason, essays that introduce a single writer in the context of a period of literary history often paint with large brushstrokes. They canvas a writer's career in order to give a sense of its scope and arc.[7] By necessity, though, such essays must forgo or foreshorten close readings, by which I mean the intense scrutiny of a poem's constituent parts and their arrangement. I would argue that it is precisely this type of intense scrutiny that is most challenging and essential to the permanent recovery of nineteenth-century women's poetry.[8] In what follows, I attempt to model a reading practice that, to borrow Adela Pinch's helpful phrase, might be called "contextualized, gender-sensitive formalism."[9] In other words, I pay close attention to the poems' language and its complicated relationship to historicized notions of gender. Looking closely at a handful of poems that address themselves to female authorship by way of the images and rhetorical stances associated with women poets in the nineteenth century, I seek to understand how conventions in Piatt's poetry illuminate and dramatize the conditions of her own authorship. This scrutiny troubles our ability to divide her work into tidy categories even as it demonstrates both the complicated work of poetic convention and her nuanced understanding of it. What is more, I hope that it provides a glimpse of the joy her poems can afford their readers.

Entering the national literary marketplace in the 1850s and 1860s, first by way of the *Louisville Journal* and then by New York publisher Walter Low, Sarah Piatt wrote herself into a culture with well developed, if contradictory, expectations of female poets.[10] These expectations can be seen in various anthologies of women's poetry published in the late 1840s as Piatt came of age as well as in the reviews of Piatt's collections.[11] Anthologists and reviewers alike explicitly oppose female and male authorship. Unlike the cerebral male poets whose minds are, to use Rufus Griswold's language, "impatient of the fetters of time, and matter, and mortality," the female poets express "the vivid dreamings of an unsatisfied heart" and the "natural cravings of affections."[12] Thomas Buchanan Read describes female poets as "forms of fairer mould" who "[pour] songs for vern pleasure – / Songs their hearts could not withhold" and features them in an elaborate illustration as women playing lyres alongside pastoral scenes.[13] Reviews of Piatt's poems likewise underscore the decidedly "feminine" characteristics of her poems. Of her first singly authored collection of poems, *A Woman's Poems*, the very title of which overtly foregrounds her gender and marks the collection as distinctively and generically "female," one reviewer writes, "Mrs. Piatt's book is rightly named, for the finest feminine qualities characterize its contents. Here we may see faithfully and delicately pictured girl, sweetheart, wife, and mother."[14] Of that same collection, William Dean Howells writes in the pages of *The Atlantic Monthly*, "We shall be far from making it a cause of offence in the author that she has not written like a man. It appears to us that the only quality which it is worthwhile for women to contribute to literature is precisely this feminine quality."[15]

The "feminine qualities" to which the reviewers and anthologists refer are now associated with what modern scholars call the "Poetess tradition," a tradition that I would like to position Piatt's poetry in dialogue with rather than in opposition to.[16] Despite what may be a modern critical desire to situate Piatt exclusively as subverting the Poetess tradition with its trappings of submission and conventionality, she does fit the Poetess mould in certain important and undeniable ways. A number of different print sources, for example, refer to Piatt as a "Poetess."[17] What is more, Piatt's ongoing use and examination of the conventions associated with Poetesses bespeak an engagement that is far more conflicted and multifaceted than an overwhelmingly subversive reading of her poems might suggest.

Take, for instance, Piatt's oft-reprinted poem "The Fancy Ball," which William Dean Howells singles out in his review of *A Woman's Poems* as "perfectly feminine." This particular poem is an intriguing choice for Howells given its ostensible critique of images one might associate with "perfectly feminine" poetics. Although his identification of this poem as an exemplary "feminine" poem might suggest to us that "The Fancy Ball" openly embraces conventions associated with Poetesses and, therefore, situates Piatt in the "herd," the poem itself appears to hinge on the rejection of precisely those conventions and to stake out an identity in opposition to them and the herd they conjure. A careful scrutiny of the poem, though, reveals that the language of "embracing" and "rejecting," of "herd" and "not herd," fails to account accurately and adequately for the complex work of convention within the poem and within the print culture in which it circulates. Rather than blindly accept or willfully jettison "perfectly feminine" conventions, the poem dissects, scrutinizes, and analyzes them.

"The Fancy Ball" stages a dialogue in which a speaking "I" declines to wear a set of costumes offered by a "you." By the end of the poem, the "I" refuses to wear any costume at all. I quote the poem in full:

> As Morning you'd have me rise
> On that shining world of art;

You forget: I have too much dark in my eyes –
And too much dark in my heart.

"Then go as the Night – in June:
Pass, dreamily, by the crowd,
With jewels to mock the stars and the moon,
And shadowy robes like cloud.

"Or as Spring, with a spray in your hair
Of blossoms as yet unblown;
It will suit you well, for our youth should wear
The bloom in the bud alone.

"Or drift from the outer gloom
With the soft white silence of Snow:"
I should melt myself with the warm, close room –
Of my own life's burning. No.

"Then fly through the glitter and mirth
As a Bird of Paradise:"
Nay, the waters I drink have touch'd the earth;
I breathe no summer of spice.

"Then — " Hush: if I go at all,
(It will make them stare and shrink,
It will look so strange at a Fancy Ball)
I will go as — Myself, I think![18]

Presented as a domestic personal exchange, the poem's diction and imagery invite us to read it as a meditation on publication and poem making. The second line aligns the fancy ball with the public, rather than private, world of art, of which poetry in the nineteenth century was decidedly a part. The fancy ball as an event presents us with a metaphor for print publication: to attend the ball is to appear in print. One might argue, then, as others have, that in refusing certain costumes that perpetuate a particular and stereotypical ideal Piatt's poem offers a thinly veiled critique of "the gendered expectations placed on nineteenth century women's poetry."[19] The final stanza certainly presents itself as playfully defiant and appears to reject conventions often associated with women's poetry. Instead of the costumes of convention, the poem proposes a "self" – even if that self might appear "so strange at a Fancy Ball" and "make them stare and shrink." In this way, the poem appears to echo Piatt's declarations in the letter to Stedman quoted above. The poem's "I," it would seem, is not one to go with the herd.

But to end a reading there would be to oversimplify the work of convention that the verbs "stare and shrink" clarify. Together the verbs suggest both attraction and repulsion. Whereas the others at the ball might not be able to take their eyes off the "I," they might also and at the same time shrink from that "I" in fear, distaste, or even horror. Given this coincidence of fascination and aversion at the "I's" "self," Piatt's choice of the pronoun "it" in the final lines is significant. On the one hand, "it" might be read as referring to the act of independence that going to the ball as herself would constitute. In this sense, the "I's" refusal to wear the conventions of women's verse leads the dancers at the ball "to stare and shrink."[20] However, the "it" of the penultimate and antepenultimate lines might also refer specifically to "Myself." In doing so, "it" neuters the self or, perhaps more accurately, reflects the grammatical fact that "I," that marker of self, is not gendered: the first-person pronoun, in all of its forms, draws its gender from its referent. Here, though, we have no specific referent for "I"; rather, we decipher its gender by way of the costumes it rejects. In other words, we deduce the gender of the poem's speaking "I" largely by way of the conventions that the "you" suggests the "I" wear. Absent those conventions, we have before us an ungendered "I" and an ungendered "self." Whatever it might look like, an ungendered self at the "Fancy Ball" of print publication might, indeed, have appeared both captivating and monstrous. Read in this way, the poem's final lines are not so much a playful rejection of convention as they are a scrutiny of the gendering of particular conventions and the relationship between those conventions and the notion of a poetically rendered self.

As the first poem in *A Woman's Poems*, "The Fancy Ball" foregrounds the ways in which Piatt's first singly authored book of poetry complicates and illuminates the relationship between convention and gender. Given that beginning, the final poem in the book, " – To – ," with its self-conscious scrutiny of the conditions under which Piatt labored, might rightly be seen as a conclusive gesture, an ending of sorts. But both the poem itself and its extended republication history suggest that this poem, perhaps more than any other, represents the qualities of Piatt's verse that made it, at once, so conventional and, to recall the penultimate line of "The Fancy Ball," so "strange."[21] I quote the poem in full:

> Sweet World, if you will hear me now:
> I may not own a sounding Lyre
> And wear my name upon my brow
> Like some great jewel full with fire.
>
> But let me, singing, sit apart,
> In tender quiet with a few,

And wear my fame upon my heart,
A little blush-rose wet with dew.
(*A Woman's Poems*, p. 127)

Like "The Fancy Ball," " – To – " is constituted by conventions. The lyre, her heart, the "little blush-rose" recall not only the Spring and Morning of "The Fancy Ball" but also Thomas Buchanan Read's "forms of fairer mould." By way of these conventions, " – To – " presents a posture familiar to readers of the mid-nineteenth century. The image of the lyre and the characterization of the "I" as singing "in tender quiet" with a "few" evoke Sappho, the poetess of Ancient Greece whose poems and image circulated widely in the nineteenth century and were associated with the Poetess tradition.[22] Although the lyres and jewels of Piatt's " – To – " are not identical to the costumes that "The Fancy Ball" ostensibly rejects, they are images associated with the same kind of female authorship. Like "The Fancy Ball," " – To – " makes cunning use of grammatical units and syntactical relationships to scrutinize the relationship between the poem's "I" and its constitutive gendered conventions. More specifically, it uses the grammatical structure of the conditional in order to clarify and make visible its own conditions of production and of Piatt's authorship.

In " – To – ," each of the stanzas presents itself as a complete grammatical unit, the first of which is a conditional (an if/then sentence), the second a hortative imperative (a softened command). The meaning of the conditional first stanza depends on how the reader understands the colon at the end of line one. Conditionals articulate a logical relationship in a speculative situation. "If" this happens, "then" that will follow. "That" depends on "this." "This" enables "that" to happen or be. The conditional "if" appears in the poem's first line: "Sweet World, if you will hear me now." But, importantly, the second line of the poem lacks the adverb "then" that often (though not necessarily) begins the main clause of a conditional: "Sweet World, if you will hear me now: / I may not own a sounding Lyre."

This absence is noteworthy. On the one hand, the colon that appears at the end of the first line acts as an elided then-clause. That is, it does the grammatical work of the second half of the conditional. If you will hear me now, then you will hear the following three lines, the beginning of the poem, which, as it turns out, offer a rhetorical act of self-deprecation. If you will hear me now, you will hear me acknowledge what I lack – namely, "a sounding Lyre." Here, the word "sound" resonates with multiple meanings. Under the first definition of "sound," the *OED* lists the following: "to make or emit a sound"; "to resound; to be filled with sound"; and "to give call or summons to arms." The eighth definition is "to utter in an audible tone … Sometimes implying loudness of voice." Not to own a sounding lyre, then, could suggest that the "I's" lyre is silent (something the fact of the poem belies) or that it is muted or that it is not martial. But "sounding" also has a nautical definition ("to ascertain the depth of the sea") and is often used figuratively to mean "to penetrate or pierce" or "to make inquiry or investigation."[23] These definitions would suggest that the "I" may not own a lyre that lends itself to a probing exploration of an idea, the idea, say, of authorship. If the colon at the end of the first line is taken as the second half of the conditional, then " – To – " begins by implying that it is not the kind of poem that sounds.

The absence of the adverb "then" also opens up another possibility – namely, that the last three lines of the first stanza be read as the second half of the conditional set up in line one. In this sense, the colon replaces the missing "then." The lines might well read: "Sweet World, if you will hear me now, then I may not own a sounding Lyre." Read in this way, the main verb ceases to be subjunctive and becomes permissive: if the "I" is to be heard, then it is not permitted to own a sounding lyre. If the poem is to be read, it may not *sound* in certain ways. According to this reading, the lines no longer self-deprecate but rather articulate clearly the condition of their own reception: the poem's "I" must invariably self-deprecate in order for the sweet world to hear it. Again, it bears pointing out that the poem's "I" nowhere explicitly declares its gender; rather that gender emerges by way of the conventions that constitute the poem, conventions bound to the poem's ostensible inability to sound.

More than an ironic instance of the conventions of self-effacement,[24] these lines capture in their grammatical doubleness one of the defining conditions of Poetess authorship in the nineteenth century: that in order to be heard one must speak according to a particular set of conventions, even if those conventions would purport to mute the poem itself (and the Poetess as well). What Piatt's poem reveals is that those conventions are neither inevitable nor static but rather conditional and dynamic, capable of being brought into provocative and illuminating relationship with one another. " – To – " claims not to possess a lyre that sounds; and yet, in that proclamation, the poem gives voice to (sounds) precisely the conditions under which it was produced and circulated. In doing so, the poem discerns and clarifies (sounds) those conditions and the conventions that maintain and are maintained by them. Again the poem does not merely ironize those conventions; which is to say, it does not simply use them to articulate their opposite. Rather, Piatt turns those conventions so that they might speak doubly and draw attention to their particular logic.

The fact that at least one reviewer understood " – To – " as an expression of Piatt's own "modest hope" points to yet another aspect of Poetess authorship more generally and Piatt's authorship particularly that I have not yet addressed – namely, the degree to which readers mapped a Poetess's personal identity onto her poems.[25] Piatt was always a shadowy antecedent to which her poem's first-person pronouns might refer. Though to read a poem's "I" as Piatt's own may be to engage in an interpretive act of fiction, the pervasiveness of that reading practice in the nineteenth century, particularly with respect to women writers, necessarily influenced how Piatt thought about the written "I," particularly her own.[26] The significant fluidity between the author's identity and a poem's "I" finds powerful expression in a poem entitled "A Coin of Lesbos," in which Sappho acts as a tool through which Piatt examines the complicated dynamics and dilemmas of her own authorship. She does so by creating a poem in which the speaking "I" identifies with Sappho all the while acknowledging and capitalizing on her own (Piatt's) fraught identification with both the "I" and Sappho in the poem. I quote the poem in full:

> I think how long she held it with a smile
> (Her jealous lyre complaining on her breast),
> Dust thick on everything, and she, the while,
> Forgetting it and Phaon and the rest.
>
> With those great eyes, that had not longed as yet
> To lose their tears in kindred brine, ah me!
> Fixed on its precious glimmer, "It will get —
> What will it get?" she murmured. "Let me see.
>
> "Some jewel that will more become my head
> Than withering leaves of laurel? Nay, not so.
> At least, I think, some lovelier robes," she said,
> "Than any woman weareth that I know!"
>
> So, years ere that deep Glass wherein she gazed
> With her last look had flashed it to the sun,
> So mused, I fancy, the most over-praised
> Of women who have ever sung on earth – save one![27]

Though in the first stanza the speaking "I" distinguishes clearly between herself and Sappho, the second stanza blurs that distinction. There the "I" moves from thinking about Sappho holding her "lyre complaining on her breast" to imagining Sappho's later suicide, the moment at which Sappho would lose her tears and herself in the kindred brine of the ocean. The acknowledgment of Sappho's self-annihilation, of which the poem's Sappho is strikingly unaware, engenders a reaction from the speaking "I" encapsulated in the mournful phrase "ah me!," evidence of the "I's" emotional identification with Sappho. The breathy "ah me!" invites us to consider that

Sappho's tears may be "kindred" not only to the salt water of the ocean but also to the salt tears of the "I" which the thought of Sappho's death provokes.

Not only an expression of the "I's" apparent sympathetic identification with Sappho, the phrase "ah me!" bespeaks other forms of identification of which the "I" may not be aware but Piatt most certainly is. The phrase itself is a kind of convention – a transportable interjection signifying an emotive reaction that accrues more specific meaning in a particular context. Here, the phrase "ah me!" corresponds strikingly with the poem's portrayal of Sappho in the first stanza: Sappho might be easily imagined to sigh "ah me!" as she sits with her "lyre complaining on her breast." Indeed, the participial adjective "complaining" means "to produce a mournful sound," which is precisely what "ah me!" is presented as being.[28] One might argue that the speaking "I," in remembering Sappho's death, writes herself into the Sapphic posture with which the poem begins. She identifies with Sappho insofar as she sympathizes with and draws identity from her. So in a loose sense, the first-person accusative "me" in the interjection might be said to refer to both the "I" and Sappho with whom she identifies.

If Piatt acknowledged the degree to which she herself was a shadowy antecedent to her poem's first-person pronouns, then it follows that she herself also becomes, to some extent, a referent for the poem's "ah me!" I do not mean to suggest the kind of easy conflation of author and "I" that would read "ah me!" as an unmediated expression of the author's apparent sorrow. Rather, I would argue that the phrase "ah me!" in opening a space for Piatt to inhabit signifies a moment of complicated recognition that underscores Piatt's ambivalent relationship to both the "I" and Sappho. "Oh, look," Piatt appears to be saying, "there I am – a written 'I' voicing convention, a woman poet remembering the fate of another woman poet, and a writer whose fate is unknown to her but plain to her later readers." Both the "I" and Sappho do, indeed, exemplify dynamics of authorship that Piatt knew all too well. The poem's "I" gives expression to the forms of identification and conventions that made Piatt's poem recognizably "feminine," to borrow Howells's word, while Sappho embodies Piatt's ineluctable ignorance of her own fate – how her life will end and what will become of her poems – that will condition how later generations read and remember her and her work. Twenty-first-century readers may see Piatt's fate – her relegation to dusty shelves, her long exclusion from the thing called "American poetry" in the wake of modernism – written clearly in the arc of literary history; such is the benefit of hindsight. But Piatt would, of course, have had no way of knowing with certainty how the future would deal with her or her writing. Characteristic of Piatt's treatment of convention more generally, the easily transportable "ah me!" here is freighted with a kind of intellectual and emotional heft that it is not normally imagined to carry.

In acknowledging Piatt's inevitable ignorance of her fate, literary and otherwise, I do not mean to minimize her own clear understanding of the degree to which her authorship and therefore literary fate were determined largely (though not exclusively) by things beyond her control, by something scholars now call "print culture." Piatt's own understanding of the print culture's impact on her life and legacy manifests itself in one of the most provocative instances of grammatical flexibility I have come across in her poems: the poem's concluding phrase "save one!" Both a prepositional phrase and an imperative, "save one!" embeds in an overtly conventional gesture a compelling recognition of the cost of the very authorship that is defined by gestures of that sort.

Read as a prepositional phrase, "save one" performs a conventional act of self-deprecation, reminiscent of Piatt's earlier poem " – To – "; it implies that, like Sappho, though to an even greater degree, the "I" has been "overpraised." In this reading, the "one" refers modestly and elliptically to the poem's "I" and, for readers, to Piatt herself even as it refers more generally to any woman poet other than Sappho. The fact that one reviewer felt compelled after reading this poem to assure Piatt that she was not, in fact, overpraised confirms both the trend of grafting Piatt's personal identity onto the poem's first-person pronoun and of reading overtly conventional moments as unmediated expressions of the author.[29]

Read as a command, "save one" doubles its pronouns and takes as its organizing relationship not the comparison between Sappho and the "one" but the dynamic between its own subject and direct object. As is the case with any imperative, the subject of "save one" is the implied and invisible "you" commanded by an also invisible "I" that has no grammatical place in the sentence: "[I command, (you)] save one!" In printed imperatives, that "you" takes the reader as one of its referents and therefore the subject of the sentence; any one act of reading, then, constitutes a different specific referent for "you." As a result, the commanded "you" is, at once, singular and plural, specific and general, identified and anonymous, qualities that likewise apply to the poem's "one." That is, the "one" refers to a written "I," to a particular writer (Piatt), and to women writers more generally; "one" is a grammatical unit, an identifiable someone, and an anonymous idea.

The qualities of the "you" – its invisibility, its boundedness to printed matter, its inherent plurality as well as its apparent ability to act on the "one" – recommend that we read it as referring not only to any one reader but also synecdochically to the more amorphous and multifarious print culture that exerted such powerful influence on the lives of all writers. In doing so, we would read the poem as taking as its addressee an abstraction that takes on material, though always partial, form in a number of different agents of which the writer is, importantly, one. The fact that the writer is part of the print culture she inhabits and the poem addresses matters in reading Piatt's closing imperative because it means that, to some degree, in commanding the "you" to "save one" the "I" is addressing herself. Rather than exist independent of the print culture she addresses, the written "I" – like and as Piatt – is a part of it. That is not to say that the "I" can "save" "one" – be that "one" herself or Piatt or some other poetess – any more than any one of the other agents that in sum constitute the print culture can; but it does acknowledge the "I's" place, however limited and compromised, in the very thing she commands.

Taking the print culture as the "you's" referent, we would also read the "I" as addressing the very thing from which she commands the "one" to be saved. The poem's scrutiny of conventions associated with Poetess authorship invites us to read the poem as demanding that "one" be saved from the gendered restrictions on poetic expression embodied in the "I" and Sappho, restrictions maintained and perpetuated by the many and diverse actors that make up nineteenth-century American print culture. Given its monetary title, the phrase may be understood as demanding that "one" be saved from the fact that profitable forms of authorship required an adherence to particular conventions; that to earn the "coin of Lesbos," one must hold the complaining lyre. No publishing author, though, can be "saved" from print culture: it is the ground on which authorship stands. Moreover, while it is certainly true that Piatt felt and resisted the pressures and demands that dictated and restricted the way women wrote, it is equally true that the very conventions that ostensibly restrict her writing are also the tools she uses to illuminate and examine those restrictions. So it is with "A Coin of Lesbos." Piatt's authorship was unavoidably shaped by the image of Sappho as it circulated in the nineteenth century as well as by her readers' understanding of her own identity and that identity's relationship to her poems' "I's." But in "A Coin of Lesbos" rather than restrict her, Sappho and "I" become vehicles that enable Piatt to investigate the complicated, paradoxical, inescapable conditions of her own authorship and to demonstrate her own poetic powers. In the end, the imperative "save one!" commands its "you" not so much to rescue "one" as to recognize the cost of "one's" authorship, to acknowledge what must be done to sound the lyre and what is at stake in doing so.

Thus far, the poems that I have chosen to read have shared both a taste for syntactical play and an interest in certain conventions associated with the Poetess – conventions of modesty and submission, sentiment and emotionality. None has made use of the tropes of domesticity that were so prevalent in women's poetry in the nineteenth century, nor have any engaged in the more overt and biting forms of cultural protest that characterize a noteworthy percentage of Piatt's total poetic output. So I would like to turn now to a poem that does both: Piatt's "A Pique at Parting." The dialogic structure that organizes so many of Piatt's poems and which we saw in "The Fancy Ball," is, in "A Pique at Parting," central to revealing the complicated process by which conventions gather and transport meaning, including those imposed by a restrictive patriarchal culture.[30] In "A Pique at Parting," this process relies explicitly on the demonstrative pronoun "that." I quote the poem in full:

Why, sir, as to that — I did not know it was time for the moon to rise,
    (So, the longest day of them all can end, if we will have patience with it.)
One woman can hardly care, I think, to remember another one's eyes,
    And — the bats are beginning to flit.
    ...We hate one another? It may be true.
    What else do you teach us to do?
    Yea, verily, to love you.

My lords – and gentlemen – are you sure that after we love quite all
    There is in your noble selves to be loved, no time on our hands will remain?
Why, an hour a day were enough for this. We may watch the wild leaves fall
    On the graves you forget ... It is plain
    That you were not pleased when she said —Just so;
    Still, what do we want, after all, you know,
    But room for a rose to grow?

You leave us the baby to kiss, perhaps; the bird in the cage to sing;
    The flower on the window, the fire on the hearth (and the fires in the heart) to tend.
When the wandering hand that would reach somewhere has become the Slave of the Ring,
    You give us – an image to mend;
    Then shut with a careless smile, the door –
    (There's dew or frost on the path before;)
    We are safe inside. What more?

If the baby should moan, or the bird sit hushed, or the flower fade out – what then?
    Ah? the old, old feud of mistress and maid would be left though the sun went out?
You can number the stars and call them by names, and, as men, you can wring from men
    The world – for they own it, no doubt.
    We, not being eagles, are doves? Why, yes,

We must hide in the leaves, I guess,
And coo down our loneliness.

God meant us for saints? Yes – in Heaven. Well, I, for one, am content
  To trust Him through darkness and space to the end – if an end there shall be;
But, as to His meanings, I fancy I never knew quite what He meant.
  And – why, what were you saying to me
  Of the saints – or *that* saint? It is late;
  The lilies look weird by the gate.
  … Ah, sir, as to that – we will wait.[31]

"A Pique at Parting" ostensibly stages a conversation between a speaking
"I" and her companion "sir." The subject of their dialogue is the elusive
"that." The poem begins with what appears to be a kind of romantic pique,
the precise source of which – "that" – remains unspecified. Like the bats in
the poem's fourth line, the speaker flits from one topic of conversation to
another – from the moon to the day to the other woman to the bats – circ-
ling "that" without ever specifying it. The fact of another's woman's eyes,
we are invited to imagine, may be the source of the conflict between the
speaking "I" and the "you." The "I" cannot remember – or, more precisely,
does not care to remember – the eyes that her companion may or may not
have taken note of. If in line three the speaking "I's" defensiveness or irrit-
ability appears to be directed at the other woman, the last three lines of the
first stanza complicate the system of allegiances. Although the speaking "I"
acknowledges the likely enmity between herself and the other woman – "We
hate one another? / It may be true"– this ambivalent (and subjunctive) recognition also involves the acknowledgment of "your" hand in that rivalry:
"What else do you teach us to do? / Yea, verily, to love you." In other words,
the speaker implies that the "sir" dictates and restricts the relationship
between the two women as a way of maintaining his own relationship with
both. The last lines of the first stanza also signal to the reader a more general
address embedded in what appears to be an intimate exchange. That is, the
poem's addressee (its "you") is, at once, singular and plural, a point made
explicit in the first line of the next stanza. As the first stanza ends, we seem
to be moving away from a supposed particular conflict between individuals
(signified by "that") toward a more general conflict between gendered social
expectations.

  That general conflict appears to be about the various forms of "teaching"
men do. Replete with images of conventional literary domesticity – birds,
babies, flowers, the fires of the hearth and heart – stanzas two, three, and
four protest how the "lords – and gentleman" of the poem teach "us" not
only to hate "one another" but also to live and write. The poem suggests

that the patriarchal cultural and economic powers restrict and dictate the lives and writing of women by providing them with a set of predetermined plotlines and images by which to live and, just as important, with which to represent those lives. Poems that made use of and, therefore, circulated these conventions educated women as wives and mothers, readers and writers. Not surprisingly, however, according to the poem, these plotlines and images fail to coincide with the lived experience of the poem's "we."

The correlation between the life that "you" gives "us" and the language that "you" gives "us" to represent it finds expression in the poem's third stanza: "You leave us the baby to kiss, perhaps; the bird in the cage to sing; / The flower on the window, the fire on the hearth (and the fires in the heart) to tend." The baby and bird, like the flower and fire on the hearth, are, of course, material objects associated with female domesticity. What is more, they are conventional images that characterized – indeed, consti-tuted – much nineteenth-century women's poetry, including a great deal of Piatt's own. The dual grammatical role of the bird of line fifteen as both subject and direct object of the infinitive "to sing" exemplifies the way in which the bird, baby, flower, and fire signify concurrently material things and their poetic representation: "You leave us ... the bird in the cage to sing" can mean both you leave us the bird in the cage so that it might sing and so that we might sing it – so that we might cast it into verse.

Moreover, these poetic images not only constitute a set of conventions with which to sing domesticity; they also seem to be intended as a salve for the discontentment one might feel within the plotlines "left" by the "lords – and gentlemen": "When the wandering hand that would reach somewhere has become the Slave of the Ring, / You give us – an image to mend" – that is, you give us an image so that it might mend us, restore us in some way. However, the very fact of the protest belies the efficacy of the image to mend: it bespeaks the dissatisfaction that the images were presumably intended to assuage. Furthermore, it insists that the static images fail to correspond to the dynamic material objects to which they refer: the baby of a poem may wait passively to be kissed, but the baby of lived experience might moan or laugh or wail or vomit or, likely, all of the above as it waits to be kissed. Even the image used in protest – "the Slave of the Ring" – itself rings wooden and awkward. It reduces the complexity of a marriage, even one in a decidedly patriarchal society, flattening out the complicated and competing forms of power and negotiation at work in that type of relation-ship. Here, too, the image suggests a form of stasis that the lived experience complicates and contradicts. One cannot help but wonder if the "wandering hand that would reach somewhere" reaches for a pen but finds itself "the Slave of the Ring," which is to say finds itself the slave of an image as static and, therefore, inadequate as those that came before. In this way, the poem insists and performs that images, in fact, do not mend.

According to the reading I have just sketched, the particular conflict signified by the word "that" is little more than a pretext for scrutinizing and protesting the more general conflict between the "lords – and gentlemen" and the "mistress[es] and maid[s]"; "that" is merely a place for the "I" to begin and end. And yet, "that" remains, somehow, central to the poem. It tempts the reader, leaves traces of itself throughout the poem. It flits through the lines, changing shape as it moves; it shadows other gestic words, and, in the end, leaves the reader waiting. Grammatically and dramatically, "that" demands attention from the first line to the last. It is precisely this intersection between the unfolding drama the poem presents and the curious grammatical role played by "that" that troubles any reading of this poem as merely a feminist protest against certain forms of patriarchal power. Images, perhaps, cannot mend the poem's "I," but the poem itself can clarify and scrutinize the work of the images.

By definition, the demonstrative pronoun or deictic "that" refers to something else. It stands in the place of its antecedent. In the case of "A Pique at Parting," "that" gestures to something lying beyond the edges of the poem. So, here, perhaps obviously, "that" has meaning because of something else. The way that Piatt uses "that" – as both the thing that joins the speaking "I" and her companion and the very thing the speaking "I" dodges defining – underscores a truth about language more generally: that meaning is determined through and emerges out of webs of context. By withholding "that's" antecedent, the poem emphasizes "that's" relationship to a series of other diverse elements – the "I," the "you," the moon, the other woman's eyes, the bats – all of which shape our thinking about what "that" is. We are left to infer the meaning of "that" and to confront, quite literally, its various possibilities. "That" achieves a kind of complexity not by revealing its antecedent but rather by performing the referential nature of language and making visible the manifold agents involved in generating meaning.

The conventional poetic images at the heart of the poem function in much the same way: they, too, are presumed to have referents in the material world, something akin to an antecedent to which they refer. However, the images of babies, birds, flowers, and fires circulated so widely in nineteenth-century print culture that they ceased to stand for much of anything but themselves. They gesture not so much to material objects but rather to other images that constitute other poems that circulated in the literary marketplace. Regardless of whether, in the moment of composition, these images referred directly to the material world, once they began to circulate by way of various print media those images became part of a literary economy that shapes what and how the poems mean. That economy rendered the bird, baby, flower and fires, as it were, pure convention.

It is in this way that the poem challenges most directly the terms of the protest it ostensibly makes. On the one hand, the poem appears to protest the various forms of control that men – "the lords – and gentlemen" of society and, particularly, of the publishing industry – exert over the domestic and literary lives of women, including the tropes available to them to describe that world. Said differently, the poem objects to the fact that men "give" women "image[s] to mend." Yet, in light of the complex functioning of the word "that" and its relationship to the play of the conventions in the poem, "A Pique at Parting" suggests that men do *not* in fact "give" women images. Such a linear system of exchange oversimplifies how the American print culture created and maintained the poetic conventions that defined women's verse. Indeed, the poem demonstrates that the world of print cannot be reduced to "the lords – and gentlemen" who give and the maids and mistresses who receive. An understanding of images as given by men and received by women isolates two agents involved in the exchange and suggests that they (the agents) as well as the act of exchange itself possess a kind of discreteness that the poem stridently refuses to accept. Divorced from any one actor (author, editor, reader, poem) and enmeshed in an intricate web of agents, the conventional images that Piatt both renders and rends in "A Pique at Parting" circulated neither inevitably nor accidentally and their meaning, like the meaning of "that," emerged out of and in relationship to a web of diverse agents. In this sense, "that" functions as pronouns have elsewhere in the poems I have examined: it lays bare the conditions and conventions of meaning-making.

As a way of closing, I would like to return to Piatt's letter to Stedman. My chapter has attempted to trouble Piatt's own dichotomy of herd and not herd and to reveal, by way of a careful consideration of her poems, that this type of dichotomy cannot account fully for the complexity of Piatt's work. Piatt's poems defy easy categorization – they stand both among and apart from the herd. But I confess that I love reading her letter to Stedman. There is something in me that relishes her unambivalent and witty fury. Piatt's own poetry, though, has taught me to be wary of any unambivalent expression of her defiance precisely because it would have us look away from poems that partake of and anatomize the very things she elsewhere claims to reject. And there are many such poems. Moreover, a desire to hear her defiance might lead us, in some shadowy and inchoate way, to believe that her more overtly subversive poems body forth a version of Piatt that is less mediated by language and convention, less a product of a particular set of conditions than her apparently conventional poems. Said differently, it might lead us to believe that in her more defiant poems we hear her "authentic voice." I believe we should be wary of seeking out authenticity in poetry, for succeeding in doing so too often means we have merely recognized in the past something that accords with our notions of ourselves. Her "authentic" voice is as likely a fiction as a reality given the challenge any of us have of writing ourselves truly and wholly into language.

What we have left of Piatt's mind and voice and spirit are her poems, and those poems have much more to teach us about the printed "I's" that endure and the voices those "I's" evoke, erase, and engender than about some shadow of authenticity lost to us in the unprinted world of the past. The "I's" of even Piatt's most seemingly personal poems are the creation not only of her poetic capacities but of the culture of print itself. Piatt wrote many strikingly complicated and powerful poems. But these poems, like all the others she wrote, were and are mediated by convention. They draw their meaning and whatever identities they have from a complex collective process, of which the author, though perhaps most important, is only a part. Authors can manipulate and shape this process, but they cannot ultimately control it. This is a truth of which Piatt appears profoundly aware. Like the "that" in "A Pique at Parting," the "I's" in her poems take their meaning from what lies within the poems and from the world beyond their edges. Those "I's," like the lyre and by way of the lyre, sound and in sounding reveal to us the very things that might enable us to hear.

NOTES

I want to thank the Princeton Americanist Colloquium for having invited me to give a version of this chapter as a talk. The chapter certainly benefited from their attention.

1 Born on a Kentucky plantation in 1836, Sarah Morgan Bryan started publishing poems in the local newspaper while attending New Castle Female Seminary in the 1850s. She later married poet John James Piatt in 1861 after a literary courtship in the *Louisville Journal* and began what would become her itinerant adulthood. With their family in tow, Piatt and John James moved north to Washington, DC and then south to Ohio before journeying to Cork, Ireland in 1882. After a decade abroad, the Piatts returned to Ohio once more. Her adult life was a time of incredible loss and productivity: she lost four of her seven children before her death and published constantly. In the wake of John James's death, Piatt moved to New Jersey to live with her son Cecil where she then died in 1919. For biographical information regarding Piatt, Jean Allan Hannawalt's unpublished dissertation entitled "A Biographical and Critical Study of John James and Sarah Morgan (Bryan) Piatt" remains the most comprehensive resource (University of Washington, 1981).

2 Sarah Piatt, "Letter to Edmund Stedman," Edmund Clarence Stedman Papers, 1840–1960, Rare Book and Manuscript Library, Columbia University in the City of New York.

3 *Ibid*. For treatment of Piatt as a periodical poet see Paula Bernat Bennett, "Not Just Filler and Not Just Sentimental: Women's Poetry in American Victorian Periodicals, 1860–1900," in Kenneth Price, ed., *Periodical Literature in Nineteenth-Century America* (Charlottesville: University Press of Virginia, 1995); Bennett, *Poets in the Public Sphere* (Princeton University Press, 2003); Matthew Giordano, " 'A Lesson from' the Magazines: Sarah Piatt and the Postbellum Periodical Poet," *American Periodicals: a Journal of History, Criticism, and Bibliography*, 16.1 (2006), 23–51.

4 Piatt's poems also appeared in Mary Tardy's *Living Female Writers of the South* (Philadelphia: Claxton, Remsen, and Haffelfinger, 1872); John Greenleaf Whittier's *Song of Three Centuries* (Boston: J. R. Osgood, 1876); Edwin A. Alderman and Joel C. Harris's *Library of Southern Literature* (New Orleans: Martin and Hoyt, 1907); and Emerson Venable's *Poets of Ohio* (Cincinnati, OH: Robert Clark, 1912), to name a few.

5 See, for instance, poems of Piatt's included in contemporary anthologies of infant elegies. Piatt's "His Share and Mine," "The Butterfly's Message," "The Favorite of Five," and "No Help" all appeared in the 1876 anthology *Little Graves* alongside poems by Felicia Hemans, Lydia Sigourney, and Henry Wadsworth Longfellow. For treatment of Piatt's elegies as subversive, see Mary McCartin Wearn's *Negotiating Motherhood in Nineteenth-Century American Literature* (New York : Routledge, 2008).

6 See "Art Versus Heart," review of *Voyage to the Fortunate Isles* by Mrs. S. M. B. Piatt, *Scribner's Monthly* (August 1874), 501–2; "Current Literature," review of *A Voyage to the Fortunate Isles*, *Overland Monthly*, 13 (September 1874), 295–96; William Dean Howells, "Recent Literature," review of *A Woman's Poems, Atlantic Monthly*, 27 (June 1871), 773–75; "Mrs. Piatt's Poems," review of *Complete Poems, The Literary World*, 25 (August 1894), 279; "Minor Book Notices," *The Literary World* (July 1874), 27.

7 For this type of treatment of Piatt, see Paula Bernat Bennett's Introduction, *The Palace-Burner: The Selected Poetry of Sarah Piatt* (Urbana-Champaign: University of Illinois Press, 2001).

8 The tenuous status of recovered authors can be seen in the fact that Piatt appears in the 6th edition of the *Norton Anthology of American Literature* (2003) but not in the 7th edition (2007) published only four years later.

9 Adela Pinch, *Strange Fits of Passion: Epistemologies of Emotion, Hume to Austen* (Palo Alto: Stanford University Press, 1996) p. 12.

10 Piatt co-authored her first book of poems with her husband: *The Nests at Washington and Other Poems* (New York: Walter Low, 1864). For a careful treatment of Piatt's early poems in the *Louisville Journal*, see Susan Grove Hall, "From Voice to Persona: Amelia Welby's Lyric Tradition in Sarah M.B. Piatt's Early Poetry," *Tulsa Studies in Women's Literature*, 25.2 (Fall 2006), 223–46.

11 Rufus Wilmot Griswold's *Female Poets of America*, Caroline May's *The American Female Poets*, and Thomas Buchanan Read's *Female Poets of America* were all published for the first time in 1848. Although the first editions of these collections predate the publication of Piatt's first book by almost fifteen years, both Griswold's and Read's collections went into numerous editions through the 1880s. As a result, their vision of female authorship circulated well into

the latter half of the century, shaping the context in which Piatt's poems were written, circulated, and read.

12 Rufus Wilmot Griswold, Preface, *Female Poets of America*, ed. Griswold, additions by R. H. Stoddard (New York: James Miller, 1878), p. 3.

13 Thomas Buchanan Read, "Proem," *Female Poets of America* (Philadelphia: E. H. Butler, 1848).

14 Review from the *Cincinnati (Ohio) Gazette* appears in the back matter of Piatt's *Voyage to the Fortunate Isles and Other Poems* (Boston: Houghton Mifflin, 1886).

15 William Dean Howells, "Recent Literature," review of *A Woman's Poems*, by Sarah Piatt, *Atlantic Monthly* 27 (June 1871), 773–75.

16 For recent discussions of the "Poetess tradition," see Yopie Prins and Virginia Jackson, "Lyrical Studies," *Victorian Literature and Culture*, 27 (1999), 521–30; Yopie Prins, *Victorian Sappho* (Princeton University Press, 1999); Laura Mandell, "Introduction: the Poetess Tradition," *Romanticism on the Net*, 29–30 (February 2003); Eliza Richards, *Gender and the Poetics of Reception in Poe's Circle* (Cambridge University Press, 2004); Virginia Jackson and Eliza Richards, "'The Poetess' and Nineteenth Century American Women Poets," *Poetess Archive Journal* 1.1 (April 2007), www.poetessarchive.com; Virginia Jackson, "'The Story of Boon' or the Poetess," *ESQ*, 54.1–4 (2008), 241–68; Tricia Lootens, "States of Exile," in Meredith McGill, ed., *The Traffic in Poems* (New Brunswick: Rutgers University Press, 2008).

17 See reviews from *The Independent*, the *Cincinnati Inquirer*, and the *Philadelphia Evening Bulletin* reprinted in the back matter of Piatt's *Voyage to the Fortunate Isles and Other Poems*; Stedman identifies her as a Poetess in Edmund Clarence Stedman, ed., *Poets of America* (Boston: Houghton, Mifflin, 1885).

18 Sarah Piatt, *A Woman's Poems* (Boston: Osgood, 1878), pp. 1–2. A further quotation from this edition appears parenthetically in the text. Piatt's *A Woman Poems* was first published anonymously by Osgood in 1871. It then appeared in a new edition in 1878.

19 Giordano, "'A Lesson from' the Magazines," p. 12.

20 The way that the poem's second stanza alludes to Lord Byron's "She Walks in Beauty Like the Night" indicates the degree to which male and female poets made use of similar conventions to describe female figures.

21 It is the first poem to appear in her section of *Nests at Washington* and the last poem to appear in the first volume of her two-volume *Poems* (1894), a significant but by no means comprehensive selection of her work. It also appeared in several other of her own collections as well as Stedman's later *An American Anthology* (1900) and Emerson Venable's *Poets of Ohio* (1912).

22 For a study of the place of Sappho in nineteenth-century literary culture, see Yopie Prins, *Victorian Sappho* (Princeton University Press, 1999).

23 "sound, v." *Oxford English Dictionary*, 2nd edn., 1989. *OED Online*, Oxford University Press, accessed March 10, 2010.

24 For a reading of Piatt's poetry in which irony plays a central role, see Paula Bernat Bennett's "Irony's Edge: Sarah Piatt and the Postbellum Speaker," in *Poets in the Public Sphere: The Emancipatory Project of American Women's Poetry, 1800–1900* (Princeton University Press, 2003).

25 Review of *Complete Poems*, by Sarah Piatt, *The Literary World*, 25 (August 1894), 279.

26 For a discussion of this trend, see Augusta Webster's "Poets and Personal Pronouns" in the *Examiner* (March 12, 1878), 268–70.

27 *Lippincott's Monthly*, 32 (June 1887), 998. I am particularly indebted to Susan Wolfson and Sara Smilko for their thoughtful comments and observations regarding this poem.

28 "complain, v." *Oxford English Dictionary*, 2nd edn., 1989. *OED Online*, Oxford University Press, June 15, 2010.

29 Review of *Poems*, by Sarah Piatt, *Irish Monthly*, 22 (November 1894), 613–14.

30 "A Pique at Parting" is a particularly interesting example of Piatt's use of the dramatic monologue, a form she used often and to great effect.

31 Sarah Piatt, *Dramatic Persons and Moods* (Boston: Houghton, Osgood and Company, 1880), 13–15.

10

JOHN D. KERKERING

Poe and Southern poetry

Their respective ties to the Southern United States alone might lead us to assign Edgar Allan Poe, Henry Timrod, and Sidney Lanier to a single Southern tradition. As we shall see, however, these writers were connected by a deeper tie that is evident in their engagement with each other's work on the topic of poetics. The mutual engagement among these authors yields a conceptual tradition, but one in which, as we shall see, different emphases arise: Poe reveals a transcendental concern with romantic aesthetics, Timrod reveals a nationalist concern with Southern Confederate autonomy, and Lanier reveals a racial concern with Anglo-Saxon ethnic difference. In what follows I will treat each of these writers in turn, moving chronologically through Poe and Timrod to Lanier in order to sketch the differing views that emerge from these authors' engagement with each other.

Edgar Allan Poe was born in 1809 in Boston and was educated at the University of Virginia and West Point. His education was primarily in ancient and modern languages, which gave him access to poetic works indirectly, but he did not make the study of poetry itself a central academic pursuit. Instead, his poetic collections appeared in a manner that was ancillary to his academic work. These collections included a first in 1827, a second in 1829, a third in 1831, and a fourth in 1845, with several uncollected poems rounding out his total output. Poe's poetic writings form just a fraction of his total written work, much of which consists of prose short stories. These poetic works, however, hold a special place in his *oeuvre* because he considered his status as poet to be of particular importance. As Floyd Stovall observes, "[Poe] is now most esteemed as a writer of short stories, but by temperament and inclination he was first and always a poet. He turned to fiction and adopted the career of a magazine editor from sheer necessity, not from choice."[1]

Poe's poetics subdivides human consciousness into three distinct modes, and the purpose of poetry, in his view, is to effect the isolation of one of these modes, the feeling or sentiment of the beautiful. The other two modes of consciousness are the true, the isolation of which is effected by the rational contemplation of questions about truth and falsehood, and the good, the isolation of which is effected by the moral contemplation of questions about proper ethical conduct. It follows that the sentiment of the beautiful, if it is to be isolated from these other two states of mind, should not be mixed with questions of rational truth or moral goodness; poetry in its pure form, if it is to effect only one of these modes of consciousness – the mode of the beautiful rather than the good or the true – should be neither scientific nor didactic. (Poe derives much of this poetic theory from his reading of others, principally Samuel Taylor Coleridge's 1814 work *Biographia Literaria*.)[2] This position would later strike the imagination of Charles Baudelaire, for whom Poe was the inspiration for an aestheticized pursuit of art for art's sake. As Poe would later write, "under the sun there neither exists nor *can* exist any work more thoroughly dignified – more supremely noble than this very poem – this poem *per se* – this poem which is a poem and nothing more – this poem written solely for the poem's sake."[3]

Poe's later prose writings on poetry are equally explicit about this three-part subdivision of consciousness. In a review of Longfellow, for instance, Poe observes, "Dividing the world of mind into its most obvious and imme-diately recognizable distinctions, we have the pure intellect, taste, and the moral sense," where "Poesy is the handmaiden but of Taste."[4] In his review entitled "Drake-Halleck," to take another example, Poe describes a "faculty" "perceptible" "in all human beings," one that is responsible for a "primitive sentiment" or "instinct" that he calls "the sentiment of Poesy."[5] It is worth noting the similarity of this vocabulary – "sentiment" and "instinct" – to Ralph Waldo Emerson's in his essay "Self-Reliance," a similarity that can lead one plausibly to align them with each other as fellow transcendental-ists. There is even a relation to Emerson in the religious eschatology found in Poe's definition of poesy: "Poesy is the sentiment of Intellectual Happiness here, and the Hope of a higher Intellectual Happiness hereafter."[6] But while Emerson's writings derive from his training as a Christian minister and draw consistently on a religious logic, Poe is more consistently concerned, as we've begun to see, with an aesthetic logic in his writings.

Poe's vocabulary is, in his own way, just as elusive as Emerson's; at one point, for instance, he uses the terms "soul," "heart," and "intellect" to cor-respond to his notion of the beautiful, the good, and the true, and at other points he uses the terms "taste" and "duty" to refer to the domains of the beautiful and the morally good, respectively.[7] Other synonyms arise else-where in his prose writings about poetry. Similarly, Poe's disposition to make fine discriminations of terms – he distinguishes passion from sentiment, for instance, and distinguishes both from the faculty of "Veneration" – leads one to wish to understand him as articulating fully thought-out faculty psychology whereas his vocabulary, from essay to essay, appears to be less systematic than this would require.[8] Despite Poe's reiteration of this subdivision of consciousness, his notion remains elusive; viewed in the context of traditional aesthetic discourse, his notion of the beautiful as an elevated sentiment might be understood as resembling the Longinian notion of sublimity, where one gets an effect of elevation from passages of writing. Addressing Longinus' view of the sublime, Edgar Olson writes,

> The soul is elevated by sublimity to joy and exultation; the reader feels an identification with the author, for the soul feels [quoting Longinus] "as though itself had produced what it hears"; hence what does not elevate at all would not even be false sublimity, and that which elevates only temporarily and has a diminishing force forever after is false sublimity, while that which has a permanent force and which provides a perpetual nourishment for the soul is the sublime itself.[9]

While Poe never invokes Longinus by name in his poetic theory, he does write that "I need scarcely observe that a poem deserves its title only inasmuch as it excites, by elevating the soul. The value of the poem is in the ratio of this elevating excitement."[10] In the same essay he writes that "I make Beauty, therefore – using the word as inclusive of the sublime – I make Beauty the province of the poem."[11] Poe differs from Longinus, however, in that Longinus does not reserve this sublime elevation for the notion of the beautiful, as distinct from the true and the good.

Poe is consistent with Coleridge, at least, when distinguishing actual poetry from "the sentiment of Poesy": "since Poetry, in this new sense, *is* the practical result, expressed in language, of this Poetic Sentiment in certain individuals, the only proper method of testing the merits of a poem is by measuring its capabilities of exciting the Poetic Sentiment in others." "For a poem is not," he continues, "the poetic faculty, but the *means* of exciting it in mankind," and we can "test ... [a poem] by its measure of exciting the Poetic Sentiment."[12] Here Poe's point is to stress the instrumentality of a poem in exciting someone's passions for the beautiful to be raised to this elevated condition. This should be distinguished from Poe's slightly different notion, expressed elsewhere, that poetry is the product of the exercise of this faculty. "It is a passion to be satiated by no sublunary sights, or sounds, or sentiments, and the soul thus athirst strives to allay its fever in futile efforts at *creation* ... And the result of such effort, on the part of souls fittingly constituted, is alone what mankind have agreed to denominate Poetry."[13] Yet in "Drake-Halleck" Poe asserts that the fact of being created by someone experiencing this sentiment of veneration for the beautiful need not guarantee a piece of writing's utility in inducing others to that sentiment. Indeed, he suggests that someone with a deliberately methodical approach to writing poetry (someone, he writes, with greater "metaphysical acumen" and little of the "faculty of Ideality") would be better equipped to produce poetry than someone readily moved by poetry because the former person would be drawing upon "the powers of Causality" while the latter would not.[14] Such a person would be better suited to producing poetry even if ill-suited for experiencing it because poetry causes this sentiment rather than being caused by it.

We see this account of poetry's genesis to be present in what is perhaps Poe's best-known essay on poetry, "The Philosophy of Composition," in which he discusses his approach to writing the poem "The Raven" as exemplary of his poetic composition process generally. Poe's concern here is the audience for poetry and the poet's effort to awaken that audience to what he has been describing as the sentiment of the beautiful. Perhaps the most important aspect of this essay is Poe's focus on "effects": "I prefer commencing with the consideration of an effect ... afterward looking about me (or rather within) for such combinations of event, or tone, as shall best aid me in the construction of the effect."[15] What is "within" is not his emotional state but his rational deliberation about how words are to be combined so that effects are elicited. His poetry is not, then, about communicating a particular idea from the private consciousness of the poet to the reading public. Poe's own private consciousness is in principle irrelevant to the goals of the poetry. In practice, the story may be a bit different since many critics suspect that Poe was motivated to write certain of his poems in response to biographical circumstances,[16] but the force of Poe's theory in this essay is to set aside such idiosyncratic personal concerns in favor of viewing the composition process as a rigid protocol or procedure for producing effects in readers: "It is my design to render it manifest that no one point in ["The Raven"'s] composition is referable either to accident or intuition – that the work proceeded step by step, to its completion with the precision and rigid consequence of a mathematical problem."[17] So while it is common in discussions of this essay to emphasize this notion of "totality, or unity, of effect" that Poe describes as achievable only by works characterized by "brevity," my point here is to emphasize that what is totalized or unified is an effect on readers, not a communication of information to them.[18]

This principle will be important for the poem "The Raven" itself: there the raven's repeated enunciation of "nevermore" in the poem's refrain is not a vehicle for anyone's ideas – since the bird has presumably learned to imitate the sound of a word without learning to use the word as language – but is instead a source of effects on that poem's speaker. The raven is thus an appropriate poetic speaker precisely because it ultimately has no content to convey; it is instead the occasion for responses in others. The speaker's well-known drama of response to the raven in this poem thus stages, more generally, a reader's response to a poem. The speaker is first interrupted by the raven when he is falling asleep over a volume of "forgotten lore";[19] this reading material is deliberately staged here as something from which the speaker will turn away upon the arrival of the raven. The raven is thus an allegorization of a poem, the arrival of which takes a reader away from "lore" whose concern is propositional content (and thus either truth or goodness). By contrast, the language of the raven – i.e. the word "nevermore" – is important for its sound pure and simple; the things that this sound might mean – if it is to mean anything at all instead of being, say, musical – are open-ended. And this occasions the speaker's turn to a sentiment not of truth or goodness but of beauty. For Poe, in this essay, a poem "most closely allies itself to *Beauty*" with the turn of the speaker's thoughts to "the death of a beautiful woman," his beloved Lenore, since, as Poe asserts, "the death, then, of a beautiful woman is, unquestionably, the most poetical topic in the world."[20] It is possible, then, to read the poem as its own allegorized philosophy of composition, with the raven acting as poems in general act and the speaker responding as readers in general would respond to poems – with a dynamic experience of effects.

"The Raven" was originally prefaced by a brief editorial comment that is commonly attributed to Poe, a comment that refers to the poem as "one of the most felicitous specimens of unique rhyming which has for some time met our eye."[21] In this editorial preface Poe asserts the importance of sound effects to the poem, which he describes as follows: "It will be seen that much of the melody of 'The Raven' arises from alliteration, and the studious use of similar sounds in unusual places."[22] In relation to this focus on sound, he writes more generally that "The resources of English rhythm for varieties of melody, measure, and sound, producing corresponding diversities of effect, have been thoroughly studied, much more perceived, by very few poets in the language."[23] Poe himself would undertake such a study in his essay on versification, "The Rationale of Verse" (1848), where he depicts verse form as a subject that lends itself to rational or deliberate thinking. But he qualifies this deliberation by underscoring verse form's immediate availability to all listeners, a form he refers to as "quantity": "The fact is that *Quantity* is a point in whose investigation the lumber of mere learning may be dispensed with, if ever in any. Its appreciation is universal. It appertains to no region, nor race, nor era in especial. To melody and to harmony the Greeks hearkened with ears precisely similar to those which we employ for similar purposes at present."[24] Here Poe again articulates a transcendental aesthetic stance (one that turns out to be, we note, primarily Eurocentric), and he goes on to suggest affinities between versification's effects and the sound qualities of music: "The perception of pleasure in the equality of *sounds* is the principle of *Music*," he writes, and he speaks of "*verse*, which cannot be better designated than as an inferior or less capable Music."[25] It is music that serves as the standard, for Poe; it best of all – and verse too, to the extent that it is like music – provides the inducement to the elevated sensation that one is in the presence of beautiful ideality. This is the position Poe would articulate in his final and most thorough articulation of his aesthetic theory of poetry, his essay "The Poetic Principle." There Poe writes,

> Contenting myself with the certainty that Music, in its various modes of metre, rhythm, and rhyme, is of so vast a moment in Poetry as never to be wisely rejected – is so vitally important an adjunct, that he is simply silly who declines its assistance, I will not now pause to maintain its absolute essentiality. It is in Music, perhaps, that the soul most nearly attains the great end for which, when inspired by the Poetic Sentiment, it struggles – the creation of supernal Beauty.[26]

Poe thus concludes with the following definition: "I would define, in brief, the Poetry of words as *The Rhythmical Creation of Beauty*."[27] Poems in which this emphasis on the musicality of sound is evident include "The Bells," "To Helen," and "Annabel Lee." In "The Bells" Poe experiments with sound in a variety of ways, as the following passage suggests:

> Keeping time, time, time,
> In a sort of Runic rhyme,
> To the tintinnabulation that so musically wells
> From the bells, bells, bells, bells,
> Bells, bells, bells –
> From the jingling and the tinkling of the bells.
>
> (*Poems*, p. 435)

Here the musicality of the verse is evident in the alliteration ("Runic rhyme"), the repetition (of "time" and "bells"), and in the end rhyme ("wells" and "bells"). Indeed, it is a musical instrument – the bell – that is the very focus of the poem. The effort to reproduce the bells' repeated ringing in the repetition of the word "bells" suggests an onomatopoetic impulse in Poe's writing.

Something quite different is apparent in the poem "To Helen," where the musicality is more restrained yet present nonetheless in the form of blank verse – an unrhymed sequence of lines in iambic pentameter (where an "iamb" is a two-syllable unit of sound in which the first syllable is short or unstressed and the second syllable is long or stressed, and where "pentameter" means that there are five of these iambs per line):

Clad all in white, upon a violet bank
I saw thee half reclining; while the moon
Fell on the upturn'd faces of the roses,
And on thine own, upturn'd – alas, in sorrow!
(*Poems*, p. 445)

Here the first two lines have what are problematically called masculine end-ings (i.e. ending in a long or strong stress syllable) and the final two lines have what are correspondingly called feminine endings (i.e. ending in a short or weak stress syllable). The sound quality is subtle, and it contributes to an effort to create a mood associated with the encounter with Helen in this enchanted garden.

In "Annabel Lee" Poe experiments with sound in yet another manner, using an intermittently anapestic meter (that is, three-syllable units of sound in which the first two are short or unstressed and the third is long or stressed) incorporated within a traditional ballad meter (of seven long or stressed syl-lables per pair of lines):

It was many and many a year ago,
    In a kingdom by the sea,
That a maiden there lived whom you may know
    By the name of Annabel Lee; –
And this maiden she lived with no other thought
    Than to love and be loved by me.
(*Poems*, p. 477)

Here the ballad meter reinforces the archaic implication of "many a year ago" and the rhyme scheme gives musicality to the verse. In the case of this poem, as with "The Bells" and "To Helen," Poe is drawing variously upon sound effects in order to cause in readers the elevated state of "Ideality" and sensation of the "Beautiful" that his transcendental aesthetics underscores.

Poe was explicitly hostile to the notion that literary works of a writer such as himself should be viewed as a badge of honor for that writer's nation. Thus Poe laments, "we ... often find ourselves involved in the gross paradox of lik-ing a stupid book the better, because, sure enough, its stupidity is American."[28] In such a frame of mind, "we forget, in the puerile inflation of vanity, that *the world* is the true theatre of the biblical histrio" – where, again, the focus on a universality of reference is confined to a Eurocentric viewpoint.[29] A more restricted focus on nation – the Confederacy rather than America – would eventually, however, come to be the mode of poetry most congenial to Henry Timrod. The contrast between Poe and Timrod was the focus of Timrod's fel-low Southern poet, Paul Hamilton Hayne, in whose memorial remembrance of Timrod (published in 1873) he writes the following:

> Timrod's productions ... do not appeal, like too many of Edgar Poe's, to our sense of rhythmic harmony *alone*; nor are they charming, but mystic utterances, which here and there may strike a vaguely solemn echo in the heart of the visionary dreamer. No! beneath the surface of his delicate imagery, and rhythmic sweetness of numbers, rest deeply imbedded the "golden ores of wisdom."[30]

This notion of "wisdom" is consistent with Edd Winfield Parks's assessment that Timrod was an ethical poet, whereas ethics was something that, as we have seen, Poe associated with the good rather than the beautiful and therefore excluded from the domain of Poesy. Such a focus on the thematics of the good was something Poe associated with "the heresy of *The Didactic*" – the term "heresy" here indicating his displeasure with this approach to poetry.[31]

Henry Timrod was born in 1828 and died in 1867, a period which spans the conflict and resolution of the US Civil War, and as this conflict brewed, as we will see, Timrod's allegiances to a Southern Confederacy took shape. In his prose writings about poetry, however, Timrod is focused more on aesthetic than overtly political concerns. In his essay "A Theory of Poetry," for instance, Timrod explicitly invokes Poe in order to take issue with his notion that brevity is essential to poetry, arguing that a long poem – such as Milton's *Paradise Lost* (the example Poe invokes) – is a poem throughout its extended length and not, as Poe argues, just a series of short poems.[32] But in addition to addressing this issue of a poem's proper length, Timrod also writes the following in reference to Poe's three-part division of consciousness and his isolation of beauty as the sole province of poetry:

> I think, when we recall the many and varied sources of poetry, we must, perforce, confess that it is wholly impossible to reduce them all to the simple element of Beauty. Two other elements, at least, must be added, and these are Power, when it is developed in some noble shape, and *truth*, whether abstract or not, when it affects the common heart of mankind ... It is, then, in the feelings awakened by certain moods of the mind, when we stand in the presence of Truth, Beauty and Power, that I recognize what we all agree to call poetry.[33]

Timrod's view is thus distinct from Poe's in that, while he admits that consciousness can be subdivided into component faculties, he does not isolate one of these as the sole province of poetry. In this way his view is perhaps more akin to Longinus than Poe ultimately is – and Timrod uses the term "sublimity" in his essays on poetry – since Longinus likewise, as we have seen, does not subdivide his sublime state of elevation according to distinct mental faculties.[34]

Ultimately, Timrod most differs from Poe in relation to Poe's emphasis on "effects": while Poe wants the poem to affect a reader, Timrod wants some sort of environmental phenomenon – e.g. the natural world – to affect the poet, whose poetry in turn expresses this environmental effect on him. As Timrod writes in his essay "What is Poetry," "Coleridge remarks that the question, What is poetry? is very nearly the same with, What is a poet? The distinctive qualities of poetry grow out of the poetic genius itself."[35] A poem that is worth dwelling upon for its contemplation of the poet's own sensitivity is Timrod's "A Vision of Poesy." This is the story of a boy who, having been endowed with a preternatural poetic gift, seeks to accede to a poetic vocation. The story is ultimately one of qualified success for this outsetting bard, and insofar as it articulates the basis of that failure, it is instructive about Timrod's poetic theory. The boy presents himself, while a child, in terms reminiscent of Wordsworth's "Ode: Intimations of Immortality":

> O mother! Somewhere on this lovely earth
> I lived, and understood that mystic tongue,
> But, for some reason, to my second birth
> Only the dullest memories have clung.[36]

He learns the language of "human words" but is aware that "other sounds there be / Which seem, and are, the language of a life / Around, yet unlike ours" (p. 140). The child's mother draws a distinction between the boy's intuition and a religious or spiritual endowment because, while "God … freely gives / All that we need to have, or ought to know," the child is forced to wonder about this mysterious language (p. 142). Instead of God, there is a "lady" who is the child's poetic muse (p. 142). One night years later the boy has a vision of Poesy in the form of a "mortal maiden"; "in heaven, wherefrom she took her birth, / They called her Poesy, the angel of the earth" (p. 147). Here is what Poesy describes as her charge in thus visiting the youth:

> I sow the germ which buds in human art,
> And, with my sister, Science, I explore
> With light the dark recesses of the heart,
> And nerve the will, and teach the wish to soar;
> I touch with grace the body's meanest clay,
> While noble souls are nobler for my sway.
>
> (p. 148)

More than just experiencing this exploring and soaring himself, the purpose of the poet is to translate this inspiration to those for whom such a state is unavailable, so the poet is ultimately a messenger of thematic content to those who cannot share his elevated experience: "And what thou mayst discover by my aid / Thou shalt translate unto thy brother man." She says, "Into thy soul my soul have I infused; / Take care thy lofty powers be wisely used" (p. 150).

A late-life reckoning with whether the boy has "wisely used" those powers is featured in Part II of "A Vision of Poesy." Now an adult, the man is revisited by the spirit of Poesy, who tells him, "Thy songs were riddles hard to mortal ear" (p. 159). The basis of this reproach is that the bard sought his own idiosyncrasy – "thy own peculiar difference" – rather than seeking communion with mankind: "nor didst thou care to find / Aught that would bring thee nearer to thy kind. // Not thus the Poet, who in blood and brain / Would represent his race and speak for all" (p. 159). Although the verdict is that "Thou mightst have been," the consolation is that "Thy life hath not been wholly without use": "though thy name shall pass away," "Thy life shall bear its flowers in future times" (p. 161). For Timrod, the poet responds sensitively to the world (and conveys this response in poems) whereas for Poe, the reader responds sensitively to the poem (the poem eliciting this response, or these effects, in readers). Timrod thus would not consider poetry as reducible to the effects of sounds, as is suggested by the "nevermore" sound of Poe's raven.

Increasingly, the thematic focus for Timrod became martial in nature as the conflict between North and South approached a military form. In honor of the occasion of a secessionist gathering – what an earlier title of the poem referred to as "the meeting of the first southern Congress, at Montgomery, February, 1861" – Timrod wrote a poem that he came to call "Ethnogenesis":

> At last, we are
> A nation among nations; and the world
> Shall soon behold in many a distant port
> Another flag unfurled!
> Now, come what may, whose favor need we court?
> And, under God, whose thunder need we fear?
>
> (pp. 100–01)

Shortly after writing this poem Timrod joined the South Carolina military regiment to fight on behalf of the South in the Civil War; he later became a war correspondent.[37] Exempted from service due to poor health, he served as editor of the *Daily South Carolinian* and wrote editorials on such topics as "Southern Nationality."[38] In one such editorial he wrote the following:

> One purpose alone has actuated us in the conduct of this journal. It is to contribute all that journalists can contribute to the achievement of the complete, unqualified, and lasting independence of the Confederate States. In comparison with that object, everything else that makes life precious is, to us, a matter of secondary consideration, for the simple reason that, upon the attainment of that object, the permanent preservation of everything that makes life precious, absolutely depends.[39]

As was similarly stated by Paul Hamilton Hayne, author of a biographical sketch prefacing Timrod's collected works, "The objection [to Timrod's poetry in the North] is that the majority of his pieces, and the ablest, deal with Confederate topics, and praise Confederate heroes."[40] This martial spirit is evident in such Timrod poems as "A Call to Arms" and "Carolina."[41] Timrod would ultimately be designated as "Poet Laureate of the Confederacy" by H. T. Thompson.[42]

The focus on the Southern Confederacy was likewise important for the early life of Sidney Lanier, who served in the Confederacy's military. But what is most distinctive about Lanier's poetics is his later switch in allegiance away from a Confederate nationalism and toward loyalty to the re-unified Union. This was effected by his transformation of how we understand the United States' Union – not as the "North" as distinct from the "South" but as selected Northerners combined with selected Southerners. And for Lanier these selected representatives of the Federal Union were ethno-racial, i.e. were Anglo-Saxons. In other words, Lanier rewrote the sectional conflict between North and South into a racial conflict between black and white, and he unified the whites, North and South, into the population of Anglo-Saxons whom he conceived of as the true Americans. Thus his ultimate focus was only incidentally national and was fundamentally racial. Lanier was developing his racial views during the period of "Redemption," a time when the civil rights advances of the Reconstruction period (1865–77) were being gradually undermined by segregationist and white supremacist positions. Specifically, terrorist racial violence perpetrated by the Ku Klux Klan was intimidating black voters from the polls, and supreme court rulings were rolling back the post-war civil rights legislation.[43]

For his racialist thinking Lanier relied on a focus on music, a focus in some ways similar to Poe's but ultimately quite different. For Lanier, the sound of poetry is itself a kind of music, ultimately distinguishable from the words and meanings that make it up; in this sense it resembles the meaningless sound of Poe's raven. In his essay "From Bacon to Beethoven" Lanier writes the following:

> With the great majority of the human race the musical tones which are most frequently heard are those of the human voice. But these tones – which are as wholly devoid of intellectual signification in themselves as if they were enounced from a violin or flute – are usually produced along with certain vowel and consonantal combinations which go to make up words, and which consequently have conventional meanings. In this way significations belonging exclusively to the *words* of a song are often transferred by the hearer to the tones of the melody. In reality they are absolutely distinct.[44]

Lanier demonstrates his point by replacing words with "the meaningless particle *la*" in order to show that the pitches of the voice-as-instrument remain even when meaningful words have been eliminated.[45] Poetry, for Lanier, is just like such a song: instead of having "conventional meanings," it consists of the music of these word sounds. And as such sounds, it has, moreover, an intrinsic racial nature or essence. As Lanier would later write, in his *The Science of English Verse* (1880),

> I think no circumstance in the history of aesthetics is so curious as the over-powering passion of the English ear for 3-rhythm as opposed to 4-rhythm. From the beginning of English poetry with the *Song of the Traveller*, which we may perhaps refer to the 6th century: or, speaking within the more certain bounds of poetic history, from our father Caedmon: through all the wonderful list down to the present-day, every long poem and nearly every important short poem in the English language has been written in some form of 3-rhythm.[46]

The tradition of Anglo-Saxon poetry (which, for Lanier, extended uninter-rupted from the tenth century to his present-day poets like Tennyson and Whitman) was embodied by what he calls "3-rhythm" – "the mighty rhythm which beats through all these songs."[47]

Lanier writes extensively about the racial essence of this Anglo-Saxon sound effect. One very public venue for this writing is an 1876 letter to the editors of the *New York Times* about the libretto he wrote to a cantata to be performed on the occasion of the national centennial in Philadelphia. Lanier's libretto, he argues, is to be understood as music, and as music it is to be understood as containing the "abrupt vocables" of "Saxon words," so the choir singing these words is making Anglo-Saxon music.[48] Thus Lanier is writing for a national centennial but is himself interested in a much longer, and particularly racial, tradition, one that excludes ethnic minorities from what is no longer a geographic (i.e. Northern and Southern) nation but is now instead a racial (i.e. Anglo-Saxon) diaspora. This notion of an Anglo-Saxon race is different from the "ethnos" implied by Timrod's poem "Ethnogenesis": while Timrod considered his Confederacy's ethnic genesis to be originating in 1861, Lanier considered his Anglo-Saxon ethnic genesis to date back to the earliest phases of Anglo-Saxon poetry. Lanier's centen-nial cantata was thus, in his mind, neither a genesis nor a centennial but a millennial reaffirmation of Anglo-Saxon racial continuity, a continuity made manifest in the unbroken persistence of metrical-musical form.

Lanier's poetry of the Reconstruction period directly addressed the pol-itical tensions of the period; see, for instance, his "Laughter in the Senate," "Civil Rights," or "Them Ku Klux." He is perhaps better known, however, for a poem like "Song of the Chattahoochee," but if this poem is thematically unconcerned with the racial politics of the period, it is just as much engaged, formally, with Lanier's Anglo-Saxon "3-rhythm" and is thus just as much an assertion of white or Anglo-Saxon supremacy. Here is the first stanza of "Song of the Chattahoochee":

> High o'er the hills of Habersham,
> Veiling the valleys of Hall,
> The hickory told me manifold
> Fair tales of shade, the poplar tall
> Wrought me her shadowy self to hold
> The chestnut, the oak, the walnut, the pine,
> Overleaning, with flickering meaning and sign,
> Said, *Pass not, so cold, these manifold*
> *Deep shades of the hills of Habersham,*
> *These glades in the valleys of Hall.*[49]

The idea that I am suggesting here is that the sound of this "song" has, according to Lanier's poetic theory, nothing at all to do with the "manifold / Fair tales" told by the hickory or the "flickering meaning and sign" conveyed by the other trees. Once translated into verse, what matters is not the sound of nature but the sound of culture – of (for Lanier) a distinctively Anglo-Saxon culture that speaks through every line of the poem insofar as every line embodies his characteristic 3-rhythm. This poem is thus less about the landscape of the South than it is about the Anglo-Saxon race shared by white Northerners and Southerners alike. Lanier consequently reflects the white supremacist solution to sectional conflict, a solution that still is being reckoned with in the United States today.

We have seen that Timrod wrote in response to Poe (rejecting Poe's restriction of poetry to the domain of beauty alone), and Lanier also engaged with both of these predecessor authors in a similarly critical fashion. In response to the metrical theories of Poe (as set out in Poe's "The Rationale of Verse") Lanier writes that "we find Poe's essay permeated by a fundamental mistake quite fatal to the usefulness of even the shrewd detached glimpses occurring here and there."[50] Poe's mistake, according to Lanier, is his decision to think of accented and unaccented syllables rather than long and short ones, the latter approach alone admitting the kind of musical treatment that is central to Lanier's poetic theory.[51] Similarly, when commenting on the poetry of Henry Timrod, Lanier writes that Timrod "had never had time to learn the mere craft of the poet – the technique of verse."[52] In both of these cases Lanier is interested in verse technique, or the musicality of poetry, so it is Lanier's most salient contribution to subsequent discussions of verse – his foregrounding of the musicality in verse structures – that provides the ground of his disagreements with Poe and Timrod. Because of these disagreements, each writer is able to articulate his own distinctive theory of poetry. But it is ultimately in spite of these disagreements, and because of their critical engagement with each other, that these poets come together to form a Southern tradition of poetic thought.

NOTES

1 Floyd Stovall, *Edgar Poe the Poet: Essays New and Old on the Man and his Work* (Charlottesville: University Press of Virginia, 1969), p. 63.
2 *Ibid.*, pp. 126–74.
3 Edgar Allan Poe, "The Poetic Principle," in *Selected Writings of Edgar Allan Poe,* ed. Edward H. Davidson (Boston: Houghton Mifflin Co., 1956), p. 468.
4 Edgar Allan Poe, "Ballads and Other Poems," in *Selected Writings*, p. 436.
5 Edgar Allan Poe, "Drake-Halleck," in *Selected Writings*, p. 420.
6 *Ibid.*
7 Edgar Allan Poe, "The Philosophy of Composition," in *Selected Writings*, p. 456; Poe, "The Poetic Principle," p. 469.
8 Poe, "Drake-Halleck," p. 420.
9 Edgar Olson, "The Argument of Longinus' 'On the Sublime,'" in R. S. Crane, ed., *Critics and Criticism: Ancient and Modern* (University of Chicago Press, 1952), p. 243.
10 Poe, "The Poetic Principle," p. 464.
11 *Ibid.*, p. 471.
12 Poe, "Drake-Halleck," p. 421.
13 Poe, "Ballads and Other Poems," p. 437.
14 Poe, "Drake-Halleck," p. 421
15 Poe, "The Philosophy of Composition," p. 453.
16 Dwayne Thorpe, "The Poems: 1836–1849," in Eric W. Carlson, ed., *A Companion to Poe Studies* (Westport, CT: Greenwood Press, 1996), p. 103.
17 Poe, "The Philosophy of Composition," p. 454.
18 *Ibid.*, p. 455.
19 Poe, "The Raven," in *The Poems of Edgar Allan Poe*, ed. Thomas Ollive Mabbott (Cambridge, MA: Harvard University Press, 1980), p. 364. Further quotations from this edition are cited parenthetically in the text.
20 Poe, "The Philosophy of Composition," p. 458.
21 Poe, "By – Quarles," in *The Norton Anthology of American Literature*, 4th edn., vol. 1, ed. Nina Baym *et al.* (New York: W. W. Norton & Co., 1994), p. 1447.
22 *Ibid.*
23 *Ibid.*
24 Edgar Allan Poe, "The Rationale of Verse," in *The Complete Tales and Poems of Edgar Allan Poe* (New York: Random House, 1975), p. 913.
25 *Ibid.*, p. 914.
26 *Ibid.*, p. 470.
27 *Ibid.*
28 Poe, "Drake-Halleck," p. 419.
29 *Ibid.*, p. 418.

30 Paul H. Hayne, "Memoir of Henry Timrod," in *The Poems of Henry Timrod*, ed. Paul H. Hayne (New York: E. J. Hale & Son, 1873), p. 66.
31 See Edd Winfield Parks, *Henry Timrod* (New York: Twayne, 1964); Poe, "The Poetic Principle," p. 468.
32 Poe, "The Philosophy of Composition," p. 455.
33 Henry Timrod, "A Theory of Poetry," in *The Essays of Henry Timrod*, ed. Edd Winfield Parks (Athens: University of Georgia Press, 1942), pp. 117–18.
34 *Ibid.*, p. 106.
35 Henry Timrod, "What is Poetry?" in *The Essays of Henry Timrod*, p. 73.
36 Henry Timrod, "A Vision of Poesy," in *The Poems of Henry Timrod*, p. 141. Further quotations from this edition are cited parenthetically in the text.
37 See Walter Brian Cisco, *Henry Timrod: A Biography* (Madison, WI: Fairleigh Dickinson University Press, 2004), pp. 73, 78.
38 *Ibid.*, p. 95.
39 Quoted *ibid.*, p. 100.
40 Quoted *ibid.*, p. 125.
41 Hayne, "Memoir of Henry Timrod," pp. 37–38.
42 Quoted in Parks, *Henry Timrod*, p. 115.
43 See Eric Foner, *Reconstruction: America's Unfinished Revolution, 1863–77* (New York: Harper and Row, 1988) and Joel Williamson, *A Rage for Order: Black/White Relations in the American South Since Emancipation* (New York: Oxford University Press, 1986).
44 Sidney Lanier, "From Bacon to Beethoven," in *The Science of English Verse and Essays on Music*, The Centennial Edition of the Works of Sidney Lanier, ed. Paull Franklin Baum (Baltimore: Johns Hopkins University Press, 1945), p. 277.
45 *Ibid.*
46 Sidney Lanier, *The Science of English Verse*, in *The Science of English Verse*, p. 110.
47 *Ibid.*, p. 112.
48 Sidney Lanier, "The Centennial Cantata," in *The Science of English Verse*, pp. 272–73.
49 Sidney Lanier, "Song of the Chattahoochee," in *Poems and Poem Outlines*, The Centennial Edition of the Works of Sidney Lanier, ed. Charles R. Anderson (Baltimore: Johns Hopkins University Press, 1945), p. 104.
50 Lanier, *The Science of English Verse*, pp. 11–12.
51 *Ibid.*, p. 11 note 2.
52 Sidney Lanier, *Florida*, in *Florida and Miscellaneous Prose*, The Centennial Edition of the Works of Sidney Lanier, ed. Philip Graham (Baltimore: Johns Hopkins University Press, 1945), p. 161.

I I

IVY G. WILSON

The color line: James Monroe Whitfield and Albery Allson Whitman

> Let no man who loves the Negro race then decry poetry, for it is by this
> and other proofs of genius that our race will be enabled to take its place
> among the nations of the earth.
>
> Katherine Tillman[1]

In her 1897 review of "Afro-American Poets and Their Verse," Katherine
Tillman, writing for the African Methodist Episcopal *Church Review*,
notes that Albery Allson Whitman was one of a growing number of writers
whose increasing presence in the arts marked the increasing progress of the
race. Whitman's "The Freedman's Triumphant Song," Tillman commented,
abounded in "graceful metaphors" and contained "an easy flow of words."[2]
Tillman's praise for Whitman was as much about his particular versification
as it was with his having delivered the poem at the 1893 World's Fair that
many African Americans saw as the approach of a new dawn with the *fin
de siècle*. Indeed, linking Whitman with the revered Frances Ellen Watkins
Harper and a host of younger writers, Tillman viewed poetry as an index
to the race.

Joining other prominent African Americans in Chicago, Whitman read
"The Freedman's Triumphant Song" at the "Colored American Day" of the
World's Columbian Exposition. "The Freedman's Triumphant Song" chronicles the perseverance and loyalty of African Americans to the nation. Like
William Cooper Nell's *Colored Patriots of the American Revolution* (1855)
and William Wells Brown's *Negro in the American Rebellion: His Heroism
and His Fidelity* (1867), Whitman references Bunker Hill and Valley Forge
to accentuate the bond of African Americans to the country by underlining
their military service.

> Fear not, Columbia! Never fear
> The Negro's well-known presence here.
>
> ...

208

Fear not pollution from *his* touch.
But foreign contact, fear it much.[3]

Whitman's belief in the United States was unduly, almost blindingly, strident, so much so that he exploited a sense of nativism to underscore his proclamation of black patriotism in the poem.[4] Beyond underscoring their loyalty and fidelity, Whitman underlines African Americans' organic relationship to the country by emphasizing the fact that most were native born. Anticipating the "cast down your bucket" rhetoric of Booker T. Washington's 1895 "Atlanta Compromise" speech, Whitman's poem implores white America to turn first to their African-American counterparts immediately before them in their very midst. In the wake of the failures of Radical Reconstruction and, importantly, preceding Booker T. Washington's famous "Atlanta Compromise" by two years, Whitman's "The Freedman's Triumphant Song" romanticized the past relationship between African Americans and white Americans to portray an idealized future vision of the US national landscape.

Beyond its encomiums for the present moment of African-American writers, Tillman's review also offered a brief outline of the literary history of black poets from the revolutionary period to the end of the nineteenth century. Tillman's article, however, does not review, let alone mention, a single poet between Phillis Wheatley and Frances Harper in the first half of the nineteenth century. Furthermore, the poets that she mentions in the second half of the nineteenth century, including Josie D. Heard, Robert Clayton, Mamie Eloise Fox, and Cordelia Ray, all emerged in the post-Reconstruction era.

While studies of nineteenth-century African-American literature often privilege the slave narrative, recent work on poetry has compelled a reassessment of the multiple genres – and, importantly, multiple themes – of nineteenth-century African-American letters. The emergence of the North Carolinian George Moses Horton is one of the most compelling examples of how the broader field of African-American literary history might be reassessed though specific attention to the question of genre. In terms of genre, a host of scholars such as Mary Loeffelholz, Eliza Richards, and Meredith McGill have been advocating the need to advance an understanding of nineteenth-century US poetry that moves beyond the Walt Whitman/Emily Dickinson dyad. If studies of the slave narrative are demarcated by the publication of Frederick Douglass's 1845 *Narrative*, studies of nineteenth-century African-American verse might be delineated by the arrival of Harper. The long nineteenth century of African-American poetry, in this regard, is divided by Wheatley's 1773 *Poems on Various Subjects, Religious and Moral* and Harper's 1853 *Poems on Miscellaneous Subjects* on the one hand and

Paul Laurence Dunbar's *Lyrics of Lowly Life* in 1896 on the other hand. By focusing on the literary careers of James Monroe Whitfield and Albery Allson Whitman, this chapter analyzes how a focus on poetry and poetics compels a reconsideration of nineteenth-century African-American literary history. Whereas Whitfield's last probable poem was published in 1870, Whitman's first volume was a year later in 1871; their literary production, thus, spans the entire length of the second half of the nineteenth century. More importantly, by amplifying the voice of Whitfield and Whitman as two of the many unknown bards of whom James Weldon Johnson spoke in his poem "O Black and Unknown Bards" (1922), this chapter offers a view of how the African-American literary canon began to reconstitute itself in the wake of the decline of the slave narrative.

The circulation of James Monroe Whitfield

In the opening years of the Civil War in 1861 and 1862, Martin Delany surreptitiously incorporated a number of poems by his friend and fellow black emigrationist James Monroe Whitfield into *Blake; or The Huts of America*. Whitfield has remained in relative obscurity ever since, having received neither much commercial success in his lifetime nor subsequent critical attention for his 1853 volume *America and Other Poems*. But the dearth of criticism on Whitfield belies his importance as a poet, which did gain increased recognition when he moved to California in the early 1860s.

Whitfield was born to free blacks in 1822 and worked as a barber for the majority of his life but long aspired to be a poet exclusively. Douglass published a number of Whitfield's poems in *The North Star* and *Frederick Douglass' Paper*, encouraging him to abandon manual labor for the *belles lettres* of poetry. The first known poem published by Whitfield was entitled "Self-Reliance," which appeared in *The North Star* on December 14, 1849, followed the next week by one entitled "The North Star." Another six poems appeared in Douglass's periodicals between 1850 and 1852. In the antebellum period, he also published in Garrison's *Liberator* and Julia Griffiths's collection *Autographs for Freedom*, culminating with the appearance of his volume *America and Other Poems*, published by the James S. Leavitt Company of Buffalo, New York. One of the most conspicuous aspects of much of Whitfield's early poetry is how little it concerns race or slavery. In "Self-Reliance," Whitfield depicts a man whose sense of conscience is informed by Christianity; "To A – H – " is a paean to a noble figure whom even the gods admire; and "Ode to Music" finds Whitfield illuminating the aurality of nature. Furthermore, Whitfield's "Morning Song," a poem published after *America and Other Poems*, extends his interest in nature and the pastoral.

Whitfield probably reached his largest audience, then and now, because of his republication in Martin Delany's *Blake*. Delany's novel appeared serially in the *Anglo-African Magazine* and the *Weekly Anglo-African* and, as Eric J. Sundquist notes, he absorbed a host of Whitfield poems only to have them ventriloquized throughout the novel.⁵ In *Blake*, Whitfield's poem "Prayer of the Oppressed" is rendered through the mouth of the Cuban Placido. Other Whitfield poems featured in *Blake* include "To Cinque," "Yes! Strike Again the Sounding String," and "How Long." The assimilation of Whitfield in Delany's story signals one way in which political ideology can become strategically discursive, and the intertextuality of genres whereby verse is modified by the conventions of the novel.

By foregrounding the idea of intertextuality, the circulation of Whitfield's verse illustrates how the conventions of the novel and poetry influence each other. "Prayer of the Oppressed" and "To Cinque" were initially published in Whitfield's 1853 volume, but both "How Long" and "Yes! Strike Again the Sounding String" take more circuitous itineraries en route to Delany's *Blake*. "How Long" was originally published in Griffiths's *Autographs for Freedom*, which also featured poems by Harriet Beecher Stowe, John Greenleaf Whittier, and J. M. Eells. "Yes! Strike Again the Sounding String" was originally published in the March 15, 1850 issue of *The North Star*. After Whitfield included it in his volume, Douglass subsequently republished it whole in the advertisement for *America and Other Poems* in the July 15, 1853 issue of his newspaper. In the case of "How Long," the poem migrated from gift book to volume to magazine; in the case of "Yes! Strike Again the Sounding String," the poem migrated from newspaper to volume to newspaper to magazine. In both instances, the poems circulated from the specific context of their initial publication in newspapers to be later recontextualized within the format of a serialized novel. Furthermore, when Delany puts these poems into the mouth of Placido, he figuratively moves them from out of the ostensibly personal domain of an individual reader and into the public domain of social performance and demonstration.

Stylistically, the transfer of "To Cinque" and "Prayer of the Oppressed" to chapters 60 and 61 respectively of *Blake* illuminates the common elements of poetry, oratory, and song as part of a similar cultural genealogy in the mid nineteenth century. When Placido utters words from Whitfield's "Prayer of the Oppressed" before the Grand Council in Cuba, he does so with a tone of noticeable authority and gravitas, almost as if it were a declamation – "At the signal of the Chief, the poet, stepping upon the elevation on which were seated the orchestra, amidst a deathlike silence of anxious listeners and fond

admirers, read in a loud, impressive, and solemn manner."[6] As a performance, Whitfield's poem is transformed into a formal speech. By contrast,
Whitfield's "To Cinque" is illustrated as a communal and extemporaneous
performance in chapter 60 – "Suddenly, as if by magic, the whole company
simultaneously rose to their feet. With silent and suppressed demonstrations, men and women waved hand and handkerchief, Blake and Placido
entering at the instant when the amateur orchestra, instrumental and vocal
commenced in strains most impressive."[7] The transliteration of Whitfield's
poetry into *Blake* is a figurative act of transubstantiation, one where the discursive routes of its rearticulation in narrative form through the periodical
format is symbolic of a proleptic collectivity that Delany hopes will engender his reading audience to mobilize against chattel slavery.

While there is some evidence that Whitfield may have traveled to Central
America in search of land for a black colony from 1859 to 1861, it is probable that he reemerged in California in the summer of 1862. On August 23,
1862, the *Pacific Appeal*, one of the earliest and most important black periodicals in California, acknowledged that it had a correspondent under the
initials "J. M. W." and a "J. M. Whitfield" is listed in the "Our Contributors"
column of the first page of the paper, beginning on March 14, 1863. In
the midst of the Civil War, Whitfield altered his former emigrationist position to champion black participation in the Union cause, as he articulated
in an editorial for the *Pacific Appeal* in the August 9, 1862 issue. He also
continued writing as a poet, publishing "To A – Sketching from Nature"
on May 23 the following year. "To A – Sketching from Nature" was both
an opportunity to reflect upon the transcendence of nature as much as a
reflection that California itself might be the perfect embodiment of nature, a
new Eden where African Americans might be able to start anew. As much as
Whitfield's interaction with the *Pacific Appeal* reveals about his own position
as a writer, it can also help to illuminate the history of Northern California's
African-American communities in the years during and after the Civil War.

Whereas Whitfield's lengthiest poem had been "The Vision," his verse for
the San Francisco *Elevator* was more extended and protracted. In 1867, he
published "A Poem, Written for the Celebration of the Fourth Anniversary of
President Lincoln's Emancipation Proclamation" for the *Elevator*. His only
previously published periodical poem before then was probably "To A –
Sketching from Nature" more than three years earlier. Whitfield's "Fourth
Anniversary" was a 400-line poem, written in iambic tetrameter and published in two parts on January 4 and 11. It was also published as a small volume under separate cover with Ezra R. Johnson's "Emancipation Oration"
in the same year. The poem outlined the history of the country from the
beginning to the present. Rather than depict emancipation as simply the

freeing of America's black subjects, Whitfield conceptualized the poem as an illustration of how the Emancipation Proclamation liberated the country writ large, freeing the idea of liberty from a slavocracy which held the nation in bondage.

> One century and a half had flown
> > When Freedom gained the first great fight;
> Defied the power of the throne,
> > And bravely proved the people's might,
> > > When banded in a righteous cause,
> > > To overthrow oppressive laws.
> 'Twas then, when struggling at its birth,
> > To take its proper place beside
> The other Nations of the earth,
> > The rule of justice was applied;
> > And all mankind declared to be
> > Inheritors of Liberty;
> > With right to make their freedom known,
> > By choosing rulers of their own.
> But when it came t' enforce the right,
> > Gained on the well-contested field,
> Slavery's dark intrigues won the fight,
> > And made victorious Freedom yield.[8]

Whitfield's poem implies that slavery separated the USA from the teleology of modernity enjoyed by "The other Nations of the earth" because it tied the country to an anachronistic temporality. In the poem, Whitfield enumerates, almost in the vein of one of Walt Whitman's catalogs, a litany of national and regional identities that comprise the USA and that have worked to preserve the Union and abolish slavery. In contrast to his position as recently as a decade earlier regarding the necessity of black emigration, Whitfield's message and tone here are more than nominally patriotic, a difference in perspective due as much perhaps to being on the other side of the Civil War as well as the other side of the country.

Whitfield continued underscoring progress as a theme in his last known published poem by accentuating the USA as the apotheosis of the sign of the times. In an untitled poem for the *Elevator* appearing on May 6, 1870, Whitfield distills much of the "Fourth Anniversary" poem.

> To lead the van of Freedom's march,
> > Till on the earth there shall remain,
> Nowhere beneath the heaven's blue arch
> > A single slave to clank his chain;
> Till all around, from east to west,

From north to south, on land and sea,
Like us, the nations shall be blest
With equal laws and liberty.[9]

Published in the midst of Radical Reconstruction, Whitfield's concluding lines intimate that only after the end of slavery could the USA come to embody a "city upon a hill," as a model for the rest of the world to emulate. Here, Whitfield's poem moves beyond a national anthem into a kind of transcendent paean.

Albery Allson Whitman and narrative poetry

While Whitfield's poetry could only adopt an appreciation of the nation after the beginning of the Civil War, Albery Allson Whitman's poetry made less use of an explicit critique of the USA. Whitman clearly wanted to be a national poet in the vein of John Greenleaf Whittier or Henry Wadsworth Longfellow and his long narrative poems aspire to develop into epic form. Experimenting with blank verse, dialect verse, *ottava rima*, Spenserian stanzas, iambic, trochaic and anapestic lines in three to five feet, Whitman had an appreciation for various metrical and stanzaic forms. Whitman's experimentation with different poetic forms was propelled by his desire to master the "high" literary art of poetry as much as it was by a belief that poetry as a genre could best affect social change. Indeed, Whitman believed that the world was at the beginning of a "poetical revolution":

> As we understand it to-day, I think poetry is the language of universal senti-ment. Torch of the unresting mind, she kindles in advance of all progress. Her waitings are on the threshold of the infinite where, beckoning man to listen, she interprets the leaves of immortality ... Poesy is free, and knows not of hire. Beauty is her inspiration, – her creed is Truth, Goodness her Divinity.[10]

While not quite a theory of poetics, Whitman's words here amount to a manifesto for poetry. By "language of universal sentiment," Whitman means that poetry could become a lingua franca to articulate any number of emotions and thereby translate them as universal. Noticeable too here in Whitman's estimation of poetry is the idea of the sublime and its relation to beauty. In the most direct sense, Whitman saw man merely as the medium of true poetry but there is also a degree in which he sees both poetry and man as instruments of God.

Whitman produced a prodigious amount of poetry. Assumed to be published around 1871, his first volume, *Essay on the Ten Plagues and Miscellaneous Poems*, according to Whitman sold about one thousand cop-ies; however, no copies remain. His next volume, *Leelah Misled*, emerged two years later in 1873, followed by *Not a Man, and Yet a Man, with Miscellaneous Poems* in 1877. *The Rape of Florida* was published in 1884 and again with slight revisions as *Twasinta's Seminoles; or, Rape of Florida* in 1885. In 1890, Whitman published a combined edition of *Twasinta's Seminoles* that included *Not a Man, and Yet a Man* as well as a new collection of poems entitled *Drifted Leaves*. His last major volume, *An Idyl of the South*, was published at the beginning of the new century in 1901.[11] Along with the long narrative poems of *Leelah Misled, Not a Man, and Yet a Man, The Rape of Florida*, and *An Idyl of the South*, Whitman also produced lyrics, sonnets, and other poems.[12]

Among these works, Whitman published two dialect poems, pieces that reveal the range of his literary experimentation. He included both "Uncle Saul's Resolve" and "Tobe's Poem" in *Drifted Leaves*. Earlier in 1877, Whitman attempted a German dialect in his humorous ballad "Solon Stiles." Whitman's publication of "Uncle Saul's Resolve" and "Tobe's Poem" in 1890 was part of a movement by African-American writers over the decade, including Paul Laurence Dunbar and James Edwin Campbell, to recover the tenor and rhythms of dialect speech for complex literary effect.[13]

Whitman was keenly aware of the British poets. While *The Rape of Florida* is clearly influenced by Lord Byron's *Childe Harold* (1812–18), Whitman refers to a host of other English and Scottish writers throughout his works, including Sir Walter Scott, Robert Burns, and Thomas Campbell. Part of the reason that these poets appealed to Whitman, as Joan Sherman notes, is because of their depiction of a pastoral world, a pastoral world that Whitman wanted to show had been "clearly marred by race prejudice."[14] Although the curriculum at Wilberforce University underscored a classical education, Whitman's reading extended well beyond that to which he could have been introduced during his brief time there, and he might, in this regard, be considered an autodidact. In the words of Blyden Jackson no other poet before Dunbar, save perhaps Horton, "seems to have been so much born a poet."[15]

While it seems excessive to identify Whitman as a mockingbird poet, as Vernon Loggins and Charles E. Wynes have done, it is clear that he was enamored of the high British romantics and popular American poets like Whittier and Longfellow.[16] For Whitman, mastery of the classical forms of high poetry was paramount. But the preoccupation of American writers with classical forms of poetry was ruptured with the publication of Walt Whitman's *Leaves of Grass* in 1855, which changed forever the landscape of American poetry. Albery Whitman's attachment to the form of epic and his allusions to the Bible seemed antiquated, if not tied to another milieu altogether.

With its various references to classical English writers, *Leelah Misled* might be an indication of Whitman's reading in his early days as an aspiring poet. As would become apparent in his next volume *Not a Man, and Yet a Man*, Whitman's influences included Tennyson, Scott, and Byron, poets to whom he was most likely exposed during his brief time at Wilberforce University. Many of these poets had written poems of extended length that would have appealed to Whitman because of his attraction to epic and heroic themes. Along with Byron and Scott, William Shakespeare, Edmund Spenser, and John Milton are mentioned in *Leelah Misled* and it seems that Whitman was more than nominally familiar with their work. Milton's *Paradise Lost* (1667), for example, would have certainly appealed to Whitman as a literary example that displayed a command over meter and for its thematic concern with theology.

The influence of Whittier and Longfellow is more perceptible in his 1877 volume *Not a Man, and Yet a Man* than in the earlier *Leelah Misled*. As Benjamin Brawley notes, "The Old Sac Village" and "Nanawawa's Suitors" both shadow Longfellow's *The Song of Hiawatha* (1855) and Vernon Loggins finds links to Longfellow's "Paul Revere's Ride" (1861) in *Not a Man, and Yet a Man* as well.[17] Indeed, Whitman wrote to Longfellow twice, hoping to receive an endorsement. Whitman imagined his poetry to be a nationalist enterprise, one focused on the particular predicaments and promises of the USA. as a model for the rest of the world. The second stanza of *Leelah Misled*, for example, opens with the lines "Nor sing to me of distant climes, O muse! / Nor foreign cities, groves nor empires great, / But from my own Columbia fair, I choose / A song bearing with it of truth the force and weight."[18]

As Blyden Jackson has noted, both *Not a Man, and Yet a Man* and *The Rape of Florida* come out of the literary world of saga and epic and one might note that a perceptible degree of melodrama runs through all of Whitman's major narrative poems.[19] *Leelah Misled* follows the tribulations of a young woman whose virtue is compromised by a man who betrays her. His next volume, *Not a Man, and Yet a Man*, centers on frontier settlement life and chattel slavery and depicts the heroic exploits of an all-but-white slave named Rodney. The early parts of the poem are set on the frontier during the early nineteenth century where Rodney is owned by the wealthy Sir Maxey, a prominent member of the white settler community in Saville, Illinois. Not far from Saville is a village of Sac tribe Native Americans led by chief Pashepaho.

While Whitman exploits some of the most commonplace literary conventions in nineteenth-century African-American letters – most notably the trope of the tragic mulatta and the figure of the heroic masculine subject – the Native-American subplot of *Not a Man, and Yet a Man* explores a little-studied episode of US history. In rather stark terms, these episodes represent the collision of the "savage" and the "civilized" as the inevitable consequence of the nationalizing imperatives of western expansion. The Sac Indian subplot of *Not a Man, and Yet a Man* is not only an ostensible image of frontier America – of life on the border, as it were – but it illustrates the complex machinations of US racial codes that stratified Native and African Americans in relation to the idealized position of the normative white American subject proper. *Not a Man, and Yet a Man* is one of a few literary texts by African Americans to take up Native America as a topic in the nineteenth century, along with, for example, Ann Plato's poem "The Natives of America" (1841). Many of Whitman's readers would have already held an image of the Native American in their mind either through Longfellow's *Hiawatha* or the broader discourse about the "noble savage." Readers in the Midwest, in particular, would have readily recalled the episode of the War of 1812 where Fort Dearborn was burned to the ground. Whitman must have had this in mind when he described Rodney approaching the smoking ruins of Saville.

Although Whitman portrays the Sac Indians as idyllic and peaceful, he nonetheless sets them up as the foil against which he can initiate Rodney's own claim for an American identity. Whitman overdetermines Rodney's masculinity by making it a product of his physical strength and fortitude as much as it is a condition of his being dutiful and loyal. While Rodney does not identify with the white settlers of Saville, he also does not intuitively sympathize with the Sac Indians. Before he is sent to Fort Dearborn he conveys his own sentiments about the anomalous state of being "colored" and a slave and the contradictions of being a man and yet not a man.

> If I, an alien to your house and hearth,
> The ignoble sharer of a slavish birth,
> Had I a single treasure dear to me,
> A single home joy bright, or, even were
> I wonder of my life, my arm I'd bare,
> And thrust my fingers into peril's hair.
> But none of these, and not a cheer within
> My darkened breast, what may I hope to win?
> Own me a man, and trust a manly breast.
> For be assured, although your slave am I,
> He will not cower, who will dare to die;
> He sees no terror in menace's eye.
> The gaping wounds I for my master wear,
> Already warn me that I unrewarded bear.[20]

Described as being of 85 percent Saxon blood, Rodney is figuratively between camps but, quite literally, constitutive of neither. His loyalty might be simply read as an illustration of personal fidelity. But, given Whitman's Prologue, where he is at pains to underscore the alliance between blacks and whites during the American Revolution and Civil War as a paradigmatic sign of patriotism, Rodney's heroism and fidelity are correlated here as a precursor to being enfolded into the national body politic.

While Whitman uses Native Americans as a foil to establish Rodney's initial position as a national subject, his next volume, *The Rape of Florida* (1884), illuminates a different genealogy between African and Native Americans where they come together as a coalition. Divided into four cantos, *The Rape of Florida* is comprised of 257 Spenserian stanzas that are obviously indebted to Byron's *Childe Harold*. Although Whitman borrows the form of *Childe Harold*, none of his major characters embodies the conventional image of the Byronic figure who, while heroic, is also somewhat flawed. Rather Whitman has all of his heroes approach perfection. *The Rape of Florida* tells the story of Palmecho, his daughter Ewald, and Atlassa, a gallant warrior between the first (1816–18) and second (1835–42) Seminole Wars. Its main action focuses on the trials of Ewald and Atlassa, who are consumed with rescuing Palmecho from US soldiers. Under a flag of truce, Palmecho attends a peace conference in St. Augustine, where he is imprisoned a second time. When he is captured a third time, he is packed with other Seminoles and maroons (or runaway blacks) onto a ship. Unlike his previous volume which features near-white black heroes, *The Rape of Florida* depicts alliances between maroons and Seminole Indians as they attempt to resist incursions by the US Army, incursions that would eventually result in the removal of both blacks and Natives to San Augustine, Texas and then Santa Rosa, Mexico.

Both *Not a Man, and Yet a Man* and *The Rape of Florida* call attention to what the epic might have meant to Whitman as a both a poet and a "colored" American.[21] The two works signal Whitman's desire as a poet to craft a volume that might merit being placed alongside Whittier's *Snow-Bound* and Longfellow's *Hiawatha* and suggest that he had much more in common with them formally than any other African-American poet of his day, including Harper. The two poems, however, indicate how Whitman as a "colored" American uses the epic to invert it as an apparatus of nationalism; the conclusion of *Not a Man, and Yet a Man* intimates that Rodney might soon become a US American, while all of the colored heroes of *The Rape of Florida* are relocated to the margins of the USA on the opposite side of the border of Mexico.

Whitman's last major volume, *An Idyl of the South*, returns the reader to the familiar theme of black and white race relations. Published in 1901, it is divided into two sections: "The Octoroon" and "The Southland's Charms and Freedom's Magnitude," both written in *ottava rima*. The latter is a plea for conciliation between former slaves and masters that recapitulates many of Whitman's sentiments about solidifying the bond between black and white Americans articulated in *Not a Man, and Yet a Man* and "The Freedman's Triumphant Song," among other places. Generally considered to be one of Whitman's best poetic achievements, "The Octoroon" narrates the story of Lena, a blue-eyed slave, who is loved by her young master, Sheldon Maury. When Maury's father learns of his son's feelings for Lena, he sells her to a profligate army officer named Major Royall. She escapes with the help of a slave named Andy (reminiscent of Andy from Harriet Beecher Stowe's *Uncle Tom's Cabin*) but dies shortly thereafter from exhaustion.

Throughout his poetry, Whitman stages a theory of African-American poetics, one where a concern with aurality remains a central preoccupation. This preoccupation with sound is evident in *Leelah Misled*, his second volume of poetry. In the latter quarter of the poem, Whitman devotes more than ten stanzas to a soliloquy by Leelah's distraught father when he learns that his daughter has been betrayed. Like the majority of the poem, the soliloquy is comprised of modified odes consisting of two quatrains followed by a couplet. But the most remarkable part of the poem is Leelah's response, which is conspicuously rendered in song:

> I would my happy ma could come,
>   And whisper in my ear,
> The words I used to hear at home,
>   "Don't weep my Leelah, dear,"
> Or that I could beside her be,
> Beneath the weeping willow tree,
> I would I never had been moved,
>   Though handsome men I met,
> I would I never could have loved,
>   Or that I could forget.
> But I was young, my heart was free,
> My love as pure as love could be.
>
> *(Leelah Misled*, pp. 30, 32)

Thematically, the song is a lamentation about the fall of a young woman who can only find solace in the echo of her mother's words and the thought of being eventually buried next to her. Formally, the song consists of six verses joined by a refrain that Whitman divides through different stanzaic and metrical configurations. Each verse is composed of a ballad stanza (abab) followed by a rhymed couplet in iambic tetrameter. The refrain consists of a short rhymed couplet accompanied by a variation on the envelope stanza (abba). Critically, although considerably shorter than her father's meditative soliloquy, Leelah's song functions to counteract her father's words and they, therefore, operate contrapuntally.

As an anecdote that closely shadows Leelah's predicament, the song is not simply an allegory but a subtextual commentary on Whitman's theory of poetics. Rather than being a pre-scripted song imported for the occasion, Leelah's bears the mark of being intuitive and extemporaneous. It is almost as if the delicacy of the situation, indeed of Leelah's own heart, demands that a song be created – almost as a literalization of Whitman's later declaration that "the subtle evolutions of thought must be expressed in song."[22] Given the various formal and thematic similarities described above, Leelah's song produces an echo effect, signaling the importance of the sonic medium for Whitman's poetry. Thus, *Leelah Misled* underscores the larger centrality of aurality to Whitman's poetic endeavors, not only with rhyme and rhythm but with the representation of songs themselves as art in his poetry.

One of the most noteworthy aspects of *Leelah Misled* as a text is what it discloses about Whitman's understanding of poetry and poetics. The multitudinous metrical configurations that Whitman employed from *Leelah Misled* to *An Idyl of the South* reveal that he was consumed with the aesthetics of sound. Most of his major volumes read like novels in verse and their length afforded him the latitude to experiment with patterns within the precincts of different sections or cantos. These experiments with stanzaic patterns might be thought of as variations on movements within a larger musical score. *Leelah Misled* furnishes an early pronouncement of Whitman's understanding of the uses of sound within poetry.

> My fetters broken, I began to sing.
> Who bears my strain, then, mark the happy cause
> Thus prompting me; and, as my lay I bring,
> Think not that I thus come to win applause;
> For as a bird just fledged would swell its throat,
> Warble a song, and warble it again,
> Careless of who mark an imperfect note:
> So sing I now, and will I sing again,
> But since so many bards have shamed their muse
> By aims too high, a humbler course I choose.
>
> (*Leelah Misled*, p. 5)

For Whitman, the effectiveness of poetry depended upon how it achieved a degree of sonic accord and harmony. In striving for the ostensible perfect note, Whitman sought to deliver the content of his poetry through a discernible sound system. Above we see the image of the "warble," perhaps now most associated with Walt Whitman's "When Lilacs Last in the Dooryard Bloom'd" (1865) as well as the impression of the caged bird that echoes in Horton from the first half of the nineteenth century and anticipates Dunbar and Maya Angelou. Whitman's poetics were influenced by a sense of aurality, articulated here by the speaker's proclamation of a desire to sing.

"To make a poet black, / and bid him sing!"

Like much of Whitman's poetry, the lead poem of Whitfield's volume *America* is also preoccupied with the question of sound and song. The eponymous poem "America" opens with a set of visceral lines, ones that lull the reader with a degree of familiarity and anticipation only to have that familiarity immediately dissolved – "AMERICA, it is to thee, / Thou boasted land of liberty, – / It is to thee I raise my song, / Thou land of blood, and crime, and wrong."²³ Whitfield's "America" echoes Samuel Francis Smith's "My Country, 'Tis of Thee" (1831) and, in departing from the anticipated tone of Smith's song, Whitfield illuminates the contrast between the America celebrated in "My Country, 'Tis of Thee" and his poem, between a romanticized America and a real America.

Both Whitfield and Whitman published poetry in the forty-year period after slavery that is the focus of Tillman's essay in the African Methodist Episcopal *Church Review*. In Tillman's estimation, African Americans had progressed considerably during this period and she predicted that more might be expected under more favorable circumstances. Although black America had yet to produce a Milton or Shakespeare, she lamented, she understood the race to have accomplished enough that soon "the Afro-American poet will contribute to the world's literature."²⁴ The promise of the African-American contribution to the world's literature is not only marked in someone like Dunbar but in figures like Whitfield and Whitman who word by word refashioned the lines of poetry to both explore and cross the color line.

NOTES

1 Katherine Davis Chapman Tillman, "Afro-American Poets and Their Verse," African Methodist Episcopal *Church Review*, 14 (1898), 422.
2 *Ibid.*, p. 425.
3 Alberry Allson Whitman, "The Freedman's Triumphant Song," in *World's Fair Poem* (Atlanta: Holsey Job Print, 1893), p. 6.

4 Furthermore, Africa has only a nominal presence in Whitman's writings. In the elegy "The Lute of Afric's Tribe," Whitman outlines how the "sweet warblings" of Africa migrated across the Atlantic and found their way to Joshua McCarter Simpson, author of *The Emancipation Car* (1874) (Albery Allson Whitman, "The Lute of Afric's Tribe," in *Not a Man, and Yet a Man* [Springfield, OH: Republic Printing Company, 1877], p. 221). But the Whitman work where Africa has the greatest presence is "Poem to Bishop H. M. Turner" (1892). Although the poem does address Africa, it can only do so by recalibrating the USA as the epicenter of the black diaspora and, as such, works to reify the nationalist subtext of much of Whitman's verse. The poem was written in celebration of Henry McNeal Turner's return from Africa. Like Daniel Alexander Payne before him, Turner was one of the most well-known and highly respected bishops in the African Methodist Episcopal Church. Early lines in the first stanza intimate a new connection with Africa, perhaps even one with possible emigration intentions – "To our despised and injured race. / Two worlds clasp hands across the sea, / The mother and her child; / The heavens rejoice for earth is free" ("Poem to Bishop H. M. Turner," p. 3). Whitman's language here exploits the rhetoric of the family so intrinsic to emigration calls to return to Africa; but as the poem continues, it becomes evident that, while mother and child may have been reunited, there would be no permanent return to the ancestral house.

> So Afric, in her children blessed,
> Looks to the New World in the West,
> And treasures more than Egypt knew,
> Are hers in wealth and learning, too.
>
> (p. 9)

Turner went to Africa to establish a satellite of the A.M.E. Church and Whitman's poem intimates that such a religious mission would pull the continent into the orbit of black America and thereby into the orbit of Western European culture as well. The poem is undergirded by a figurative regal concert heralding Turner's return as much as the advent of a new day.

5 Robert S. Levine has provided one of the most comprehensive outlines of the publication history of *Blake*; see Levine, *Martin Delany, Frederick Douglass, and the Politics of Representative Identity* (Chapel Hill: University of North Carolina Press, 1997), pp. 179–80. See also Eric J. Sundquist, *To Wake the Nations: Race and the Makings of American Literature* (Cambridge, MA: The Belknap Press, 1993), pp. 203–04.

6 Martin Delaney, *Blake; or, The Huts of America*, ed. Floyd J. Miller (1861–62; rpt. Boston: Beacon Press, 1970), p. 259. For more biographical details concerning Whitfield, see Robert Levine and Ivy G. Wilson, eds., *The Works of James M. Whitfield: America and Other Writings* (Chapel Hill: University of North Carolina, 2011), pp. 1–27.

7 *Ibid.*, p. 250.

8 James M. Whitfield, "A Poem Written for the Celebration of the Fourth Anniversary of President Lincoln's Emancipation Proclamation," in *Emancipation Oration and Other Poems* (San Francisco: Published at the *Elevator* Office, 1867), pp. 25–26.

9 James M. Whitfield, "Poem by J. M. Whitfield," *San Francisco Elevator*, May 6, 1870.

10 Albery Allson Whitman, *The Rape of Florida* (St. Louis: Nixon-Jones, 1884), p. 5.

11 Beyond these longer narrative poems, Whitman also produced a number of shorter verses, most of which are collected in *Miscellaneous Poems* and *Drifted Leaves*. Many of these are occasional poems like "The Great Strike" about the labor upheaval and civil unrest of 1877 and "Hymn to the Nation," a celebration of the centennial of the USA – "Columbia has lived a hundred years / Thro' trials, hopes, and doubts and fears, / And still she lives, tho' often tempest-rocked, / Republic yet, united, one and free, / And may she live; her name the synonyme [*sic*] of Liberty!" (*Not a Man, and Yet a Man*, p. 220). There are nationalist poems like "Custer's Last Ride," reminiscent, as Benjamin Brawley notes, of Tennyson's *The Charge of the Light Brigade* (1854) ("Three Negro Poets," *Journal of Negro History*, 2 [1917], 384–92). *Miscellaneous Poems* also includes the paean "Ye Bards of England." Appended to the 1890 combined edition of *Twasinta's Seminoles*, *Drifted Leaves* features a number of pastoral poems as well as an elegy dedicated to Whitman's mother. It also includes a few pieces about the Civil War with poems on Stonewall Jackson and Ulysses Grant and another entitled "The Veteran," which would be reprinted later as one of two poems published underneath the title of *World's Fair Poem* in 1893.

12 Beyond bringing out his poems as volumes, Whitman published at least two poems in the African Methodist Episcopal *Church Review*. "Woods and Rocks – A Reverie" appeared in 1886 and "A Contrast" twelve years later in 1898.

13 Although, like Dunbar, Whitman experimented with a number of poetic forms, he never achieved the commercial or critical acclaim that Dunbar received and the majority of his poetry was put out by small publishing houses. Little is known about these houses and even less is known about Whitman's particular relationship to these firms. *Leelah Misled* was published by Richard LaRue in his home state of Kentucky, *World's Fair Poem* in Atlanta by Holsey Job Print, and *An Idyl of the South* by Metaphysical Printing in New York City. *The Rape of Florida* and its two revisions were published by Nixon-Jones Printing located in St. Louis. Given that Kate Chopin had to publish her novel *At Fault* in 1890 at her own expense with the same St. Louis press, it is conceivable that Whitman had to finance his own publication of *The Rape of Florida*, if not other volumes.

14 Joan R. Sherman, "Albery Allson Whitman: Poet of Beauty and Manliness," *CLAJ*, 14 (1971), 140.

15 Blyden Jackson, "Albery Allson Whitman," in Trudier Harris and Thadious M. Davis, eds., *Afro-American Writers Before the Harlem Renaissance* (Detroit: Gale, 1986), p. 264.

16 See Vernon Loggins, *The Negro Author: His Development in America to 1900* (New York: Columbia University Press, 1931) and Charles E. Wynes, "Albery Allson Whitman – the 'Black Mocking Bird' (?) Poet," *Illinois Quarterly*, 41 (1978), 38–47.

17 See Blyden Jackson, *A History of Afro-American Literature: The Long Beginning, 1746-1895*, vol. 1 (Baton Rouge: Louisiana State University Press, 1989), pp. 272–92, 415, 440.

18 Albery Allson Whitman, *Leelah Misled* (Lexington, KY: Richard LaRue, 1873), p. 2. Subsequent references will be cited parenthetically in the text.

19 Jackson, *A History of Afro-American Literature*, p. 283.

20 Whitman, *Not a Man, and Yet a Man*, p. 81.

21 As Whitman wrote in the Preface to the 1885 edition of *Twasinta's Seminoles*: "I am in active sympathy with the progressive colored man. I have a mind to think that he has a calling among his fellow-men. It may be noticed here that I use the words, colored man, instead of the word Negro. I do this because *my* feelings decide in favor of *colored* man by a vote of eight to seven. I am in active sympathy with America's *coming* colored man."

22 Whitman, *The Rape of Florida*, p. 5.

23 James M. Whitfield, *America and Other Poems* (Buffalo, NY: James S. Leavitt, 1853), p. 9.

24 Tillman, "Afro-American Poets," p. 428.

12

DONALD PEASE

Colonial violence and poetic transcendence in Whitman's "Song of Myself"

This chapter originated as an inquiry into the site of enunciation of Whitman's "Song of Myself." Throughout "Song of Myself," the poet took up a trans-subjective stance that enabled him to straddle heterogeneous places and historical periods indifferent to the determinations of time and place. Was there a passage in the poem in which he acquired this freedom from the determinations of time and place?

My attempt to answer this question coincided with my effort to explain why Whitman had included the memory of the colonial violence that took place in Goliad within "Song of Myself." Over time these seemingly incompatible processes of inquiry merged into the discovery that Whitman's poetic witness to the mass slaughter at Goliad located the otherwise unclaimable site of enunciation for "Song of Myself."

This chapter constitutes an effort to find terms to explain the complicated relationship between the site of enunciation of Walt Whitman's "Song of Myself" and the colonial violence that this literary formation at once disavowed yet revealed. What Walter Mignolo has described as the "dark side" of the American Renaissance came to light in the antebellum United States when the rebirth of classical legacies within the so-called masterworks of the United States' literary tradition coincided with colonial expansion.[1]

In what follows, I will discuss this formerly obscured dimension of the American Renaissance through the discussion of a passage from Walt Whitman's "Song of Myself" in which the recollection of a scene of colonial violence coincided with the discovery of resources within his poetic personality that Whitman called the "me myself."

The remarks that follow are divided into sections that turn on two interrelated claims: that colonial violence constituted the disavowed underside of the American Renaissance, and that this other scene was the site of enunciation for the speech acts whereby Walt Whitman celebrated the United States itself as the greatest poem.

Goliad, Texas: the needless slaughter of God's image

The chapter begins with an explanation of Whitman's association of his literary project with the effort to establish the United States' hemispheric sovereignty in the military campaign that President James A. Polk ordered General Zachary Taylor to undertake against the state of Mexico from 1846 to 1848. Whitman began this association in the editorials that he wrote while working for the *Brooklyn Eagle* from 1846 to 1848.[2]

These editorials have been disqualified by Whitman scholars as either juvenilia or as expressive of views that Whitman had either cast off or radically transformed after he assumed the mantle of the national bard. But the expressive personality that Whitman assumed in writing these editorials was animated by the structure of feeling upon which the passages I shall cite from "Song of Myself" depended for their intelligibility.

Whitman constructed a validation of the United States' presumption that the hemisphere itself was a national entitlement in the editorial he composed for the May 2, 1846 edition of the *Brooklyn Eagle*, in which he characterized the memories of the Alamo and Goliad as violations of that presumption: "The massacre at the Alamo, the bloody business at Goliad, the red butcheries which the cowardly Mexicans effected whenever they got the people of Texas in their power during the course of the sanguinary contest, should be avenged more signally than ever outrage was avenged before!"[3] At Goliad, General Santa Anna repudiated international treaties protecting prisoners of war when he ordered the mass execution of men he had taken captive. This act violated the sovereignty of the power presupposed by both of the parties who made the terms of capitulation – the prisoners and their captors. The men Santa Anna slaughtered at Goliad had actively consented to go to a war that represented their will. But Santa Anna refused to recognize their treaty of surrender. Santa Anna's command to execute the men made martyrs and assassins out of the participants in this event.

In his editorials, Whitman described the victims of this mass execution as a manifestation of the sovereign destiny of the American people. In articulating his condemnation of Santa Anna's actions, Whitman invoked Mexico's violation of international rules of war understood to be binding for all sovereign nations. Whitman represented Polk's appropriation of Mexican territory as redress for the martyrdom sustained by the Texans who occupied it.

In his May 2 editorial, Whitman remembered the 1836 massacres at Goliad and the Alamo as justifying motives for the US–Mexican War. Both of these "red butcheries" ruptured the progressive narrative underwriting the ideology of Manifest Destiny. Whitman's editorial gave expression to his readership's righteous indignation as the affective basis for the redemptive violence President Polk directed against a Mexican state. The shame and collective outrage that emerged with this violation of the image of the United States' exceptional place in providential history "should be avenged more signally than ever outrage was avenged before."

Imperial conquest as an Anglo-Saxon practice of freedom

While I shall discuss Whitman's vexed relationship to the battle at Goliad in greater detail when I turn to his account of the events that took place there in "Song of Myself," just now I need to provide a schematic account of the incident. The Battle of Goliad was part of the Texas Revolution that culminated in the Independence of Texas in April 1836. Goliad marked the conclusion to a much larger battle that took place in Coleta, Texas on March 19–20, 1836. On March 27, 1836, 354 American prisoners from the battle were executed under the command of General Santa Anna. The difference between the mass deaths at the Alamo and Goliad was that the soldiers who died at Goliad signed a treaty of surrender but the former did not. Yet the militia at Goliad endured the same catastrophic fate as had the soldiers at the Alamo.[4]

Goliad named an historical event – the slaughter in cold blood and burning of the bodies of 354 Texans after their commander had signed an agreement that their Mexican captors treat them as prisoners of war – that could not be claimed as an American event. The scene was inhabited by a sacrificial body politic. The members of the militia who died at Goliad had surrendered their will to their commander, Colonel Fannin, who represented it in the treaty of surrender he signed with the Mexican state. The members of Fannin's militia voluntarily enlisted in a war to take possession of Mexican territory. Whitman's editorials depicted the rangers as having died for the freedom of the soil. But he dismissed the Mexicans' right to defend their territory as a barbaric claim.

Goliad was discontinuous with the nation-making violence of the expansionist present and discontinuous with the nation-founding violence of the revolutionary past. The events at Goliad took place in the gap between the United States as a civi-territorial compact and this field of violence. The people-annulling violence that took place there emerged out of the violation of a people's right to have rights.

Goliad also named the colonial practices that had to be excluded from the nation's official history in order for the national compact to appear democratically inclusive. Upon calling attention to this rupture in the nation's moral economy, Whitman positioned himself at the site of a violation of

America's providential history so that he could effectively reinvest his readers' moral outrage at the young men's deaths in the regenerative colonial violence the state directed against those who supposedly had no right to the land and who did not deserve to live.

Colonial relations differ from democratic relations in that they are grounded in the distinction between those whose lives must be defended and those whose lives are not worth living. Whitman's editorials turned the memory of Goliad into a practice of colonial violence when he invoked it to justify President Polk's war with Mexico. After representing them as apart from the American body politic, Whitman's editorials relocated Mexicans within a territory that was uninformed by justice or liberty.

In redescribing the militia who were executed at Goliad as sacred martyrs whose blood called out for vengeance, Whitman evoked the memory of Goliad to reestablish a norm of hemispheric dominance whereby the United States represented its standing in terms of the refusal to recognize the sovereignty of any of the other territorial states within the hemisphere.[5] The militia's voluntary surrender at Goliad rendered that site extraterritorial to both the United States and Mexico. The men who were interned at Goliad inhabited the status of raw biological life. Their encampment there rendered them utterly vulnerable to the will of their captors. At the most intimate level of their being, they were given over to a field of power that conditioned them absolutely.[6]

Although Whitman represented General Santa Anna's violation of the treaty of surrender as grounds for the derecognition of Mexico's standing as a sovereign state, it was in fact the Texas Rangers' acts of looting that had violated the sovereignty of the Mexican state.[7] The Texans' offer of surrender at Goliad had embroiled General Santa Anna in an intractable performative contradiction. After the fall of San Antonio on December 30, 1835, Santa Anna issued a punitive decree declaring that all "armed foreigners who entered Mexico with the intention of attacking the government would be executed as pirates upon capture."[8] Santa Anna had published the edict of San Antonio so as to avoid the political difficulties in which the Texan militia taken as captives at Goliad subsequently embroiled him. Santa Anna could not treat the Texans as prisoners of war without transforming what he described as "their acts of piracy" into an incident of war between sovereign states; and Santa Anna could not treat the Battle of Goliad as an incident in a war between sovereign nation states (rather than a police action involving small bands of pirates) without also turning the Texas militia into representatives of the United States government.[9] When he revoked the agreements protecting prisoners of war, Santa Anna represented the men taken as prisoners at Goliad as pirates who were voided of the protection of a sovereign state.

The United States achieved its self-declared standing as the hemispheric sovereign at the outset of the so-called Mexican–American War when it deprived the Mexican state of the power to exercise control over its populations and spaces.[10] After the United States stripped the Mexican government of this capacity, it reduced the peoples of Mexico to the condition of raw biological life. In the editorials that he published in the May 6 edition of the *Brooklyn Eagle*, Whitman exploited this categorization when, in the name of redressing the outrage the Mexican state putatively enacted at Goliad, Whitman reduced all of Mexico to a terrorizing geography inhabited by non-humans from whom the citizens of the United States society had to be defended:

> Though Mexico is called a Republic, the inhabitants have neither the real possession of true liberty nor any tangible idea of it. As a people, their character has little or nothing of the noble attributes of the Anglo-Saxon race (we say this more in regret than in contempt for it is true), never developing the sturdy independence of the English freeman, their Spanish and mulatto ancestors have lent them craft, subtlety, passionate spite, deceit and voluptuousness enough – but no high patriotism, no doubtless devotion to great truths, no energy to overcome obstacles, no lusty independence, preferring a home in the wild to giving up even a trifling principle. The Mexicans are a hybridous race withal – Only a small proportion are of purely Spanish or any other European extraction. Nine-tenths of the population are made up of various intermixtures formed from white, Indian and black parentage, in all its mottled varieties. Nothing possessed by such a people can stand for a moment before such a power as the United States.[11]

Having described Goliad as a bloody example of the Mexicans' violation of the rules of war in his May 6 editorial, Whitman generalized the scene of the war crime to include the entirety of the territorial state of Mexico, that was thereby rendered a just target for the United States' acts of retributive violence. By way of the characterizations of them in his May 8 editorial, Whitman turned the people of Mexico into the negative referents of a biopolitical settlement in which the capacity to be killed was rendered inherent to the condition of being Mexican.[12] In passages like the following, Whitman arrogated the power to break into the domains of hemispheric life, armed with the biopolitical power to decide who would live and who would die:[13]

> May 8, 1846: We who pay shot for our soldiers want something for our money – some little glory in one way or another; a dozen or twenty dead Mestizos now and then, at least. In all conscience, we cannot think General Taylor justified unless he transmits the account of a skirmish out of which our tongue-patriots can manufacture the glory, forthwith.[14]

Following this biologization of the conflict, Whitman's representations of the practice of Anglo-Saxon freedom entailed the right of conquest of the Mexican territory. Upon describing the Mexicans as a "hybridous race" who were perforce lacking in the "noble attributes of the Anglo-Saxon race," Whitman endowed Zachary Taylor's army with the biopolitical mandate to accomplish the United States' sovereign right to propagate "the Empire for Liberty" by whatever means necessary.

Whitman invoked the memory of Goliad to reestablish a norm of hemispheric dominance premised on the United States' systematic derecognition of the sovereignty of other state territories.[15] Goliad supplied President Polk with an excuse for declaring a war between two hostile races with different institutions and different interests. After their violation of a binding agreement concerning the treatment of prisoners of war, Whitman eliminated the Mexicans from inclusion within a civilized body politic. Since they were unable to conform to basic norms of justice, Mexicans could never become part of civil society.

In his May 19, 1846 editorial, Whitman endowed Anglo-Saxons with a mythic right of conquest and therefore a right to spread liberty throughout the hemisphere. In formulating this mythology, Whitman reduced the peoples of Mexico to racial stereotypes as the supplemental rationale for effecting the ineradicable equivalence between Anglo-Saxon liberty and the conquest of Mexican territory:

> Any body with brains in his head cannot help seeing that the United States must conquer. Why what a comparison. This republic, the richest nation on earth – the fullest of means, of men, of moral power – running over with the elements of which great victories are made – the nation of nations – this to be pitted against such a state as Mexico – a land of zamboes and mestizoes – distracted, impoverished, with no reality about it – when the very freedom they are fighting for is not understood – where the officers and priests are despotic and the people slavish! What can be expected of such a contest, while the natural laws are not suspended? and what doubt can there be of who will win the day?[16]

Whitman's editorial redescribed the war of colonial domination pursued by the men who died at Goliad as an Anglo-Saxon practice of liberty. In so doing he transfigured the dead militia into representatives of the United States Republic who had been subjected to an oppressive and dominative foreign power. He thereby linked the memory of Goliad to the much higher intentionality of the divine vengeance executed by Polk's declaration of war. Whitman contended that the Mexican state that had ignored the sovereign authority of the signed treaty deserved to be overruled by Polk's imperial war.

The biopolitics of the Mexican–American War

In his reflections on questions of political sovereignty, Giorgio Agamben focuses upon what he has described as the concealed points of convergence between the juridico-political and biopolitical models of power. In *Homo Sacer*, Agamben traces the origins of the biopolitical body that he calls "bare life" to a figure known in Roman law as the *homo sacer*, defined as "he who can be killed with impunity but who cannot be sacrificed." "This figure," as Agamben explains, "names what is included within the juridico-political realm precisely as what must be excluded from it."[17]

Now it is Agamben's contention that the inclusion of bare life in the political realm constitutes the original – if occulted – core of sovereign power. "It can even be said," Agamben explains, "that the production of a biopolitical body is the original activity of sovereign power."[18]

To be sure, Agamben's historical generalizations are quite wide-ranging, but they eventuate in accounts of a variety of zones of abandonment – internment camps, detainment centers, Nazi concentration camps, slave ships, impromptu relocation areas – in which the normative conditions of human lifeworlds underwent radical suspension. What Agamben calls the *nomos* of the camp describes spaces in which individuals are reduced to bare life insofar as they are included within the calculations of the state only in order to be abandoned by those calculations. The American state's positioning of Mexicans within a localization lacking a principle of order not only supplied another powerful historical example of what Agamben has named a zone of abandonment, but that positioning was also quite literally productive of the United States border in the middle of the nineteenth century.

In proposing that Goliad should also be construed as the uncanny location from within which Whitman enunciated "Song of Myself," however, I need to explain the relationship between the space from within which Whitman sings and celebrates and what Agamben calls a "sovereign exception." Agamben draws the concept of the sovereign exception from Carl Schmitt. According to Schmitt, the exception "is an element in law that transcends positive law in the form of its suspension."[19] As such the exception enacts the sovereign power that grounds and enforces the rule of law as such. As the solely authorized enactor of the powers immanent to the space of exception, the sovereign, according to Schmitt, is positioned at one and the same time within and without the juridico-political order over which he presides:[20] "He simultaneously founds and guarantees the legal order; yet exceeds it."[21]

Agamben elsewhere extends Schmitt's analysis of sovereignty to explain the paradoxical relationship between localization and ordering in general and specifically with references to the juridico-political constructions that produced the representations of the New World. According to Schmitt, the connection between localization and ordering that was constitutive of what he called the "*nomos* of the earth" inevitably produced a region or zone that was excluded from law. Such spaces assumed the shape of a free and juridically empty space in which the sovereign power no longer knows the limits fixed by the *nomos* of the territorial order.[22]

In the classical epoch of the *Ius Publicum Europaeum*, this zone corresponded to the New World, which was identified with the state of nature in which everything was possible.[23] In *Homo Sacer* Agamben elaborates upon Schmitt's paradox to explain why this process of "localization-ordering" must perforce assume the form of the generalization of the state of the exception. "The state of nature and the state of the exception," Agamben explains,

> are nothing but the two sides of a single topological process in which what was presupposed as external (the state of nature) now reappears as in a Moebius strip or a Leyden jar, on the inside (as the state of exception) and the sovereign power is this very impossibility of distinguishing between inside and outside, *physis* and *nomos*, nature and exception. The state of exception is thus not so much a spatio-temporal suspension as a complex topological figure in which not only the exception and the rule, but also the state of nature and the law, the outside and the inside pass through one another.[24]

The border that Whitman's editorials had installed between the United States and Mexico produced a concrete instance of this complex topological figure. Whitman's imaginary border was not an arbitrarily inscribed boundary line; it was the concrete figuration or projection of an imaginary membrane. This boundary line specified something that was included within the US juridico-political order as a zone of indistinction between the chaos of barbarism (to which he consigned the state of Mexico) and the normal state of US civil society, resulting in an outside that is brought within as what must be excluded from the normal order.

In his several accounts of the Battle of Goliad, Whitman deployed his representations of it to materialize this literal underside of the national territory. Goliad named a space of generalized violence that Whitman included within the territorial United States to delineate what its civil order must exclude, so as to render discernible its ineluctable differences from the Mexican territories that Whitman characterized as non-civilizable:

May 11, 1846: We have dammed up our memories of what has passed in the
South years ago – of the devilish massacres of some of our bravest and noblest
sons, the children not of the south alone, but of the north and west – massacres
in defiance not only of ordinary humanity, but in violation of all the rules of
war. Who has read the sickening story of those brutal wholesale murders, so
useless for any purpose except gratifying the cowardly appetite of a nation of
bravos, willing to shoot down men in the hundreds in cold blood – without
panting for the day when the prayer of that blood should be listened to – when
the vengeance of a retributive God should be meted out to those who so ruth-
lessly and needlessly slaughtered His image.[25]

In this editorial, Whitman summoned God to avenge, remember, and make
efficacious the injustice suffered by these victims. The occasion for this
editorial was the absence of any compensating event by which the Goliad
atrocity could be rendered consistent with a providential view of American
history. The massacre at Goliad called into question God's providence with
respect to his elect as well as God's ability to avenge atrocities performed
against those under his care.

When Whitman remade the volunteers who were "needlessly slaughtered"
as manifestations of God's image, he designated the Mexicans who violated
the divine image as the targets of God's retributive justice. If history was the
evidence of God's providential rationality, this outrage demanded vengeance
as the compensating intelligibility that would restore meaning to an historical
atrocity that threatened the American way of life with meaninglessness.

Having described Goliad as a bloody example of the Mexicans' violation
of the rules of war in his May 6 editorial, on May 11, Whitman generalized
the scene of the war crime to include the entirety of the territorial state of
Mexico, that was thereby rendered a just target for the United States' acts
of retributive violence. Whitman's description of the Goliad massacre as the
needless slaughter of God's image in this editorial supplied President Polk's
campaign of imperial aggression with a sacred mission. After Whitman portrayed the US–Mexican War as the vindication of the sacred memory of
those who were murdered at Goliad, he supplied Polk's invasion of Mexico
with a retroactive justification as redress for the martyrdom sustained by the
rangers who invaded it.

By turning the men's passive suffering into intelligible sacrifice, the editor compensated their incomparable pain by undoing the incommensurabil-
ity between glorious merit and abhorrent destiny. The Mexican–American
War was thereafter made to fulfill a sanctifying function: it retroactively
transformed meaningless death by slaughter into the meaningful death of
martyrdom.

The "dammed-up" memory of the fact that this massacre had indeed taken place was supplanted by the editor's outrage over the loss of the fiction through which the nation recognized itself as an Empire of Liberty. After the bodies of the dead militia disappeared into editorials that articulated the political theology of the state, the violence directed against them became expressive of the rationale for the United States' self-aggrandizement.

As a prisoner of war camp, Goliad lay outside the control of Mexicans. It was regulated by international agreements that dictated how prisoners should be treated. Their voluntary surrender positioned them within a space that in being protected by international rules applicable to prisoners of war was extraterritorial to both the US and Mexico.

In becoming the virtual historical witness to the soldiers' martyrdom, Whitman inhabited the zone of indistinction between barbarity and civilization that Whitman's several accounts of it correlated with Goliad's "out of placedness."[26] The men who lost their lives there died in a place that, as a prisoner of war camp, named an order lacking localization in either the United States or Mexico. But this site lacking localization nevertheless becomes Whitman's means of territorializing the border in between the United States and Mexico.

In Whitman's narrative of their fate, the Texans who were killed and the Mexicans who killed them underwent a drastic change in their biopolitical status. Whereas the Mexicans reduced the Texans to the condition of bare life, Whitman, in his retelling of their story, effected the transformation of these "sacred martyrs" into the representatives of the sovereign desire for freedom upon which the United States body politic was founded. Whitman thereafter represented the state's appropriation of Mexican territory during the US–Mexican War as redress for the martyrdom sustained by the US citizens who occupied it.

Overall, Whitman's editorials translated the Texans' collective sacrifice into the agency responsible for the soil's annexation. This land became the United States' possession when the prisoners at Goliad lost the lives that they had pledged to the agreement. Goliad named the space in which the Texans who had been reduced to the condition of raw biological life provided the pretext for Whitman's transfiguration of the entirety of the United States into the condition of what Giorgio Agamben called the sovereign exception.

The emergence of the poet out of the ashes of Goliad

The chief differences between the poet and the editor became evident in their incompatible ways of representing what took place at Goliad. Whitman's editorials portrayed the "martyrs'" demand for vengeance as the affective energy needed to justify a war after which the United States annexed a large swath of Mexican territory. At the time its memory underwent transposition into the poetry, the reality of what happened at Goliad had been subtracted from the nation's transmissible history. The questions raised by the massacre at Goliad – who would count as a person, whether this soil would be free or slave soil – prefigured the crisis of representation that would result in the Civil War. But Goliad's status as a place that lacked placement within a recognizable territorial site or a transmissible history supplied the poet with a site outside space and time for the enunciation of transhistorical poetic speech acts that were comparably unlocatable.

By the time he had begun composing *Leaves of Grass*, Whitman conceived of the mass murder at Goliad as a hideous prefiguration of the impending War of Secession. In section 34 of "Song of Myself," Whitman recounted the horrifying singularity of what had happened without the explanatory logic of a historically referential past.

Now I tell what I knew in Texas in my early youth,
(I tell not the fall of Alamo,
Not one escaped to tell the fall of Alamo,
The hundred and fifty are dumb yet at Alamo,)
'Tis the tale of the murder in cold blood of four hundred and twelve young men.

Retreating they had form'd in a hollow square with their baggage for breastworks,
Nine hundred lives out of the surrounding enemy's, nine times their number, was
   the price they took in advance,
Their colonel was wounded and their ammunition gone,
They treated for an honorable capitulation, receiv'd writing and seal, gave up
   their arms and march'd back prisoners of war.

They were the glory of the race of rangers,
Matchless with horse, rifle, song, supper, courtship,
Large, turbulent, generous, handsome and affectionate,
Bearded, sunburnt, drest in the free costume of hunters,
Not a single one over thirty years of age.
The second First-day morning they were brought out in squads and massacred, it
   was beautiful early summer,
The work commenced about five o'clock and was over by eight.

None obey'd the command to kneel,
Some made a mad and helpless rush, some stood stark and straight,
A few fell at once, shot in the temple or heart, the living and dead lay together,
The maim'd and mangled dug in the dirt, the new-comers saw them there,
Some half-kill'd attempted to crawl away,
These were despatch'd with bayonets or batter'd with the blunts of muskets,

A youth not seventeen years old seiz'd his assassin till two more came to release
him,
The three were all torn and cover'd with the boy's blood.

At eleven o'clock began the burning of the bodies;
That is the tale of the murder of the four hundred and twelve young men.[27]

What I find most compelling about Whitman's account of the Battle of Goliad
has reference to its placement in the poem. Whitman's positions his tale of
the Battle of Goliad within a series of passages in "Song of Myself" wherein
Whitman's identification with the bodies of the wounded, the impoverished,
the enslaved, or the imprisoned rupture the continuity between the self, body,
and nation his song had heretofore presupposed. Whitman's most accomplished critics and interpreters have characterized the sequence of passages
that begins with the assertion "I am the man, I suffer'd, I was there" and that
concludes with "I sit shame-faced and beg" as unassimilable to the logic of
celebratory identification underwriting the rest of the poem. James E. Miller,
Jr., to name but one of those commentators, has described this series of passages as giving expression to the dark night, the despair that is the underside
of Whitman's celebratory stance.[28]

Goliad occupied a site of transition in between the dissipation of one
socio-symbolic arrangement and the emergence of another. The events at
Goliad took place in the gap between the construal of United States as a
democratic republic whose citizens were bound together by a shared civi-
territorial compact and as an imperial state formation. The people-annulling
colonial violence that took place there represented what had to be excluded
from the history of the democratic republic.

Unprecedented in its extremity, Goliad violated conditions of historical
representation. This dislocated colonial locale could neither be officially
remembered nor truly forgotten. Lacking placement within US history and
US geography, the events that took place at Goliad appealed to Whitman's
poetry for placement.

Although two historical currents – racial warfare, and the practice of state-
sponsored genocide – coincided in this exceptional catastrophe, Whitman's
poem did not situate Goliad within a pre-existing historical narrative. This
tale disrupted the continuity of the sequence of recollected narratives in
which it appeared in that it neither took place at the time of the Revolution
nor commemorated a successful battle. Goliad took place in between two
wars. In the four decades of revisions to "Song Of Myself," Whitman did
not link it either to the Civil War that would soon follow it nor to the
Revolution and French and Indian wars that preceded it. Goliad signaled a
form of temporal discontinuity that demanded a different future.

Santa Anna's subjugation of a helpless population of Americans at Goliad had inspired Whitman to write editorials representing the Mexican–American War as an emancipatory crusade whose participants reenacted the American Revolution. In 1855 the contestation between the Free Soil Party and Slave Power over the political status of Texas and other southwestern territories eclipsed this characterization.[29] But if the men's deaths in 1836 had already been avenged during the US–Mexican war, why did the speaker even feel obliged to recall the murder of 412 men?

He did so in part, I would argue, because this melancholic scene supplied Whitman the affective resources needed to separate himself from the perspective of the editorial writer and become the poet of *Leaves of Grass*. As an editor, Whitman had covered over the hole Goliad had opened up in the symbolic network by placing it in the psychically restorative context of a patriotic frame narrative. The poet's recollection of the events that transpired at Goliad was marked by the absence of both the stirring patriotic rhetoric and the providential frame narrative with which the editor had come to terms with them. In place of the reciprocal relationship between violence and retribution, the poet encountered only the terrible contingency at the heart of the event.

Nine years after the termination of the Mexican–American War, Whitman withdrew the words upon which he had formerly staked his profession as an editor, and he enjoined his readers to participate in collective witness to this scene of catastrophic loss. The memory of Goliad pulled him into the precincts of a nameless place on the outskirts of a prisoner of war encampment where "assassins" mowed down scores of the "race of rangers," gathered their mangled bodies into piles, and burned the corpses like so many sheaves of wheat. On this Potters Field where the ashes of the uncelebrated dead were scattered across a scorched landscape, bereft of grass, the sun itself seemed to have stood still, and America was driven from its course.

The editor of the *Brooklyn Eagle* could not fathom this act of democide without converting it into the basis for political action. But the poet tarried at the site of this grim harvest of ashes and dust to draw in the resources of anomie as the nothing out of which his poetry emerged. The poet came into being in the presence of this void. Rather than integrating this atrocity within the political metaphysics of Manifest Destiny underwriting the editor's sense of historical continuity, Whitman's poetry took away the power of naming the event from politics pursued like a national religion. Having abandoned the triumphant frame narrative through which the editor had represented it, the poet grappled with the real catastrophe that took place on this traumatized landscape.

But if he did not wish to reject language or to abandon life, how could Whitman substantiate the event? How could he choose words that would prevent others from becoming consumed by grief or despair?

Poetry as an alternative constitutional power

The distinction between Whitman's personae as editor and poet turned on his different attitudes to the violated treaty of surrender. The editor avenged the violated compact by transfiguring it into a motive for war, but the poet of "Song of Myself" became the trans-subjective witness to the people who lost their lives at the breach of their treaty of surrender. The poet's witness to the violence done to the men who "treated for an honorable capitulation" unloosed the ties binding him to the imperial war upon which Whitman had staked his profession as a newspaper editor and established a poetic compact with the men who were about to die.

Santa Anna's order to execute the men whose safety he had guaranteed upon signing the writ of capitulation opened up a space of exception in which the sheer force of law had suspended the forms of law. His edict resulted in a condition of law in which, on the one hand, the norm – in this case adhering to the rules pertaining to the treatment of prisoners of war – was in force but it was not applied – hence exerted no actionable force. And on the other hand, an act that did not possess the form of a legal rule – mass execution of the men imprisoned at Goliad – acquired the force of law.[30] Whitman's poetic compact might be understood as an effort to restore the relationship between the men's forms and the terms securing them that had been catastrophically disrupted within this exceptional space.

Construed from the standpoint of language practices, the state of exception refers to a condition of anomie in which the potential for the successful accomplishment of expressive communication is separated from the communicative act that empowers speech to become meaningful for another speaker. In both cases, the state of exception marks a threshold at which the logic and praxis blur with each other.

Just as there are linguistic elements without denotation that they acquire only in discourse, so in the state of exception the norm is in force without any application. The concrete linguistic activity becomes intelligible through the presupposition of something like a language. This passage from *langue* to *parole* is not logical, it is practical – it is the assumption of *langue* by a speaking subject and the implementation of that complex apparatus Emile Benveniste called the enunciative function.[31] In the act of enunciation, language is formed through a suspension of concrete practice and its semanticization in its immediate reference to the real.[32]

Giorgio Agamben describes what takes place when "pure violence without logos claims to realize an enunciation without any real reference" as the linguistic equivalent of the anomie resulting in the wake of the sheer force of law suspending lawful forms. Words are always haunted by an intrinsic violence brought on by their difference from phenomena. Words possess a material presence that signifies the absence of the thing within the exterior world that language cannot internalize.[33]

In language the relation between the general (the potential for expressive communication) and the particular (the communicative act) is not reducible to merely a logical operation of subsuming the particular under the general rule as an instance. What is instead at issue is language's relation to world in the passage from a generic proposition having a merely virtual reference to a concrete reference to a segment of reality.

Whitman transformed the anomie precipitated by the broken treaty into the pure violence of a poesis that took the place of force of the norms of law that would have rendered the conditions of the treaty legally binding. It was Santa Anna's violent separation of the Texans from the already constituted terms and rules of the treaty to which he was a co-signatory that placed them in need of the reconstituting power of Whitman's poetry. The poet acquired this constituent power by reentering the space of extreme anomie, where the force of law has separated from its forms. In this space of exception Whitman took up the place of the witness to the force that rendered the treaty inapplicable and became the recipient of the pure violence that guaranteed the men's survivability within and as his tale. Because the already constituted forms of the treaty lacked the force of law capable of ensuring the men's survival, the poet's speech acts alone were capable of investing them with linguistic viability.

Santa Anna's mandate had violated the sovereign authorizing power presupposed by both of the parties who agreed to the terms of capitulation. The men's captive bodies were inhabited by the sovereign force of law that Santa Anna's dictum dissevered from its forms. In standing in for the universal subject who bore witness to the binding power of the treaty of surrender, the poet reengaged this terrible violence but voided of the viewpoint through which the editor had transmuted it into the language of militant revenge. The poet's speech acts thereafter assumed the function of the nexus that should have connected the terms of the treaty with the figures to which they applied. They animated the tie, the uptake of the enunciative function ("I cling to you so that you cannot unloose me" [*Complete Poetry*, p. 186]) linking the prisoners' constituted forms to the re-constituting force of the poet's speech acts.

After the rangers died into the place that memorialized the violation of their entreaty, Whitman articulated the dead men's collective demand for a viable compact to his poetic speech acts. They lived on through the tropes that Whitman made out of their entreaty. Whitman was transformed into a poet through the tropes he created to realize their demand. His speech drew upon the secondary constituent power of poesis to bind the men's forms to the act of narration through which they remained memorable.

The narrator-poet who bore witness to the traumatizing effects of the rangers' violated compact transposed his narration into an intersubjective compact binding the doomed rangers with Whitman's readers. Insofar as the dialogical relationship between poet and reader partook of this traumatizing eventfulness, it threatened to embed both the poet-narrator and his narratees within its catastrophizing orbit. Lacking anchorage within history's Real, this event was inscribed in the "Now" of poetic enunciation.

Now I tell

"Now I tell what I knew in Texas in my early youth" involved the poet in a tacit dialogue that brought his readers into the zone of an unfolding narrative rather than a finished report. When Whitman wrote "*Now* I tell," he eradicated the distinction between the race of rangers who lost their lives *then* and the narrator remembering them *now*. The poet would appear to have been seized by the deep unconscious, involuntary memory that lay outside of history understood as a consciously remembered experience. "Now I tell" summoned the poet to bear witness to this horrific event that was perforce subtracted from yet nevertheless haunted all other events within "Song of Myself" as their negated inside.

Whitman's editorials sacralized the trauma as the terrible revelation of the slaughter of God's image. But Whitman's poetry did not endow the disaster with meaning. Its traumatizing affects opened up a disjunction between what happened *then* and the memory overtaking him *now*. The suddenness with which the pent-up memory condensed within "Now I tell" grabbed hold of the speaker also suspended the reader's attention within an assemblage of unassimilable time that generated an alternative sense of space.

The traumatic memory that had broken into the present lived on in the empty materiality of poetry where it survived in a form that was otherwise than historical. Inscribing it as a contingent happening whose cause was suppressed in favor of its continuing effects, the poem did not situate this event. It disclosed the intensity of the object loss of its history. When he reached the end of the narration that began "Now I tell" with the phrase "That is the tale of the murder of the four hundred and twelve young men," Whitman sequestered a trauma that he did not want to pass on. But in living on in the "Now" of the poet's language, the traumatic eventfulness of the event became ever more eventful.

The interruption of history that this event portended also gave the poet access to his vision. It was his love of the Goliad dead who had lost their powers of self-representation that inspired the poet to sing their story. After the men's deaths, the poet had to discover the poetic resources with which to re-present them. The dead lived on through the tropes that Whitman made out of their will to survive, and Whitman was revitalized through the tropes he created to facilitate that will. Whitman's song transmuted their bodies into expressions of poetic voice rather than biological processes.

As he told their story, the poet inhabited an affective site informed by the terrible anxiety of the men's response to extreme danger. His efficacy as the event's witness depended upon his own exposure to annihilation in the scene that had taken possession of him. In what might be described as the "Call me Ishmael moment" of "Song of Myself," the poet tarried within this traumatizingly mortal space to communicate what survived. Rather than endowing the catastrophe with meaning, his words withdrew into the event's mode of eventuation. Since the poet's words were uttered from within the scene he narrated, the event seemed on the verge of happening again. Poised in the anguish of bearing witness to the event, the poet transported his readers to an inner landscape where the event never stopped taking place.

The unclaimable events that the poet narrated within the spot of time opened up by "Now I tell" interrupted the flow of homogeneous time and made it possible for the poet to reactivate other times. By its very persistence "Now I tell" also generated an alternative sense of space.

The men whose collective fate the poet memorialized were in close enough psychological proximity to the poet to be all but looking at him. They were demanding that he sing their song as the implicit promise of renegotiating the relationship between the living and the dead. The voices of these dead men cried out for the entreaty of the poetry as compensation for the violation of their treaty of surrender. Their demand that he sing their song placed the recognitional acts his poetry supplied outside the social world in which the living and the dead cannot know one another.

In witnessing the event, through a subjective lens, Whitman found words that enabled him to achieve a fragile mastery over the immobilizing fascination of the spectacle. In doing so, he endowed the scene with an afterlife. Holding the memory of Goliad within the oblivion to which history had consigned it required Whitman to invent a poetic practice whereby he transfigured its traumatic features into an evanescence that shone through everything.

As the image of a vulnerable population on the verge of mass execution faded from memory, disparate aspects of the event arose at different levels of legibility throughout other scenes. Unassimilated and unassimilable, elements of this dissociated memory drifted into other sections of "Song of Myself." The vivid image of a boy, who, like Whitman, was not yet seventeen years old when he was assassinated on this beautiful summer day in 1836 recalled the following passage from section 5 of "Song of Myself":

I mind how once we lay such a transparent summer morning,
How you settled your head athwart my hips and gently turn'd over upon me,
And parted the shirt from my bosom-bone, and plunged your tongue to my bare-
stript heart,
And reach'd till you felt my beard, and reach'd till you held my feet.

Swiftly arose and spread around me the peace and knowledge that pass all the
argument of the earth.[34]

In section 34, Whitman imagined himself witnessing the moment of the boy's death. As he imagined the boy grappling in the dirt with the two blood-covered assassins dispatched to kill him on this beautiful early summer morning, the poet all but lay down next to the boy to replace the assassins' knives with his words. In section 5 he described the embrace of a companion who lay down beside him as the experience of being taken up by a language without logos and without referent ("Swiftly arose and spread around me the peace and knowledge that pass all the argument of the earth"). Was the companion who plunged his tongue into the poet's "bare-stript heart" a prefiguration of the seventeen-year-old boy that the poet's words brought back to life? Has the poet taken the place of the boy's assassins in lying beside him on the grass? Are not the companion's plunging tongue and reaching grasp metaphors of the reading process? Is the boy being brought back into life through sensual identification with the words through which the poet has remembered him? In this scene, has the experience of being read by an intimate companion worked up the poet's senses so excitingly because he felt his words bring this beloved friend back into the life of his poetry?

The specter of the young men whose corpses were thrown to the flames in section 34 also haunted the poet's narration of the the bodies of twenty-eight young bathers stroked by an invisible hand in section 11. Indeed, parts of this site upon which the poet witnessed the death of the nation are discernible in all of the other sections of "Song of Myself." As the speaker is assumed by the inflooding memories of the lives that demanded celebration, he also is celebrating the self through whom these inalienable memories have become singer and song as well as the substance of what's sung. "I celebrate myself and sing myself / And what I assume you shall assume" (*Complete Poetry*, p. 25).

Whitman deployed this moment from the past into a site of transition in the present so as to engage American literature in a practice of transfiguration that turned this mortalized site into an ongoing celebration of ongoing poesis. But the poet did not accomplish this rededication until he found himself on the sacred ground between the living and the dead in section 38 of "Song of Myself":

> Enough! enough! enough!
> Somehow I have been stunn'd, Stand back!
> Give me a little time beyond my cuff'd head, slumbers, dreams, gaping,
> I discover myself on the verge of a usual mistake.
>
> That I could forget the mockers and insults!
> That I could forget the trickling tears and the blows of the bludgeons and
> hammers!
> That I could look with a separate look on my own crucifixion and bloody
> crowning!
>
> I remember now,
> I resume the overstaid fraction,
> The grave of rock multiplies what has been confided to it, or to any graves,
> Corpses rise, gashes heal, fastenings roll from me.
>
> I troop forth replenish'd with supreme power, one of an average unending
> procession.
> Inland and sea coast we go, and pass all boundary lines,
> Our swift ordinances on their way over the whole earth,
> The blossoms we wear in our hats the growth of thousands of years.
>
> Eleves, I salute you! come forward!
> Continue your annotations, continue your questionings.[35]

The ceremony at work in this section of the poem resituated the event that had traumatized him as a young man within a site of passage ("on the verge of a usual mistake") in which the poet discovered that his transfixed relation ("That I could look with a separate look") to this mortifying trauma ("my own crucifixion") posed an impediment to his poetic process. Representing that process as comparable to the resurrection of the dead supplied conditions within the poem for the transformation of the self-shattering trauma ("the overstaid fraction") into the ongoingness of Whitman's poesis. The poet's refusal to look with a look that separated the events that took place then from these transfigurative processes turned the earlier scene into this transformational site of passage. The self-transformative utterance ("That I could look with a separate look on my own crucifixion and bloody crowning!") produced the singer as the celebratory witness through whom the dead never stopped resurrecting in and as his song.

If we link the editorial writer's metaphor of a dammed-up memory with the poet's representation of his utterances as speech floods, we can see how the singer within section 38 of "Song of Myself" has retroactively assumed the men's unachieved will to escape death within the fluency of his resurrection song. Rather than aligning his poem with the Christian mysteries, however, Whitman deployed this moment from the past as a site of transfiguration in the present so as to engage his poetry in a practice of endless celebration.

By returning to this overstaid moment, the singer re-experienced this site of mass slaughter as the occasion for the renascence of poesis. Whitman's remembering of the dead through the addition of this figure has transfigured his speech acts into an endless procession of tropes.[36] In passing through inscription within the figures of his song, the dead rangers have arisen from their mass grave (the burning of the field has turned soil into rock) as an unending procession trooping across the globe.

This poetic ritual retroactively subsumed the event that had been subtracted from history within a resurrection song whose singer was quite literally composed out of the re-membering of the dead. "I remember now, / I resume the overstaid fraction" and "what I assume you shall assume." Devoid of all other predicative traits, the singer thereafter was entirely absorbed in the process of becoming anything that came into appearance through and as his song.

The fact that the song was written became as important as what was said. The poet has written his words down so as to raise up the figures of the dead. The holocaust enacted on a field of grass may have turned men into ashes and dust. But the poet's exercise of his faith in the act of marking his word enabled him to sow words out of this grim harvest. Conjuring tropes out of a deadened landscape, he let the scorched earth express itself as the pages of *Leaves of Grass*.

The pages of *Leaves of Grass* supplied the ground upon which he admitted and recreated his readers. The soil's uttering leaves became an emblem of the acts of writing and reading. These leaves produced a vision of the world as an open book that was to be enlarged through repeated acts of reading. The labor of reading reaped an immeasurable and instantaneous crop.

The underside of Whitman's song

It has been the burden of this chapter to articulate two claims: first, that Whitman's "Song of Myself" took place in between the speaker's witness of mass execution at Goliad and the song through which the dead replenish the national body politic, and second, that the colonial violence that Whitman represented as having taken place at Goliad constituted a disavowed underside of the American Renaissance.

In section 38, the singer's remembering of the mass murder turned the body of the singer into the celebrative portal through which the dead returned. The men who died at Goliad longed for an absolute freedom. But in relocating the dead within his immortal song, he subtracted this space from the social order that was immortalized through it. In Whitman's song, the site that had been deprived of any part of the earth's territory became the site upon which he sang the "Song of Myself."

At the site in which he experienced the demand to remember the men who died there, Whitman literally regenerated the US body politic out of the forgetting of Goliad as an instance of colonial violence and the remembering of it as the site of the celebratory enunciation of his song. His self was sung into existence here as the poetic medium through which the race of rangers' absolute longing for freedom constituted the affective substance at the core of what Whitman calls "me myself." The singer celebrated "me myself" through the glorification of the dead out of whose infinite longing for freedom the living were reborn. It was their rebirth in and as the tropes of Whitman's song that celebrated the US nation as the remembering of the dead by and as the living and that celebrated living through this song.

The locus of enunciation for Whitman's poetry was structured in the non-coincidence of a scene of colonial violence with this poetic festival that emerged from yet obstructed that scene. But there was a difference between the material level in which the soldiers remained dead and the symbolic level in which the body politic was reborn. The redemptive figures that the poet has generated out of these immolated victims compete with the ashes and dust into which these young men have disintegrated. In thematizing the oscillations between these levels of representation, the poem's structure of exchange transferentially redescribed the event in a way that at once obscured and revealed the colonial violence that took place there.

As the space that was included within the American Renaissance as what must perforce be excluded from its official self-representations, Goliad continues to regulate the order of American Renaissance eventuation from which it has been removed. If Goliad names the permanent site of re-nascence from the state of nature to the empire of liberty, this site of permanent emergency might also be described as continuing to haunt our present historical conjuncture.

NOTES

1 Walter Mignolo, *The Darker Side of the Renaissance: Literacy, Territoriality, and Colonization* (Ann Arbor : University of Michigan Press, 1995).
2 *The Collected Works of Walt Whitman: The Journalism*, ed. Herbert Bergman, Douglas A. Norer, Edward J. Recchia (New York: Peter Lang, 1998), vol. 1: 1834–46.
3 *Ibid.*, p. 342.
4 Thom Hatch, "Surrender and Massacre at Goliad," in *Encylopedia of the Alamo and the Texas Revolution* (Jefferson, NC: Mcfarland and Company, Inc., 2007), pp. 99–106.
5 Judith Butler discusses US norms of dominance with an account of the ways in which those norms are experienced most profoundly at the instant of their loss: "What kind of loss is this? It is the loss of the prerogative, only and always to be the one who transgresses the sovereign boundaries of other states, but never in the position of having one's own boundaries transgressed." *Precarious Life* (New York: Verso, 2004), p.39.
6 Butler discusses this condition of primary vulnerability within the context of prisoner of war camps in the chapter "Violence, Mourning, Politics." *Ibid.*, pp. 19–49.
7 Hatch, "Atrocities Committed during the Texas Revolution," in *Encylopedia*, p. 41.
8 *Ibid.*, p. 42.
9 *Ibid.*
10 For a splendid account of Tejanos's perspectives on the United States' violation of Mexico's sovereignty, see Arnoldo DeLeon, "Tejanos and the Texas War for Independence: Historiography's Judgment," *New Mexico Historical Review*, 61 (April 1986).
11 *Walt Whitman: The Journalism*, vol. 1: 1834–46, p.349.
12 "Whose lives count as grievable lives? What makes for a grievable life?" Judith Butler correlates these questions with reflections on Foucault's association of the state's biopolitical power with the decision over who it will let live and let die. *Precarious Life*, pp. 20–21.
13 "If a life is not grievable, it is not quite a life; it does not qualify as a life and is not worth notice. It is already the unburied, if not the unburiable." *Ibid.*, p. 34.
14 *Walt Whitman: The Journalism*, vol. 1: 1834–46, p. 354.
15 "When the United States acts, it establishes a conception of what it means to act as an American, establishes a norm by which that subject might be known. In recent months a subject has been instated at the national level, a sovereign and extra-legal subject, a violent and self-centered subject; its violence constitutes the building of a subject that seeks to restore and maintain its mastery through the systematic destruction of its multilateral relations, its ties to the international community." Butler, *Precarious Life*, p. 34.
16 *Walt Whitman: The Journalism*, vol. 1: 1834–46, pp. 366–67.
17 Giorgio Agamben, *Homo Sacer: Sovereign Power and Bare Life*, trans. Daniel Heller-Roazen (Stanford University Press, 1998), pp. 8, 11.
18 *Ibid.*, p. 6.
19 *Ibid.*, p. 15.

20 *Ibid.*, p. 17.

21 *Ibid.*

22 *Ibid.*, p. 35.

23 *Ibid.*, p. 36.

24 *Ibid.*, p. 37.

25 *Walt Whitman: The Journalism*, vol. I: 1834–46, p. 359.

26 On a discussion of the ways in which Whitman's various accounts of these events served his performing the role of cultural diplomat, see Kirsten Gruesz's *Ambassadors of Culture: The Transamerican Origins of Latino Culture* (Princeton University Press, 2002), pp. 121–35.

27 *Walt Whitman, Complete Poetry and Collected Prose*, ed. James E. Miller, Jr. (Boston: Houghton Mifflin Company, 1959), p. 53. Subsequent quotations from this edition will be cited parenthetically in the text.

28 James E. Miller, Jr., "Introduction," in *ibid.*, p. xlviii.

29 Both sides in the Civil War were united in their opposition to the threat that Mexico posed to the civil order. Both the Southerners and Northerners who fought over the future of the nation's state were nevertheless united in their opposition to an enemy that would subordinate the national territory to an alien will. In representing the Mexican War as what the Civil War constituted itself through excluding, Whitman transformed the Mexican War into the regulative underside or regulative boundary of the Civil War. As its scapegoated other, the Mexican war underwrote the Americanness of the Civil War. The Northerners and Southerners who died in the Mexican war proleptically renewed and renovated the country by way of their joint sacrifice.

30 Giorgio Agamben, *State of Exception*, trans. Kevin Attell (University of Chicago Press, 2005), pp. 36–37.

31 Cited in *ibid.*, p. 39.

32 *Ibid.*, p. 38–40

33 Philip Fisher discusses the significance of these passages in the chapter "Democratic Social Space," in *Still the New World: American Literature in a Culture of Creative Destruction* (Cambridge, MA : Harvard University Press, 1999), pp.82–86.

34 *Walt Whitman, Complete Poetry and Collected Prose*, p. 28.

35 *Ibid.*, p.56.

36 For a fine recent discussion of this form of poesis, see Rob Wilson, *Be Always Converting, Be Always Converted: An American Poetics* (Cambridge, MA: Harvard University Press, 2009).

13

CRISTANNE MILLER

Emily Dickinson's "turbaned seas"

Most popular and scholarly accounts of Dickinson represent her at home –
that is, on 280 Main Street in Amherst, Massachusetts, Dickinson's residence from 1830 to 1840 and from 1855 until her death in 1886.[1] By the
age of 30, in 1860, she was relatively reclusive, and in 1865 she wrote
to Thomas Wentworth Higginson that "To an Emigrant, Country is idle
except it be his own ... I do not cross my Father's ground to any House
or town" (L330).[2] Cartoonists have memorably portrayed Dickinson as
running a travel agency advertising special deals for staying at home, or
keeping a schedule that marks as momentous plans to go to the pantry
or the garden. This notorious reclusiveness has encouraged scholarly neglect of ways that Dickinson's writing was shaped by the world beyond
Amherst. Such neglect is being remedied in relation to the Civil War, an
increasingly obvious influence on Dickinson's writing.[3] No one would
now repeat Thomas H. Johnson's infamous dictum that Dickinson "did
not live in history and held no view of it."[4] Very little attention has been
paid, however, to the ways in which the international spectrum of cultures
and events played into her poetics. Dickinson did not write poems "about"
international exchange but she was part of a community that perceived its
material pleasures, republican principles, and beliefs in relation to global
commerce. Moreover, Dickinson's personal circumstances as the well-edu-
cated daughter of a state and national Congressman and devoted reader of
newspapers and periodicals made her a more than usually active observer
of the cultural energies of her time.[5]

Between 1858 and 1881, Dickinson wrote over seventy poems referring to
the "Orient" or mentioning people, animals, or products from Asia – sometimes echoing popular stereotypes and sometimes countering them. Like
many of her era, Dickinson imagined South, West, and East Asia as places of
extravagant wealth and beauty. She also, however, writes poems that demonstrate knowledge of the contemporary politics of Asia and that critique
Western assumptions and attitudes. In the first eight years of her serious

writing (1858–65), and especially between 1860 and 1863, she invoked the East with remarkable frequency, constructing images that have less to do with ethnocentric universality or Western privilege than with creative self-transformation and a romanticized natural wealth and ability.[6]

News about foreign lands was delivered daily to the Dickinson household through the pages of the *Springfield Republican* – among the nation's most influential and internationally focused newspapers, edited by Samuel Bowles, one of Austin Dickinson's best friends and an important friend of the poet herself, to whom she wrote many letters and sent several poems; seven of the ten poems published during her lifetime appeared in Bowles's *Republican*.[7] Books imagining, describing, and translating Asian cultures and religious scriptures into idioms accessible to nineteenth-century Americans were also part of the Dickinson family library – including the *Koran* (the first US edition, 1806, translated in 1649 by Alexander Ross), Hiram Bingham's *A Residence of Twenty-one Years in the Sandwich Islands* (1848), David Allen's *India Ancient and Modern* (1856), Francis L. Hawks's *Narrative of the Expedition ... to the China Seas and Japan, 1852–1854* (1856), and many Orientalist poems and tales.[8] She teased her brother about his "kindled imagination" when he was reading the *Arabian Nights* (L19 and L22, 1847–48), and refers to this text herself in three other letters (L335, 438, 698). Reminders of Asia also abounded in more direct and material forms. As Daniel Lombardo notes, from the 1820s on, Amherst was known for sending missionaries around the world, and Mount Holyoke produced a "disproportionate number of graduates" who married missionaries to South and East Asia.[9] Dickinson's friend Abbie Wood moved with her husband to Syria in 1855. Dickinson herself visited a Chinese Museum in Boston in 1846, and in Monson, where her mother grew up, three Chinese students attended the Academy in 1847.[10] "Charge to the Heathen, by the Pastor! Front seats reserved for Foreign Lands!" Dickinson writes in mockery to Jane Humphrey in 1855, pleading to her friend, "don't let your duty call you 'far hence' " (L180). Frazar Stearns, a close friend of Austin's, traveled to India between October 1859 and August 1860.[11] Daneen Wardrop writes that in the late 1850s women's "tabletop poetry collections often featured drawings of women in Turkish outfits with other images of eastern exotica" and "Turkish trousers" was a popular name for bloomers in 1851–52.[12] These aspects of material culture developed out of what has been called the Oriental Renaissance of the late eighteenth and early nineteenth centuries, when the printing of Sanskrit texts in Europe stimulated an explosion of interest in cultures of Asia.[13] Encounters with those who had travelled, news about foreign lands, objects from Asia, and Orientalist literature provided Dickinson with a vocabulary and model for the knowledge and inspiration she associated with leaving home and the beauty of anything rare or unexpected.

During the late 1850s and early 1860s, Asian lands once primarily associated with exotic romance were a regular feature of the more staid spheres of war, politics, and finance. As the *Republican* announced in relation to the laying of the Atlantic telegraph cable in 1858, innovations in communication and transportation were bringing "the world into a nutshell ... wherever commerce spreads her sails ... will some time, and soon, be a network of wires ... transforming the world into a vast community" (August 7, 1858). Yet it also reports, "Notwithstanding the multitude of books on China, it is still an unknown country to most of us" (July 25, 1859). This was true of all Asia. As Dickinson first began preserving her work in manuscript books (1858), Asia was frequently in the news. During the Second Opium War (1856–60), the United States negotiated with China to gain access to more ports and agreement that China would house its ambassador in Beijing. The Sepoy Mutiny in India began in 1857. Although the *Republican* is openly Western in its perspective, it at times sympathizes with Asian peoples against European colonizing powers – in ways characteristic of the complex currents of US Orientalism at the time.[14] On May 16, 1857, the *Republican* notes that the (first) Opium War was profitable for England and the present war is "unhuman," and a January 1, 1859 article refers to the battle at Salimpore as "The Butcheries in India," noting that 700 Indian men, women, and children were killed but only two Europeans. In 1858, Japan signed the Harris treaty, which began the process of opening that country to foreigners, and in 1860, the Tokugawa Shogunate of Japan sent its first delegation to the United States. Walt Whitman's "A Broadway Pageant" describes the welcome parade for the Japanese in New York: "Comrade Americanos! To us, then, at last the Orient comes." Dickinson would have read nearly daily reports of the visit, including that New York spent $100,000 hosting it.[15]

News from Asia could be puzzling, however, because of the lag time between when events occurred and when news reached the USA, making even basic accounts unreliable. In the *Republican*, events in Asia were reported at least a month after they occurred, and many reports were partial. A headline one day might be contradicted by a bulletin on the next. On September 27, 1859 "The New Chinese War" reports that the French and English claim they have been treacherously attacked at Peiho while the Chinese bemoan British "ill-advised proceedings" in going up the wrong branch of the river. Frequent reports follow, quoting British, French, and Chinese sources – with radically different accounts of the incident. An October 3 account is taken from a July 4 dispatch. Whereas the telegraph made transportation of news within the USA relatively quick and reliable, no Atlantic Cable would be successfully in place until 1866, which meant that even news from England arrived slowly. The frequency of reports from China, Japan, India, and Turkey made these places seem near, while the uncertainty of the news kept one in suspense as to what was happening and what it meant, perhaps inadvertently supporting assumptions about Oriental mystery. The *Republican* also published periodic cultural reports on foreign lands, for example, "Female Life in Turkey" (April 11, 1857) or "The Wonders of Japan" (January 21, 1860). Such reports engaged in Orientalist description but also critically disrupted the popular imagination of a timeless, sensual, and spiritual East by describing events and people in a complex contemporary world. "Railroads in Asia," for example, describes massive construction projects underway, concluding "One thing is certain, a new era is inaugurated in Asia. The caravan routes ... will soon be replaced by railway and steam engine."[16] Seen in this context of daily news, some of Dickinson's poems take on distinct political overtones.

The most markedly political of Dickinson's Asia poems mixes fanciful description with an implied political stance. "Some Rainbow – coming from the Fair" (F162, 1860) likens spring flowers and creatures to emigrants, querying: "Whose multitudes are these? / The children of whose turbaned seas – / Or what Circassian Land?" In 1860, the people of the northwest Caucusus (including what is now Chechnya) were embroiled in the Russian–Circassian war of 1763–1862. The final years of this war involved Russian massacres of the Circassians and their forced deportation to various parts of the Ottoman Empire. Circassians were the focus of myth, literature, and news. Lord Byron's *Don Juan* (1818–24) describes the slave auction of a beautiful Circassian woman; Lucretia Davidson's 1829 "Amir Khan" depicts a romance between the King of Kashmir and a captured Circassian. The *Republican* describes Circassians as "a race of men so vigorous and graceful in form and women so beautiful that eastern nations say they are the original and uncorrupted stock from which all the races of men descended" – a claim repeated three months later.[17] On July 6, 1859, this information accompanies a news story about a signal success of "the brave Circassian chief, Schamyl" against Russia, "the great power that seeks to subvert their national independence," calling this struggle for national liberty a "good example for the world to contemplate." Numerous stories about the "tribal" Circassians describe the land as long persecuted by greater powers attempting unsuccessfully to conquer it and the religion as "a curious mixture of paganism, Mohammedanism, and Christianity," with Islam prevailing.[18] Reports of August 1859 and January 1860 tell of Circassian emigrants to Turkey, including a shipwreck killing two or three hundred, and placing the number of recent emigrants at over 60,000.[19] To be the child of a "Circassian Land" was to belong to a besieged Islamic people celebrated for their love of liberty and mythologized as exceedingly beautiful.

"Some Rainbow – coming from the Fair," written in 1860, begins with romantic exoticism:

> Some Rainbow – coming from the Fair!
> Some Vision of the World Cashmere –
> I confidently see!
> Or else a Peacock's purple Train
> Feather by feather – on the plain
> Fritters itself away!

This spring landscape is carefree ("Fritter[ing] itself away!"), ephemeral as the rainbow, luxurious as wool from Kashmir, and as gorgeously bright as peacocks, native to South Asia. Such description echoes popular association of beauty with the Orient, especially flowers with the sensuality of harems: in the third stanza, Dickinson's "Orchis" dons spring garb to lure "her old lover."[20] By the second stanza, however, the poet introduces martial imagery into the prototypically oriental "dreamy," "Lethargic," and erotic spring:

> The dreamy Butterflies bestir!
> Lethargic pools resume the whirr
> Of last year's sundered tune!
> From some old Fortress on the sun
> Baronial Bees – march – one by one -
> In murmuring platoon!
>
> The Robins stand as thick today
> As flakes of snow stood yesterday –
> On Fence – and Roof – and Twig!
> The Orchis binds her feather on
> For her old lover – Don the sun!
> Revisiting the Bog!
>
> Without Commander! Countless! Still!
> The Regiments of Wood and Hill
> In bright detachment stand!
> Behold, Whose multitudes are these?
> The children of whose turbaned seas -
> Or what Circassian Land?
>
> (F162)

The "multitudes" of flowers, bees, and birds are soldiers of "platoon[s]," "Regiments," "Without Commander!" (perhaps a sign of their independence, or lawlessness) and "Countless!" – therefore impossible to conquer.

One might have thought that such life was lost in the harsh winter, meta-phorically a defeat in nature's battles, but they "stand as thick today" as in previous times – returning or emigrating "From some old Fortress on the sun." These "Regiments of Wood and Hill" defeat winter; they bring both themselves and "Vision" of softness and color (cashmere and peacocks). At the most mundane level, such language implies that the familiar har-bingers of spring seem exotic after months of winter – like something from a "turbaned" land, with the grace and elegance of the fabled Circassians. On the other hand, the insistent military language complicates any simple association with Oriental sensuality; these representatives of spring point directly to the war for independence waged for years by actual Circassian regiments. Moreover, the poem's echo of Isaiah's "lost ... children" of exile seeking a home, and biblical exclamation, "Behold," further establish the pathos of diaspora.[21] This landscape poem sympathizes with a people for whom spring means a return to literal battle, and who aggressively popu-late the world (they "march"). Yet such martial immigration brings color and beauty to New England hills and allusion to the children of Israel, not threat of foreign menace. This erotic and martial spring indirectly praises "Mohammedans," described by the *Republican* as "a half civilized race," as apparently indomitable in their continuing military stance and hardy sojourn across "turbaned seas." [22]

Circassians reappear as a political referent in a poem of 1864. "Color – Caste – Denomination –" (F836) admonishes the living to be as egalitar-ian as "Death," who with his "Democratic fingers" pays no attention to the shade of the life he takes. Curiously, however, in this Civil War poem about "Color," the only race mentioned is the Circassian: "If Circassian – He is careless – / If He put away / Chrysalis of Blonde – or Umber / Equal Butterfly – // They emerge from His Obscuring –"; upon resurrection, all emerge "Equal" and with the multiple colors of the butterfly, not the rela-tive monotone of human skin. Dickinson's signifiers for "Color" are neither typical nor dichotomous: "blonde" was more often used to refer to lace that was neither white nor black than to hair color in the mid nineteenth century; it was not yet an archetypal designator for whiteness.[23] "Umber" is a medium brown pigment, named for its source in Umbria, Italy. These colors are in between the polarized distinctions of American racism, perhaps suggesting a more accurate depiction of skin tones than is acknowledged by racial stereotype or multiple shades of beauty in the human "Chrysalis." Similarly, Circassia seems to figure as a racial borderland: a tribal Muslim people of the Caucasian mountains, reputedly the most beautiful people in the world, and associated with "turbaned seas," hence neither entirely Eastern nor Western, appropriate as representing humanness to be valued for intrinsic beauty rather than hierarchical identity categories.[24] Dickinson evades the issues of US politics by avoiding language that points directly to American racism, but she nonetheless cuts to the heart of the matter by identifying the problem of classifying people by skin "Color" and does so by valorizing a non-Christian people.

"The lonesome for they know not What / The Eastern Exiles – be –" (F326; 1862) may also allude to Circassians – in this case, through a description of the colors of sunrise that cross an "Amber line" (like the meridian or lines of latitude) and then strive "in vain" to recross "the purple Moat" and return to "Heaven" on "Some Transatlantic Morn." The poem's conclusion suggests that we are all "Eastern Exiles," all diasporic wanderers taught by "Blessed Ether" to stray from "Heaven" and then incapable of regaining that native land. Again, the extravagant colors of sunrise are consonant with popular Orientalism in mid nineteenth-century America, but the idea that the bright gorgeousness suggests a literal displaced population and moreover a displacement that is typical of all human experience goes beyond popular representations of the East. Because of ongoing wars and exploitation such as the Coolie trade (frequently in the news), Asians were being forced into exile; Dickinson uses this "Eastern Exile[]" as a figure for all mortality, represented daily in the sun's "Transatlantic" journeying.[25]

Dickinson's representations of the East often correspond to the Western ethnocentric perspective in which the Orient figures as an admirable albeit "half-civilized" region, associated with the ageless and eternal, and particularly with natural wealth; she does not follow popular stereotype in imagining Asia as representative of cruelty, deceit, or danger. According to Malini Johar Schueller, American fascination with the Far East culminated in the 1850s and 1860s in the works of Northern and New England writers. Dickinson gives no evidence of having engaged in the serious reading of Asian scripture, literature, or philosophy as did contemporaries such as Ralph Waldo Emerson, John Greenleaf Whittier, Bayard Taylor, and Lydia Maria Child. Unlike Emerson and other transcendentalists, she is not interested in the Far East as a source of spiritual inspiration.[26] Unlike Whittier, she is not primarily interested in humanitarian goals – what Marwan Obeidat describes as his moral desire "to help his fellow men, Christian and Muslim alike, maintain and enjoy their freedom."[27] Unlike Whitman, she is not interested in Asia as a natural partner to or goal of (masculine) American expansion and does not personify the continent. In extolling the Japanese embassy visit, Whitman describes Asia as "The Originatress ... the bequeather of poems"; "venerable Asia" is "the all-mother," "rapt with musings, hot with passion, / Sultry with perfume," now meeting the "young" and "ever hot Libertad," or USA ("A Broadway

Pageant").²⁸ While Dickinson does distinctly identify poetry with Asia in a few poems, she imagines Oriental eroticism as revealing the same human passions she associates with all warm climates.

Dickinson's Orientalism borrows from the racist symbolic geographies of her era, which portrayed peoples in relation to stereotyped coordinates of the South, North, East, and West.²⁹ Her Amherst Academy textbooks corroborated such stereotypes. S. G. Goodrich's 1841 *A Pictorial Geography of the World*, for example, explains "the liberty of Europe, and the slavery of Asia'" as a result of the fact "that Asia has no temperate zone, no intermediate region between very cold and very hot climates. The slaves inhabit the hot, and the conquerors the elevated and cold regions." Every geographical area has its racial typology:

> The character of the Arabs is founded upon that of Ishmael. In the desert they are robbers, and in cities cheating is a substitute for robbery. They are, however, very courteous and polite ... The Hindoos are gentle, polished, and courteous in their manners; temperate, simple, frugal, industrious, lively, and intelligent. Yet the long oppression of foreign races, and the servile subordination of inferiors to their superiors, often render them treacherous, selfish, and cruel.³⁰

When Dickinson writes in 1863 that "A still – Volcano – Life –" is too "subtle" to be perceived "By natures this side Naples," she participates in this geographical assigning of attributes (F517). When she refers to the summertime bee's "jaded" philandering as "His oriental heresies" she similarly participates in this symbology (F1562, 1881). Her far more frequent invocation of the Orient as representing that which is precious and only fleetingly to be possessed, however, departs from these stereotypes, even while remaining parallel to them in its basic romantic orientation. The imagery of exile in "Some Rainbow" and "The lonesome for they know not What" departs even farther from common stereotypes in depicting Asians not as hermetically sealed off from contemporary civilizations but instead as currently emigrating across "turbaned seas" to the rest of the world, including Amherst.

The metaphor of "turbaned seas" is particularly significant in that it represents the sea itself as "turbaned," oriental, foreign. To enter the expanse of the sea, regardless of the ship's goal, is to enter foreignness, perhaps become foreign. A similar assumption grounds "Exultation is the going / Of an inland soul to sea" (F143, 1860), where the soul rejoices at journeying "Into deep Eternity," the prototypical image of the timeless East. This exultation, however, is the experience only of the "inland" soul; the "sailor" – who presumably has a sea-soul – may never feel this "divine intoxication" or release from ordinary inhibitions and boundaries because for the sailor the sea is not foreign. It seems paradoxical that, during the years when she is becoming increasingly reclusive, Dickinson imagines this sea-going entry into the unknown as "Exultation." Yet that very withdrawal might give all sense of journeying a sharper foreignness. "[T]urbaned seas" may also suggest enticing strangeness in its maleness, since the turban was traditionally worn by men. This 1860 metaphor invokes adventurousness, new possibilities or modes of perception – an excitement consonant with the shifting geopolitics of southwest Asia, the opening of trade opportunities in East Asia, the potential for eroticism, and Dickinson's own new seriousness about writing poetry.

No other Dickinson poem refers to current Asian politics, but "She died at play –", another poem of 1860, invokes Orientalism in an implied critique of the Christian resurrection narrative. In this poem, what appears to be a butterfly wanders "o'er the hill" at death: she "Gambolled away / Her lease of spotted hours, / Then sank as gaily as a Turk / Opon a Couch of flowers – " (F141). While the poem's second stanza does not follow up on this simile, the Orientalist hedonism implied in the subject's death gives it an erotic hue, in clear opposition to the Christian heaven of salvation and holiness the poet frequently shunned: in a letter of 1861 Dickinson exclaims "heaven is so cold!" (L234), and in 1862 she writes "I don't like Paradise –" (F437). This subject's hours were "spotted," perhaps suggesting licentiousness, except that to a nineteenth-century Christian all human life is "spotted"; she lived, however, in innocent "Gamboll[ing]," and at death "Her ghost strolled softly o'er the hill" while her "vestments" became "as the silver fleece," images evoking purity. For nature's "spotted" subject, death brings Eastern gaiety, beauty, and sensual pleasure. The point of this analogy would seem to be that such a death truly has no "sting," but the release from pain is distinctly not Christian.[31] At the same time, this invocation of the "Turk" could only come from stereotype since around 1860 the *Republican* reports only political tension in Turkey. Typical headlines read: "The Turkish Insurrection" (October 20, 1859); "Turkey, The Sick Man of Europe" (November 12, 1859); and "Terrible Civil War in Asiatic Turkey" (July 10, 1860). As in "Some Rainbow," Dickinson here imagines nature as Oriental, hence logically the Orient as natural in its "ga[y]" proclivities; restrictions against such "gaiety" are then, logically, unnatural.

For Dickinson, desire is often more powerful than possession, and joy is precious because it is by nature ephemeral, as she notes in "Delight is as the Flight" (F317, 1862). The distance of Asia – even as experienced through reports in the newspaper – makes it the perfect figure of desire, but also of states of inspiration and knowledge that cannot be taken for granted or unequivocally possessed. Dickinson never makes Asia the source of poems,

as Whitman does, but in "It would never be Common – more – I said –"
(F388, 1862) she associates poetry with "India." This poem's speaker first
celebrates her state of uncommon exhilaration, when she is born by poetic
meter rather than "The feet – I former used –"; then, however, "suddenly"
"the Wilderness roll[ed] back / Along my Golden lines –" and she is faced
with the "Sackcloth" of uninspired daily life, questioning, "But where my
moment of Brocade / My – drop – of India." Uncommon moments of poetic
inspiration bring wealth resembling the essence of India. "Of all the Sounds
dispatched abroad" uses an Orientalist metaphor to describe the music of
the wind, "that old measure in the Boughs –" (F334, 1862). While the wind
is musical rather than verbal (it is "Phraseless"), Dickinson claims that these
tunes are also "Permitted Gods – and me –" and are "Inheritance ... to us
... Beyond the Art to Earn." One may learn from this "Fleshless Chant" but
only through un-earned boons like inspiration. The last stanza concludes by
likening the moment of hearing this music to that when "some Caravan of
Sound / Off Deserts in the Sky – / Had parted Rank – / Then knit and swept
/ In Seamless Company –."[32] Here it is not the poet's inspiration but nature's
art that is ephemeral and Oriental, bringing temporary pleasure, as would a
caravan in the desert. "To learn the Transport by the Pain –" (F179, 1860)
more broadly imagines that the art of all "Laureates" depends on learning
from "homesick – homesick feet" that stay on "a foreign shore," or the experience of foreignness.

Five poems written between 1858 and 1862 use a pearl diver to represent
wealth beyond the speaker's grasp. In "The feet of people walking home –"
the phrase "Pearls are the Diver's farthings – / Extorted from the sea –" begins
two stanzas of analogies presenting "figures" for the distance to "immortality"; pearls are the "farthings" one pays in order to gain "Resurrection,"
and the danger of diving is the cost of gaining such coin (F16, 1858). In
"Her breast is fit for pearls," the speaker regrets "I was not a 'Diver'" and
is therefore incapable of adorning his or her lover's "breast" appropriately
(F121; 1859). "One life of so much consequence!" gives the pearl greater
significance (F248; 1861). Here the imagined "life" of extraordinary value
is epitomized as "One Pearl ... so signal / That I would instant dive –" even
if it "cost me – just a life!" The speaker knows that "The Sea is full," but the
particular "Pearl" of her or his life is "distinct from all the row –." Diving for
this pearl entails risking full engagement to achieve a life of "consequence,"
but the poem does not tell us if the speaker will risk that dive; it merely
indicates the ambition to enter the unknown territory of the "Sea" as a
route to achieving its desire. Following the biblical parable of the "pearl of
great price" representing the kingdom of heaven, pearls typically symbolized
purity, and often virginity.[33] These poems may allude to the scriptural pearl

as well as to its ocean counterpart, but it is noteworthy that in every case the focus is less on the pearl than on diving, making an activity associated with Asia represent virtuous and fulfilling life.

"Removed from Accident of Loss / By Accident of Gain" (F417, 1862) pursues an extended analogy with "the Brown Malay" "unconscious ... Of Pearls in Eastern Waters – / Marked His –" to speculate on the speaker's – or human – unconsciousness of the potential fortune to be discovered in one's local environment. As in "*One life* of so much consequence," the pearl diver or Malay is a figure for humanity, not a figure of contrast to the speaker, and diving suggests the necessity of risking the unknown in order to achieve the knowledge and wealth fundamental to any creative or significant act. As in the previous poem, the diving may be entirely psychological: the "Waters" to be tested are private ("Marked His"), but if one has the "power to dream" of what they hold then one might risk the "Accident of Gain" dependent on diving. Even an art like poetry, this figure suggests, demands the "power" to dream and the discipline to dive in order to reach the "Pearls" or "Riches" of one's own "Waters." The insistent capitals in the stanza introducing the "Brown Malay" (thirteen of eighteen words in the stanza are capitalized) intensifies his allegorical function. There is definite Orientalism in present-ing the Malay as archetypally "slow" in "conception," but the slowness is shared by the New England speaker who is "as unconscious / As the ... Malay."

Much has been written about "The Malay – took the Pearl" (F451, 1862) but the focus has been largely on Dickinson's views of slavery and on racism against African Americans, since she refers to the pearl diver as "The Negro" in stanza three.[34] The Asian content of the poem is all but ignored, although the widespread fascination with pearl divers – as well as Dickinson's other poems on this figure – makes it far more likely that Dickinson's association here is not primarily with American racial issues. This poem is as close as Dickinson comes to constructing an Oriental tale, complete with Eastern setting – although the setting contains no prototypical sensuality, luxuri-ousness, or beauty: the "Swarthy" Malay carries the pearl "Home to the Hut!" where it resides on a "Dusky Breast –." Here in dramatic monologue form reminiscent of Robert Browning's "My Last Duchess," the "Earl" ill-temperedly claims the pearl as "my Jewel" and insists on the unfairness of a lower-class Asian diver's owning what he imperialistically assumes should be his own, because he wants it. The successful Malay is again ignorant – but this time only of the speaker's competition for his prize ("The Negro never knew ..."). This "Earl" admits his unfitness for winning the pearl: "I – feared the Sea – too much" and was "Unsanctified – to touch –." In contrast, the diver is naturally capable, logically "[]sanctified – to touch –" since he

258

gets the pearl, independent of the colonizing Earl's power, and stereotypically "unconscious" of the complex longing, inadequacy, and ambition of the white Westerner.[35]

Pearl divers appeared frequently in Orientalist literature. *Harper's Monthly Magazine* (a periodical also subscribed to by the Dickinsons) prints a story called "Pearl Divers" about a competition between divers over a beautiful woman, frequently mentioning the "hut" in which the narrator of the story lives (June 1851); "Mother of Pearl" in the *Hampshire and Franklin Gazette* features a diver who saves the child of a white couple who can't swim (February 10, 1860); the November 1860 *Harper's Monthly* included an article on pearl divers called "Pearls and Gems"; and J. T. Field's "Diamonds and Pearls" relates the story of a "little negro boy in 1560, who obtained his liberty by opening an oyster" because he found "the rarest of priceless pearls" (*Atlantic Monthly*, March 1861). Dickinson's use of this stock figure focuses on the strength, agility, and success of the diver – characteristics not typically associated with the Orient – with the further twist of making him represent the pursuit of various kinds of value in life, or afterlife. Her diver is unselfconsciously capable, in true romantic stereotype, but his riches are for the most part psychological, not plunderable. This wealth is "Marked His" territorially and legally, or it is imperialistically claimed by the West ("my Jewel") but nonetheless inaccessible; it can be gained only at great price – again making it the perfect figure for an "inland" soul's ambition and longing. One hears the newspaper-reading lawyer's daughter in every capitalized element of the phrase "Eastern Waters – / Marked His –."

Several poems of the late 1850s and early 1860s refer to Asian things or people in ways commensurate with this pattern of asserting Eastern wealth, skill, and exile as a figure for all human experience or as a romanticized, natural state preferable to the colonizing Christian West. "Tho' my destiny be Fustian –" (F131, 1860) presents a speaker who "far prefer[s]" "my little Gipsey being" with its "Fustian" (stout, plain cloth) and "sunburnt bosom" to "damask ... a silver apron –" or a "Rosier" bosom, because this hardy "Gipsey being" can withstand "Frosts" and therefore "Bloom Eternally!" The positive identification of the speaker with a gipsy in this poem is strikingly at odds with the negative associations of Dickinson's beloved lexicon; Webster defines "gipsies" as "a race of vagabonds which infest Europe, Africa, and Asia, strolling about and subsisting mostly by theft, robbery and fortune-telling ... their language indicates that they originated in Hindoostan," and as "implying artifice or cunning" in a woman.[36] Dickinson's "little Gipsey being," in contrast, is natural and plain – suggesting an honest character, neither artificial nor sensual. She is comfortable in her native setting, and therefore "Bloom[s]." In "Civilization – spurns – the

Leopard!" (F276, 1862), the speaker similarly identifies with a natural being of the East: the line "Pity – the Pard – that left her Asia!" clarifies that the "Spotted," "Tawny" "nature" of the leopard cannot thrive in climates that do not support "her Customs" – suggesting that Asia may also be the natural home for a female poet who is "bold" and sometimes felt "her Customs" to be foreign to Amherst and herself to be an "Emigrant" (L330). Somewhat more typically, "A something in a summer's Day" (F104, 1859) imagines the "Transcending exstasy" of day in relation to "Azure," "perfume," and the "East" with "her amber Flag – / Guid[ing] still the sun along the Crag / His Caravan of Red –" – in other words, the morning is Oriental in its nomadic gorgeousness. In "The Love a Life can show Below" (F285, 1862), the poet defines love as that which "enamors in the East," and "Your Riches taught me – Poverty" (F418, 1862) imagines the privilege of "look[ing] on You" as "India – all Day."

After 1865, Dickinson's references to the East are more conventional, involving images of wealth and rest, without implied cultural critique of imperialist colonization, Christianity, or a life of prose in contrast to that of poetry. In 1878, "His Mind like Fabrics of the East" (F1471) presents wealth "Displayed to the despair" of all but the rare "humble Purchaser" as Asian; this wealth is intellectual and clearly admired, but creates "despair" in others and the analogy to Oriental "Fabrics" may suggest the complexity of duplicity as well as great value and beauty. "A Mine there is no Man would own" (F1162, 1869) and "How destitute is he" (F1509, 1879) both associate that which is most valued with "Indies" and "India." The 1881 poem "No Autumn's intercepting Chill" (F1563) suggests that death brings "African Exuberance / And Asiatic Rest" to a "Tropic Breast" – revising the 1860 "She died at play –" to assign gaiety or "Exuberance" to a non-Asian continent. In contrast, the 1865 "Always Mine!" (F942) comments "Old, indeed, the East" but then follows this line with an anti-Orientalist assertion of the East's continuing masculine vigor: "Yet opon His Purple Programme / Every Dawn, is first."

That Dickinson would eventually invest Asian imagery with largely transhistorical, Orientalist resonance is reasonable given both her increasing seclusion and cultural change in the USA at the time. It is not that daily newspapers contained less foreign news; indeed there was increased cultural exchange between Asia and New England in the 1870s and 1880s. Rather, at mid-century, the excitement of encounters with ideas and cultures radically different from her own through news reports and other means contributed to the general cultural ferment of the period: the world seemed to be changing at a rapid rate and in ways suggesting at least the possibility of continuing enlightenment or progress. In the early 1860s, the conjunction of Orientalist enthusiasm, the high profile of Asian lands in the news, and her own sense of adventure in starting out on her serious poetic explorations encourage Dickinson to represent the East as a complex figure for humanity, nature, and desire. After the Civil War, the national nostalgic, anti-immigrationist, and less romantically racist mood would have been less likely to stimulate imagination of the self as wild, bold, foreign, and powerfully uncivilized, or of nature and beauty as products of foreignness, emigrants from across "turbaned seas." Both early and late, Dickinson for the most part assumes the perspective of Western consciousness in contrast to Eastern beauty, peace, and natural wealth or ability. Nonetheless, the early poems sympathetic to pearl divers' plumbing of the riches in their own waters and to the literal emigration or exile of Asian peoples – later allegorized as the leopard forced to leave "her Asia" – suggest a questioning of ethnocentric universalities, especially in light of the 1865 letter to Higginson identifying herself as an "Emigrant." Dickinson's poems manifest some degree of sympathetic identification with contemporary Asians, even while participating in the Orientalist romanticization of Asia as a figure for the place or moment in which all (Western) longing can be fulfilled.

NOTES

1 See Alfred Habegger's *My Wars are Laid Away in Books: The Life of Emily Dickinson* (New York: Random House, 2001) on Dickinson's life in the Pleasant Street house (1840–55) and time away from Amherst, especially her trip to Philadelphia and Washington, DC in 1855, and treatment by a Boston opthalmologist in 1864 and 1865. The present chapter is part of a longer chapter in *Reading in Time: Dickinson in the Nineteenth Century* (Amherst: University of Massachusetts Press, 2012).

2 Dickinson's letters are quoted from Thomas H. Johnson and Theodora Ward's *The Letters of Emily Dickinson* (Cambridge, MA: Harvard University Press, 1958), identified in the text with L and the Johnson number; poems are from Ralph W. Franklin's *The Poems of Emily Dickinson* (Cambridge, MA: Harvard University Press, 1998), identified in the text with F and the number and date Franklin assigns. Although Franklin bases many dates on Dickinson's handwriting, he asserts that between 1858 and 1865 she copied poems into manuscript books within a few months of composition (p. 39).

3 For a review of scholarship on this topic see Faith Barrett, "Public Selves and Private Spheres: Studies of Emily Dickinson and the Civil War, 1984–2007," *Emily Dickinson Journal*, 16.1 (2007), 92–104. Hereafter abbreviated *EDJ*.

4 Johnson, *Letters*, p. xx.

5 Edward Dickinson was elected to the US House of Representatives in 1852 and served one term.

6 Susan Nance argues that nineteenth-century Americans were generally interested in the East as consumers, not proto-imperialists; *How the Arabian Nights Inspired the American Dream* (Chapter Hill: University of North Carolina Press, 2009), pp. 11, 21, 66.

7 The *Republican* contained remarkable international coverage both in daily omnibus sections with titles such as "Four Days Later from Europe" or "Foreign Matters" and under specific headlines such as "Our Minister to China" (October 12, 1859) or "Anarchy in Eastern Turkey" (January 26, 1860). While Dickinson sometimes disdained politics, she was an enthusiastic reader of the family's newspapers. Subscriptions to the *Republican* and the local *Hampshire and Franklin Express* stopped during the month after her death; Joan Kirkby, "'[W]e thought Darwin had thrown "the Redeemer" away': Darwinizing with Emily Dickinson," *EDJ*, 19.1 (2010), 1–29; 3. For an alternative view, see Shannon Thomas, "'What News must think when pondering': Emily Dickinson, The *Springfield Daily Republican*, and the Poetics of Mass Communication," *EDJ*, 19.1 (2010), 60–79. Thomas regards Dickinson as sharing Emerson's view that new communication technologies impeded the development of the soul (p. 10).

8 There is no evidence that Dickinson read the Koran or these travel books but she would have heard her father or brother talk about them; she did read Orientalist writers like Edgar Allen Poe and Harriet Prescott Spofford; Spofford's "The Amber Gods" and "Pomegranate-Flowers" were published in the *Atlantic Monthly* (January–February 1860 and May 1861). The *Atlantic* published several Orientalist poems, including, in 1860, "Abdel-Hassan" (Benjamin R. Plumly, January), "The Water of El Arbain" (Caroline Crane Marsh, February), "Prince Adeb" (George H. Boker, August), and "The Song of Fatima" (Thomas Bailey Aldrich, September) and essays using Orientalist description and analogies, including Higginson's "April Days" (April 1861).

9 Lombardo, *A Hedge Away: The Other Side of Emily Dickinson's Amherst* (Amherst: Daily Hampshire Gazette, 1997); Malini Johar Schueller, *U. S. Orientalisms: Race, Nation, and Gender in Literature, 1790–1890* (Ann Arbor: University of Michigan Press, 1998), p. 79.

10 Karen Sanchez Eppler, "Copying and Conversion: A Connecticut Friendship Album from 'a Chinese Youth,'" *American Quarterly* 59.2 (2007), 302. Dickinson writes of this museum visit to Abiah Root (L13). See also Hiroko Uno, "Emily Dickinson's Encounter with the East," *EDJ*, 17.1 (2008), 43–67. Ronald Zboray and Mary Saracino Zboray claim that the Chinese Museum "espoused a philosophy of enlightened relativism that invited visitors to see Chinese artifacts and the ways of life they represented on par with their own"; the products it displayed and its Chinese informants "invited visitors to imagine China more as a complex civilization amenable to diplomatic trade relations than as a culturally destitute land ripe for Euro-American conquest." "Between 'Crockery-dom' and Barnum: Boston's Chinese Museum, 1845–1847," *American Quarterly*, 56.2 (2004), 271–307; 272, 273.

11 Frazar Stearns's journal of this voyage is housed at the Jones Library, Amherst.

12 Daneen Wardrop, *Emily Dickinson and the Labor of Clothing* (Manchester: University of New Hampshire Press, 2009), pp. 196, 141.

13 Schueller, *U.S. Orientalisms*, p. 25.

14 Schueller provides excellent historical background to Orientalist writing in the USA in relation to international events and European Orientalism, as theorized by Edward Said in his seminal 1978 *Orientalism*. New England writers in the 1850s, she argues, have an "indigenous interest in the Far East" because of the well-developed Asian trade and want to mark their distinctive participation in

the "Oriental Renaissance" (*U.S. Orientalisms*, pp. 142–43). Nance similarly understands US Orientalism to change over time and differ from that of Europe, claiming that Asia "provided and inspired among Americans a tradition of extravagant and sumptuous creativity" in part because Eastern tales presented self-transformation "in robust language that closely matched the promise of consumer capitalism" (*How the Arabian Nights*, p. 12). Zhaoming Qian and Cynthia Stamy present US Orientalism as part of its historical project to distinguish itself from Europe in, respectively, *Orientalism and Modernism: The Legacy of China in Pound and Williams* (Durham, NC: Duke University Press, 1995) and *Marianne Moore and China: Orientalism and a Writing of America* (Oxford University Press, 1999).

15 *Republican*, July 3, 1860.

16 The article continues by claiming that the "incomparably higher civilization of Christendom" will now have further opportunity to influence "the old homestead of the race" (*Republican*, August 25, 1859).

17 "Schamyl Still Lives," *Republican*, July 6, 1859 and "Schamyl, the Hero of Circassia," *Republican*, October 11, 1859. In contrast, in "Barbarism and Civilization," Higginson comments that "the Circassians, the purest type of the supreme Caucasian race, have given nothing to history but the courage of their men and the degradation of their women" (*Atlantic Monthly*, January 1861, 51–61; 52). Earlier, in "The Maroons of Jamaica," Higginson calls Maroons "the Circassians of the New World," claiming that Maroons are even more devoted to fighting for their liberty (*Atlantic Monthly*, February 1860, 213–22; 213).

18 "Schamyl, the Hero of Circassia."

19 August 24, 1859, "The Russian and Circassian War"; November 15, 1859, and January 29, 1860 (no headlines).

20 Elizabeth Petrino notes that the symbolic use of flowers in China and Japan long predated that in the USA and carried a range of sexual and emotional connotations; *Emily Dickinson and Her Contemporaries: Women's Verse in America 1820–1885* (Hanover, NH: University Press of New England, 1998), pp. 129–60. Paula Bennett notes that many nineteenth-century women used Oriental settings or metaphor to write erotic verse (*Poets in the Public Sphere: The Emancipatory Project of American Women's Poetry, 1800–1900* [Princeton University Press, 2003], pp. 159–80).

21 Isaiah 49:20–21: " ... give place to me that I may dwell. Then shalt thou say in thine heart, Who hath begotten me these, seeing I have lost my children, and am desolate, a captive, and removing to and fro? and who hath brought up these? Behold, I was left alone ... "

22 "Schamyl, the Hero of Circassia."

23 Wardrop, *Emily Dickinson and the Labor of Clothing*, p. 184.

24 Schueller argues that Americans were fascinated with Southwest Asia because "it was composed of racial and cultural borderlands" of Christianity and Islam, giving them an indirect way to face their own urgent racial politics (*U.S. Orientalisms*, p. 78). Nance points out that Turks, Persians, and Arabs were often regarded as "white" (*How the Arabian Nights*, p. 15).

25 *Republican*, April 7, 1860, "The Coolie Trade"; May 18, 1860, "The Coolies in China."

26 Despite his admiration for Persian poets and knowledge of Eastern scripture, Schueller argues that Emerson increasingly represented Asia as transhistorical and passive in relation to a "westerly movement of civilization" (*U.S. Orientalisms*, pp. 185, 165, 159).

27 Marwan Obeidat, *American Literature and Orientalism* (Berlin: Klaus Schwarz Verlag, 1998), p. 89. As Obeidat acknowledges, this humanitarian desire is "occasionally colored by ... cultural misconceptions and stereotypes." See also Arthur Christy, "Orientalism in New England: Whittier," *American Literature*, 1.4 (1930), 372–92, and "The Orientalism of Whittier," *American Literature* 5.3 (1933), 247–57.

28 Whitman Archive, *Leaves of Grass*, 1867, subtitled, "(Reception Japanese Embassy, June 16, 1860)," www.whitman.org/criticism.

29 Rebecca Patterson includes chapters on "Geography" and "Cardinal Points" in *Emily Dickinson's Imagery*, although with no mention of Orientalism or Asian politics (Amherst: University of Massachusetts Press, 1979).

30 S. G. Goodrich, *A Pictorial Geography of the World* (Boston: C. D. Strong and Company, 1841), pp. 891, 925, 946.

31 Dickinson knew the passage "O death, where is thy sting?" from 1 Corinthians 15:55; she quotes from 1 Corinthians 15 in "'Sown in dishonor'!" (F153), written the same year.

32 In contrast, Patterson argues that Dickinson typically reads the East as "arid" desert when it occurs in contrast to the West (*Emily Dickinson's Imagery*, p. 195).

33 Matthew 13:46; Petrino, *Emily Dickinson and Her Contemporaries*, p. 141.

34 Betsy Erkkila, "Emily Dickinson and Class," *American Literary History*, 4.1 (1992), 1–27; Vivian Pollak, "Dickinson and the Poetics of Whiteness," *EDJ*, 9.2 (2000), 84–95; Bennett, "'The Negro never knew': Emily Dickinson and Racial Typology in the Nineteenth Century," *Legacy*, 19.1 (2002), 53–61.

35 Here Dickinson associates the East with what Peter Wollen has called the creative ideal of the "ultra-natural" in "Fashion/Orientalism/The Body," *New Formations* 1 (1987): 5–34; 27.

36 Emily Dickinson's Lexicon, http://edl.byu.edu/webster/term/445604.

SELECTED GUIDE TO FURTHER READING

Critical works

Adams, R. P. "Romanticism and the American Renaissance." *American Literature*, 23.4 (1952), 419–32.

Allen, Gay Wilson. *American Prosody*. New York: American Book Co., 1935.

Arakelian, Paul G. "Personality and Style: Options in Nineteenth-Century American Poetry." *Language and Style: An International Journal*, 24.2 (1991), 239–50.

Arms, George Warren. *The Fields were Green: A New View of Bryant, Whittier, Holmes, Lowell, and Longfellow; with a Selection of their Poems*. Stanford University Press, 1953.

Auden, W. H. "American Poetry." *The Dyer's Hand and Other Essays*. New York: Vintage, 1968.

Avallone, Charlene. "What American Renaissance? The Gendered Genealogy of a Critical Discourse." *PMLA*, 112.5 (1997), 1102–20.

Bennett, Paula B. *Poets in the Public Sphere: The Emancipatory Project of American Women's Poetry, 1800–1900*. Princeton University Press, 2003.

Bennett, Paula Bernat, Karen L. Kilcup, and Phillip Schweighauser, eds. *Teaching Nineteenth-Century American Poetry*. New York: Modern Language Association of America, 2007.

Bercovitch, Sacvan, and Cyrus R. K. Patell, eds. *The Cambridge History of American Literature: Nineteenth-Century Poetry, 1800–1910*. 4 vols. Cambridge: Cambridge University Press, 2004.

Blasing, Mutlu Konuk. *American Poetry: The Rhetoric of its Forms*. New Haven, CT: Yale University Press, 1987.

Bloom, Harold. *Poetry and Repression: Revisionism from Blake to Stevens*. New York: Oxford University Press, 1976.

Blount, Marcellus. "The Preacherly Text: African American Poetry and Vernacular Performance." *PMLA*, 107.3, Special Topic: Performance (1992), 582–93.

Brodhead, Richard H. *Cultures of Letters: Scenes of Reading and Writing in Nineteenth-Century America*. University of Chicago Press, 1993.

Buell, Lawrence. *Literary Transcendentalism: Style and Vision in the American Renaissance*. Ithaca, NY: Cornell University Press, 1973.

"American Literary Emergence as a Postcolonial Phenomenon." *American Literary History*, 4.3 (1992), 411–42.

Carlin, T. Kindlilien. *American Poetry in the Eighteen Nineties: A Study of American Verse, 1890–1899*. Brown University Studies, vol. xx. Providence, RI: Brown University Press, 1956.

Cavitch, Max. *The Poetry of Mourning from the Puritans to Whitman*. Minneapolis: University of Minnesota Press, 2007.

Churchill, Suzanne W. *The Little Magazine Others and the Renovation of American Poetry*. Burlington, VT: Ashgate, 2006.

Cushman, Stephen. *Fictions of Form in American Poetry*. Princeton University Press, 1993.

Donoghue, Denis. *Connoisseurs of Chaos: Ideas of Order in Modern American Poetry*. New York: Columbia University Press, 1984.

DuBois, Andrew. "Historical Impasse and the Modern Lyric Poem." *American Literary History*, 15.1 (2003), 22–26.

Duffey, Bernard I. *Poetry in America: Expression and its Values in the Times of Bryant, Whitman, and Pound*. Durham, NC: Duke University Press, 1978.

Egan, Ken, Jr. "The Machine in the Poem: Nineteenth-Century American Poetry and Technology." *Weber Studies: An Interdisciplinary Humanities Journal*, 12.1 (1995), 70–81.

Elliott, Emory. General Editor. *The Columbia Literary History of the United States*. New York: Columbia University Press, 1988.

Fletcher, Angus. *A New Theory for American Poetry: Democracy, the Environment, and the Future of Imagination*. Cambridge, MA: Harvard University Press, 2006.

Fredman, Stephen. *The Grounding of American Poetry: Charles Olson and the Emersonian Tradition*. Cambridge University Press, 1993.

Fussell, Edwin S. *Lucifer in Harness: American Meter, Metaphor, and Diction*. Princeton University Press, 1973.

Gates, Rosemary L. "Forging an American Poetry from Speech Rhythms: Williams After Whitman." *Poetics Today*, 8.3/4 (1987), 503–27.

Gelpi, Albert J. *The Tenth Muse: The Psyche of the American Poet*. Cambridge, MA: Harvard University Press, 1975.

Gilbert, Roger. "The Dream of a Common Poetry." *American Literary History*, 8.2 (1996), 350–63.

Golding, Alan C. *From Outlaw to Classic: Canons in American Poetry*. Madison: University of Wisconsin Press, 1995.

Gruesz, Kirsten Silva. *Ambassadors of Culture: the Transamerican Origins of Latino Writing*. Princeton University Press, 2002.

Harrington, Joseph. "Why American Poetry is not American Literature." *American Literary History*, 8.2 (1996).

Huddleston, Eugene L. "Topographical Poetry in the Early National Period." *American Literature*, 38.3 (1966), 303–22.

Kete, Mary Louis. *Sentimental Collaborations: Mourning and Middle-Class Identity in Nineteenth-Century America*. Durham, NC: Duke University Press, 2000.

Kramer, Aaron. *The Prophetic Tradition in American Poetry, 1835–1900*. Rutherford, NJ: Fairleigh Dickinson University Press, 1968.

Kreymborg, Alfred. *A History of American Poetry: Our Singing Strength*. New York: Tudor, 1934.

Larson, Kerry. *Imagining Equality in Nineteenth-Century American Literature.* New York: Cambridge University Press, 2008.

Lee, Maurice S. "Writing through the War: Melville and Dickinson After the Renaissance." *PMLA,* 115.5 (2000), 1124–28.

"Re-Canonizing Nineteenth-Century American Poetry." *Minnesota Review: A Journal of Committed Writing,* 55–57 (2002), 327–30.

Leypoldt, Günter. "Democracy's 'Lawless Music': The Whitmanian Moment in the U.S. Construction of Representative Literariness." *New Literary History,* 38.2 (2007), 333–52.

Loeffelholz, Mary. *From School to Salon: Reading Nineteenth-Century American Women's Poetry.* Princeton University Press, 2004.

"Anthology Form and the Field of Nineteenth-Century American Poetry: The Civil War Sequences of Lowell, Longfellow, and Whittier." *ESQ: A Journal of the American Renaissance,* 54. 1–4 (2008), 217–40.

Matthiessen, Francis Otto. *American Renaissance: Art and Expression in the Age of Emerson and Whitman.* New York: Oxford University Press, 1941.

McGill, Meredith, ed. *The Traffic in Poems: Nineteenth-Century Poetry and Transatlantic Exchange.* New Brunswick: Rutgers University Press, 2008.

Miller, James E., Jr. *The American Quest for a Supreme Fiction: Whitman's Legacy in the Personal Epic.* University of Chicago Press, 1979.

Morgan, A. E. *The Beginnings of Modern American Poetry.* London: Longmans, Green and Co., 1946.

New, Elisa. *The Regenerate Lyric: Theology and Innovation in American Poetry.* Cambridge University Press, 1993.

Parini, Jay, ed. *The Columbia History of American Poetry.* New York: Columbia University Press, 1993.

Pearce, Roy Harvey. *The Continuity of American Poetry.* Princeton University Press, 1961.

Petrino, Elizabeth A. *Emily Dickinson and Her Contemporaries: Women's Verse in America, 1820–1885.* Hanover, NH: University Press of New England, 1998.

Ramey, Lauri. *Slave Songs and the Birth of African American Poetry.* New York: Palgrave Macmillan, 2008.

Rehder, Robert, and Patrick Vincent. *American Poetry: Whitman to the Present.* Berlin: Gunter Narr Verlag, 2006.

Renza, Louis A. *Edgar Allan Poe, Wallace Stevens, and the Poetics of American Privacy.* Baton Rouge: Louisiana State University Press, 2002.

Richards, Eliza. *Gender and the Poetics of Reception in Poe's Circle.* Cambridge University Press, 2004.

Rohrbach, Augusta (ed. and introd.), and Martha Nell Smith (afterword). " 'A Blast that Whirls the Dust': Nineteenth-Century American Poetry and Critical Discontents." *ESQ: A Journal of the American Renaissance,* 54. 1–4 (2008), 1–285.

Rubin, Joan Shelley. *Songs of Ourselves: The Uses of Poetry.* Cambridge, MA: Harvard University Press, 2007.

Sherman, Joan R. *Invisible Poets: Afro-Americans of the Nineteenth Century.* Urbana: University of Illinois Press, 1974.

Shucard, Alan. *American Poetry: The Puritans through Walt Whitman.* Amherst: University of Massachusetts Press, 1990.

Shucard, Alan, Fred Moramarco, and William Sullivan. *Modern American Poetry, 1865–1950.* New York: Twayne, 1990.

Sorby, Angela. *Schoolroom Poets: Childhood, Performance, and the Place of American Poetry, 1865–1917.* Hanover, NH: University Press of New England, 2005.

Spengemann, William C. "Melville the Poet." *American Literary History,* 11.4 (1999), 569–609.

Three American Poets: Walt Whitman, Emily Dickinson, and Herman Melville. Notre Dame, IN: University of Notre Dame Press, 2010.

Thomas, Joseph M. "Late Emerson: 'Selected Poems' and the 'Emerson Factory'." *ELH,* 65.4 (1998), 971–94.

Turco, Lewis P. *Visions and Revisions of American Poetry.* Fayetteville: University of Arkansas Press, 1986.

Waggoner, Hyatt H. *American Poets from the Puritans to the Present.* Boston: Houghton Mifflin & Co., 1968.

American Visionary Poetry. Baton Rouge: Lousiana State University Press, 1982.

Wardrop, Daneen. *Word, Birth, and Culture: The Poetry of Poe, Whitman, and Dickinson.* Westport, CT: Greenwood Press, 2002.

Whitley, Edward. "Whitman's Occasional Nationalism: 'A Broadway Pageant' and the Space of Public Poetry." *Nineteenth-Century Literature,* 60.4 (2006), 451–80.

Wilson, Rob. "Lexical Scapegoating: The Pure and Impure of American Poetry." *Poetics Today,* 8.1 (1987), 45–63.

American Sublime: A Genealogy of a Poetic Genre. Madison: University of Wisconsin Press, 1991.

Wolosky, Shira. "The Claims of Rhetoric: Toward a Historical Poetics (1820–1900)." *American Literary History,* 15.1 (2003), 14–21.

Anthologies

Axelrod, Steven Gould, Camille Roman, and Thomas J. Travisano, eds. *The New Anthology of American Poetry: Traditions and Revolutions, Beginnings to 1900.* Volume One. New Brunswick, NJ: Rutgers University Press, 2003.

Barrett, Faith, and Cristanne Miller, eds. "*Words for the Hour": A New Anthology of American Civil War Poetry.* Amherst: University of Massachusetts Press, 2005.

Basker, James, ed. *Amazing Grace: An Anthology of Poems about Slavery, 1660–1810.* New Haven: Yale University Press, 2002.

Bennett, Paula, ed. *Nineteenth-Century American Women Poets: An Anthology.* Malden, MA: Blackwell Publishers, 1998.

Cady, Edwin Harrison, ed. *The American Poets, 1800–1900: An Anthology.* Glenview, IL: Scott, Foresman, 1966.

Conarroe, Joel, ed. *Six American Poets: An Anthology.* New York: Random House, 1991.

Foster, Edward Halsey, ed. *Decadents, Symbolists, & Aesthetes in America: Fin-De-Siècle American Poetry: An Anthology.* Jersey City, NJ: Talisman House, 2000.

Haralson, Eric L., and John Hollander, eds. *Encyclopedia of American Poetry. The Nineteenth Century.* Chicago: Fitzroy Dearborn, 1998.

Hayward, John, ed. *Nineteenth Century Poetry: An Anthology.* London: Chatto & Windus, 1950.

Hoffman, Daniel, ed. *American Poetry and Poetics; Poems and Critical Documents from the Puritans to Robert Frost.* Garden City, NY: Anchor Books, 1962.

Hollander, John, ed. *American Poetry: The Nineteenth Century, I: Philip Freneau to Walt Whitman.* New York: Library of America, 1993.

The Nineteenth Century, II: Herman Melville to Trumbull Stickney: American Indian Poetry; Folk Songs and Spirituals. New York: Library of America, 1993.

Kane, Paul, ed. *Poetry of the American Renaissance: A Diverse Anthology from the Romantic Period.* New York: G. Braziller, 1995.

Kreymborg, Alfred, ed. *Lyric America: An Anthology of American Poetry (1630–1941).* New York: Coward-McCann, 1941.

Lee, Robert A., ed. *Nineteenth-Century American Poetry.* Totowa, NJ: Barnes & Noble, 1985.

Parker, Robert Dale, ed. *Changing Is Not Vanishing: A Collection of American Indian Poetry to 1930.* Philadelphia: University of Pennsylvania Press, 2011.

Spengemann, William C., and Jessica F. Roberts, eds. *Nineteenth-Century American Poetry.* New York: Penguin Classics, 1996.

Untermeyer, Louis, ed. *American Poetry from the Beginning to Whitman.* New York: Harcourt & Brace, 1931.

Walker, Cheryl, ed. *American Women Poets of the Nineteenth Century: An Anthology.* New Brunswick, NJ: Rutgers University Press, 1992.

Weiss, Shira Wolosky, ed. *Major Voices: 19th Century American Women's Poetry: Selected Poems.* New Milford, CT: Toby Press, 2003.

Wood, Marcus, ed. *The Poetry of Slavery: An Anglo-American Anthology, 1764–1865.* New York: Oxford University Press, 2003.

INDEX

Cambridge Companions to...

AUTHORS

Andrew Marvell edited by Derek Hirst and Steven N. Zwicker

Herman Melville edited by Robert S. Levine

Arthur Miller edited by Christopher Bigsby (second edition)

Milton edited by Dennis Danielson (second edition)

Molière edited by David Bradby and Andrew Calder

Toni Morrison edited by Justine Tally

Nabokov edited by Julian W. Connolly

Eugene O'Neill edited by Michael Manheim

George Orwell edited by John Rodden

Ovid edited by Philip Hardie

Harold Pinter edited by Peter Raby (second edition)

Sylvia Plath edited by Jo Gill

Edgar Allan Poe edited by Kevin J. Hayes

Alexander Pope edited by Pat Rogers

Ezra Pound edited by Ira B. Nadel

Proust edited by Richard Bales

Pushkin edited by Andrew Kahn

Rabelais edited by John O'Brien

Rilke edited by Karen Leeder and Robert Vilain

Philip Roth edited by Timothy Parrish

Salman Rushdie edited by Abdulrazak Gurnah

Shakespeare edited by Margareta de Grazia and Stanley Wells (second edition)

Shakespearean Comedy edited by Alexander Leggatt

Shakespeare on Film edited by Russell Jackson (second edition)

Shakespeare's History Plays edited by Michael Hattaway

Shakespeare's Last Plays edited by Catherine M. S. Alexander

Shakespeare's Poetry edited by Patrick Cheney

Shakespeare and Popular Culture edited by Robert Shaughnessy

Shakespeare on Stage edited by Stanley Wells and Sarah Stanton

Shakespearean Tragedy edited by Claire McEachern

George Bernard Shaw edited by Christopher Innes

Shelley edited by Timothy Morton

Mary Shelley edited by Esther Schor

Sam Shepard edited by Matthew C. Roudané

Spenser edited by Andrew Hadfield

Laurence Sterne edited by Thomas Keymer

Wallace Stevens edited by John N. Serio

Tom Stoppard edited by Katherine E. Kelly

Harriet Beecher Stowe edited by Cindy Weinstein

August Strindberg edited by Michael Robinson

Jonathan Swift edited by Christopher Fox

J. M. Synge edited by P. J. Mathews

Tacitus edited by A. J. Woodman

Henry David Thoreau edited by Joel Myerson

Tolstoy edited by Donna Tussing Orwin

Anthony Trollope edited by Carolyn Dever and Lisa Niles

Mark Twain edited by Forrest G. Robinson

John Updike edited by Stacey Olster

Virgil edited by Charles Martindale

Voltaire edited by Nicholas Cronk

Edith Wharton edited by Millicent Bell

Walt Whitman edited by Ezra Greenspan

Oscar Wilde edited by Peter Raby

Tennessee Williams edited by Matthew C. Roudané

August Wilson edited by Christopher Bigsby

Mary Wollstonecraft edited by Claudia L. Johnson

Virginia Woolf edited by Susan Sellers (second edition)

Wordsworth edited by Stephen Gill

W. B. Yeats edited by Marjorie Howes and John Kelly

Zola edited by Brian Nelson

TOPICS

The Actress edited by Maggie B. Gale and John Stokes

The African American Novel edited by Maryemma Graham

The African American Slave Narrative edited by Audrey A. Fisch

African American Women's Literature edited by Angelyn Mitchell and Danielle K. Taylor

Allegory edited by Rita Copeland and Peter Struck

American Crime Fiction edited by Catherine Ross Nickerson